ALL YOU CAN EAT

ALL YOU CAN EAT

How Hungry is America?

JOEL BERG

SEVEN STORIES PRESS

NEW YORK • LONDON • MELBOURNE • TORONTO

Seven Stories Press
140 Watts Street
New York, NY 10013
www.sevenstories.com

In Canada: Publishers Group Canada, 559 College Street, Suite 402, Toronto, ON M6G 1A9

In the UK: Turnaround Publisher Services Ltd., Unit 3, Olympia Trading Estate, Coburg Road, Wood Green, London N22 6TZ

In Australia: Palgrave Macmillan, 15–19 Claremont Street, South Yarra, VIC 3141

College professors may order examination copies of Seven Stories Press titles for a free six-month trial period. To order, visit http://www.sevenstories.com/textbook or send a fax on school letterhead to (212) 226-1411.

Book design by Jon Gilbert

Library of Congress Cataloging-in-Publication Data

Berg, Joel.
All you can eat : how hungry is America? / by Joel Berg. -- 1st ed.
    p. cm.
Includes bibliographical references and index.
ISBN 978-1-58322-854-8 (pbk.)
1. Food relief--United States. 2. Hunger--United States. 3. Poverty--United States. 4. Public welfare--United States. 5. Political culture--United States. I. Title.
HV696.F6B453 2008
363.80973--dc22

2008040838

Printed in the USA

9 8 7 6 5 4 3 2 1

For my mother, Belle, and my father, Bernard, who gave my mind a hunger for learning, while ensuring that my body would never, ever be hungry for food

There is little evidence of poverty-induced malnutrition in the United States.

—Robert Rector, senior research fellow, Heritage Foundation[1]

There is no hunger crisis in New York City. None whatsoever. . . . Nobody of sound mind goes hungry in New York.

—Editorials, *New York Post*[2]

Who are you going to believe? Me, or your own eyes?

—Chico Marx, Marx brother[3]

CONTENTS

PROLOGUE II

INTRODUCTION Hunger Amidst Plenty: A Problem as
American as Apple Pie 13

Section I —THE PROBLEM

CHAPTER I   Who is Hungry in America?: The Politics of
Measuring Hunger 25

CHAPTER 2   How Hunger Costs *All* of Us 45

CHAPTER 3   Why Brother (and Sister) *Still* Can't Spare a Dime:
A Short History of Domestic Hunger 53

CHAPTER 4   The Tattered (But Still Existing) Federal Hunger Safety Net 83

CHAPTER 5   Let Them Eat Ramen Noodles: One Week Living on
$28.30 of Food 99

CHAPTER 6   Are Americans Hungry—Or Fat? III

CHAPTER 7   Dickens Revisited: Life in the New Gilded Age 127

CHAPTER 8   Let Them Eat Sound Bites: The Polarized
Politics of Welfare Reform 157

CHAPTER 9   The Poverty Trap: Why It Is So Hard to Escape
Poverty in America 175

CHAPTER 10   The Charity Myth 191

CHAPTER II   How Media Ignores Hunger (Except During
Holidays and Hurricanes) 217

Section II —THE SOLUTION

CHAPTER 12   Here It Is: The Plan to End Domestic Hunger 237

CHAPTER 13   Bolstering Community Food Production and Marketing 259

9

CHAPTER 14   A New War on Poverty 275

CHAPTER 15   How All of Us (Including *YOU*) Can End Hunger
in America 283

APPENDIX A   Hunger and Poverty-Fighting Resources 295

APPENDIX B   Revised Rules for Radical Centrists: Tips for Activists
on How to Organize and Craft Messages for Successful
Advocacy Campaigns 303

ACKNOWLEDGMENTS 315

NOTES 319

INDEX 341

PROLOGUE

T his is a true story: There was once a man panhandling outside the subway station in Brooklyn right in front of where I live, asking for "money for food." I introduced myself and gave him a map showing the food pantries and soup kitchens in the neighborhood, but also encouraged him to apply for food stamps, since food stamp benefits are much more substantial than pantry or kitchen allotments. That's the kind of guy I am. He then said—and this is a direct quote: "I can't apply for food stamps because my family would be ashamed if I got help from the city." That's the kind of country this is. Only in America would someone be less ashamed to beg for help from his neighbors than to obtain government benefits to which he is legally entitled.

He probably didn't even think about the times when he had worked and paid payroll taxes—nor all the times he had bought things and paid sales tax. He probably didn't think about the fact that his own tax dollars would have paid for his food stamp benefits, nor consider that, when government helps, it is merely a more organized and fairer way of getting help from his neighbors.

If even hungry Americans don't believe that government aid is the solution to hunger, what does that mean for the rest of us? This books aims to change that thinking. While charities, businesses, and private citizens all have vital roles to play in the fight against hunger, this book argues that only government has the size, scope, resources—and yes, the legitimacy—to take the lead in actually solving the problem. And make no mistake: Government *can* solve the problem.

But until the problem is solved, I'll know that there will always be men, women, and children without enough food right outside my home. In New York City, where I live, there are 1.3 million people in such straits. In the country in which I live, there are 35.5 million.

Sometimes, at night, with the Brooklyn streets just below my window and hungry people all around me, I can't sleep. I bolt out of bed and I begin to type. This book is the product of my conscience prodding me awake.

If this book is even minimally effective, by the time you've finished reading it, I hope you too will have just a little harder time sleeping.

But if I've really accomplished the main goal of this book—both convincing you that this country has a practical and affordable way to rapidly end hunger and engaging you in a new national movement to make it happen—then the man outside my home and tens of millions like him may have all the food they need. Then we can all sleep at night, soundly.

HUNGER AMIDST PLENTY
A Problem as American as Apple Pie

We have long thought of America as the most bounteous of nations . . . [t]hat hunger and malnutrition should persist in a land such as ours is embarrassing and intolerable. More is at stake here than the health and well being of [millions of] American children. . . . Something like the very honor of American democracy is involved.

—President Richard Nixon, May 6, 1969, Special Message to Congress Recommending a Program to End Hunger in America[1]

Try explaining to an African that there is hunger in America. I've tried, and it's not easy.

In 1990, while on vacation, I was wandering alone through the dusty streets of Bamako, the small capital of the West African nation of Mali, when a young man started walking alongside me and struck up a conversation. At first, I thought he wanted to sell me something or ask me for money, but it turned out he just wanted to talk, improve his English, and learn a little about America. (He had quickly determined by my skin color that I was non-African and by my sneakers that I was American.)

When he asked me whether it was true that everyone in America was rich, I knew I was in trouble. How could I explain to him that a country as wealthy as mine still has tens of millions suffering from poverty and hunger? How could I explain to him that America—the nation of Bill Gates, "streets paved with gold," Shaquille O'Neal, and all-you-can-eat buffets—actually has a serious hunger problem? That—in a country without drought or famine and with enough food and money to feed the world twice over—one in eight of our own people struggles to put food on their tables?

In Mali, such a statement was a hard sell. While that nation has one of the planet's most vibrant cultures, it also has one of the least-developed economies. The country has a per capita annual income of only $470, meaning the *average* person makes $1.28 per day—and many earn far less than that, eking out subsistence livings through small-scale farming or other backbreaking manual labor.[2] With the Sahara desert growing and enveloping ever-increasing swaths of Mali, the nation frequently suffers from widespread drought and famine. According to the UN, 28 percent of Mali's population is seriously undernourished.[3]

I tried to tell him that not all Americans were as rich as he thought, and that much of the wealth he saw was concentrated among a small number of people while the majority toiled to make a basic living. I explained that living in a cash economy such as America's presents a different set of challenges than living in a subsistence and barter-based economy that exists in much of Mali. That in America, you have to pay a company for oil, gas, and all other basic necessities. You must pay a landlord large sums of money to live virtually anywhere. That while many workers in America earn a minimum wage equaling less than $11,000 a year for full-time work (the US federal minimum wage was then $5.15 per hour), they often pay more than $1,500 per month in rent, which equals $18,000 per year. So, many actually pay *more* in rent than they earn. Then they have to figure out a way to pay for health care, child care, transportation, and yes, food. When Americans have expenses that are greater than their income, they must go without basic necessities.

I thought I was very persuasive, but I still don't think I ultimately convinced him. Given that English was likely his third or fourth language, perhaps he didn't precisely understand what I was saying. Perhaps concepts such as paying for child care didn't resonate with him since few Malians pay others to care for their children. Moreover, I bet that—all my caveats aside—$11,000 a year sounded like a great deal of money to him.

Standing there in Africa, for the first time in my life I briefly had a hard time convincing even myself that hunger in the US was something that I should seriously worry about given that things were obviously so much worse elsewhere. After all, I was forced to consider that, as bad as hunger is in America, US children rarely starve to death anymore, while they still do in parts of the developing world.

But then I recalled all the people I had met throughout America who couldn't afford to feed their families—who had to ration food for their children, choose between food and rent, or go without medicine to be able to buy dinner—and I reminded myself that, just because they weren't quite dropping dead in the streets, that didn't mean that their suffering wasn't significant indeed. And then I further reminded myself that America *was* the nation of Bill Gates—and more than 400 other billionaires, not to mention more than 7 million millionaires—so it was particularly egregious that my homeland allowed millions of children to suffer from stunted growth due to poor nutrition. I thus came back to the same conclusion I reach every day: while hunger anywhere on the planet is horrid and preventable, having it in America is truly unforgivable.

It is not surprising that it is often difficult to convince average Americans that there is a serious hunger problem in the United States. Our nation tends to think of hunger as a distant, overseas, Third World problem. Our collective mental images of hunger are usually of African children with protruding ribs and bloated bellies—surrounded by flies and Angelina Jolie—sitting in parched, cracked dirt. When I try to explain US hunger to Americans, some automatically assume that I am inflating the extent of the problem. They simply don't see it in their daily living. They know that America is the richest and most agriculturally abundant nation in the history of the world. They can't believe that a place with so much obesity can have hunger. And besides, they assume that I am exaggerating because I am an advocate, and it is my job to exaggerate.

THIRTY-FIVE AND A HALF MILLION . . . AND COUNTING

When people look at the facts for themselves, they discover the shocking reality: hunger amidst a sea of plenty is a phenomenon as American as baseball, jazz, and apple pie. Today in the United States—because tens of millions of people live below the meager federal poverty line and because tens of millions of others hover just above it—35.5 million Americans, including 12.6 million children, live in a condition described by the federal government as "food insecurity," which means their households either suffer from hunger or struggle at the brink of hunger.[4]

Primarily because federal antihunger safety net programs have worked, American children are no longer dying in significant numbers as an immediate result of famine-like conditions—though children did die of malnutrition here as recently as the late 1960s. Still, despite living in a nation with so many luxury homes that the term "McMansion" has come into popular usage, millions of American adults and children have such little ability to afford food that they do go hungry at different points throughout the year—and are otherwise forced to spend money on food that should have been spent on other necessities, like heat, health care, or proper child care.

Most alarmingly, the problem has only gotten worse in recent years. The 35.5 million food-insecure Americans encompass a number roughly equal to the population of California. That figure represents a more than 4-million-person increase since 1999. The number of children who lived in such households also increased during that time, rising by more than half a million children. The number of adults and children who suffered from the most severe lack of food—what the Bush administration now calls "very low food security" and what used to be called "hunger"—also increased in that period from 7.7 million to 11.1 million people—a 44 percent increase in just seven years.[5]

While once confined to our poor inner cities (such as Watts, Harlem, Southeast DC, the Chicago South Side, and the Lower Ninth Ward of New Orleans) and isolated rural areas (such as Appalachia, the Mississippi Delta, Indian reservations, and the Texas/Mexico border region), hunger—and the poverty that causes it—has now spread so broadly it is a significant and increasing problem in suburbs throughout the nation.

Meanwhile, just as more people need more food from pantries and kitchens, these charities have less to give. Since the government and private funding that they receive is usually fixed, when food prices increase, charities are forced to buy less. When those fixed amounts from government actually decrease (as they have in recent years), the situation goes from worse to worser.

In May 2008, America's Second Harvest Food Bank Network—the nation's dominant food bank network (which, in late 2008, changed its name to Feeding America)—reported that 100 percent of their member agencies served more clients in the previous year, with the overall increases estimated to be between 15 to 20 percent. Fully 84 percent of food banks were unable to meet the growing demand due to a combination of three factors: increasing number of clients; decreasing government aid; and soaring food prices.[6]

The number of "emergency feeding programs" in America—consisting mostly of food pantries (which generally provide free bags of canned and boxed groceries for people to take home) and soup kitchens (which usually provide hot, prepared food for people to eat on site)—has soared past 40,000. As of 2005, a minimum of 24 million Americans depended on food from such agencies.[7] Yet, given that more than 35 million Americans were food insecure, this statistic meant that about 11 million—roughly a third of those without enough food—didn't receive any help from charities.

We live in a new gilded age. Inequality of wealth is spiraling to record heights and the wealthiest are routinely paying as much as $1,500 for a case of champagne—equal to five weeks of full-time work for someone earning the minimum wage. While welfare reform is still moving some families to economic self-sufficiency, families being kicked off the rolls are increasingly ending up on the street. Homelessness is spiking. Poverty is skyrocketing. And the middle class is disappearing.

Meanwhile, soaring food prices made it even more difficult for families to manage. Food costs rose 4 percent in 2007, compared with an average 2.5 percent annual rise for the 1990–2006 time period, according to the US Department of Agriculture (USDA). For key staples, the hikes were even worse: milk prices rose by 7 percent in 2007 and egg costs rose by a whopping 29 percent.[8]

It was even tougher for folks who wanted to eat nutritiously. A study in the Seattle area found that the most nutritious types of foods (fresh vegetables, whole grains, fish, and lean meats) experienced a 20 percent price hike, compared to five percent for food in general.[9] The USDA predicted that 2008 would be even worse still, with an overall food price rise that could reach 5 percent, and with prices for cereal and bakery products projected to increase as much as 8.5 percent.[10]

As author Loretta Schwartz-Nobel has chronicled in her 2002 book *Growing Up Empty: The Hunger Epidemic in America*, the nation's hunger problem manifests itself in some truly startling ways. Even our armed forces often don't pay enough to support the food needs of military families. Schwartz-Nobel describes a charitable food distribution agency aimed solely at the people who live on a Marine base in Virginia and includes this quote from a marine: "The way the Marine Corps made it sound, they were going to help take care of us, they made me think we'd have everything we needed. . . . They never said you'll get no food allowance for your family. They never said you'll need food stamps . . . and you still won't have enough."[11] Schwartz-Nobel even quoted a Cambodian refugee in the Midwest as saying, "My children are hungry. Often we are as hungry in America as I was in the (refugee) camps."[12]

AMERICA'S DIRTY SECRET COMES OUT OF HIDING

From 1970 to 2005, the mass media ignored hunger. But due to the surge of intense (albeit brief) media coverage of poverty in the aftermath of Hurricane Katrina, and subsequent reporting of food bank food shortages and the impact

of increasing food prices on the poor, the American public has been slowly wak-
ing to the fact that hunger and poverty are serious, growing problems
domestically. Plus, more and more Americans directly suffer from hunger, have
friends or relatives struggling with the problem, or volunteer at feeding charities where they see the problem for themselves.

Harmful myths about poverty are also starting to be discredited. While
Americans have often envisioned people in poverty as lazy, healthy adults who
just don't want to work, 72 percent of the nation's able-bodied adults living in
poverty reported to the Census Bureau in 2006 that they had at least one job,
and 88 percent of the households on food stamps contained either a child, an
elderly person, or a disabled person.[13] It is harder and harder to make the case
that the trouble is laziness and irresponsibility. The real trouble is the inability
for many working people to afford to support their families on meager salaries,
and the inability of others to find steady, full-time work.

FUNDAMENTALLY A POLITICAL PROBLEM

As far as domestic issues go, hunger is a no-brainer. Every human being needs
to eat. Hunger is an issue that is universally understandable. And everyone is
against hunger in America. Actually, you'd be hard-pressed to find anyone in
America who says they're *for* hunger.

Unlike other major issues such as abortion, gun control, and gay marriage—
over which the country is bitterly divided based on deeply held values—Americans
of all ideologies and religions are remarkably united in their core belief that, in a
nation as prosperous as America, it is unacceptable to have people going hungry.

Even ultraconservative President Ronald Reagan, after being embarrassed
when his top aide Edwin Meese suggested that there was not really hunger in
America and that people were going to soup kitchens just so they could get a
"free lunch," was quickly forced to issue a memo stating his abhorrence of
domestic hunger and his intention to end it.[14] Since then, Presidents George
H. W. Bush, Bill Clinton, and George W. Bush—and high-profile members of
the Senate and the House—have all given speeches laced with ringing denun-
ciations of domestic hunger.[15] Even right-wing think tanks—which often
minimize the *extent* of hunger or say that hunger is the fault of hungry people—claim they do want to end any hunger that may exist.

So why haven't we ended this simple problem? One word: *politics*.

If we were to put the American political system on trial for its failures, hunger would be "Exhibit A." Unlike other books that have argued that domestic hunger is a very unique problem, this book posits that it is actually emblematic of our society's broader problems. The most characteristic features of modern American politics—entrenched ideological divisions, the deceptive use of statistics, the dominance of big money, the passivity and vacuity of the media, the undue influence of interest groups, and empty partisan posturing—all work in tandem to prevent us from ending domestic hunger.

If we can't solve a problem as basic as domestic hunger—over which there is so much theoretical consensus—no wonder we can't solve any of our more complicated issues such as immigration and the lack of affordable health care. In 1969, reaching a similar conclusion, Senator George McGovern, then-chairman of the Senate Select Committee on Nutrition and Human Needs, put it this way:

> Hunger is unique as a public issue because it exerts a special claim on the conscience of the American people. . . . Somehow, we Americans are able to look past slum housing . . . and the chronic unemployment of our poor. But the knowledge that human beings, especially little children, are suffering from hunger profoundly disturbs the American conscience. . . . To admit the existence of hunger in America is to confess that we have failed in meeting the most sensitive and painful of human needs. To admit the existence of widespread hunger is to cast doubt of the efficacy of our whole system. If we can't solve the problem of hunger in our society, one wonders if we can resolve any of the great social issues before the nation.[16]

It is not surprising that liberal George McGovern would make such a statement, but it is a bit shocking that Republican Richard Nixon—McGovern's opponent in the 1972 presidential election—made similar statements during his presidency, after having denied that hunger was a serious problem. The reason Nixon finally acknowledged domestic hunger—and ultimately took serious action to reduce it—was that he was forced to do so by a combination of grassroots citizen agitation and concentrated national media attention on the issue.

In more recent decades, we've gone backwards, and our modern elected officials deserve most of the blame. While, in the 1970s, the newly instituted federal nutrition safety net that Nixon and McGovern helped create ended starvation conditions and almost eliminated food insecurity altogether, in the early

1980s, President Reagan and a compliant Democratic Congress slashed federal nutrition assistance and other antipoverty programs. Reagan also began the multi-decade process of selling the nation on the false notion that voluntary and uncoordinated private charity could somehow make up for a large-scale downsizing in previously mandatory government assistance. Predictably, hunger again rose.

Both Bush administrations and the Newt Gingrich Congress enacted policies that further worsened America's hunger problem. But when a somewhat more aggressive Democratic Congress took over in 2007, they did little more than undo some of the worst damage by the Republicans and offer a few tepid improvements. To be fair, in 2007, Congress slightly raised the minimum wage and added a bit more money for the Special Supplemental Nutrition Program for Women, Infants, and Children—better known as the WIC food program—and, in 2008, they somewhat increased food stamp benefits. Certainly, small advances under Democratic leadership were much better than the consistent setbacks under the Republicans. But even liberal Democratic leaders have proved unlikely to propose bolder efforts because they worry that such a focus might turn off middle-class "swing voters," and because big money donors—who now control the Democratic Party nearly as much as they control the Republican Party—have different priorities.

Even when elected officials of both parties *do* want to do something substantive to address hunger and poverty, they usually get bogged down in all-but-meaningless ideological debates, rhetorical excesses, and score-settling partisan antics.

Certainly, it's not just elected officials who are to blame. Many religious denominations that denounce hunger also teach their congregations (consciously or unconsciously) that hunger is an inevitable part of both human history and God's will. While it should be ameliorated with charitable acts, they sadly teach, it can't really be eliminated. Businesses that donate food to charities often oppose increases in the minimum wage and other government policies that would decrease people's need for such donated food. The news media, funded by ads from both businesses and the politicians, rarely point out these discrepancies, and focus instead on cheerleading for superficial, holiday-time charitable efforts.

But most harmfully, Americans all over the country have been tricked into thinking that these problems can't be solved and that the best we can hope for is for private charities to make the suffering marginally less severe.

THE GOOD NEWS: WHAT POLITICS BROKE, POLITICS CAN FIX

America *can* end hunger. Moreover, as this book argues in detail, by imple-
menting a bold new political and policy agenda to empower low-income
Americans and achieve fundamental change based upon mainstream values,
America can end hunger quickly and cost-effectively. That achievement would
concretely improve tens of millions of lives, and, in the process, provide a blue-
print for fixing the broader problems of our entire bilge-ridden political system.

Outside the Taylor Grocery and Restaurant (which serves the world's best
grilled catfish) in Taylor, Mississippi, there is a sign that says, "Eat or We Both
Starve." Not only is that slogan a good way to sell catfish, it is a great way to sum
up why our collective self-interest should compel us to end domestic hunger.

No society in the history of the world has sustained itself in the long run
with as much inequality of wealth as exists in America. Growing hunger and

poverty, if left unchecked, will eventually threaten the long-term food security, finances, and social stability of all Americans, even the ones who are currently middle class or wealthy. At the dawn of a new presidency, as the nation clamors for change and a new direction, hunger is a problem too simple and too devastating to ignore. I hope that this book will help give us a framework to work toward a happier, healthier, better-fed America.

THE PROBLEM

CHAPTER I

WHO IS HUNGRY IN AMERICA?
The Politics of Measuring Hunger

A single death is a tragedy, a million deaths is a statistic.
—Soviet dictator Joseph Stalin[1]

*If you're in denial about it, if you're minimizing it, if you're triv-
ializing it, if you're conning yourself about it, then you'll never get
where you need to be.*
—"Dr. Phil" McGraw[2]

From Dr. Phil to your Aunt Florence, anyone giving you self-help advice can
tell you that the first step toward solving a problem is admitting that you
have one. That's why the politics of ending hunger is tied inexorably to the politics of measuring it.

While social reformers began measuring the extent of domestic hunger in
the early 1900s, it is telling that, as late as the mid-1960s, the federal government still had not attempted to significantly measure the problem on its own.
As the Citizens' Board of Inquiry Into Hunger and Malnutrition in the United
States reported in 1968, "Society uses the lack of data as the basis for its inability to move quickly toward a solution. And some officials have turned ignorance
into confirmation that malnutrition does not constitute a serious or pervasive
problem."[3]

The United States Department of Agriculture (USDA), which had the lead
federal responsibility for national antihunger programs, and which routinely
collected voluminous data on a wide range of matters, had never even come

close to measuring the hunger problem nationwide. When the department gin-
gerly attempted to assess the extent of the problem in just a handful of states,
a department bureaucrat who opposed the move tipped off the powerful head
of the House Appropriations Subcommittee on Agriculture, the racist and reactionary Congressman Jamie Whitten of Mississippi. Whitten made one call
back to the department, and Mississippi was removed from the list of states to
be surveyed, even though then (as now) it clearly had one of the nation's highest rates of hunger.[4]

Other, more progressive parts of the government, such as the US Commission on Civil Rights Commission, were at the same time trying to get answers,
particularly about whether food aid was being improperly denied to nonwhites.
Frustrated at its inability to force the USDA to provide data regarding that problem, the Commission wrote the following to the Department in 1965:

We note that the Consumer and Marketing Service has developed data
collection systems which can inform it of the number of pounds of
selected types of cigar wrapper tobacco products each year, as well as
the number of pounds of goat meat condemned after re-inspection for
being tainted, sour, or putrid. We can only ask that the same amount
of imagination that can develop a system to collect data such as this
be applied to the critical area of equal opportunity and program participation in food programs.[5]

While the USDA did not immediately jump to study hunger, it did produce
a "Food Consumption Survey" in 1965 that found that 63 percent of households with incomes under $3,000, and 57 percent of households with incomes
from $3,000 to $4,999, had diets that were deficient in one or more of USDA-
recommended nutrients. Not focused solely on low-income people, the survey
also found that 37 percent of households with incomes above $10,000 (about
$63,000 in 2006 dollars) lacked such nutrients.[6]

In 1967, at the instigation of antipoverty advocates, Congress mandated that
the federal Department of Health, Education, and Welfare (HEW)—pointedly
not the USDA—conduct a national nutrition survey to obtain the first hard federal antihunger numbers in a few benchmark states. The survey turned up
shocking results. In testimony before the Senate in 1968, study director Dr.
Arnold Schaefer noted similarities in malnutrition between poor Americans and
people in the Third World, saying, "Our studies to date clearly indicate that there

is malnutrition (in America)—and in our opinion it occurs in an unexpectedly large proportion of Americans."[7] Said author Nick Kotz who followed the hunger issue closely: "The doubters were now confronted with that kind of evidence this nation worships—truths found in tubes and tabulated by computers."[8]

This study—combined with widespread media coverage of it and of similar private studies by doctors at around the same time—was largely responsible for the public outrage that prompted federal policy makers to create the modern nutrition assistance safety net. But, just when advocates were hoping this study would be expanded to all fifty states, the Nixon administration ended it as a cost-cutting measure.

Several years later, President Reagan appointed a commission to study hunger that denied there was a serious hunger problem in America. It was widely recognized as a whitewash. Reagan administration political appointees also intervened to rewrite a USDA report that had originally demonstrated the effectiveness of the Women, Infants, and Children (WIC) program (a program providing food to mothers and young children that they had cut), removing positive conclusions and highlighting minor criticisms.[9]

In the late 1980s, the Food Research and Action Center (FRAC)—a national antihunger lobbying and research organization—started a multiyear project to develop the Community Childhood Hunger Identification Project (CCHIP) to more accurately assess the unique types of food shortages faced by low-income American children. The second and final CCHIP study was based on surveys conducted at eleven sites in nine states and the District of Columbia between 1992 and 1994. It found that 4 million American children under age twelve were hungry, and another 9.6 million were at risk of hunger. The study received widespread media coverage and surprised Americans who had thought domestic hunger was no longer a major problem. The study also provided the first truly nationwide data proving that hungry children were far more likely to experience health problems and miss school than their low-income peers who were not hungry.[10]

USDA FOOD SECURITY DATA

Advocates subsequently succeeded in getting Congress to enact legislation requiring the USDA, which had improved its reputation somewhat on the hunger front, to collect and publish data on the extent of domestic hunger. In

1995, the USDA, using data collected by the US Census Bureau, first published numbers on the extent of hunger and "food insecurity" in America. The report was compiled based on a US Census Bureau questionnaire that annually asks households a detailed series of questions about foods eaten, meals skipped, the amount and cost of foods purchased, and worries about hunger. The report has since been issued every year, and, although the timing of its annual release and some of its terminology have changed over time due to political and other considerations, it is remarkable that the study's basic methodology has stayed mostly the same in that time, allowing the United States to have its first true annual indication of falling or rising hunger.

Under the original terminology, American households were classified as either "food secure" or "food *insecure.*" Then, to make matters more confusing, households that were "food *insecure*" were originally divided into two subcategories: "food insecure *with* hunger" and "food insecure with*out* hunger." In other words, everyone who was "hungry" was also "food insecure," but not everyone who was "food insecure" was also "hungry," at least under the official government definition of the word.

I'll be the first to admit that the term "food insecurity" is bureaucratic, academic, and just plain awkward. But I do think it is a very useful term, helping the nation understand food insufficiency in its uniquely American context. The USDA describes households as food insecure if they are "at times, uncertain of having, or unable to acquire, enough food for all household members because they had insufficient money and other resources for food."[11] We are able to show quite precisely that—because people can't afford to pay for housing, health care, transportation, child care, other basic expenses, as well as all the food they need—they are forced to frequently ration food.

How is that different from hunger? Hunger was defined by the USDA as "the uneasy or painful sensation caused by a recurrent or involuntary lack of food." In other words, hunger is when people don't eat for significant periods of time because they can't afford enough food.

So it's easy enough to understand what constituted a household that was "food insecure with hunger," but what was a household that was "food insecure with*out* hunger?" In such a household, people might occasionally skip meals; reduce portion sizes; buy more filling but less nutritious foods; or worry about where they will get their next meal, even if, for the time being, they were not going for long periods of time with *no food at all.* In other words, these households were at the brink of hunger.

Many families who are food insecure slip in and out of hunger at various times because of job losses, medical problems, divorces, among other reasons. Another way of describing people who are food insecure but not hungry is that they are one or two setbacks away from hunger.

Fully 16.6 million households (10.9 percent of all households), containing 35.5 million Americans, suffered from food insecurity in 2006.[12] It is vital to note that, when a household experienced food insecurity sometime during the year, that does not mean it suffered from the condition daily throughout the year. Usually, families suffer from hunger only sporadically during the year or at a certain points in each month (such as near the end of the month, when their benefits run out). On *any given day*, according to the USDA, the number of Americans with low food security or "very low food security" (their new term for "hunger," as I will explain later) is far smaller than the number of people who face those conditions sometime during the year:

> When interpreting food security statistics, it is important to keep in mind that households are classified as having low or very low food security if they experienced the condition at any time during the previous 12 months. The prevalence of these conditions on any given day is far below the annual rates. For example, the prevalence of very low food security on an average day during the 30-day period from early November to mid-December 2006 is estimated to have been between 0.5 and 0.8 percent of households (600,000 to 877,000 households).[13]

LIES, DAMN LIES, AND STATISTICS

Interpretation of food insecurity data provides a perfect example of how, in today's hyper-divided political culture, ideologues on both sides characterize these statistics in a way most likely to support their previously held beliefs. Thus, whether you see the statistical glass (or stomach) as half empty or half full depends upon whether you want to prove that poverty in America is outrageously high or acceptably minimal.

The conservative think tank the Heritage Foundation concluded in 2004: "According to the USDA, on a typical day, less than one American in 200 will experience hunger due to a lack of money to buy food."[14] Heritage didn't point out that the small-sounding one in 200 figure actually represented a whopping 1.5 million Americans. Surely Heritage wouldn't say, for instance, that although there were 17,034 people murdered in the US in 2006, since only one out of 6.4 million Americans were murdered on a *typical day*, murder isn't a serious problem.[15]

While Americans don't generally suffer from hunger each and every day, such experiences are usually frequent and reoccurring. On average, households that are food insecure during the year know this condition in six different months during that same year. One-fifth of food-insecure households are in that state often or almost every month.

Of the 16.6 million food-insecure households, 4.0 million households, containing 11.1 million people, suffered from hunger or very low food security at least *sometime* during the year.[16] In these households, "the food intake of some household members was reduced, and their normal eating patterns were disrupted because of the households' food insecurity."[17] On average, these families suffered these conditions seven months out of the year.[18]

This does not mean that everyone in each of those households suffered from what the USDA used to call hunger. Often parents go hungry themselves, but make sure to feed their children. In addition, on school days, most children have access to government-subsidized school lunches, and an increasing number obtain school breakfasts and afterschool snacks. In 2006, 12.6 million children lived in food-insecure households, equaling one in six American households, truly a startling statistic. Yet a far smaller number—430,000 children—suffered from hunger or very low security.[19] This is an unconscionably high number, but conservatives (few of whom ever experience hunger themselves or even see it in their daily lives) claim it is small and point out that it is less than 1 percent of all US children. I guess it's easy to see the nation's hunger statistics as half full if your own stomach is always full.

EXAGGERATIONS BY ADVOCATES

Unfortunately, advocates are not immune from misrepresenting the facts either. One antihunger group in New York included in its newsletter a piece of artwork featuring two emaciated-looking silhouettes holding empty bowls, with the slogan below: "Feed My Starving Children." Another New York agency, a kosher soup kitchen, sent out a fundraising e-mail headlined: "More Jews Starving in New York City."

Yet another in Ohio had this statement posted prominently on its Internet home page: "Would you believe that 1 in 6 children in Ohio go to bed hungry every night?" Unfortunately, there are three reasons why that statement wasn't true.

First, the one in six children figure refers to the fact that one in six children in the state lived in households that suffered from food insecurity, but most of the children who were in food-insecure households did *not* suffer from what the USDA then called hunger.

Second, even in food-insecure households that *do* suffer from hunger, it's not safe to assume that all the children suffer from hunger.

Third, just because a child goes hungry at least sometime during the year does not mean the child is going to bed hungry *every night*.

To be more accurate, the group *should* have said: "One in six children in our state are hungry or at risk of hunger." Why would a highly respected organization make such a misleading claim, fudging over statistical fine points? Because they want to attract as much media attention and as many donations as possible.

Sometimes advocates even admit to fudging the facts. Michael Harrington wrote in his pioneering book, *The Other America: Poverty in the United States*:

If my interpretation is bleak and grim, and even if it overstates the case slightly, that is intentional. My moral point of departure is a sense of outrage, a feeling that the obvious and existing problem of the poor is so shocking that it would be better to describe it in dark tones rather than to minimize it. No one will be hurt if the situation is seen from the most pessimistic point of view, but optimism can lead to complacency and the persistence of the other America.[20]

As an advocate who struggles every day to get the public to care about poverty, I certainly understand the desire to exaggerate to make a point more forceful. But I believe that not only is shading the truth morally wrong—no matter the broader importance of a cause—such misrepresentation actually harms the movement in the long run.

The American public increasingly finds itself caught between both sides of the statistical battlefield. Given that the media now merely reports all claims as if they were equally credible, the public no longer has a factual referee, and is likely to either believe assertions that reinforce their preconceived notions or, even worse, assume both sides are lying, and become more cynical than ever.

When the public suspects that advocates are exaggerating, they often tune out the message. Americans know we don't have masses of people starving in the streets here, so when antihunger champions try to insinuate otherwise, the public will refuse to believe anything else that advocates have to say. If America can't believe advocates with regards to the extent of the problem, no wonder their solutions are received with skepticism.

The truth—that in the richest nation in the history of the world, tens of millions of Americans, including millions of American children, face hunger or the threat of hunger, either frequently or occasionally—is appalling enough to warrant widespread attention.

SO, WHO IS HUNGRY IN AMERICA?

Virtually all hungry Americans are poor or near poor, but not all poor Americans are hungry. While 10.9 percent of all households are food insecure, 36.3 percent of those living below the federal poverty line are.[21] That means that nearly two-thirds of all poor people in the US somehow manage to *escape* the threat of hunger by juggling bills, getting help from friends and neighbors, obtaining food from government nutrition assistance programs, growing their own food, or going to food pantries and soup kitchens.

The problem also greatly affects the nearly poor. In 2006, fully 27.3 percent of families living below 185 percent of the poverty line (meaning that, in 2007, for a family of three, they earned less than $31,600) were food insecure.[22] The struggles for such families are exacerbated because, if their family income tops 130 percent of the poverty line (meaning that, in 2007, for a family of three, they earned more than $22,300), they almost always have too much income to obtain food stamps.

The USDA report also tells us that hunger defies geographical stereotyping. While hunger is, as we would expect, highest in cities and in rural areas, even in the nation's suburbs—which were not too long ago bastions of middle- and upper-class comfort—one in eleven households suffer from food insecurity. And even though the South still has the worst hunger problem, the Midwest, West, and Northeast are not far behind.[23]

While states have varying rates of food insecurity (in the years 2004–2006, Mississippi had the highest rate of food insecurity, 18.1 percent, while North Dakota had the lowest rate, 6.4 percent), in no state was food insecurity faced by anything close to a majority of households and in no state was the number negligible.[24] It is truly a nationwide problem.

States with the highest food insecurity rates tend to be states with high poverty rates. But that's not always the case. Some states, such as New York, have a food insecurity rate significantly lower than the poverty rate. Others, like Oregon and Washington, have food insecurity rates higher than their poverty rates. Researchers have found that state-level differences in food insecurity reflect both differences in demographics mostly beyond the control of each state (such as the income, employment, age, education, and family structure of their residents), as well as differences in factors greatly controlled by each state (such as economic conditions, the accessibility and use of government food assistance programs, and tax policies). One particularly interesting finding was that high state tax burdens (including the combined effects of property, sales, and income taxes) can increase food insecurity.[25]

THE ACCURACY OF THE USDA HUNGER NUMBERS

Is the USDA food insecurity methodology accurate? It is fair to say about it what Winston Churchill said about democracy: "It is the worst possible system except when compared to all others." It is certainly the best measure yet developed to assess the extent of these problems nationwide, and both government officials and advocates benefit greatly from having at least one annual benchmark for these problems. Yet, by their very nature, hunger and food insecurity defy precise measurement, and the USDA food insecurity methodology has many significant flaws, not the least of which is that it measures only people who are living in "households" and who are willing to self-report to government information gatherers.

Many are overlooked. Homeless people, for example, are not counted. Thus, if a low-income family that was food insecure (but not yet hungry) was still barely living in a dwelling in 1996, they could be counted as food insecure by the methodology. But, if by 2002, they had become homeless and hungry, even though had become *more* food insecure, they would no longer be counted as food insecure because they would not be counted at all. Given the spiking homelessness nationwide, this is not a hypothetical issue. The USDA acknowledges this flaw: "The omission of homeless families and individuals from these daily statistics biases them downwards, and the bias may be substantial relative to the estimates, especially for the most severe conditions."[26] For instance, in New York City, on just one night (December 27, 2007), at least 35,081 people slept in city homeless shelters.[27] When you add the large number of homeless people in the city sleeping on streets, in parks, in subways, doubled-up in the homes of friends or relatives, or in abandoned buildings, the number of people who are homeless and hungry but not counted by the government as food insecure is significant.

Furthermore, low-income families, and especially immigrant families, are disproportionately likely to live doubled- and tripled-up—often illegally—in dwellings that were originally designed for one family. Such families are surely less likely to volunteer their existence to government data collectors, even though they have a far higher-than-average likelihood of suffering from food insecurity and hunger.

There is also ample evidence that Census data from which the food insecurity data is derived undercounts key poverty indicators. For instance, in 2006, there were 9.1 million households that reported to the Census American Community Survey that they had obtained food stamp benefits but USDA official statistics showed that 11.6 million had done so. On the vital matter of food stamp participation, the Census data was a whopping 23 percent below the actual data. Who knows how much the Census-collected food security data undercounts reality?

HUNGER IN AMERICA'S SHADOWS

Supplementing the USDA's hard data are eyewitness reports of hunger by the few reporters and writers who care to look. In chronicling living conditions for families that had left welfare in the late 1990s, *New York Times* reporter and author Jason DeParle wrote:

> I was struck by how many working families complained about facing depleted cupboards—or about just plain going hungry. I spent some time with Michelle Crawford, the Milwaukee woman Tommy Thompson [the then-governor of Wisconsin] featured in his legislative address. ("I want to run for president," she remembered him telling her, "and I want you on my team.") While her pride in landing a job was real, so were her struggles to buy a commodity as basic as milk. To

fool the kids, she sweetened a powdered mix and hid it in store-bought jugs. "Then we ran out of sugar," she said. Food wasn't on my mind when I stopped by Pulaski High School to talk to some students with welfare-to-work moms. But it was on the mind of the kids, who commandeered the conversation with macabre jokes about Ramen noodles and generic cereal. When I asked how many had recently gone to bed hungry, four out of the five raised their hands. "Go to my house, look into the refrigerator—you'll be lucky if there's a gallon of milk," said a senior named Tiffany Fiegel. Then she burst into tears.[28]

Author and activist Barbara Ehrenreich, who worked at jobs that paid at or near the minimum wage in order to write her classic book, *Nickel and Dimed: On Not Getting By in America*, described a low-wage coworker who ate only half a bag of Doritos per day, who couldn't afford eighty-nine cents to buy a soda, and who, when asked whether she was hungry at the end of an eight- or nine-hour workday said, "Well, I get dizzy sometimes."[29]

GROWING FOOD PANTRY AND SOUP KITCHEN USE

Another way to measure hunger is to count the number of people who use food pantries and soup kitchens. Ironically, out of the tens of millions of Americans forced to utilize charitable pantries and kitchens, not all are characterized by USDA's methodology as suffering from food insecurity or hunger. One reason may be that the food they received from charities prevented them from lacking sufficient food. Yet, most Americans would likely consider anyone forced to go to a soup kitchen or food pantry as hungry even if they didn't meet the government's formal definition of the term.

A study of feeding programs released by the USDA in 2002 found that even while the economy was growing, the use of services had gone up 11 percent at food rescue organizations, 4 percent at soup kitchens, and 5 percent at food pantries.[30]

The most comprehensive study of the people using pantries, kitchens, and feeding programs at emergency shelters was conducted in 2005 by America's Second Harvest—the nationwide network of food banks and food rescue organizations. This report found that, even during a then-booming economy, the America's Second Harvest system served an estimated 24 to 27 million unduplicated people annually, with a midpoint of 25.3 million, a significant increase over the 2001 midpoint figure of 23.3 million. On any given week in 2005, this network served 4.5 million different people, of whom 36 percent were children and 10 percent were elderly. More than a third of the households had at least one employed adult. Only 12 percent were homeless. The report stated:

> Hunger in America 2006 shows that America's Second Harvest network members serve some of the most vulnerable populations in America. Based on the findings of this study, the millions of people served by our Network do not meet the stereotypical profile of a hungry person. The data shows that hunger reaches into virtually all communities across the United States, affecting even the least likely of victims.[31]

It is true that the America's Second Harvest report, like the USDA annual reports, dispels geographical stereotypes, proving that hunger is a serious problem in every state of the nation, and throughout urban, rural, and suburban America. But that isn't the same as saying that people forced to use pantries and kitchens are just like everyone else in America. As Chart 1A shows, fully 68 percent of households that used emergency feeding programs had incomes below the meager federal poverty line, compared to 10 percent of all American families. Only 28 percent of all adults using such programs were working, compared to 66 percent of all the nation's adults. Seventeen percent of the adults using the agencies were older than the age of sixty-five. If we were to assume for the sake of argument that all of the people above the age of sixty-five were retired, which is certainly not true, that would mean that 55 percent of eighteen- to sixty-five-year-old food recipients didn't work outside the home. While some may be unwilling to work, most of these people are permanently disabled, raising children full time, unable to find work, or too ill to work. These facts dispel the myth that everyone hungry is just too lazy to work, as well as the alternative myth sometimes advanced by advocates that everyone hungry is already working.

The America's Second Harvest study also found that 63 percent of adult charitable food recipients had a high school degree or higher (compared to 84 percent of the adult population as a whole), but only 5 percent had a college degree or higher (compared to 24 percent in the US). Thirty-seven percent had less than a high school degree (compared to 15 percent in the US). High school dropouts were thus eight times more likely than college graduates to face hunger, although it is important to note that high school dropouts were usually born into much lower income families than were college graduates. While food clients were mostly white, African Americans were a far higher percentage, and Hispanics were a slightly higher percentage, of food recipients than they were of the US population as a whole.[32]

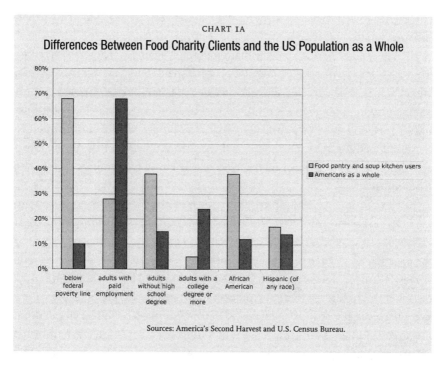

CHART IA

Differences Between Food Charity Clients and the US Population as a Whole

Sources: America's Second Harvest and U.S. Census Bureau.

Thus, while hunger organizations often say that hunger can "happen to anyone" in order to increase sympathy from the non-hungry public, in truth, hunger is much more likely to happen to people who live in poverty and suffer from other poverty-related conditions. Yes, there is the occasional wealthy stockbroker who loses everything due to an addiction, mental illness, or losing a job, and then falls so far that he or she must use a soup kitchen. But most people who started out wealthy have enough assets saved—and have family and friends with enough resources—to prevent them for truly hitting the skids when they are down. Low-income people are far less likely to have such backup resources. The sad reality is that most people who use food pantries and soup kitchens are poor because their parents were poor.

FOOD BANKS, FOOD PANTRIES, AND SOUP KITCHENS RUNNING ON EMPTY

As a result of a weakening economy, increasing food prices, and high costs for fuel, the needs at emergency feeding programs are soaring. The United States Conference of Mayors found that, during 2007, sixteen major cities (80 percent of those responding to their survey) experienced increased requests for emergency food assistance. Among the cities that provided data, the median increase was 10 percent.[33]

By late 2007, it became clear that emergency feeding programs were facing a new crisis, with the number of people forced to use them skyrocketing, and with their food supplies slashed. Despite President Bush's repeated calls for the country to support the "faith-based armies of compassion," his administration severely cut the poundage of USDA "bonus buy" food provided to nonprofit feeding agencies, most of which were faith-based. Private donations also decreased as a result of both the economic slowdown and changes in the food industry.

In New York City, the number of people who use food pantries and soup kitchens skyrocketed in 2007, while food stocks drastically declined, forcing at least half of these programs to ration food, according to the annual survey by the organization I manage, the New York City Coalition Against Hunger. The survey estimated that pantry and kitchen use increased by 20 percent in 2007, on top of the 11 percent increase in 2006 estimated by the previous year's survey. Fifty-nine percent of agencies—a record number—said they lacked the resources to meet their growing demand in 2007, a sharp increase from the 48 percent who lacked such resources in 2006.[34] Given that hunger continued to increase in the city even when the stock market was still strong in 2006, it is no wonder that, when economic indicators weakened, lines at pantries and kitchens got even worse. When the economy gets a cold, people in poverty get pneumonia.

The problem is spreading fast to even formerly comfortable suburbs, such as Long Island, where 259,000 people needed help from food pantries in 2007. One pantry's need grew by 150 percent over the last twelve years.[35] Just across the Hudson River from New York City, in suburban New Jersey (one of the wealthiest states in the nation), pockets of hunger are growing:

> "Our people don't have enough to eat for the rest of the month," said Sandra Ramos, director of Strengthen Our Sisters, a Passaic County bat-

tered women's shelter. . . . "There was a time when two dozen home-less persons would show up for meals at Hope House of Catholic Charities in Dover," said Joann Tyler, who helps run the shelter. "These days, it's not uncommon to find double that lining up for meals," she said.[36]

When I grew up in Rockland County, New York, a suburb about twenty miles north of New York City, in the 1960s through 1980s, it was mostly solidly middle class, with a few pockets of great wealth and a few smaller pockets of poverty. Due to largely stagnant wages and a huge influx of low-paid immi-grants, the poverty rate in Rockland more than doubled from 1990 to 2006, rising from 6.4 percent to 12.9 percent. There were very few food pantries and soup kitchens needed in Rockland when I was growing up, but there are now more than fifty-one different feeding sites.[37] Given that the county only has about 294,000 people, it has a higher per capita number of pantries and kitchens than New York City. In addition, many extra free feeding programs spring up in Rockland around each holiday season, including one in the Vil-lage of Haverstraw, where, in 2007, people started lining up for food an hour before the doors opened.[38]

Hunger is a growing problem in upstate New York as well. In and around Buffalo, as factories shuttered one after another, the region entered an eco-nomic and social tailspin. Bonnie Giammusso, the coordinator of a local food pantry said, "The need never ends." A pantry volunteer, Harold Mante, said, "We are trying to stamp out hunger, but the lines of the people keep getting longer every year."[39]

These problems are not unique to New York. In Wichita, Kansas, the num-ber of people who are in severe poverty increased by 88 percent between 2001 and 2006. The Bread of Life food pantry served 25,000 people in the first ten months of 2007, 3,500 more people than in the same period the previous year. Catholic Charities in Wichita fed 7,529 people in the first six months of 2007, about 1,300 more than during the same period the previous year.[40]

In Boston, Catherine D'Amato, president and chief executive officer of the Greater Boston Food Bank, said that 2007 was "one of the most demanding years I've seen in my 30 years in the field." The Vermont Foodbank said its sup-ply of food was down 50 percent from the previous year. "It's a crisis mode," said Doug O'Brien, the bank's chief executive. At the New Hampshire Food Bank, demand for food was up 40 percent over the previous year and the supply was down 30 percent. "It's the price of oil, gas, rents, and foreclosures," said Melanie Gosselin, executive director of the food bank.[41] "In Washington, DC," wrote the *Independent*, "three of the city's largest charities—a shelter for 300 men, a community kitchen that feeds 4,000 every day, and a food bank that supplies the basic needs of 108,000 people a year—revealed sharply reduced donations and a sense of desperation for the future."[42] "Hunger is a problem everywhere in Alaska," according to Shawn Powers of the statewide food bank, "but the results for rural Alaska [are] especially heartbreaking. Eleven percent of adults and 14 percent of children in rural Alaska had to skip or cut down on meals [in 2006] because there was not enough money for food. Twenty-six percent of rural Alaskans reported that they could not afford to eat balanced meals, and 34 percent struggled to make their food last through the month."[43]

In the deepening recession of 2008, there were sharp hikes in pantry and kitchen use in every corner of the country. Reported MSNBC: "The story is retold over and over again: 40 percent more clients at the Salvation Army in Panama City, Florida; 20 percent more for Urban Ministries of Raleigh, North Carolina; almost 200 percent more for the Community Food Ministries Food Pantry in Boise, Idaho."[44]

THE GREAT HUNGER COVER-UP

In my travels for the USDA while serving under the Clinton administration, I saw with my own eyes conditions I didn't expect in America. As late as 1994, I witnessed African-American communities in Mississippi, white enclaves in Kentucky, and Native American pueblos in New Mexico all lacking running water. Employment was scarce, and the jobs that did exist barely paid the minimum wage. People went hungry. And the faces of the children were drained of hope.

I'll never forget visiting the home of an elderly woman in one impoverished New Mexico pueblo. Her tiny living room was proudly adorned with photos of children and grandchildren whom she had sent off to fight in America's wars. But the nation had not reciprocated by providing her with even basic necessities of life.

So I wasn't surprised at all when, in 1999, the USDA released the first-ever federal report on state-by-state levels of food insecurity in America and found that the highest levels of hunger were in places with historically high levels of poverty: New Mexico, Mississippi, and Texas.[45]

Secretary of Agriculture Dan Glickman (my then-boss) and myself made it clear to the media that the report's most important finding was that hunger was a significant problem in *all* fifty states, and that we were pointedly *not* assigning any blame to states with the highest hunger rates. Glickman said, "During this, the most prosperous economy in decades, it should shock most Americans to know that hunger persists and is in every state."[46] Still, no American should have been surprised that states with higher poverty also had higher hunger.

Unfortunately for hungry Americans, that *was* a big shock for two key Republican elected officials: New Mexico Congressman Joe Skeen and Texas Governor George W. Bush, who had already begun his run for the presidency.

On a campaign swing through New Hampshire, Bush was asked by a reporter about the study. His response: "I saw the report that children in Texas are going hungry. Where? You'd think the governor would have heard about it if there were pockets of hunger in Texas." Retorted a newspaper in Bush's hometown of Austin: "Indeed, you would, especially if one of those pockets is just a few miles from his front door."[47] Bush also added, "I'm surprised that a report floats out of Washington when I'm running a presidential campaign."[48]

Skeen was then the chair of the House Appropriations Subcommittee on Agriculture, which controlled virtually all of the USDA's spending. In his tenure as chair, Skeen's top priority usually was providing more government aid to large-scale livestock operations, similar to the one owned by his family.

You might have hoped that the new findings on the staggering amount of hunger in his home state would have prompted Skeen to use his awesome power as the chief funder of the nation's largest nutrition assistance programs to immediately propose ways to expand these efforts to a size that could actually end hunger. But he did just the opposite. He trashed the findings of the study, took them as a personal attack designed to embarrass him, and then worked to *end* some USDA antihunger activities.

Given that the data in the report was collected over a number of years by numerous nonpolitical career civil servants at the US Census Bureau, and compiled over years by nonpolitical career civil servants at the USDA—and further given that the final report detailed problems in all fifty states—it was truly absurd to believe that it was nothing more than a political conspiracy to embarrass two men.

In revenge, Chairman Skeen quickly wrote into a bill, which passed in the House of Representatives then led by Newt Gingrich and Tom DeLay, language that specifically eliminated funding for my position and the Community Food Security Initiative—which was building partnerships between the federal government and grassroots antihunger groups—that I was running at the USDA.[49] Yet my real concern wasn't losing my job. I was much more worried about the department's ability to continue the vital work of the initiative. The Clinton White House was able to get that provision stripped out of the final bill that became law, thus temporarily saving my position. But the whole dustup did make it impossible for the department to ever obtain any of the staff or program funding that it sought to expand and institutionalize the initiative, which Bush eliminated when he became president.

Stung by the campaign embarrassment, once Bush took office his administration used every opportunity to continue to shoot the messenger by undermining the USDA food insecurity methodology. The administration discontinued the tradition, started by the Clinton administration, of annually releasing the national food security and hunger numbers for the previous year on World Food Day in October, instead holding off the annual release until after each November's elections.

Going around the department's own bureaucracy and further dumping on their own department's research, administration appointees at the USDA asked the Committee on National Statistics (CNSTAT) of the National Academies to examine the validity of the methodology. The statistics mavens at the Academies couldn't get over the concept that hunger in the US was not as severe as hunger in the Third World, so they said the word "hunger" shouldn't be used here. Such a step reflected a greater change in social science research from personal observation to numbers crunching, as pointed out by author Jason DeParle:

> With economists in control [over the last few decades of poverty research], most poverty academics had gotten out of the business of talking to poor people altogether; tenure passed through data sets, not inner-city streets. The experts spoke a desiccated, technical language, mostly to themselves.[50]

Using the statisticians as an excuse, administration appointees at USDA then decided to replace the term "hunger" with the term "very low food security." In opposing the change, I pointed out that the word "hunger" was frequently used in the press, in advertisements, and in general American conversation on a casual basis. Ambitious athletes, businesspeople, and politicians who very much want to win in their fields are called "hungry." People waiting to be fed at a restaurant often complain that they're "hungry," or even "starving." But you won't hear anyone say that they "have so much food insecurity they could eat a horse." And the Bible does not say, "For I was suffering food insecurity and you gave me food." The word is "hungry." It is a powerful word, clearly, instantly, and universally understood. Given how much has already been taken away from them, surely those Americans who are too poor to afford all the food they need ought to at least retain possession of the word in the English language that most accurately describes their condition.

Of course, the main reason the administration wanted to bury the data and no longer use the word "hunger" was that the true facts made them look terrible. As Chart 1B shows, the number of Americans facing very low food security/hunger started to tick up again near the end of the Clinton administration, and it skyrocketed upward under George W. Bush, rising from 3.3 million people in 2001 to 4.6 million in 2006, a 39 percent increase.[51]

CHART 1B

Soaring US Hunger from 1999 to 2006

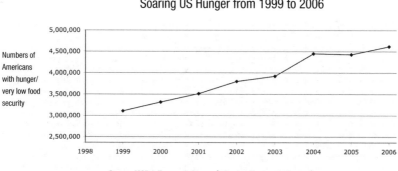

Source: USDA Economic Research Service, Economic Research

The administration's attempt to underplay the issue entirely backfired. The *Washington Post*, which had in the past given the yearly USDA numbers little or no coverage, ran a front-page story headlined, "Some Americans Lack Food, but USDA Won't Call Them Hungry."[52] The national media further amplified the story. Keith Olbermann on MSNBC unfairly slammed the USDA author of the revised survey, Mark Nord, as the "Worst Person in the World" even though he was a career civil servant who developed the original survey that used the word "hunger" and had little control over the nomenclature decision by political appointees. Seventy members of Congress wrote the USDA blasting the nomenclature change. Ultimately, the change in terminology resulted in an *increased* use of the term "hunger" by the media and politicians to describe USDA's annual findings. Under the old methodology, because "hunger" was a subset of "food insecurity," it should have been clear to anyone who cared to make the distinction that it was not accurate to conflate the two. But now that the USDA no longer uses the term "hunger" at all, the vast majority of people who describe the USDA food insecurity report now say that the 35.5 million food-insecure Americans are 35.5 million "hungry" Americans. It's the sort of irony fit for a bureaucrat.

CHAPTER 2

HOW HUNGER COSTS *ALL* OF US

Food insecurity is strongly associated . . . (with) increased num-
bers of hospitalizations. I would point out that a single 48-hour
hospitalization, besides being traumatic for child and family, costs
federal (health) benefit programs more than a year's food stamp
benefits for a child!

—Dr. Deborah Frank, director, Grow Clinic for Children at Boston Medical
Center[1]

Even though the US has more than 35 million food-insecure residents, given
that the nation's overall population is about 301 million people, this means that
266 million Americans (about 88 percent of the population) have enough food.
So why should the non-hungry 88 percent of Americans care?

Reason one: Although most people who face hunger were poor or near-poor
their whole lives, people who are now middle-class Americans may still face hunger
themselves someday. Job losses, divorces, bad mortgages, illnesses, and plain bad
luck often contribute to sudden drops in financial wellbeing, particularly if the people facing the setbacks previously had significant debt and limited assets (as is the
case with many middle-class Americans today). So the first reason to worry about the
nation's hunger problem is that the crisis might someday be your own.

Reason two: The high prevalence of food insecurity in America has a devastating impact upon our economy and international competitiveness by
increasing our nation's spending on health care and reducing our productivity
and educational performance. Hunger also makes it nearly impossible for people to escape poverty. A recent study written by Dr. J. Larry Brown of the
Harvard School of Public Health concluded:

The cost burden of hunger in the United States is a minimum of $90 billion annually. This means that on average each person living in the US pays $300 annually for the hunger bill. On a household basis this cost is $800 a year. And calculated on a lifetime basis, each of us pays a $22,000 tax for the existence of hunger. And because the $90 billion cost figure is based on a cautious methodology, we anticipate that the actual cost of hunger and food insecurity to the nation is higher.[2]

On the basis of that study, I calculated that, in New York City alone, city residents pay an estimated $2.65 billion per year, or about $335 per resident, resulting from indirect costs of the city's 1.3 million food-insecure residents. People in every city, county, and town of America must pay their own share of the massive national costs of hunger.

Reason three: The national economy, like a skyscraper, is only as strong as its foundation. It would make sense that ensuring a brighter future for America would include empowering and enabling its citizens to succeed and contribute. Even Henry Ford—no great liberal—understood that workers needed to be paid at least well enough to buy his cars. It significantly weighs down the entire economy when large numbers of people are too poor and too hungry to purchase goods and services, or to be as innovative or productive as they can be.

HUNGER HARMS PEOPLE IN EVERY PHASE OF THE LIFE CYCLE

In recent decades, scientists have produced vast amounts of data proving that hunger and food insecurity harm low-income Americans at each stage of their lives. Not only does hunger impair physical growth and health, but it saps energy and makes it impossible to concentrate, thereby compromising performance at school, work, and home. All those factors then fuel feelings of despair and inadequacy.

The Nutrition-Cognition National Advisory Committee—a panel comprised of doctors, nutritionists, and other experts on the effects of hunger—concluded in 1998 that problems with poor nutrition start even before birth:

Pregnant women who are undernourished are more likely to have low birth weight babies. Along with other health risks that are common to low birth weight babies, these infants are more likely to suffer developmental delays. In the case of very low birth weight infants, permanent cognitive deficiencies associated with smaller head circumference may reflect diminished brain growth.[3]

According to pediatrician Dr. Deborah Frank, malnourished mothers are more prone to have children with birth defects:

Micronutrient deficiencies that arise from inadequate maternal nutrition—even in the presence of adequate maternal weight gain in pregnancy—can have devastating consequences. There is a well-established relationship between inadequate maternal folate intake at the time of conception and the risk of neural tube defects (spina bifida) in children.[4]

Clearly, if you want fetuses to develop properly, you should support expansion of the Women, Infants, and Children (WIC) program, which provides food to young children and mothers, and has a spectacular track record of ensuring exactly that. I can't help but note the irony in the fact that, when Congress voted in 2005 to cut funding for the WIC program, most of the members of Congress who claimed to be pro-life voted for the cut.

After birth, problems associated with hunger are only compounded, as Dr. Frank noted:

Child hunger is a health issue, a very serious one. My kids [at the clinic] don't have AIDS but they function as if they did. The difference is that their immune system was fine until they become malnourished. Now they just continue to decline and decline.[5]

The Nutrition-Cognition National Advisory Committee described it this way:

Under nutrition impacts the behavior of children, their school performance, and their overall cognitive development. . . . Undernourished children decrease their activity levels and become more apathetic. This in turn affects their social interactions, inquisitiveness, and overall cognitive functioning. Even nutritional deficiencies of a relatively short-term nature influence children's behavior, ability to concentrate, and to per-

form complex tasks. . . . [Child hunger] is capable of producing progressive handicaps—impairments which can remain throughout life. . .
. By robbing children of their natural human potential, under nutrition
results in lost knowledge, brainpower and productivity for the nation.
The longer and more severe the malnutrition, the greater the likely loss
and the greater the cost to our country.[6]

Dr. J. Larry Brown explained further:

The research shows that youngsters from food insecure and hungry
homes have poorer overall health status: they are sick more often,
much more likely to have ear infections, have higher rates of iron defi-
ciency anemia, and are hospitalized more frequently. In short, going
hungry makes kids sick. . . . They miss more days of school and are
less prepared to learn when they are able to attend. . . . Further exac-
erbating this interactive impairment of young bodies and minds are
the emotional and behavioral impacts.[7]

A study at urban medical centers in five states and the District of Columbia
found that food-insecure children had odds of "fair or poor health" nearly twice
as great, and odds of being hospitalized since birth almost a third larger, than
food-secure children."[8] Another study concluded that food-insufficient children
scored significantly lower on arithmetic tests, were more likely to repeat a
grade, were more likely to see a psychologist, and had greater difficulty getting
along with other children.[9]

Beyond the direct physical and psychological impact upon children due to
the deprivation of nutrients, simply knowing that your family faces hunger—
even if your parents take great pains to feed you before they feed themselves,
as is often the case—can take its toll. One study found

Children as young as 11 could describe behaviors associated with food
insecurity if they had experienced it directly or indirectly. . . . Psychological aspects included worry/anxiety/sadness about the family food
supply, feelings of having no choice in the foods eaten, shame/fear of
being labeled as poor, and attempts to shield children. Social aspects
of food insecurity centered on using social networks to acquire food
or money and social exclusion.[10]

Even more so than simply being poor, one study found that being food insecure is associated with increased mental illness and behavioral problems
among children:

> Hungry children were three times more likely than at-risk for hunger
> children and seven times more likely than not hungry children to
> receive scores indicative of clinical dysfunction. . . . The same pattern
> of at least doubling of risk was found for other indicators of psy-
> chosocial dysfunction like special education and repeating a grade. . . .
> Hungry children were seven to 12 times more likely to exhibit symp-
> toms of conduct disorder than not hungry children.[11]

Another study that looked at a broad variety of factors found that food insecurity
generally decreases heath-related quality of life and physical function for children.[12]

As children move into adolescence, a lack of food continues to have devastating effects. One study found that simply being poor didn't make teenagers
more suicidal than those who were nonpoor, but being hungry or suffering
from food insecurity did make them more suicidal.[13]

Facing hunger also makes it more difficult to be a good parent. Food-insecure
parents have higher rates of depression and more significant stress, and this has
a negative impact upon their parenting.[14] The percentage of mothers with either
major depressive episodes or generalized anxiety disorder increases with increasing food insecurity.[15] A study in Oregon found that "adults in food insecure
households were more than twice as likely to suffer depression as adults in households with adequate food."[16] One study in large cities found a vicious cycle: food
insecurity made women more depressed, but because they were more depressed
they were less able to take the steps necessary to end their food insecurity.[17]

In adults, food insecurity and hunger are also closely tied to poor heath. Only
11 percent of people who use food pantries, soup kitchens, and homeless shelters in America reported that their health is "excellent," compared to 16 percent
who say their health is "poor" and 30 percent who say their health is only "fair."
Twenty-one percent of all the adults who obtain food from these emergency
programs reported that they had no health insurance. Forty-one percent of the
food recipients reported unpaid hospital and medical bills. Nearly one in ten
clients reported that they had been refused medical care because they could
not pay or because they had a Medicaid or Medical Assistance card during the
previous twelve months.[18]

All of these effects of hunger inhibit one's ability to make a living. Finding and keeping a job is hard enough—it is even harder on an empty stomach. It is no wonder that hunger is so harmful to worker productivity. Nobel Prize–winning economist Robert Fogel estimated that 20 percent of the population in England and France was effectively excluded from the labor force around 1790 because they were too weak and hungry to work. Improved nutrition, he calculated, accounted for about half of the economic growth in Britain and France between 1790 and 1880. As a result, he has pointed out that hungry people cannot work their way out of poverty.[19] A more recent study of low-income urban women found that "food secure women tended to have better employment and income outcomes than food insecure women, and they also tended to be less socially isolated."[20]

In 2006, fully 619,000 American seniors, living on their own, suffered from food insecurity, a condition especially difficult for elderly people who must rely on help from pantries and Meals-on-Wheels programs that often provide food that is too high in both sodium and sugar.[21]

The impact grows greater still among people battling life-threatening diseases. A study of low-income cancer patients found that food-insecure patients had higher levels of nutritional risk, depression, and financial strain, and lower quality of life compared with food-secure patients. Fifty-five percent of food-insecure cancer patients reported not taking a prescribed medication because they could not afford it, versus 13 percent of food-secure patients.[22] Many seriously ill people must choose between paying for either medicine or food. I can't imagine a more awful dilemma. The only thing worse is being able to afford *neither.*

HUNGER MAKES IT IMPOSSIBLE TO ESCAPE FROM POVERTY

Noting how some people question whether hunger is truly a problem distinct from poverty, author Nick Kotz, writing in 1969, retorted by pointing out that "if hunger is, in fact, a new metaphor for looking at the problems of abject poverty, it is the most basic one."[23]

It is common for people to question whether ending hunger would reduce poverty. But, only someone who has never known it could ask such a question. Hunger makes it harder for children to learn, for parents to parent, and for workers to work. It causes frustration and hopelessness. It makes it nearly impossible for sick people to get well. Put simply, being hungry makes it more difficult for a person or family to escape poverty. It is a huge actor in the cycle of poverty that traps more and more people in this country every year. Ending hunger is an achievable goal that can help to break that cycle, offer people the fighting chance we all deserve, and move us toward ending poverty in America.

CHAPTER 3

WHY BROTHER (AND SISTER) *STILL* CAN'T SPARE A DIME
A Short History of Domestic Hunger

(One of the children was) an Italian boy with a continual pain in his chest and a bad cough which lasted two years. The father is a cobbler making $7 or $8 a week, and the family lives in the basement rooms back of the shop. The lad with the pain in his chest lives in a semi-dark, damp room and eats little besides macaroni, bread, and coffee. One further element of hopelessness is that he has now turned fourteen, has taken his working papers, and must get a factory job at once.

—Frances Perkins, "A Study in of Malnutrition in 107 Children from Public School 51 (New York City)," 1910[1]

In the early 70s, the United States sharply reduced hunger, partly by strengthening food assistance programs. But progress against hunger has not continued, and hunger has increased over the last several years.

—Former Senate Majority Leader Robert Dole, Republican from Kansas, 2005[2]

Hunger in America has not been static over time. It has been transformed considerably as a result of changes in economic conditions and government policies.

Hunger in the US first appeared as a pervasive condition during the Industrial Revolution, when parents didn't earn enough to pay rent and feed their families, and countless American children, such as the Italian boy described above, lived on little each day besides a few scraps of food and coffee. Hunger grew to famine-like proportions during the Depression, but was sharply reduced by the postwar economic boom in the 1940s through the 1960s. It was almost eliminated by the introduction of the modern federal nutrition safety net in the late 1960s and mid-1970s. In the 1980s, it started growing again as a result of downsizing and structural changes in the US job market and cuts in federal nutrition programs. Since those trends were never fully reversed in the 1990s, and since poverty started growing again after 2000, domestic hunger is significantly greater today than in it was in 1979. However, since we still *do* have the nutrition safety net (albeit in a tattered form) that didn't exist at all before the New Deal, there is far less hunger in America today than in 1910.

Hunger in America has never been caused by a lack of food. Ironically, despite the Dust Bowl, a key cause of the nationwide collapse of the farm economy in the 1930s was a *surplus*, not a lack, of food. Then, as now, the main reason people went hungry is that they didn't have the money or government support necessary to access the abundance all around them.

PRE-INDUSTRIAL AGE

Hunger in America dates back thousands of years to periodic famines faced by Native Americans, and then played a central role in the stories of the first European settlers, including the thirteen men at Jamestown who died from starvation. But the emerging nation rapidly developed a vast agricultural abundance. By 1707, the image of America as a bountiful garden was already known around the globe.[3] The nation soon achieved its status as "breadbasket to the world."

This bounty of course did not extend to African slaves who received barely enough food rations to keep them alive, nor to Native Americans, whose primary sources of food, most significantly buffalo meat, were systematically destroyed by settlers. Meanwhile, as most early European Americans worked on farms and were able to grow their own foods, there were some pockets of poverty early in US history. These poor people were treated particularly harshly since the early colonial leaders had brought with them the English tradition of blaming the poor for their poverty, including the practice of throwing people who owed money into debtors' prisons.

BRITISH IMPORTS: INDUSTRIAL REVOLUTION AND WIDESPREAD HUNGER

The pattern for how America's leaders would deal with hunger and poverty among its residents—and particularly among oppressed minorities—was, in many respects, set by how the British treated the starving Irish people during the potato famine of the 1840s. While the immediate cause of the one million deaths in Ireland was a natural failure of the potato crop, British economic and governmental policies on food exports, land ownership, and famine relief greatly increased the extent and severity of the suffering when they refused needed aid in order to prevent the starving masses from becoming too "dependent."

As Christine Kinealy documents in her definitive history of the famine, the world's first soup kitchens were created in response to the Irish famine, primarily because serving soup was cheaper and more efficient than serving actual meals. People were usually only given food in exchange for work, but some people were so weak from hunger that they were unable to work, and thus got less food, and thus progressively weaker, and became less able to work . . . until they died.[4]

As the Irish famine death toll mounted, British officials preached the gospel of local community responsibility and personal self-reliance. Charles Trevelyan, British officer in charge of famine relief, wrote:

> . . . indirect advantages will accrue to Ireland from the scarcity, and the measures taken for its relief . . . Besides, the greatest improvement of all which could take place in Ireland would be to teach the other people to depend upon themselves for developing the resources of the country, instead of having recourse to the assistance of the government [of Britain] on every occasion. If a firm stand is not made against the prevailing disposition to take advantage of this crisis to break down all barriers, the true permanent interests of this country will, I am convinced, suffer in a manner which will be irreparable in our time.[5]

Similarly, Charles Wood, the British Chancellor of the Exchequer, wrote:

> What has brought them [the Irish], in great measure at least, to their present state of helplessness? Their habit of depending on government. What are we trying to do now? To force them upon their own

resources. Of course, they mismanage matters very much. . . . If we are to select the destitute, pay them, feed them, and find money from hence, we shall have the whole population of Ireland upon us soon enough.[6]

Thus, a philosophy emerges that the best way to aid poor people is to cut off their aid. The soup lines in Ireland were certainly harsher than even the most punitive policies in America today, but the basic concept prevails. We can see it today in New York City, where unemployed adults without dependents are cut off from food stamps after three months if they are unable to find work. Compare Trevelyan's and Wood's statements to Mayor Michael Bloomberg's when he denied food stamps to the unemployed in 2006: "I'm a believer that people should have to work for a living. You have to have a penalty if there's a requirement to work, and this penalty is one that's appropriate."[7]

THE ARRIVAL OF MACHINES—AND WIDESPREAD POVERTY AND HUNGER—IN AMERICA

After the arrival of the industrial age in America, an ever-increasing percentage of the nation's populace lived in cities, without the ability to raise their own food. Unlike workers in the previous age who may have worked on small farms or in tiny shops for an owner they or their families had personally known their whole lives, the new waves of desperate immigrant factory workers usually had no personal connection with the bosses, and were treated as such. Seven-day workweeks, child labor, and minuscule wages were all par for the course. Lacking unions or significant political power, the workers had little choice other than to generally accept their conditions, and once in a while, participate in a riot that was sure to be bloodily suppressed. Despite their paltry wages, rents weren't cheap—even for packed, disease-ridden, rat-filled tenements without hot water. But at least these Northern workers were paid wages; in the post-Reconstruction South, most African Americans lived as tenant farmers, often earning nothing for their labors except for the privilege to continue working on someone's else's land.

By the 1860s, alcoholism and homelessness became growing problems, and were most noticeable in big cities with newspapers to report on the problems. In 1866, the *New York Times* reported "large numbers of entirely homeless men and women drifting in the street [of New York City]." In 1909, the city built a Municipal Lodging House for the homeless with 964 beds. Officials painted a rosy picture of conditions there, but resident Frank Tannenbaum said: "It's not fit for a dog."[8]

Big cities also started developing the first American soup kitchens, some of which are still in operation today (such as the New York City Rescue Mission, founded 1872, and Chicago's Pacific Garden Mission, founded in 1877). In his classic realist novel *Sister Carrie*, Theodore Dreiser painted a vivid picture of the mission conditions, circa 1900: "The men waited patiently like cattle in the coldest weather, often for several hours, before they could be admitted. . . . They ate and went away again, some of them returning regularly day after day the winter through."[9] What is truly heartbreaking is that Dreiser could be almost precisely describing how those agencies function today.

In the progressive era, social reformers started ambitious attempts to better count and document the extent of hunger. In 1904, in his landmark book *Poverty*, Robert Hunter caused a major stir by estimating that there were 70,000 hungry children in New York City, and explaining, many years ahead of his time, that malnutrition significantly hindered the ability of children to learn and grow.[10] Hunter's contemporary, John Spargo, described how, eager to disprove Hunter's findings, New York school officials went into classrooms and asked children to raise their hands if they were hungry; not surprisingly, few were willing to humiliate themselves in front of their teachers and their classmates by admitting hunger. Spargo wrote:

One of the most notable of these school investigations was undertaken by this principal of a large school to "prove conclusively that there is no such thing as a serious problem of underfeeding among our school children." The principal is a devotee of the theory of the survival of the fittest and the elimination of the weak by competition and struggle. "If you attempt to take hardship and suffering out of their lives by smoothing the pathways of life for these children, you weaken their character, and, by doing so, you sin against the children themselves, and, by doing so, sin against society."[11]

Not satisfied with such official research methods, Spargo performed his own investigation. He met a captain of a Salvation Army post in New York who personally knew of several children who were "literally half starved," and told the story of children who were clearly very hungry but did not want to obtain free breakfasts at the charity because they didn't want to take a "handout."[12] Spargo estimated that eight percent of the city's school children had no breakfast at all, and another 15 percent had virtually no breakfast other than a piece of bread or crackers, but "without milk, cereals, cake, butter, jam, eggs, fruit, fish, or meat of any kind."[13] Describing the broader national problem, Spargo wrote:

> The thousands of rickety infants to be seen in all our large cities and towns, the anemic, languid-looking children one sees everywhere in working class districts, and the striking contrast presented by the appearance of the children of the well-to-do bear eloquent witness to the widespread prevalence of underfeeding.[14]

Spargo noted that other nations in Europe had long been studying the problem of child hunger, and some had even started school meals programs. "Only we in America have ignored this problem of terrible child hunger."[15]

Following up on the work of Hunter and Spargo in New York City, a young Frances Perkins (who would later go on to become the nation's first female US cabinet secretary, serving as Franklin Delano Roosevelt's secretary of labor and helping write the Social Security Act) wrote a master's thesis at Columbia University in 1910 entitled, "A Study in Malnutrition in 107 Children from Public School (P.S.) 51."[16]

She found that, during the recession of 1907–1908, there were "pathetic cases of little boys and little girls fainting in school from sheer lack of food." The doctor working with her found such symptoms as pallor, emaciation, and dark circles under the eyes in 107 children who were "bona fide malnutrition cases." Three quarters of the children had for breakfast nothing more than bread, or bread and coffee, or tea. "In some cases butter is used with the bread in the morning, but this is very rare, for butter is costly." A typical lunch was soup, possibly (but not always) with meat, and tea. A typical supper was bread and tea, some polenta, and, on some occasions, sandwiches. "Eggs, butter, and fresh milk are conspicuous by their absence from most family diets . . . very little fresh fruit and few fresh vegetables enter into the diets." Perkins summed up her findings this way: "The sight of many little children with the blight of hunger set upon their future made it impossible for the investigator and writer to forget that the material here treated in a cold, impersonal manner is nevertheless a mass of human documents full of human misery."

Perkins findings are remarkable today in a number of ways. While exact statistical comparisons of food insecurity in 1910 versus today are not possible, it is still clear that low- income children were far hungrier than they are today. They ate almost no protein on an average day, didn't have regular access to school meals, and rarely had more than some bread and coffee. Even the hungriest American kids in the modern age generally have a lot more and better food than that. Also striking is that almost all these children had mothers who worked outside the home, reminding us that the social changes in the 1960s and 1970s that brought large numbers of women into the workplace for the first time affected mostly middle- and upper-class women, since low-income woman had *always* worked outside of the home out of necessity.

Perkins's study also described the first pilot school lunch program in the US that had started a few years earlier in Chicago, through which a group of society women provided meals to "only children known to be needy and deserving." She pondered a debate that still rages today over whether all school meals should be free and universal: "Some would like to see school feeding on the same basis as public education—free, scientific, and compulsory for all. Others would provide free meals only for the children of poverty stricken parents, and still others propose a system of school meals where the children voluntarily attend and pay for the actual food they receive, leaving only the cost of administration to the public funds." She said people opposed school meals because that would "weaken parental responsibility" and "pauperize the community." But a more progressive objection is that "children undernourished represent a family in poverty, and that feeding of school children is not enough to raise the family out of poverty."

Perkins also made an argument, remarkably prescient for 1910, which also happens to be a central argument of this book: efforts to feed hungry children should not be taken as a substitute for broader societal efforts to fight poverty.

> The questions involved, in preventing malnutrition, are after all the two which are fundamental to all social reform, the question of increasing wages and the question of making education more widespread. Temporary relief is necessary, and its method may well deserve discussion, but it is after all an expedient to head off malnutrition until society adjusts itself and provides adequate incomes and adequate education to all its workers. The heading off must be done, however, and must be done at once.

Unfortunately, all this time later, we are still waiting for a society that provides adequate incomes and adequate education.

THE GREAT DEPRESSION AND THE COLLAPSE OF THE CHARITY SYSTEM

As horrible as things were in 1910 for the poor, by 1931, at height of the Great Depression, they were even worse. It was the only time in recorded US history of large-scale famine-like conditions nationwide.

Americans routinely foraged through garbage cans for food and dug up public parks to find roots they could eat. Parents reluctantly sent their children door-to-door to beg. Relief agencies nationwide lost their ability to prevent starvation. In New York City, ninety-five people diagnosed as suffering from starvation were admitted to the city's four largest hospitals in 1931. Twenty of them died.[17] The city had eighty-two separate breadlines.[18] The Municipal Lodging House for the homeless provided 408,100 lodgings and 1,024,247 meals in 1931. One year later, in 1932, it provided 889,984 lodgings and 2,688,266 meals, at a time when the entire New York City population was only 6.9 million people.[19]

Localities, expected to fund relief efforts themselves, were simply running out of money to do so. In May 1932, the average relief grant in Philadelphia—out of which people were expected to pay for food and all other basic expenses—was cut to $4.32 per family per week, equaling about $62 per week in today's money. In New York City, the average weekly relief grant fell to $2.39 (about $35 in today's money) and less than half of the unemployed heads of families received any relief at all. Baltimore gave needy families an average of 80 cents, and Atlanta provided 60 cents per week for whites and less for blacks.[20]

The nation was near the point of revolution. At times, armed men would go in large groups to stores to demand credit and, when refused, take food anyway. The term "food riot" became popular in the press. Even the president of the Baltimore and Ohio Railroad, Daniel Willard, said, "I'd steal before I starve."

Adding fuel to the fire was the country's glut of unused food. Oklahoma union activist and editor Oscar Ameringer wrote, "The farmers are being pauperized by the poverty of the industrial populations and the industrial populations are being pauperized by the poverty of the farmers." Neither farmers nor factory workers had the money to buy the products of the other. Columnist Walter Lippmann wrote, "I shall speak of the paradox at the heart of all this suffering—the sensational and intolerable paradox of want in the midst of abundance, of poverty in the midst of plenty."[21]

Today it seems obvious that government should have purchased some of the excess agricultural products and distributed them to the hungry, but at the time, opposition to government involvement in social welfare, as well as the belief in the unlimited abilities of American charities, was deeply ingrained in American thought. Consequently, the idea of the government buying food and distributing it for free seemed radical, particularly to the Republicans in charge of the nation. In 1931, when Democratic leader William McAdoo suggested that surplus wheat be distributed to the unemployed, President Herbert J. Hoover rejected the idea, saying, "I am confident that the hungry and unemployed will be cared for by our sense of voluntary organization and community service." On another occasion, in describing the choice between having local governments and charities address the problem versus having the federal government do so, Hoover said:

> It is solely a question of the best method by which hunger and cold can be prevented. . . . My own conviction is strongly that if we break down this sense of individual responsibility to the individual, and mutual self-help in the country in times of national difficulty and if we start appropriations of this character we have not only impaired something infinitely valuable in the life of the American people but we have struck at the roots of self-government.[22]

Ironically, Hoover had first become nationally known in America for his effective leadership in providing aid to starving Europeans following World War I, but he just couldn't accept the reality that his beloved United States needed that same type of help.

As America's crises worsened further, Hoover would not budge in his opposition to domestic relief. In a 1932 speech, he decried government aid, saying, "A cold and distant charity which puts out its sympathy only through the tax collector yields only a meager dole of unloving and perfunctory relief."[23] He was clearly blind to the fact that millions of Americans on the verge of starvation would have been grateful for any sort of food aid, no matter how unloving and perfunctory. Two days before the election of 1932, which he lost in a landslide to FDR, Hoover declared himself unable to "find a single locality where people are being deprived of food or shelter."[24] Hoover was the nation's first significant right-wing hunger denier. It is no wonder a conservative think tank, the Hoover Institution, is named after him.

But as much as Hoover's loss was a landslide of historic proportions (with FDR getting 22.8 million popular votes and Hoover 15.7 million), 41 percent of voters supported him despite his refusals to provide aid. In other words, at a time when an estimated one third of the country was unemployed and millions of Americans were on the verge of starving to death, nearly four in ten Americans were so opposed to government intervention that they voted for a candidate who insisted that localities and charities—not the public sector—had the prime responsibility to respond to the national crisis.

Hoover was not alone in his opposition to government food aid. Wealthy people who dominated the boards of charities complained that providing food aid would promote dependency and that private charity was more efficient than government aid.[25] Even progressive social workers believed that food aid "was an antiquated form of relief, inconsistent with modern social work practice and the dignity of the client."[26]

Yet the severity of the crisis eventually sunk in for many of our nation's leaders, and necessity trumped ideology, as even staunch Republican US Rep. Hamilton Fish supported a proposal to have the government buy excess wheat for distribution to the poor:

> "It is a disgrace and an outrage that this country of ours, with over abundance of food stuffs, should permit millions of our own people to continue to be undernourished and hungry." Citing instances in which Congress had aided the victims of disasters abroad, Fish argued that the "first function of government is to take care of its own people in time of great emergency." Permitting people to starve, he declared, was "creating a hotbed for communism."[27]

Still, congressional support was not unanimous. Rep. Charles Adkins (R-IL) challenged Fish's claim that people were starving. "There are many indigent people," Adkins conceded, "but the question is, does anybody starve?"[28] Conservatives who did support the measure went out of their way to stress that it was *not* a "dole," the word used then for welfare. Said Rep. David Glover (D-AR): "I am as much opposed to dole as any man in this Congress. But there is a difference between feeding a hungry man and dole. There is no person that would have a spark of feeling for humanity that would dare say that the government, with all this wheat in its hands and food that could be delivered to a person in distress should stand by and let them suffer." Said Rep. Oscar De Priest (R-IL): "I am against all doles but I think during these perilous times when people are hungry we ought to cut the red tape and feed the people of America."

Rep. John Flannagan of Virginia, however, made a stirring floor speech that eviscerated the hypocrisy of his colleagues rushing forward to decry food relief as "dole":

> Oh, the scarecrow in this bill seems to be that it will be considered a dole. Their statesmanship will not permit them to vote for anything that smacks of a dole. Well, I do not care what you call it . . . I am interested in feeding the hungry. It is a sad spectacle to see men who never felt the pangs of hunger, who do not know what it means to go without three good meals a day, who are living on the fat of the land . . . in the name of statesmanship, stand here and quibble over a name—over whether this is a dole or a relief measure. . . . Why if that is statesmanship all I have to say is—and I am a Presbyterian elder and believe my church will voice my sentiment—damn such statesmanship.[29]

The bill passed overwhelmingly.

After Roosevelt took office, the controversy over whether to support food aid versus other kinds of aid was not settled. His agriculture department received widespread and withering criticism for slaughtering and then discarding hogs in order to reduce supply. In response, FDR ordered the department to start distributing the meat to the hungry.

Today's liberals tend to forget that FDR repeatedly opposed giving out free money and food without requiring work—especially when they blasted Bill Clinton for supposedly betraying the New Deal tradition by supporting welfare reform. Roosevelt said direct relief was "a narcotic, a subtle destroyer of the human spirit." Instead of continuing to sponsor a "spiritual and moral disintegration fundamentally destructive to the national fiber," he said the government must find work for those in need and able to work. "We must preserve not only the bodies of the employed from destruction but also their self-respect, their self-reliance and courage and determination. Therefore, the Federal government must and shall quit this business of relief."[30]

A pragmatist who sometimes contradicted himself in order to solve pressing national problems, Roosevelt also significantly expanded the efforts—begun in the previous administration, against Hoover's will—to distribute free commodities to low-income Americans. FDR included other goods in addition to wheat and significantly increased the volume of surplus food purchased and distributed by the federal government.

FDR also supported creation of the first Food Stamp Program, in 1938. The program operated by permitting people on relief to buy orange stamps equal to their normal food expenditures; for every one dollar's worth of orange stamps purchased, fifty cents' worth of blue stamps were received. Orange stamps could be used to buy any food; blue stamps could only be used to buy food determined by the Department of Agriculture to be surplus. Over the course of nearly four years, the program reached approximately 20 million people, was located in nearly half of the nation's counties, and cost a total of $262 million (about $3 billion in 2006 dollars). The program was ended five years after it started, in 1943, as World War II brought an end to the Depression.[31]

SCHOOL LUNCH AND THE POSTWAR ERA

Even though FDR's food programs were a vast expansion of any previous food aid and even though they began to limit to mass starvation, they did not eliminate the widespread malnutrition that festered during the long Depression. When World War II arrived, General George Marshall and others noticed that American conscripts arrived at boot camp too malnourished to adequately fight. Consequently, President Harry S Truman and ultraconservative Senator Richard Russell, chair of the Senate Committee on Armed Services and a leading segregationist, teamed up to create the National School Lunch Program. While the program wasn't required in all schools and while many students still had to pay some reduced fee for lunch, it was a gigantic leap forward. Decades later, Russell said: "If I had to preserve one federal program above all others, I would still choose the School Lunch Program."[32]

Following the war, the nation experienced a tremendous long-term economic boom, which created the most prosperous middle class the world had ever known. Most Americans now assume that such growth was solely a result of the independent productivity of the private sector. But government efforts, most notably the original GI Bill, played a critical role in this growth. The GI

Bill enabled returning soldiers to obtain government help to pay for college, enabling millions of Americans, including my father, to become the first in their families to attend college. It's hard to imagine today, but leaders of some of the most elite institutions of higher education opposed that provision of the bill, assuming that people who couldn't afford to pay for college probably weren't smart enough to succeed there. The president of the University of Chicago, Robert Maynard Hutchins, said of the GI Bill, "Colleges and universities will find themselves converted into hobo jungles," and James B. Conant, president of Harvard, found the bill "distressing" because it failed "to distinguish between those who can profit most by advanced education and those who cannot."[33] Many of these same leaders later retracted their criticisms, admitting that the students who attended their institutions with GI Bill benefits were the most serious and hardworking they ever had. In the peak year of 1947, veterans accounted for 49 percent of college admissions. By the time the original GI Bill ended on July 25, 1956, 7.8 million of 16 million World War II veterans had participated in an education or training program.[34] Before the GI Bill, America's universities were exclusionary bastions for the nation's upper-crust elites. After the law, the nation's campuses were opened, at least briefly, to people from diverse economic backgrounds.

The GI Bill also helped returning veterans put a down payment on a first home or start a small business. From 1944 to 1952, the government backed nearly 2.4 million home loans for World War II veterans.[35]

While these programs and a booming economy provided for many people, there were still pockets of poverty and hunger, which were generally overlooked and neglected. In 1959, the Dwight D. Eisenhower administration reported to Congress that the USDA, when deciding how to utilize surplus commodities, gave first priority to overseas sales, second to international donations, and last priority to feeding hungry Americans.[36] Also that year, when Congress passed legislation authorizing the USDA to reestablish the Food Stamp Program, President Eisenhower refused to exercise that authority.

HUNGER "REDISCOVERED" IN THE 1960S

The next decade proved that elections truly do matter. Campaigning in West Virginia in 1960, John F. Kennedy, who had grown up in great privilege, was genuinely shocked and appalled to find hungry children with hollow eyes, living on little more than surplus lard and cornmeal. He made hunger an issue in the general election, even raising domestic hunger in the opening statement of a debate against Nixon:

> I'm not satisfied when we have over 9 billion dollars worth of food [in surplus]—some of it rotting—even though there is a hungry world, and even though 4 million Americans wait every month for a food package from the government, which averages five cents a day per individual. I saw cases in West Virginia, here in the United States, where children took home part of their school lunch in order to feed their families. . . . I don't think we're meeting our obligations toward these Americans.[37]

After winning the election, Kennedy quickly acted upon his concern. The first executive order he issued as president on January 21, 1961, doubled the number of foods on the commodity surplus list and directed the USDA to start the pilot Food Stamp Program, which Eisenhower had refused to implement, in select locations.[38] What a difference a day makes.

A year later in 1962, the publication of Michael Harrington's groundbreaking book on poverty, *The Other America*, significantly increased the nation's awareness that not all Americans were benefiting from the nation's growing prosperity. Then in 1964, President Lyndon B. Johnson launched the War on Poverty. Late that year, as a part of a deal to pass a wheat and cotton bill, Congress slightly increased the Food Stamp Program, allowing, but not requiring, any locality in the nation to run a local program. In 1966, Congress began expanding the National School Lunch Program and created the first pilot school breakfast programs.

Still, the hunger problem persisted. In April 1967, a Senate subcommittee held a hearing on poverty and the Head Start Program in the Mississippi Delta (a region comprising of parts of Mississippi, Arkansas, and Louisiana that has extraordinarily high rates of poverty and a large African-American population), and Senators Robert Kennedy (D-NY) and Joseph Clark (D-PA) decided to see poverty conditions for themselves outside of the hearing room. Given Kennedy's superstar status as the brother of the martyred president and a potential presidential candidate himself, his visit with hungry children in Mississippi attracted widespread media attention. According to Kennedy aide Peter Edelman, Kennedy saw "visible swollen bellies and running sores on the arms and legs of young children that appeared not to be healing. Kennedy asked the children what they had eaten and how many meals they ate every day. They said that they usually have one meal a day, and they had eaten whatever they were going to eat that day."[39]

Said Kennedy, "I've seen bad things in West Virginia, but I've never seen anything like this in the United States. . . . My God, I didn't know this kind of thing existed. How can a country like this allow it? Maybe they just don't know."[40] Kennedy's children later said "he came home to dinner that night deeply shaken," and that he, a man of few words so much of the time, "couldn't stop talking about what he had seen that day."[41]

A few weeks later, a team of doctors headed by Dr. Robert Coles and funded by the Field Foundation traveled to the Delta to study hunger there. Discovering Third World–style malnutrition, their findings startled the nation:

> . . . we saw children whose nutritional and medical condition we can only describe as shocking—even to a group of physicians whose work involves daily confrontation with disease and suffering. In child after child we saw: evidence of vitamin and mineral deficiencies; serious, untreated skin infections and ulcerations; eye and ear diseases, also unattended bone diseases secondary to poor food intake; the prevalence of bacterial and parasitic disease, as well as severe anemia, which resulting loss of energy and ability to live a normally active life; diseases of the heart and lungs—requiring surgery—which have gone undiagnosed and untreated . . . and finally, in boys and girls in every county we visited, obvious evidence of severe malnutrition, with injury to body's tissues—its muscles, bones and skin as well as an associated psychological state of fatigue, listlessness, and exhaustion. . . . We saw homes with children who are lucky to eat one meal a day. . . . We saw children who don't get to drink milk, don't get to eat fruit, green vegetables, or meat. . . . Their parents may be declared ineligible for the food stamp program, even though they have literally nothing. . . . We do not want to quibble over words, but "malnutrition" is not quite what we found. . . . They are suffering from hunger and disease and directly or indirectly they are dying from them—which is exactly what "starvation" means.[42]

One of the doctors on the team, Dr. Raymond Wheeler of North Carolina, included his own field report:

At one house the landlords reportedly had forbidden the tenants to have a garden although in this particular case, there was obviously ample space for one. This—from all reports—is common practice in the towns as well as on the plantations, though why this should be so in view of their well-known need for food seemed inexplicable on any ground other than outright spite. . . . Only one of the families I visited ever had milk at all and this was reserved for the "sickliest" ones. One mother summed it up: "These children go to bed hungry and get up hungry and don't ever know nothing in between."[43]

A few months later, at a US Senate hearing, Dr. Wheeler again gave a vivid description of what he saw in Mississippi. But he added an even more shocking charge, especially coming from a Southern white man—that the white ruling class of Mississippi was purposely starving African Americans in order to drive them out of state because the mechanization of cotton picking had made their labor unnecessary and because their civil rights organizing had made them a threat to the power structure. He called Mississippi "a kind of prison for a great group of uneducated, semi-starving people." His comments generated a firestorm.

THE RACIAL SUBTEXT IN OPPOSING ANTIHUNGER EFFORTS

Perhaps many Southerners were outraged that such oppressive conditions existed in their region and were thankful to Dr. Wheeler and his colleagues for having the courage to speak up, but judging from the letters to him on this topic, the greatest sentiment seems to be that they betrayed their race by raising the issue at all.[44] Read a typical hate letter written to the doctors from a woman in Neshoba, Mississippi:

Doctors! I want to . . . tell you just how cheap, rotten, lying, disgusting, and contemptible you, & all your cohorts are—in your most recent "liable attacks on Mississippi." If I just didn't know that God will see you all get your true punishment, I would <u>love</u> to personally take you on myself. . . . The "loads" of commodities the lazy Negroes carries out for their illegitimate children by the dozens & husbands too sorry & lazy to work and make a living and then drives around in some of the finest cars here is in Miss & I can't even afford a car to hold a job with & them such disciples of Satan. Forever lying and slinging mud at our Miss! All of you are of the very lowest caliber of humanity. . . . You are a Disgrace to America and also the entire medical profession!

One letter, claiming that it was "from a group of graduate students in sociology and anthropology who have been working in the field and good citizens who helped all across this land of ours," said:

Why smear the South with your headlines? (Incidentally four of us followed the Alabama march put on by Martin L. King and it was a disgraceful and degrading round of licentiousness which turned our stomachs even though we were supposed to be ready for anything as future sociologists) . . . We say to you that we are tired of working and paying taxes to support immoral Negro women producing illegitimates by the thousands for public dole—this applies to trashy whites as well. . . . What does a doctor expect to find but skin infections and parasitic diseases when people don't wash themselves? . . . Those sullied woman bring much of the trouble to their children through association with the vilest and filthiest of "men" . . . all they do is sit back and wait for the monthly check and produce more illegitimates for more disease and more suffering. They should be sterilized so that society would be gradually cleaned of its diseases, but you wouldn't recommend that, would you Doctors?

At least there are two pieces of notable "fan" mail in Wheeler archives. The first was a letter from Mrs. M. S. Vomacka of Duluth, Minnesota, thanking him for testifying before Congress and saying "you are a very 'brave' man for making such an honest statement and you have awakened the citizens of this country into just how 'awful' we really are." He also received a telegram from Dr. Martin Luther King, Jr., thanking him for his work.

The reason I provide so much text from the hateful letters is to document just how much of the underlying opposition to fighting hunger was fueled by racism (not just in Mississippi, but throughout the South, and indeed, nationwide), a situation that has not entirely ended even decades later, despite the fact that the majority of hungry Americans were (and still are) white.

It is no coincidence that many of the strongest supporters of segregation were also the fiercest opponents of increasing government support for anti-hunger efforts. Leading segregationist (and the father of a mixed-race child) Strom Thurmond almost succeeded in halting efforts to get the federal government to measure hunger, saying: "There has been hunger since the time of Jesus Christ and there always will be."[45] Powerful House Agriculture Appropriations Chair Jamie Whitten complained to Senator George McGovern that if "hunger was not a problem, Nigras won't work," and that McGovern was promoting revolution by seeking an improvement in food stamp benefits, which Whitten thought would be used for "frivolity and wine."[46] Whitten even opposed expansion of the School Lunch Program to many of the nation's poorest jurisdictions that did not yet have such programs. Sadly, for me at least, the USDA headquarters building in Washington, DC, where I worked for eight years, is now named for Whitten.

Author Nick Kotz has described how, in the 1960s, "Food and welfare aid, in minimal amounts, were available for the docile poor who 'stayed in line,' but these benefits could be withheld from anyone who challenged or threatened the institutions." Kotz explains how food aid was cut off to civil rights activists in Mississippi, how parents in Kentucky who fought for school lunches for their kids had their children denied use of a youth corps program, and how party bosses in Des Moines and Chicago used food aid to bolster their political machines.[47]

LIMITED FOOD AID AND STARVATION CONDITIONS

The opposition of key congressional committee chairs in the mid-1960s further weakened the small federal nutrition programs. As some counties switched from free commodities to food stamps, because people had to provide cash to buy a portion of their food stamps up front (when they previously got the commodities for free), the number of people getting help from the government dropped. For instance, in Sunflower County, Mississippi, in the 1960s, participation in federal food aid dropped from 18,540 persons in the commodity programs to 7,856 in food stamps. In 1967, fewer than one in six poor Americans benefited at all from the commodity or food stamp programs. More than half of all states denied food aid to many people with incomes below the poverty line (in 1967, it was $3,335 for a family of four). Localities were allowed a great deal of discretion over how they managed their programs, which encouraged eccentric rules such as the one in an Indiana township which denied commodity aid to families with dogs in the household.[48] Eligibility requirements were different in each state, but Whitten insisted on a rule that no county could have both commodities and food stamps. As a result of all those restrictions on food aid, Third World–like conditions existed in significant pockets of the nation at the time.

Following up on the Field Foundation's study of Mississippi, the Citizens' Board of Inquiry Into Hunger and Malnutrition in the United States conducted a study in 1968 in order to prove that such conditions existed throughout America and to motivate the media to focus on the issue. The cochairs of the study, Benjamin E. Mays and Leslie W. Dunbar, wrote: "No other western country permits such a large proportion of its people to endure the lives we press on the poor. . . . To make four-fifths of a nation more affluent than any people in history, we have degraded one-fifth mercilessly."[49] The report found "chronic hunger and malnutrition in every part of the United States," and that people were going without food for four or five days in a row or subsisting on powdered milk for a week at a time. Substantial numbers of newborns were dying, "from causes that can be traced directly and primarily to malnutrition." Only 5 million of the 29 million then-eligible Americans were participating in the two existing government food programs (commodities and food stamps) and, "the majority of those participating [were] not the poorest of the poor," because the poorest of the poor could not afford to buy the stamps. While noting the inherent challenge in measuring the problem, the report stated: "We face a problem which, conservatively estimated, affects 10 million Americans and in all likelihood a substantially higher number." The report concluded: "We find ourselves somewhat startled by our own findings, for we had been lulled into the comforting belief that at least the extremes of privation had been eliminated in the process of becoming the world's wealthiest nation."[50]

Despite setbacks in the last few decades, there is still far less hunger and malnutrition in the United States today than in 1968. What changed? Grassroots activists took action, the media took notice, elected officials took their cue to pass antihunger legislation—and the modern safety net was constructed. The system worked.

HUNGER STUDIES AND MEDIA COVERAGE MAKE HUNGER A "HOT ISSUE"

Dr. King launched the "Poor People's Campaign" to target poverty nationwide, and one of its top goals was to expand federal nutrition assistance programs. After King's assassination, the movement, led by Rev. Ralph Abernathy, camped out on the Washington Mall to dramatize the issue. They were able to demand and obtain meetings on hunger with key national leaders.

Later in 1968, CBS broadcast an extraordinary, hour-long, Emmy Award–winning, prime-time documentary called *Hunger in America*, based on the Citizens' Board report. Opening with a lengthy close-up of a malnourished baby literally dying as the camera rolled, the broadcast galvanized the nation. Other networks and newspapers also gave hunger great attention. NBC's *Evening News* also won an Emmy that year for its frequent hunger coverage. The issue was fully rediscovered.

The Field Foundation and Citizens' Board studies were both specifically designed to attract media coverage, which, it was hoped, would then advance legislation. The strategy worked. As a former USDA colleague of mine, Ronald De Munbrun, has proven in research, such reports set a pattern, followed until this day, by which antihunger groups issue reports specifically to obtain media coverage and thereby achieve public policy improvements.[51] That's the main reason the organization I manage in New York City regularly issues reports, many of which do generate media coverage and prompt elected official to take action.

In the late 1960s, hunger was a hot issue in Washington. The US Senate created a Select Committee on Nutrition and Human Needs (often referred to as the "Hunger Committee") chaired by liberal senator George McGovern of South Dakota. Significantly, the committee also included archconservative Robert Dole of Kansas.

A further breakthrough came when Senator Ernest Hollings of South Carolina unexpectedly disavowed his previous claims, which he had made when he was governor, that there was no hunger in his state, saying that he had previously denied the problem because he worried that companies in the North would cancel their plans to relocate to South Carolina if they knew the level of deprivation there. Hollings then said, "South Carolina's hunger is both white and black. . . . Let me categorically state there is hunger in South Carolina. I have seen it with my own eyes. Starving—that is too dreadful a term. But the result is the same. Those weakened and diseased by hunger are dying from the diseases caused by hunger."[52]

RICHARD NIXON: CROOK, DESPOT, THIEF . . . AND ONE OF HISTORY'S GREATEST (ALBEIT RELUCTANT) HUNGER FIGHTERS

In early 1969, the new president, Richard Nixon, expressed doubt that there was any serious hunger in America. A senior White House official echoed the president, saying, "There may be malnutrition in America—but real hunger on a substantial scale—I don't believe it." Nixon's director of communications publicly criticized Senator McGovern (who they suspected, correctly, would run for president) for "traipsing around the country with television cameras" and said it was disgraceful for McGovern and others to "make hunger a political cause."[53]

Yet the political pressure for Nixon to do something about hunger had increased so significantly that, in May of 1969, he sent a "Special Message to the Congress Recommending a Program to End Hunger in America." The message included the implication that the poor were hungry due to ignorance and that "people must be educated in choosing proper foods." But other than that, Nixon's antihunger rhetoric was surprisingly stirring, and most importantly, his policy proposals were progressive, concrete, and broad. He called for Congress to expand the Food Stamp Program and eliminate the requirement that even the poorest people in need of food stamps purchase them. He sought congressional authority for the USDA to have both a Food Stamp Program and a food distribution program in the same county. He announced that he had created a Food and Nutrition Service within the USDA to administer antihunger programs. And he even indicated that he had directed the USDA to start a "Special Supplemental Food Program," the forerunner to the WIC program, which would be specially aimed at aiding low-income women and infants.[54] Thus, almost entirely due to agitation from the media, antipoverty activists, and other political leaders, an administration, which doubted that hunger even existed just months prior, ended up proposing what were, at that point in American history, the most significant proposals ever made to reduce it.

Nixon placed such a high public priority on hunger issues that, later in 1969, he sponsored the first—and, as of 2007, only—White House conference on hunger, although he told his secretary of agriculture to "use all the rhetoric so long as it doesn't cost any money."[55] In order to entice a young congressman to take a job in the administration as head of the Office of Equal Opportunity, a Great Society agency with the legal mandate to ensure "maximum feasible participation of the poor" in running government antipoverty efforts, Nixon threw in the extra enticement that the individual would head up the adminis-tration's antihunger initiatives. The congressman took the job, and although he was in charge of the one federal office directly tasked with increasing the involvement of poor people in government, he actually opposed inviting rep-resentatives of the poor to the antihunger conference because he feared an embarrassing militant protest. If such a pattern of logic sounds familiar, it should. The young man in charge of the antihunger program was none other than Donald Rumsfeld.[56]

THE 1970S: BIRTH OF THE ANTIHUNGER MOVEMENT AND THE MODERN NUTRITION SAFETY NET

Most of the nation's leading antihunger groups were founded during a fourteen-year period starting in 1970: The Food Research and Action Center (FRAC) in 1970; Bread for the World in 1973; World Hunger Year (WHY) in 1975; Second Harvest (which later changed its name to America's Second Harvest and then Feeding America) in 1979; and Share Our Strength (SOS) in 1984.

Not coincidentally, the nation's greatest advances in reducing hunger came in the same decade. Not only was the fledging antihunger movement strongest in flexing its new muscles, but Senators Dole and McGovern forged a consensus across party and ideological lines to take concrete steps to reduce domestic hunger. Over a span of just a few years, the developments came fast and furious.

In 1971, Congress passed legislation that limited the purchase requirement for food stamps and, as an amendment to the Child Nutrition Action of 1972, Congress authorized the Special Supplemental Nutrition Program for Women, Infants, and Children (WIC). In 1973, Congress passed a law requiring states to expand the Food Stamp Program to every jurisdiction.[57]

The biggest advance was the passage of the Food Stamp Act of 1977, which created the Food Stamp Program as we know it today. The act completely elim-inated the purchase requirement for food stamps, making them free on a large scale for the very first time. It also established national income eligibility guide-lines at the poverty line and required outreach to enroll more people into the program. Showing the nation's ambivalence toward such matters, the act also penalized households whose heads voluntarily quit jobs. Overall, though, the bill was a major advance and resulted in more Americans getting more generous benefits.[58] In 1978, Congress permanently authorized the Child and Adult Care Food Program, which provides food to low-income children in child care and to low-income seniors in certain institutional settings.

Overall, between 1969 and 1979, as Chart 3A demonstrates, the expansion of existing programs and the start of new ones resulted in a dramatic increase in the percentage of low-income Americans who received federal help obtaining food.[59]

CHART 3A

Growth of the Federal Safety Net Programs

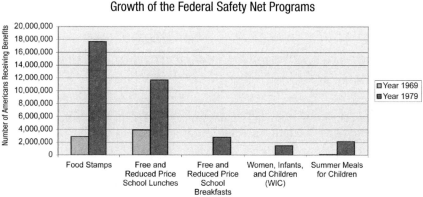

Source: USDA Food and Nutrition Service

Participation in the Food Stamp Program increased sixfold, from 2.8 million people to 17.6 million people. The number of children receiving free and reduced-price lunches tripled, from 3.9 million to 11.7 million children. The number of children receiving free summer meals increased even more dramatically, from a small pilot program feeding 99,000 kids to a major national program serving 21 million. Neither the WIC program nor free and reduced-price breakfasts paid by the federal government even existed in 1969; by 1979 there were 4 million people benefiting from WIC and 2.7 million children getting free and reduced-price breakfasts.

These expansions succeeded spectacularly in achieving their main goal: ending starvation conditions in America.

In 1979, the Field Foundation sent a team of investigators back to many of the same parts of the United States found to have high rates of hunger in the late 1960s. They found dramatic reductions in hunger and malnutrition, and concluded: "This change does not appear to be due to an overall improvement in living standards or to a decrease in joblessness in these areas. . . . The Food

Stamp Program, the nutritional components of Head Start, school lunch and breakfast programs, and . . . WIC have made the difference."[60] Had the nation built upon this progress by further expanding and strengthening these programs, it could have easily ended hunger entirely.

THE REAGAN ERA: KETCHUP BECOMES A VEGETABLE AND FOOD PANTRIES BOOM

Some say the greatest symbol of the Ronald Reagan era is the fallen Berlin Wall, even though it fell after President Reagan left office and even though Reagan's role in prompting the collapse of the Soviet Union is debatable. I think a much more apt symbol of the Reagan era is the food pantry.

The gauzy nostalgia of Reagan's "Morning in America" political campaign ads masked the reality that high unemployment, social service cutbacks, and plummeting wages brought back significant domestic hunger.

When Reagan entered office in 1981, there were only a few hundred emergency feeding programs in America, most of which were traditional soup kitchens serving mostly the people who had been historically the most hungry—single men with substance abuse or mental illness problems. Yet, as a direct result of the economic policies and social service cuts set in motion by Reagan, the number of emergency feeding programs in America skyrocketed, and continued to do so even after he left office. There are now more than 40,000 such programs in America, and roughly two-thirds of them are food pantries, where parents and their children, the elderly, and working people obtain free groceries. Pantries didn't exist in any great numbers in the years between World War II and the 1980s.

Pantries were needed because Reaganomics failed. Somehow, tax cuts for the wealthy and massive defense spending did not lead to a "trickling down" of money for the poor. In the early years of the Reagan presidency, a nominally Democratic Congress, awed by Reagan's personal affability and scared of his political popularity, approved his harsh budgets. Social programs were hit hard. Even previously moderate congressional heroes of the antihunger movement, such as Senator Dole, went along for the ride. They allowed Reagan to cut food stamps and WIC, and even prevented the Food Stamp Program from engaging in outreach. Typical of how Reagan operated, he smilingly claimed that he cut outreach funds so the money saved could go to benefits, but none of those savings were used for benefits. He also slashed funding for education, health, support services for the mentally ill, and housing. The Congressional Budget Office estimated that there were $110 billion in reductions in social services from 1982 to 1986.[61]

To add insult to injury, all these cutbacks occurred during a time of a deep recession and extensive factory closings. After some insensitive comments by Reagan and his top aides—and after it became clear that there was a sharp spike in the number of feeding charities, as well as a massive new wave of homeless people on the streets of the nation's cities—hunger was again briefly back in the national limelight.

A team of doctors once again traveled the country looking for, and finding, "severe malnutrition," and Dr. J. Larry Brown chronicled their disturbing findings. They found a day care administrator in New Haven, Connecticut, who said, "The majority of babies come here hungry." They visited a firehouse in rural Maine, which doubled as a feeding program that provided a daily hot meal to senior citizens, and the center director said that "for a majority of them, I'd say it is the only meal of the day." They met a doctor in Mississippi who said that he literally "watched a baby die from malnutrition." A Mississippi girl told them she was not happy about the start of summer vacation: "When we is in school we get to eat lunch, but in summer we only gets supper." They heard of an Alabama man undergoing dialysis treatment who said that he and his wife didn't have one bit of food for their children that night. This man said, "While I am dying it's heartache to see my children going hungry and I can't do anything about it." The doctors concluded that 20 million Americans were going to bed hungry at some time each month. Even though the team hand delivered its report to the White House, when asked about the report by the media, the White House denied they had seen it. An administration spokesperson at the USDA later said: "The problem of hunger is not widespread. The federal government is doing more to end hunger than any administration in history."[62]

But the turning point in the Reagan revolution was when the administration tried to cut funding for school lunches, and, in addition, tried to save funds by classifying ketchup as a vegetable so that it would meet the vegetable requirements of school lunches. That caused a firestorm. While people could accept cuts to food stamps, which many thought went to lazy adults, the public couldn't abide cutting food for innocent kids. Plus, the "ketchup as a vegetable" idea was so easy to ridicule that it provided persistent fodder for the nation's comics and cartoonists. The flap prompted so much media coverage and water cooler talk that even Americans who did little to follow government and politics were aware of it. Recognition of the severe domestic hunger problem finally led Congress back to its senses, and it enacted incremental improvements in the Food Stamp Program in 1985 and 1987.

A BRIEF RETURN TO SANITY IN THE 1990S

By the 1990s, the time was ripe to undo some of the worst excesses of the Reagan era. In 1992, national antihunger leaders showed rare unity by agreeing to a major national declaration to end hunger, which stated: "Many of us are moved by the belief that the United States is losing its economic leadership, and that we must invest more in our children and families to insure national productivity in a more competitive world. Others are moved by enlightened self-interest, pointing out that we can neither pay now nor pay later for preventable problems."

I was proud to serve in the Bill Clinton administration at the USDA in a variety of positions for the full eight years of 1993 to 2000, during which I focused a great deal of my efforts on fighting hunger.

The administration's first antihunger efforts were encouraging. Prompted, in part, by preliminary data from the Community Childhood Hunger Identification Project (CCHIP), which showed that 4 million American children were hungry, President Clinton convinced the still-Democratic Congress to include in the 1993 budget $2.7 billion in funding for food stamp improvements. This funding implemented significant parts of the Mickey Leland Memorial Domestic Hunger Relief Act, which had been a main objective of antihunger advocates, by increasing benefits and simplifying applications for food stamps.

After the Newt Gingrich radicals took over Congress in 1994, they tried to dismantle the nutrition assistance safety net. Again, previous hunger heroes such as Bob Dole were mostly silent, although a few true Republican heroes (such as Senator Richard Lugar of Indiana) did provide a strong defense for food stamps. In the end, two Clinton vetoes of welfare reform bills preserved the Food Stamp Program as an entitlement program with national standards. However, the final welfare reform bill that Clinton signed eliminated food stamp eligibility for most legal immigrants, placed food stamp restrictions on unemployed adults, and reduced the size of average benefits, thereby cutting billions of dollars from the program.

In 1997 and 1998, Clinton successfully pushed Congress to reverse some of those cuts. When he signed the 1998 bill, he said,

This bill . . . rights a wrong. When I signed the Welfare Reform Bill in 1996 I said the cuts in nutritional programs were too deep and had nothing whatsoever to do with welfare reform. . . . Today we reinstate food stamp benefits to 250,000 legal immigrants, including seniors, persons with disabilities, and 75,000 children. . . . None of these benefit cuts had the first thing to do with welfare reform. Reinstating them is the right thing to do.[63]

During the Clinton administration, Food Stamp Program participation plummeted from 25 million to 17 million people. Some of that drop was for the best possible reason, because people's incomes had risen so greatly with the strong economy that they were no longer eligible. But the drop in food stamp participation was far greater than the drop in poverty. It turned out that many of the people removed from the rolls not only remained eligible for the benefits, but desperately needed them. As states were legally removing people from the welfare rolls, they were removing virtually all those people from food stamp benefits as well, often illegally. This was particularly ironic because the administration understood that food stamps were actually *more*, not less, important to people when they left welfare because they supported work. In response, President Clinton and US Secretary of Agriculture Dan Glickman directed the USDA to work with states to reverse the decreasing food stamp rolls. The administration increased food stamp outreach and made it easier for people to own cars and still obtain food stamps. While such steps did not immediately reverse the decline, they did put in place policies and mechanisms that would enable the rolls to increase over the subsequent years.

Secretary Glickman, with the strong backing of the White House, also launched two unique public/private initiatives, both of which I led. The first effort—the Food Recovery and Gleaning Initiative—worked to increase the amount of excess, wholesome food donated to feeding charities from restaurants, farms, cafeterias, and food manufacturers. Out of that effort grew the Community Food Security Initiative, which built partnerships between the federal government and nonprofit groups, businesses, and communities to reduce hunger and increase local food reliance.

Most of the national antihunger groups were wary of both these efforts, worrying that the administration was tacitly accepting the Republican line that private charity, not government, was responsible for ending hunger. Speaking at the 1997 Summit on Food Recovery and Gleaning, Secretary Glickman took great pains to dispel that notion, saying, "We know the government's food programs work, and that they will continue to be the first and strongest line of defense against hunger."[64]

At the National Summit on Community Food Security in 1999, President Clinton, appearing in videotaped remarks, explained how the Community Food Security Initiative would work in tandem with government safety net programs:

> I took executive action to help families gain access to food stamps. . . .
> Our work is far from done. While the federal government continues to
> be deeply involved in the fight against hunger, our nutritional safety
> net alone can't conquer the problem. . . . Government programs
> haven't done enough to capitalize on community expertise. . . . Com-
> munity efforts have often not taken full advantage of the government
> resources available to them. This conference is about building stronger
> partnerships, about bringing all the parties to the table and forming
> stronger ties among the federal government; state, local, and tribal
> governments; the private sector; nonprofit groups; the faith commu-
> nity; and private citizens.[65]

In the closing weeks of the administration in 2000, President Clinton announced that the USDA had created a program to enable senior citizens to obtain fresh fruits and vegetables at farmers' markets, modeled on an existing USDA program that enabled WIC participants to do so. Although a number of states already had such farmers' market coupon programs for seniors, and while the USDA only put $10 million into the effort that year, it was a major advance to have the federal government make it a national initiative.

So how did the Clinton administration do in fighting hunger? As difficult as it is to do a harsh self-assessment, I'd give us about a B+ for effort and a B for results. (Our results would have been better had it not been for consistent opposition from a Republican Congress.) Because the food insecurity methodology was not used before 1997, and further because it changed in 1998, we don't know precisely how the extent of hunger changed during that time. But given that the number of Americans in poverty plummeted by 7 million people between 1993, when Clinton took office, and 1998, it's safe to assume that hunger and food insecurity decreased as well. In the years for which we do have USDA food insecurity data, 1998 to 2000, we know that the number of food-insecure people dropped by 3 million people, from 36 to 33 million.[66]

Still, as the Clinton administration left office, even though we had slashed the poverty rate, we still had more poverty than any industrialized nation on the planet. As a result, the world's wealthiest country still had 33 million people living in homes that couldn't afford enough food. Tens of millions of people eligible for food stamp benefits weren't receiving them. Despite food stamp eligibility restorations for some categories of legal immigrants, many low-income legal immigrants—working hard and playing by the rules—still were ineligible for food stamps. And the lines at soup kitchens and food pantries were increasing.

As I often pointed out in internal administration debates—sometimes to the chagrin of certain fellow political appointees who thought that offering internal criticism of administration policies was tantamount to disloyalty—our accomplishments were just not good enough. But the people who really mattered—Clinton and Glickman and my fellow appointees working on hunger issues—agreed that we needed to do more and better. Just as we started making real progress, our time ran out. Sometimes, eight years seem like a long time. But, in our fight against hunger, they were all too short.

THE BUSH ERA AND THE BATTLE-FATIGUED "ARMIES OF COMPASSION"

Of course, everything got worse, far worse, after George W. Bush took office. The promise of "compassionate conservatism" gave way to the reality of skyrocketing poverty, declining wages for the poor and the middle class, unimaginably huge tax cuts for the mega rich, and soaring inequality of wealth. A small part of President Bush's Faith-Based Initiative, designed to aid what he called the "armies of compassion," was somewhat helpful, even providing some funding to the organization I direct. But mostly the initiative hovered between being a well-intended failure and an outright fraud, a mere reelection scheme masquerading as a government program.

There were only three bright spots in Bush's record on hunger. One, consistent with the pro-immigrant stand he had taken as a governor and in his first few years in office (but later largely abandoned under withering criticism from conservatives), Bush supported Congress's action that restored food stamp eligibility to more, but still not all, legal immigrants. Second, Bush's Under Secretary in charge of the USDA nutrition assistance programs, Eric Bost, did an admirable job of improving access to the Food Stamp and summer feeding programs. And third, while the federal government's overall response to Hurricane Katrina was worse than dismal, the only part of the response that actually worked was the Disaster Food Stamp Program, which began providing massive numbers of people with emergency food stamp benefits within just a few days of the hurricane hitting.

Other than that, the picture was bleak. In 2005, the Republican Congress and the president agreed upon a 1 percent cut in all spending—excluding, of course, spending on wars and homeland security. While defenders said the cuts were "across the board" in order to make it sound like they were fair and prudent, this meant cuts to the WIC program and to commodities going to pantries and kitchens.

President Bush offered two additional budget proposals so draconian that even the Republican Congress didn't go along with them. He proposed cutting hundreds of millions of dollars out of the Food Stamp Program by eliminating the option that states have to harmonize food stamp eligibility with eligibility for other antipoverty programs, an option that a number of states had used in order to both reduce bureaucracy and help more people get benefits. By proposing to take food out of the mouths of hungry children, seniors, and other food stamp recipients, Bush certainly wasn't compassionate. By reducing flexibility for states and increasing their bureaucracies, his recommendation wasn't even truly conservative. Bush also proposed the elimination of the entire Commodity Supplemental Food Program, a proposal that would have eliminated food going to 420,000 low-income senior citizens.[67] The Republican Congress sensibly rejected both those proposals. But the Bush administration didn't quit there: in 2008, it suggested that one of the main reasons the president vetoed the new Farm Bill was that it increased food stamp benefits.[68]

By 2008—with Republicans having mostly failed to slash nutrition programs and Democrats (again in charge of Congress) unwilling to push for significant increases in them—the nation had reached a sort of uneasy equilibrium on the issue, resulting in the maintenance of a safety net of federal programs that provided enough food to prevent widespread starvation but not enough to actually end hunger in America. A major assault on hunger would have to wait until another day and another president.

CHAPTER 4

THE TATTERED (BUT STILL EXISTING) FEDERAL HUNGER SAFETY NET

I pray to the lord that I get a better job so that I don't have to go to this place [a New York City government food stamp office]. I don't make enough on my income. There are a lot of educated people that don't want to be in the system, but this is the only means of support for the time being.

—Mother of four from Brooklyn, New York, whose paperwork was repeatedly lost and whose benefits were cut off by the food stamps office

America has taken huge steps away from famine-like conditions in the early 1900s and the pockets of severe hunger in the 1960s. This is because we do have a functioning, albeit imperfect, safety net that ensures no one will starve to death. Still, the holes are large enough for millions of Americans to fall through, and that's not acceptable.

THE TRUE STORY OF AMERICA'S SAFETY NET

The myth that the safety net was entirely shredded under Reagan, Clinton, and George W. Bush is false. Cuts under Reagan, as well as cuts as a result of the welfare reform bill that Clinton signed, slowed their growth. Most of Bush's attempts to cut these programs failed. By 2006, food stamp participation had returned to levels close to the historic high in 1995, with more than 26 million people participating. As Chart 4A shows, while, in 1964, the pilot Food Stamp Program fed a number of people equal to only 1 percent of the people in poverty, in 2007 the number of people receiving food stamp benefits equaled

CHART 4A

Americans in Poverty vs. Americans Receiving Food Stamps, 1964–2007

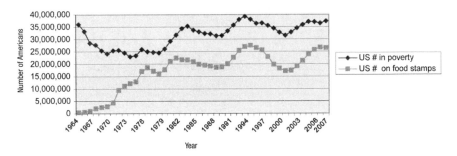

Sources: US Census Bureau Current Population Survey; USDA Food and Nutrition Service

71 percent of the people in poverty. While that's still 29 percent short, it's a huge improvement over where we were.

As Chart 4B proves, even adjusted for inflation, federal spending on the main three nutrition programs (food stamps, WIC, and school lunches) also increased over time. The spending in 1969 was equal to only about $4.5 billion in 2006 dollars, while actual spending on them in 2006 was $48 billion.

CHART 4B

Federal Spending on Nutrition Programs, Adjusted for Inflation, 1969–2006

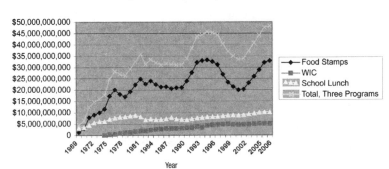

Source: USDA Food and Nutrition Service; inflation calculations by author

While it is true that spending on nutrition programs increased because poverty and need increased, Chart 4C demonstrates that nutrition spending *per person in poverty* also increased.

CHART 4C

Combined Federal Spending on Food Stamps, WIC, and School Lunch, Per American in Poverty, 1975–2006

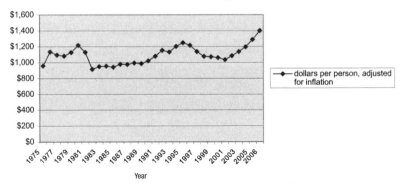

Sources: USDA Food and Nutrition Service; US Census Bureau Current Popular Survey; inflation calculations by author

So, if the programs keep increasing even when inflation is factored in, why is hunger still on the rise? One basic reason: The tens of billions spent on federal nutrition assistance programs don't even come close to making up for the hundreds of billions of dollars lost in food purchasing power of low-income Americans. Wages continue to decline. Food, health, housing, and transportation costs soar. More and more families simply cannot meet all of their needs.

HOW THE FOOD STAMP PROGRAM SAVES LIVES AND REWARDS WORK

The term "food stamps" has actually been a misnomer since the 1990s when paper coupons were replaced by Electronic Benefit Cards (EBTs), which look like, and are used like, ATM cards. This switch was a rare public policy change that pleased both sides of the ideological spectrum. Conservatives liked it because it reduced fraud, as benefits on individualized cards were far harder to trade illegally than generic coupons. Antihunger advocates liked it because it reduced the stigma in making food purchases, since the coupons that were clearly only used by poor people were replaced by cards similar to those that non-poor people use at banks.

Today, the Food Stamp Program, the bulwark of the current nutrition safety net, is not only a lifeline to tens of millions of struggling Americans, it is a huge boon to the American economy. The USDA has calculated that every five dollars in new food stamps spending generates $9.20 in community spending. A 5 percent increase in program participation nationwide would mean that $1.8 billion in new economic activity would be generated nationwide.[1]

The program can be a matter of life and death to recipients—the extra food money making a world of difference. Here's what some elderly food stamp recipients in the Seattle area have said about food stamp benefits:

"Food stamps keep the wolf away from the door."

"It's giving you better food for survival."

"With food stamps, you can pay the bills and use the stamps for food."

"It gives me money to go out and buy meat. The things I wouldn't normally be able to get at the food bank."

"When they started to give us the stamps I was able to buy fruit and other things."[2]

Food stamp benefits can act as sort of medicine, improving health and preventing illness. While far too few elderly households participate in the Food Stamp Program and the other government nutrition programs, those that do benefit greatly. A USDA study found:

> Food-insecure elders who participated in food assistance programs were less likely to be overweight and depressed than those who did not participate in food assistance programs. . . . The positive impact of participation in food assistance programs of reducing or preventing poor outcomes resulting from food insecurity will improve elders' quality of life, save on their health care expenses, and help to meet their nutritional needs.[3]

Low-income immigrant children who receive food stamps because they are citizens are 32 percent less likely to be in poor health than immigrant children from similar families that don't receive food stamps.[4]

WHO IS ON FOOD STAMPS?

While some in the public tend to think of food stamps recipients as lazy adults who just don't want to work, in the fiscal year 2005, half of all food stamp participants were children, and 8 percent were elderly. Of all food stamp households, 84 percent contained either an elderly or disabled person or a child, and these households received 89 percent of all benefits. Over 29 percent of food stamp households had earned income through work.[5] Thus, the clear majority of the people receiving help from the Food Stamp Program are either working adults, children, seniors, or people with disabilities. Lazy bums indeed!

In 2006, food stamp households were overwhelmingly poor, with a median income of just $14,773. Approximately 88 percent of food stamp households lived below the meager federal poverty line. Even if you counted food stamps as cash added to their additional income, 80 percent of food stamp recipients lived below the poverty line. Yet food stamp benefits were concentrated among *even poorer* households—40 percent of all food stamp households had a gross income less than or equal to half of the poverty guideline (less than $9,000 for a family of three), and these households received 57 percent of all benefits. Incredibly, 30 percent of households had zero net income reported.

While the public often assumes that virtually everyone on food stamps receives help their entire lives, half of the people who entered the program stayed on eight months or less, and 61 percent exited within a year.[6] Some leave because their incomes have risen. Other are still eligible, but are removed from the rolls by government due to bureaucratic snafus. Less than 15 percent of all food stamp recipients also receive Temporary Assistance for Needy Families (TANF), otherwise known as welfare. In fact, as Chart 4D indicates, between 1989 and 2005, the percentage of food stamp households receiving welfare decreased from 41.9 to 14.5, while the percentage with income from work increased from 19.6 to 29.3 percent.[7]

CHART 4D

The Number of Food Stamp Households Receiving Welfare Has Dropped and the Number of Food Stamp Households with a Worker Has Increased, Nationwide, 1989–2005

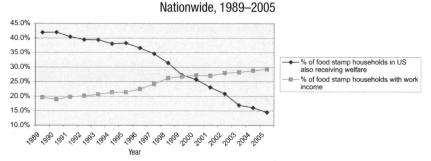

Source: USDA Food and Nutrition Service

WHY FOOD STAMPS ARE TOO HARD TO GET AND TOO QUICK TO RUN OUT

The antihunger movement's demand for increased food stamps is sort of like the old Woody Allen joke in which he complains that a restaurant has horrible food *and* the portions are too small. Despite all its success in reducing hunger, the Food Stamp Program has always been hampered in its effectiveness, as hunger researcher Peter Eisinger has written:

> People say they wish to be generous to the genuinely destitute, but they often believe that large numbers who receive public assistance are simply lazy or are cheats. . . . The program has been burdened by contradictory objectives that were designed to broaden political support but compromised its welfare aims; it has been harried by charges of fraud and abuse that opponents have used to challenge its legitimacy; it has been marked by low participation rates that stem from failures to reach the eligible, from stigma recipients were made to feel, and from complex certification processes to establish and maintain eligibility; and its level of assistance historically has been inadequate to provide genuine food security for food stamps recipients.[8]

Put another way, food stamp benefits are too small, go to too few people, are too hard to get, and too hard to keep getting, and this is permitted because they are for poor people. These factors dissuade many eligible people from applying. As the *Arkansas Democrat-Gazette* reported in 2007:

> When giving away groceries to low-income people in Carroll County, volunteers at Berryville's (Arkansas) Loaves and Fishes Food Bank try to let their clients know they might also be eligible for food stamps. But many of the families picking up potatoes, powdered milk and other staples aren't necessarily eager to sign up, said Sara Hodgson, the charity's executive director. "One complaint I've heard consistently is they get such a small amount, $10 or $15 a month." Julie Munsell, spokesman for the State Department of Human Services, said: "They may perceive it as a whole lot of administrative steps for little yield."[9]

Nationwide, in the fiscal year 2007, the average monthly food stamp benefit per person was $95.64, equaling only $23.91 per week. The minimum benefit—which often went to seniors, people living on Supplemental Security System (SSI), and people living in public housing—equaled only $10 per month, or $2.50 per week.

Food stamp recipients repeatedly tell me and other advocates that the benefits, which are supposed to last a whole month, simply don't. When clients at emergency food programs nationwide were asked how long the benefits generally lasted, 24 percent said a week or less, 30 percent said two weeks, 28 percent said three weeks, and only 17 percent said the full month.[10]

Food stamp participation is embarrassingly low. Only 65 percent of eligible people received food stamps in 2005, a significant increase from 54 percent in 2001. While this increase is encouraging, when more than a third of eligible people don't get help from the Food Stamp Program, supporters of the program have to admit that there is something very wrong with it. In comparison, I have never heard of so much as one person eligible for Social Security retirement benefits who did not start receiving them after turning sixty-five.

Because working families are subject to even more complicated participation rules, nearly half, or 47 percent, of eligible working families aren't enrolled. The truth is that low-income people are often making a rational economic decision not to apply. When you consider that it often takes two or three trips to a government office—and then people must wait for hours and hours at the office—just to obtain food stamps, when potential applicants factor all the ways they will lose money by applying (the bus or subway fare to and from the office, the wages lost by missing work those hours, and the money they will have to pay someone to look after their child while they are at the food stamp office), the decision not to apply is often a sensible one based on dollars and cents.

Many states perform even worse than the national average. In 2005, only 49 percent of all eligible people participated nationwide and, in California and Colorado, only 34 percent of eligible working households participated.[11] In some urban areas, the participation rates are truly abysmal. In 2005, the participation rate was 32 percent in San Diego, 44 percent in Las Vegas, 47 percent in Houston, and 48 percent in Denver.[12] In some rural areas, the participation rate is worse still. Even though Oregon has one of the nation's highest rates of food insecurity relative to its poverty rate, rural Wheller County, Oregon, has a food stamp participation rate of only 25 percent.[13]

A 2007 report by the USDA of Americans with very low food security (what the USDA used to call "hunger") found that, as demonstrated by Chart 4E, in one thirty-day period, 3 percent received food stamps, school lunch,

Percentage of Hungry Americans On
Federal Nutrition Assistance Programs,
2004–2005

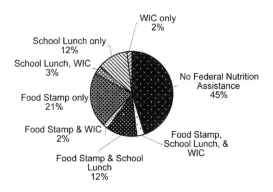

WIC only
2%

School Lunch only
12%

School Lunch, WIC
3%

Food Stamp only
21%

Food Stamp & WIC
2%

Food Stamp & School
Lunch
12%

No Federal Nutrition
Assistance
45%

Food Stamp,
School Lunch, &
WIC

Source: "Characteristics of Low-Income Households With Very Low Food Security," Mark Nord, USDA Economic Research Service, Economic Information Bulletin Number 25, May 2007

and WIC; 12 percent received food stamps *and* school lunch; 2 percent received food stamps *and* WIC; and 21 percent received food stamps *only*.[14] The report does not add those numbers together, but I did, and my simple arithmetic proved that only 38 percent of households with very low food security obtained food stamps, either alone or in combination with other federal nutrition programs. Thus, 62 percent of the very hungriest Americans don't get food stamps. When surveyed by America's Second Harvest, only 35 percent of people using emergency feeding programs nationwide said they or anyone in their household were currently receiving food stamp benefits. Twenty-three percent had applied but did not get the benefits that year.[15] Of the clients who had never applied for benefits, 43 percent thought they weren't eligible, 17 percent thought the program was too difficult to access, 15 percent said they didn't need the help, and 5 percent said that others needed the benefit more (believing, incorrectly, that if they got the benefit, the money would run out for others). Of those that *did* apply for food stamps but were not currently receiving the benefit, 41 percent said they made somewhat too much income to qualify, and 16 percent said they stopped participating in the application process because it was "too much hassle."[16]

Federal law, as well as extra rules piled on by states, counties, and cities, often make the process of applying for foods stamps a Kafkaesque nightmare. New York State's handbook for administering the Food Stamp Program is 391 pages long. While the state has bragged that it recently reduced the application form from sixteen to five pages, in New York City, people who filled out the shorter form were still required to provide caseworkers with oral answers to up to hundreds of questions. People were even asked if they owned funeral plots because, in New York, if you owned one, that would not count against food stamp eligibility, but if you owned two, that *could* count against your eligibility.

The image on the next page is a reproduction of the front of a large envelope printed by the USDA and given to potential applicants to encourage them to apply for food stamps. Notice that it has twenty-seven—yes, twenty-seven— different categories for the types of documents an applicant might need to physically bring to a food stamp office to prove his or her eligibility. And that is from an outreach tool meant to *encourage* participation.

Unlike filing federal income taxes—which can be done by mail and for which filers are not required to initially provide all receipts—the vast majority of food stamp applicants must bring with them a mountain of required documents and apply in person to a government office. In order to receive the average food stamp allotment of just $1.12 per meal, the government wants you to *prove* everything. Sometimes you even have to prove a negative—that you *don't* have a bank account or that you *don't* have a boyfriend or girlfriend living with you.

As pediatric clinic director Dr. Deborah Frank explained, "As community health providers, our teams dedicate an incalculable amount of time to assisting families with the pitfalls and traps of filling out applications, understanding requirements and recertifying for the Food Stamp Program, the application for which is much longer (and harder to understand) than the one I fill out each year for my medical license."[17]

Of course, when the system *isn't* working as it's supposed to (which is quite often), it is even more difficult for applicants. Federal law states that people are supposed to be able to apply for food stamps on their very first visit to a food stamp office, but people are often asked to come back two or three times. Federal law requires that states and counties make food stamp determinations and issue benefits within thirty days of the first application, but, in New York City in 2006, the city failed to meet the thirty-day deadline in about one in five cases. Federal law says that homeless people are supposed to be able to apply for benefits, but homeless people are often incorrectly told that they need a per-

Documents You Will Need for a Food Stamp Application

The checklist on this envelope can help you get ready for your interview with a food stamp worker You do not need everything on this list. Collect only the checked items. Bring them with you to your food stamp interview.

__ Driver's license

__ Birth certificate

__ Work or school identification card

__ Health benefits identification card

__ Voter registration card

__ Utility bills

__ Rent or mortgage receipts

__ Library card with address

__ Immigration and naturalization papers
(not required if you are not eligible to receive food stamp benefits but are applying for your children who were born in the United States)

__ Pay stubs

__ Income tax forms

__ Self employment bookkeeping records

__ Bank statements

__ Benefit award letter

__ Divorce or separation decree

__ Unemployment compensation award letter

__ Court order or other legal document for child support payments

__ Canceled checks for child support payments

__ Statement from person to whom child support payments are made

__ Paid receipts for child support payments

__ Canceled checks for child/adult care payments

__ Statement from child/adult care provider

__ Medical bills
(households with elderly or disabled members only)

__ Itemized receipts for medical costs
(households with elderly or disabled members only)

__ Medicare card showing "Part B" coverage
(households with elderly or disabled members only)

__ Repayment agreement with physician
(households with elderly or disabled members only)

__ Other:

Food Stamps Make America Stronger.

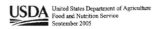 United States Department of Agriculture
Food and Nutrition Service
September 2005

manent address to apply. Many states and localities fail to provide to applicants the language translation services that are required by law. Even though all these practices clearly violate the law, and even though advocates routinely file (and usually win) court cases against such practices, there are very few mechanisms in place to force state and local governments to comply with even the most basic laws regarding program access.

Some states, like Texas, have tried to outsource their government food stamp management functions to private contractors, claiming that would improve efficiency. Of course, the real reason they did this was to try to save money and to reduce the power of public employee unions; and, of course, the system actually became less efficient and the processing backlogs increased. Caseworkers—many of whom are absurdly overworked and yelled at by clients, and thus are also victims of the system—frequently fail to return client calls, have full voicemail boxes, give applicants incorrect information, and become downright surly.

Ironically, while conservatives support such onerous practices because they keep down program participation, many social workers also believe that applicants should be subject to lengthy "case management" interviews through which the social workers can identify a full array of family problems to be solved.

It is also a reality that many nonprofit organizations—the one I head included—obtain large private grants and government contracts to navigate people through the food stamp application process, and if it were simplified, we wouldn't receive that money. Perhaps because they have a fear (either conscious or unconscious) of losing such funding, most of these groups—mine excluded—are hesitant to push too hard to simplify the Food Stamp Program.

Food stamp benefits are also difficult to keep getting once you are enrolled in the program. Many people in the program—and especially people with fluctuations in income due to employment—need to physically go to a food stamp office every few months, again with large piles of paperwork in their hands, to prove they are still eligible. I once heard a woman in New York explain how she was cut off from food stamp benefits because she had to take her daughter to the hospital on the day of her recertification interview.

Writer Jason DeParle chronicled the surreal attempt of a low-income woman to maintain her food stamp benefits in the late 1990s in Milwaukee:

Angie was broke and didn't eat all day. The loss of her food stamps left her incensed. The program required an eligibility review every three months. Arriving at her most recent appointment, she discovered her caseworker had gone on a leave of absence. In welfare jargon, that had left Angie in the "vacant zone": she no longer had a designated worker but could see whomever was free. No one was. A few weeks later Angie got a notice saying she had been cut off for failing to complete the review. "Questions? Ask your worker," it said. "Worker name: VACANT." It took two months of calling to get another appointment. When she did, the bus broke down, she got there late, and no one could see her again. Having worked until midnight the previous night, Angie was out of patience; she responded with off-color tirade that nearly got her thrown out of the office. A supervisor calmed her down, but still she had to come back the following day, when ten minutes of paper pushing restored her stamps. The fouls-ups had cost her $500.[18]

A 2007 USDA study found that people who had recently left the Food Stamp Program were actually *more* food insecure than people still in the program or those who had not received benefits recently.[19] This provides further evidence that people removed from the Food Stamp Program are far more likely to be removed as a result of administrative problems during the recertification process (missed interviews, lost letters, administrative hassles, etc.) than because they are no longer eligible. Indeed, a study in New York City in 2007 found that 80 percent of people leaving the Food Stamp Program were still financially eligible.[20]

THE STRANGE CASE OF FOOD STAMPS FINGER IMAGING

If all that wasn't bad enough, in a process that essentially treats applicants as criminals, as of 2007, food stamp applicants were required to provide finger images—electronic fingerprints—in four of the nation's largest states (California, Texas, New York, and Arizona). It is not coincidental that people never have to be fingerprinted to obtain the types of USDA aid going to less poor (and often rich) people, such as farm subsidies, money to ranchers for conservation programs, and payments to rural business owners.

In 2006, at an antihunger conference in Washington, DC, I asked then–US Secretary of Agriculture, Mike Johanns, a question that I guessed (correctly, as it turns out) he wouldn't be able to answer: "Would you support fingerprinting farmers, ranchers, and rural businesspeople in order for them to obtain USDA benefits? Assuming that your answer is 'no,' would you support ending the practice in which people are fingerprinted in order to get food stamps, especially considering that the other benefits can be hundreds of thousands of dollars and food stamps equal only about one dollar per meal?" Secretary Johanns was seemingly at a loss for an immediate response, and it seemed as though he didn't know people were fingerprinted to get food stamps, even though the Food Stamp Program constitutes more than a third of his entire budget, and even though the issue of fingerprinting Food Stamp Program applicants has been a big political and media issue. Of course, he responded that he wouldn't support fingerprinting farmers, ranchers, and rural businesspeople, and that he would "look into" whether Food Stamp Program applicants should be fingerprinted. I don't think he ever did "look into" the issue.

There are a lot of bad governmental policies out there, but few rise to the level of sheer stupidity as this one does. City officials in New York claim both that finger imaging deters fraud and that it has no negative impact upon legitimate applicants. Neither claim is true. Even under the Bush administration, the USDA has found no proof that fingerprinting significantly reduces fraud and has expressed worries that it may deter people from applying. The Urban Institute found that, in one out of twenty-three cases, otherwise eligible people don't apply solely due to finger-imaging requirements. New York detected only thirty-one cases of suspected fraud thanks to fingerprinting in 2006. Given that about 1.1 million people in the city received food stamps, that meant that finger imaging only flagged one in 34,991 Food Stamp Program applicants caught in the act of potentially committing fraud. Thus, to stop possible fraud by only one in nearly 35,000 people, the city denied benefits to one in twenty-three actual hungry people.

Even more absurd, New York City spends $800,000 yearly on finger imaging. That's right, the city spends $800,000 of its own money on a system that may prevent thirty-one people from getting benefits for which they are *not* entitled, even though it prevents 21,500 people from getting $31 million in benefits for which they *are* entitled. Furthermore, the four states that do require finger images have higher rates of payment error and lower rates of participation than those that don't. It's a lose-lose situation. For all those reasons, forty-six of the nation's fifty states don't waste their tax dollars on such an inefficient and degrading system.

Other than finger imaging, there are already a number of effective methods in use to fight fraud, such as computer matching. Fraud detection is important, but it is crucial to note that, when large-scale fraud does occur in the Food Stamp Program (an occurrence far less common than ten years ago), the perpetrators are usually food retailers, who fraudulently bill the government for nonexistent customers, or government employees, who fabricate nonexistent households. Duplicate cases created by individual food stamp recipients—the only type of fraud potentially detected by finger imaging—comprises a relatively small percentage of government money lost due to fraud.

When Eliot Spitzer ran for governor of New York in 2006, he pledged to eliminate finger imaging for public benefit applications. After he became governor, he only partially made good on his pledge. He took the far more limited approach of trying to eliminate food stamp finger imaging only for families with someone working thirty hours or more. But due to misinformed attacks from the *New York Post*, which falsely slammed him for eliminating *all* fingerprinting, and due to pressure from Mayor Michael Bloomberg, Spitzer backed down, allowing New York City to continue the finger-imaging process even for working families.

SCHOOL MEALS: WELL FED MEANS WELL READ

We've known for at least one hundred years that children who don't eat well don't tend to do well in school. Comedian and activist Dick Gregory described his experience growing up:

> The teacher thought I was stupid. Couldn't spell, couldn't read, couldn't do arithmetic, just stupid. . . . Teachers were never interested in finding out that you couldn't concentrate because you were so hungry. All you could ever think about was noontime, would it ever come? Maybe you could sneak into the cloakroom and steal a bite of some kid's lunch out of a coat pocket to bite on something. Paste. You couldn't really make a meal of paste, or put it on bread for a sandwich, but sometimes I'd scoop a few spoonfuls out of the paste jar in the back of the room. . . . Paste doesn't taste too bad when you're hungry.[21]

In contrast to such hunger, there is ample evidence that, when children receive school meals, it helps them to learn and advance. One study found "strong evidence that higher rates of participation in school breakfast programs are associated in the short-term with improved student functioning on a broad range of psychosocial and academic measures."[22] Adding to the benefit of such programs are the successful efforts over the last few decades to significantly improve both the nutritional value and the taste of school meals. A USDA study of school meals in the 2004–2005 school year found that over 85 percent of the meals met the standards for targeted nutrients and that the meals were now lower in saturated fat than they previously were.[23] There is conflicting data as to whether children continue to eat school meals when the food is healthier, but surely, if children are included in testing new recipes and schools spend enough to buy the freshest products, they can come up with foods that are both nutritious and popular with children.

Unfortunately, school meal programs are often hampered by stigma. A low-income high school dropout in Denver, describing how he felt when forced to use a different colored card to obtain a reduced-price lunch, said, "You feel low. It should not be like that. We should not have certain colors to separate us; like one rich, one poor."[24] In some schools nationwide, kids who get free lunches have to stand in different lines than those who pay for lunch; even more shocking is that, in a few schools, they have to go an entirely different room. Many children in those situations choose to go hungry rather than admit they are poor. "Lunchtime is the best time to impress your peers," said Lewis Geist, a senior and class president at Balboa High School in San Francisco. Being seen with a subsidized meal, he said, "lowers your status."[25] While school lunch programs have nearly 100 percent participation rates in elementary schools (since kids can't leave the school buildings), when the students grow older, their participation decreases.

When it comes to breakfast, participation is much worse. Research proves that children who eat breakfast at school have higher test scores, fewer school nurse visits, act up less in class, and may even suffer less frequently from obesity. Yet school breakfast participation is far lower than school lunch participation. Many suburban and rural schools don't even serve breakfast. Often it is served too early or too late, making it impractical for students to eat. Stigma is an even bigger problem, because while most kids eat lunch, everyone knows that only the really poor kids go to the cafeteria to eat breakfast. Nationwide in the 2006 school year, only 45 percent of kids eligible for free and reduced-price meals participated in free and reduced-priced breakfasts.[26] According to a 2007 report by the Food Research and Action Center, out of twenty-three big cities in the United States, fully twenty-one had rates of free and reduced-price breakfast participation below 65 percent. In eleven of those cities, the rate was below 50 percent. Many suburban and rural districts have even lower rates.

THE SAFETY NET DOESN'T MESH

While food stamps and school meals are the most far-reaching, there are fifteen different nutrition assistance programs run by the USDA alone. That number doesn't even include Meals on Wheels and other seniors' meal programs funded by the US Department of Health and Human Services. Perhaps the greatest problem with the current nutrition assistance safety net is that each program has different eligibility rules, different application forms and processes, and, quite often, different offices (sometimes across town or across the county from each other) to which people must physically go to apply. Families must earn below 130 percent of the poverty line to get food stamp benefits and free school meals, but they must live below 185 percent of the poverty line to obtain WIC benefits and reduced-price school meals. Some schools have school breakfast programs and others don't. Whether kids are eligible for free after-school snacks or free summer meals can depend either on their family's income or on the income of the people in the neighborhood in which they live. Confusing, no? That is why hungry Americans are so confused about how to get help that they are often unable to get the vital help their families need.

In 2008, responding to rising food prices and a worsening recession, Congress passed a Farm Bill that slightly increased commodities for food banks and marginally increased funding for the Food Stamp Program (while renaming it the Supplemental Nutrition Assistance Program), but did not make it significantly easier to actually signup for food stamp benefits. President Bush vetoed the bill, but Congress easily overrode him. Said conservative Republican Rep. Thaddeus G. McCotter (MI), who previously voted in near lockstep for the Bush agenda, "Twenty-five percent of my state is now in need of food assistance. I work for them, not for the president."[27]

Given the extent of the problems with our safety net, it is truly amazing how much good it has accomplished. It's certainly a relief that, because of these programs, America no longer has children living on nothing but coffee and bread. But that's a very low bar to set. With more funds, and effort, the nutritional safety net could operate at full potential, and end hunger in America entirely.

CHAPTER 5

LET THEM EAT RAMEN NOODLES
One Week Living on $28.30 of Food

It's only been twenty-four hours that I have been living on a food stamps diet and I'm already starting to see a mind-set difference. I usually don't think about food because it really is quite easy. I walk into a delicatessen or I walk into a restaurant, and I can get what I want. Now, when I wake up, I have to plan my whole day. I had to think about where I would be during lunch. Did I need to bring my lunch with me? What will I do for dinner? Do I have enough time to actually cook dinner?

—New York City Council Member Eric Gioia, describing his first day partic-ipating in the Food Stamp Challenge[1]

The Food Stamp Challenge was an advocacy strategy hatched by the Greater Philadelphia Coalition Against Hunger in 2006. They knew that if elected officials and the local media tried living for even just one week on food pur-chased with the current food stamp allotment, their efforts would call attention to the plight of low-income families who faced that struggle every week.

When Oregon Governor Ted Kulongoski accepted the challenge in April 2007 and received the first nationwide media coverage for the Food Stamp Challenge, the idea took off. Elected officials, advocates, journalists, and reli-gious leaders across country followed his lead. Everyone got in on the act. I knew a good publicity stunt when I saw one, so in May 2007, I asked a local elected official in New York, Eric Gioia, a frequent ally in antihunger fights, to join me in giving it a try.

My main goal was to dramatize the need to raise the average benefit size. I arrogantly assumed that while Gioia, the media, and the public would be educated by the challenge, given how long I had already been working on these issues, *I* wouldn't learn anything that I didn't already know.

I was wrong.

I learned that it's one thing to speak, write, research, and think about what it's like to use food stamp benefits, but it's another thing entirely to actually *live* on them.

I came to better understand that, when you are poor, many life choices, including food choices, are made *for* you, and that it takes a great deal of time— the one thing that poor people often have even *less* of than money—to find, purchase, and prepare meals that are both affordable and nutritious.

HOW THE WEEK WORKED

During the week, I would eat only $28.30 worth of food, equaling only $1.30 per meal.

I don't regularly eat meals at fancy restaurants, but the night before the challenge, I treated myself to one. I ate at one of New York's fabulous Argentinean steak houses, having a Caesar salad ($8.50), a sirloin steak ($19.95), a soda ($1.00), and a most delectable dessert of crepes filled with caramel ($6.95). Not including tip, the meal totaled $36.40, or twenty-eight times the cost of the average meal I'd have to eat the following week.

As I tried to fall asleep that night, I tossed and turned, worrying about the challenge. As someone who loved food—and lots of it—would I be able to survive the week without quitting or cheating? Could I really survive on meals at 1/28 of the cost of what I had eaten just that night? How would I deal with it when I woke up in the middle of the night and craved my usual late-night snack? Would I feel too weak to concentrate? My fears were even more oversized than my appetite. I learned my first lesson even *before* the challenge officially began: the *fear* of not having enough food can be a serious challenge.

The reason I set the cost at $28.30 was that it was the average food stamp allotment at the time for a person living in New York City, which was slightly higher than the national average of $23.91 per week.[2] Some critics pointed out that some food stamp recipients obtain higher allotments, ignoring the fact that many got less, including significant numbers of people who only received the minimum benefit, then a paltry $2.50 per week. Other critics argued that USDA guidelines say that food stamp benefits are supposed to be supplemented by food purchases made with cash. In other words, the USDA says that people aren't supposed to live only on food purchased with food stamp benefits. That is indeed USDA policy, but as pointed out even when I worked at the department, in the real world, many food stamp recipients don't have extra cash to obtain additional food. Many people rely entirely upon food they can get through food stamps or from charitable pantries and kitchens.

Even if people *are* able to supplement their food stamp purchases with their own money, current food stamp allotments still do not provide enough food for most families to adhere to what the USDA calls the "Thrifty Food Plan"—a theoretical estimate of what it would cost to purchase a minimally adequate diet. According to the Food Research and Action Center, "Although the Food Stamp Program assumes that households will be able to purchase the Thrifty Food Plan with their benefits, many studies show that food costs are so high in many areas of the country that the maximum food stamp benefit is insufficient to obtain the food allotment on that plan."[3] In fact, the USDA has found that the typical American household spends 28 percent more on food each week than the cost of the Thrifty Food Plan.[4] Given all those factors, I felt my $28.30 figure for one week was more than fair. I certainly couldn't think of any better way to at least partially walk in the shoes of a food stamp recipient for a week.

I also got a lot of help at home. Given how busy I was publicizing the challenge, my partner, Lori, who has a great deal of nutritional knowledge, shopped for me. Here's what she bought for me for at the start of the week:

Old-fashioned oats	$2.39 (18 oz. container makes thirteen 1/2-cup servings, $.18/serving; Quaker brand recommends 3/4-cup servings for a "heart-healthy" diet
Fresh corn on the cob	$1.00 (3 ears, $.33/serving, on sale)
Eggs	$1.29 (6 eggs, $.22/each)
Garlic	$.70 (1 head, about 10 cloves, $.07/each)
Ramen noodles	$1.33 (Value pack of 12, $.11/package, on sale)
Dry black beans	$.89 (1 lb. bag, 2 cups dry makes eight 1/4-cup servings dry, $.11/serving dry)
Dry brown rice	$1.50 (28 oz. bag makes nineteen 1/4-cup servings raw, $.08/serving)
Dry 12-bean soup mix	$1.29 (1 lb. bag plus seasoning packet)
Frozen broccoli	$1.25 (Store brand, 1 lb. bag makes seven 1-cup servings, $.18/serving)

Chicken thighs w/skin	$2.96 (Value pack, 8 thighs with bones $1.01/lb., $0.37/thigh, on sale)
Dry ziti	$.79 (Store brand, 1 lb makes eight 1-cup servings dry, $.10/serving, on sale)
Crushed tomatoes	$1.00 (Store brand, 28 oz. can, thirteen 1/4-cup servings, $.08/serving)
Stewed tomatoes	$1.00 (Store brand, 28 oz. can, thirteen 1/4-cup servings, $.08/serving)
Onions	$2.99 (Value pack, 6 small onions, only Vidalia available, $.50/each, on sale)
Potatoes, white	$1.50 (Value pack, store brand, 16 medium, $.09/each)
Raw kale	$.86 ($.79/lb., makes about 6 servings, $.13/serving)
Apples	$ 2.99 (Value pack, 10 small apples, $.30/each)
Olive oil	$1.79 (6 tablespoon bottle, $.30/tablespoon)

The total came to $27.22. Lori needed a few hours to shop carefully and look for sale items, and had to visit two stores to find all the items at the desired prices. Because there is no large supermarket in our immediate neighborhood in Brooklyn and because we don't own a car, she had to take a bus to the closest large supermarket. In accordance with the rules of the challenge previously set by advocates, we were able to use salt and pepper that were already in our cupboards.

Furthermore, she prepared most of my meals that week from scratch, sometimes taking more than an hour to do so. For example, dry beans prepared from scratch required overnight soaking. As a result of all her work, my week on the challenge was not quite as tough as it must have been for those who did not get such extraordinary help.

WHAT I ATE THAT WEEK

During the week, I didn't eat as fully, as nutritiously, or as deliciously—or with as much variety—as I like, but I certainly had more than enough food to survive. And I didn't even cheat. (I swear!)

Here's what I ate on two typical days of the challenge, including how much the ingredients cost (prorated to the portion size) and estimates for the meals rated nutritionally, using nutrition software called Diet Power.[5]

Thursday, May 10, 2007

Breakfast: —1-3/4 servings oatmeal, made with water ($.32)
               —1 apple ($.30)

                                                TOTAL: $.62

Lunch: —1 package ramen noodles ($.11)
               —1 serving frozen broccoli ($.18)
               —1 egg ($.22)
               —1 corn on the cob ($.33)

                                                TOTAL: $.84

Dinner: —2 servings (1-1/2 cups dry) ziti ($.20)
               —3 servings (3/4 cups) crushed tomatoes ($.24)
               —1 clove garlic ($.07)
               —1/2 serving raw kale ($.07)

                                                TOTAL: $.58

TOTAL FOR THE DAY: $2.04
• Calories: 1,457 • Fat: 28 g (sat. 10 g, trans. 0 g) • Carbohydrates: 261 g (fiber 26 g, sugar 20 g)
• Protein: 53 g • Sodium: 2,399 mg

Tuesday, May 15, 2007

Breakfast: —1-3/4 servings oatmeal, made with water ($.32)

                                                TOTAL: $.32

Lunch: —1 serving homemade 12-bean soup ($.84)

                                                TOTAL: $.84

Snack: —1 small apple ($.30)

                                                TOTAL: $.30

Dinner: —3 servings (2-1/4 cups dry) ziti ($.30)
               —3 servings (3/4 cup) stewed tomatoes ($.24)
               —4 servings (1 cup) crushed tomatoes ($.32)
               —2 garlic clove ($.14)
               —1 small onion ($.50)
               —1-1/2 servings frozen broccoli ($.27)
               —1 teaspoon olive oil ($.10)

                                                TOTAL: $1.87

Snack: —1 small apple ($.30)

                                                TOTAL: $.30

TOTAL FOR THE DAY: $3.63
• Calories: 1,838 • Fat: 20 g (sat. 3 g, trans 0 g) • Carbohydrates: 360 g (fiber 56 g, sugar 29 g)
• Protein: 73 g • Sodium: 1,364 mg

After the challenge ended, when I visited Washington, DC—along with Council Member Gioia—to lobby Congress for higher food stamp allotments, I noticed that the cost of the bagel, muffin, banana, and bottled water I purchased for breakfast at Au Bon Pain at Union Station in Washington ($5.88) equaled the cost of four meals during the challenge. Before the challenge, I would never have thought twice about my food spending.

HOW OTHER PEOPLE WHO TOOK THE CHALLENGE EXPERIENCED THEIR WEEKS

Many of the people who took the challenge reported that their grocery shopping took longer—and was more difficult—than any grocery shopping they had ever done.

A reporter in Memphis who took the challenge wrote: "In a Memphis grocery store, $22 didn't go very far. Fresh fruit such as apples at $1.79 a pound or fresh fish at $4.50 a pound takes a big bite out of the budget."[6]

A nutritionist in Michigan reported that even she had trouble living on the challenge: "The everyday green salad, a medley of greens and vegetables, that is usually a staple at my . . . dinner table, had to go."[7]

Elected officials who took the challenge received far more media coverage than advocates. Reporters seemed to assume that I did this kind of thing all the time (which I didn't) but that politicians lived high off the hog, so the challenge would be a radical departure from their daily routines. Ironically, while most elected officials earn far more than average workers, they tend to earn far *less* than mid-level corporate employees and even less than some leaders of nonprofit groups. But because of the skewed perceptions, the press seemed mesmerized that politicians would make any sort of a sacrifice, even for just a week.

Some of the ways that busy elected officials had to deal with the challenge did become comic mini-tragedies. One of the participants, Rep. Tim Ryan (D-OH), "stuck to the challenge" even as he traveled to speak at his alma mater's commencement exercises, bringing along his "pasta and sauce, as well as the last of my peanut butter, jelly, and bread." After the ceremony and late for his plane, he rushed through the airport, choosing not to check his bags to save time. He later wrote:

I step up to the metal detector, take my shoes off, place my bag through the scanner and come out the other side to the most dreaded words in travel, "Bag Check!" . . . As the agent sifted though my bag, I tried to recount what could possibly be in there that was threatening . . . my mouthwash? Toothpaste? Yeah, it was those two, but it was also my peanut butter and jelly. . . . He politely put the peanut butter and jelly to the side, closed my bag and gave it back to me. I was too astonished to talk. I took my bag and walked towards the gate thinking about the four or maybe five meals that [he] had taken from me. What am I going to do now? It's not like I can just go to Safeway and grab another jar. I have 33 cents and a bag of cornmeal to last today and tomorrow.[8]

HOW MY FOOD STAMP WEEK COMPARED WITH MY USUAL WEEK

That week I couldn't afford juice, milk, or any beverages other than tap water. I couldn't afford red meat, seafood, whole grain breads, or anything organic. I had to rely on a very limited range of food choices. As much as I once loved ramen noodles, I never want to see them again. The cheapest, most filling foods I could afford were sometimes the least nutritious. While Lori could find ramen noodles on sale, twelve for $1.33 at a grocery store several bus stops away from home, they are very high in sodium and saturated fat.

The chart below—comparing what I ate that week to a usual week—proves a few things. It's clear that I normally don't eat as nutritiously as I should, especially considering I preach nutrition for a living and I can afford any foods I need. But it also proves that, even with great care going into shopping and cooking, I wasn't able to eat as nutritiously as I should have. I couldn't afford the range of fruits and vegetables I needed and I significantly exceeded acceptable sodium levels. My daily carbs also exceeded recommended levels, demonstrating, as I will detail in the next chapter, how food-insecure people can also become obese.

While the USDA recommends two cups of orange vegetables per week, I had none that week. The USDA recommends two fruits daily, but I was only able to have one. And that one was a store-bought, mealy, nonorganic apple that wasn't very tasty. But it was the best I could get for thirty cents. Wonderful-tasting, crisp, organic apples, available just a few blocks from my apartment at one of the city's best farmers' markets, cost fifty cents a piece and were out of my price range that week. I also had less meat and fewer beans than the USDA recommends, which explains my lower protein intake.

	Typical Day Before Challenge	Two-Day Average Before Challenge (including one blow-out dinner)	Average During Challenge	USDA Limits/Guidelines[9]
Food Costs Per Meal	$6.37	$10.44	$1.10	$1.30
Food Costs Per Day	$19.10	$31.32	$3.34	$3.90
Food Costs Per Week	$133.00	$219.24	$23.45	$28.30
Daily Calories	2,521	2,913	1,965	2,000
Daily Overall Fat	71.9 g	96 g	41 g	65 g
Daily Saturated Fat	15.5 g	27 g	12 g	17 g
Daily Trans Fat	0	0	0	***
Daily Carbohydrates	364 g	371 g	330 g	271 g
Daily Sugar	83.6 g	112 g	22 g	47 g
Daily Protein	154 g	172 g	83 g	91 g
Daily Sodium	6,488 mg	5,332 mg	1,995 mg	1,779 mg
Daily Fiber	49.8 g	36 g	47 g	20–35 g/day

***No official level set by USDA, but any trans fat is generally considered harmful.

The challenge took place in May 2007. A year later, the average weekly food stamp allotment in New York City rose by only $1.95 (6 percent), to a level of $30.25. Yet, in that same year, in my neighborhood, prices rose by 45 percent for eggs, 66 percent for potatoes, and a whopping 80 percent for ramen noodles. Thus, as meager as my food stamp–level rations were in 2007, they would have been far less in 2008. When you can't even afford ramen noodles anymore, you know things are bad, really bad.

THE WEEK REINFORCED MANY OF MY PREVIOUS BELIEFS

The week proved the validity of some things I already knew from my work, such as, if you get food stamps, you won't eat like a king or a queen, but you won't starve. While some others who took the challenge complained that they felt they were running out of energy, it is nearly certain that the reason behind those feelings was psychological, not physiological. For me, because I did have nearly all the calories I needed, my physical energy level never lagged.

Given that not starving is obviously a vast improvement over starving, the experience reinforced my belief that we must do more to ensure that a greater percentage of eligible people obtain food stamp benefits. Using food stamps at one of the more than 9,000 retail outlets in New York City that accept them is better than simply relying on one of the city's 1,200 charitable food pantries and soup kitchens. While those charities perform vital and heroic work and certainly help, they can't possibly be the main solution to hunger. Many of those charities are open only a few times a month and are so strapped for resources that they provide portions that are smaller, less nutritious, and less varied than even a food stamp diet.

The week also reminded me that those who rail against the luxuriousness of food stamp allotments don't know what they are talking about. Here's a typical blog post from a newspaper Web site in West Virginia: "I was behind a man using food stamps the other day at a grocery store. He bought stuff that I could not afford with food stamps, and then pulled out a $100 bill to pay for two cartons of cigarettes. What is wrong with this picture?" First of all, given that food stamps are now delivered on plastic cards that look nearly identical to bank and credit cards, I doubt he could be sure that the person in front of him was using food stamps. Second, studies show that people on food stamps usually buy less expensive foods than everyone else. Still, conservatives never tire of claiming that they (or more usually, someone they know) saw someone buying the fanciest possible food (lobsters, they claim!) with government benefits. I hear this so frequently that you'd think there would be no more lobsters left in Maine. In reality, few stores in low-income neighborhoods even carry high-end foods, and if people can't afford juice or beef with food stamps (as I couldn't), there is no way they could ever afford lobster. But compelling myths die hard.

WHAT I LEARNED THAT WEEK

I've always had a huge appetite. I *love* to eat. The week of the experiment, I felt like Godzilla. I was ready to eat chunks of concrete. I was short-tempered and irritable. Even though the nutrition charts told me I *should* be full, I rarely *felt* completely full. I obsessed about when and what my next meal would be—even more than I usually do. It truly bothered me that I had no beverages other than water, and I felt I could never get the taste of previous meals out of my mouth, regardless of whether I liked them or not. I craved farmers' market apples and the organic chocolate soy milk that I love. It drove me nuts that, when I was waiting a long time on a platform for a subway to arrive and was increasingly thirsty, I couldn't buy a drink.

Still, I don't want to exaggerate my small sacrifice. After all, I neither had to go through the often-taxing process of applying for the benefits nor did I have to face judgmental stares from checkout counter clerks when using them. In fact, I neither shopped nor cooked that week. If I were an actual food stamp recipient who headed a family, chances are I would be a woman who shopped and cooked on top of the one or two jobs I worked outside the home to earn a living, and in addition to my paid employment, I would be caring for my children and possibly even for elderly parents.

Perhaps most importantly, I knew that, at the end of the week, I could go back to eating almost anything I wanted. Given that worrying about where you are going to get your next meal is one of the most debilitating aspects of food insecurity, the fact that I was confident I would be able to afford whatever meals I desired after just one week was likely the biggest difference between taking the challenge and actually facing hunger.

I winced when I read that a group in Minnesota claimed that one week on the challenge would teach people "what being hungry is really like." That's like saying you know what it's like to be pushed out of plane without a parachute because you once rode a rollercoaster.

One of the hurdles for me was that, since food stamp recipients can't obtain prepared food from restaurants, I couldn't either, no matter how convenient or desirable. And until that week, I never noticed just how frequently I get free food as a result of my work. At a morning meeting of a fellow nonprofit group, there were free bagels, fruit, and coffee available to all attendees. When I went to lunch meetings, there was also free food. A colleague came back from a vacation and brought back local candy. Not to mention all the evening charity receptions at which shrimp cocktail flowed almost as plentifully as the actual cocktails. It was tough, but I didn't partake of any of that food. At some wealthier corporations, the companies actually give their professional employees free meals every day so they are less likely to "waste" time going out for lunch. Just as it is ironic that millionaire Hollywood stars often receive "swag bags" of free luxury items they don't really need, people in white-collar, professional jobs—who can clearly afford to buy their own food—are offered free meals wherever they go. The Food Stamp Challenge taught me how lucky I was to have that privilege.

During the challenge, I had to plan my days around food, eating breakfast at home (even if I had an early meeting for work), carrying my prepared lunch with me, and always being home for dinner. When I met a colleague for lunch, I had to ask him to pick up food at a deli and then meet me in a park, where he guiltily ate a nice meal as he watched me eat soggy ramen noodles out of Tupperware.

People who don't face hunger take for granted that food is always a centerpiece of our social lives and holiday get-togethers. We regularly meet our friends for dinner or brunch. We plan holidays entirely around massive feasts. We take our parents out for good meals to honor them (or, to be honest, to try to get their minds off why we haven't produced grandkids). So, for example, another small difficulty for me was that Mother's Day fell during the challenge week. When I explained to my then 84-year-old mother beforehand that I would have to take her out for a celebratory meal on another day, she was disappointed but would not admit it, falling back into the "It's OK, I'll sit in the dark" routine. Before and during my visit, I explained that I would have to bring my own food and that I couldn't eat anything she offered me. I explained it repeatedly and she said she understood completely. But old habits die hard. Like a good Jewish mother, she offered me food fifteen different times (yes, I counted) and repeatedly—perhaps even a bit resentfully—brought up her desire to go out to her favorite Chinese restaurant (yes, another Jewish mother stereotype) that day. The challenge no doubt hurt her more than it hurt me. I suppose that I could have taken her out and watched her eat, but since I have minimal self-control around food (and especially around Chinese food), I just wasn't strong enough to do so. The guilt I felt at being unable to provide my mother her favorite meal paled in comparison to the guilt that must be felt by a parent when his or her children must skip a meal entirely. (I did take my mother out for a Chinese lunch the next weekend, but somehow it wasn't the same.)

One other outcome I didn't expect was that, if you spend an inordinate amount of time shopping and cooking, you actually can live on a diet only slightly less healthy than the one recommended by the USDA. But given that many food stamp households are headed by people working one or more jobs—and that many recipients are seniors or are disabled—it is not realistic to spend hours creating each meal. Many people who wrote to Gioia and me pointed out that we could have done much better if we had spent more time shopping and cooking. One told us on a radio call-in show that the answer was for low-income people to buy "slow cookers." Such comments displayed a class bias that assumed low-income people have inordinately large amounts of time on their hands to cook and shop.

Some critics complained that we didn't buy in bulk to save money, ignoring the fact that many poor people can't afford the annual membership fees that many of the big box stores require, don't have enough cash to buy in bulk, don't have cars to haul off their groceries, and don't have cabinets or refrigerators large enough to store the bulk food.

Perhaps my biggest lesson was an emotional one. Few things in life are worse to an American than lacking choice in what you eat. Throughout my life, while I have never been rich, neither have I ever lacked for basic necessities. If I am waiting on a subway platform and I get thirsty, I buy a drink. If I want to socialize with family or friends, I join them at a restaurant. If I wake up in the middle of the night or can't concentrate on work in the late afternoon because I crave a snack, I get one. By denying myself those things for just one week, I learned more than ever how much I take for granted.

Food insecurity isn't just a bit of bureaucratic nomenclature. And it's not just about not having enough food to eat. It's a feeling, both physical and psychological, and not a pleasant one.

CHAPTER 6

ARE AMERICANS HUNGRY—OR FAT?

Thankfully, poverty-induced malnutrition is virtually non-existent in the United States. In fact, poor American children today are super-nourished. . . . The poor, however, do suffer from one major nutrition-related health problem: obesity.

—Robert Rector, senior research fellow, Heritage Foundation, right-wing think tank[1]

Hungry? I've seen times when I have been. You can't buy the nutritious things you'd like to. . . . You can't really buy the food you want because you can't afford it.

—Sandy Kallok, a disabled Maine resident who uses a local food pantry[2]

When I tell people I work for an antihunger organization, people often laugh and ask why we have to put "anti" in the name. "Surely, there is no such thing as a pro-hunger group?" they ask. I respond that they have never seen the work of the Heritage Foundation or the American Enterprise Institute for Public Policy Research (AEI).

Right-wing think tanks such as these are hard at work every day generating propaganda to dismiss or deny hunger and poverty. No matter how many times they are proven demonstrably wrong, they never seem to lose credibility—at least in the world of Fox News and conservative politicians.

Heritage and AEI are exceedingly well funded and disproportionately influential. In 2005, Heritage took in $46 million in revenues and paid its president and CEO, Edwin J. Feulner, Jr., total compensation of $799,393, while AEI took in $34 million and paid its president, Christopher DeMuth, total compensation of $630,250. In contrast, the average household forced to obtain food from food pantries and soup kitchens earned $10,320, which equaled 1/77 of Feulner's salary and 1/61 of DeMuth's.[3]

Heritage and AEI opinion pieces and quotes pop up in newspapers across America, and their ideas are often parroted by leading Republican politicians at the national, state, and local levels. What is a far right-wing idea one day (such as the argument that the widespread presence of obesity proves that hunger doesn't exist in America), often seeps into mainstream American thought over time, eventually becoming accepted as conventional wisdom. For all these reasons, they have a very large influence on the nation's debates over poverty and hunger.

These think tanks consistently deny the existence, or downplay the severity, of domestic hunger. They first tried to argue that people who go to pantries and kitchens aren't really hungry. In 1983, top advisor to President Reagan, Edwin Meese (who, not coincidentally, joined Heritage Foundation as a Distinguished Fellow in 1988), told a group of wire-service reporters that stories about hunger were merely anecdotal and that people went to soup kitchens "because they don't want to pay for their lunch." Some of this denial has had a distinctly racist tinge, even though the majority of hungry people in America were (and are) white. Dr. George Graham, a member of Reagan's Commission on Hunger— which was appointed to investigate the problem after Reagan was embarrassed politically by the Meese remarks—said at the time: "As we look at the problems of our Blacks, all we have to do is look at the sports page to see who are the best nourished in the country."[4]

Today, even when right-wing think tanks sometimes do admit that more pantries and kitchens are opening and that more people are using the emergency feeding system, they deny this is happening because more people are facing hunger. Rather, they make the astonishing claim that the dramatic rise in pantry and kitchen attendance is caused primarily by an increased "supply"—a larger number of feeding organizations providing more options for obtaining food, as well as an increase in the amount of food available at many existing pantries and kitchens—thus making it easier and more desirable for people to obtain charitable food even though they don't really need it.

If they would spend so much as five minutes speaking to actual people receiving food at a charity, they'd know that argument is hogwash. Even at the best run, most generously stocked, and least patronizing kitchens and pantries in America, obtaining charitable food is usually a humiliating experience. People may have to take lengthy rides on public transportation or walk long distances, often with bulky shopping carts and children in tow, to get to these agencies. They often have to wait in line for hours just to get one meal or a few days' worth of groceries. They usually have to take whatever food is given to them, with very little choice involved. They frequently have to provide personal information to an intake caseworker. And after all of that, sometimes they then find that the charity just ran out of food. The bottom line is that most people only go to these agencies when they are at the end of their ropes and have no other options.

Another right-wing argument is that domestic hunger may exist on a very small scale, but there's no such thing as food insecurity, and because the US has far less hunger than the Third World, there is really nothing we should worry about anyway.

Citing only smaller hunger numbers but ignoring the far larger food insecurity numbers, Robert Rector of the Heritage Foundation wrote:

> It is frequently alleged that hunger and malnutrition are widespread in the United States. But while hunger does exist in the United States, it is relatively restricted in scope and frequency. For example, [federal] survey data . . . show[s] 96 percent of US households report they had "enough food to eat."[5]

You almost have to marvel at his chutzpah for using the word "alleged." But then you should be outraged that this statement blithely ignores that 4 percent of the population facing hunger at that time equaled more than 10 million people.

The percentage game misleadingly discounts the impact of truly traumatic events in peoples' lives, such as the crisis of lacking enough food. Would Rector say that more than 99.99 percent of the US population did *not* die in the September 11 terrorist attacks? Of course not, even though this percentage would be as statistically correct as the one he uses for hunger. Most people agree that even one death from a terrorist attack—or one American going hungry—is one too many.

The think tanks also dispute the government's food insecurity methodology, suggesting that, if families merely worry about whether they have enough food, it is not really a problem. They also claim that since the food insecurity methodology is based only on what people *say* about what food they may or may not eat, it's not reliable. In testimony before Congress in 2003, AEI analyst Douglas Besharov said that the USDA food insecurity methodology is "an artificial construct based on answers to eighteen different questions that express some uncertainty about having sufficient financial resources to obtain enough food to meet the needs of all household members *even once* in the past year."[6]

Besharov's argument has been proven unfounded by USDA studies that measure what people actually eat or don't eat, which have produced very similar findings to the food insecurity methodology. Moreover, his argument ignores that studies show that food-insecure people do limit or alter their food intake due to lack of money. In addition, a USDA study found that, in low-income households, especially those containing the elderly, people were far more likely to be hungry in areas with high heating costs in the winter and in areas with high air-conditioning costs in the summer, proving the "eat or heat hypothesis." The study found "it is important to understand the extent to which households make tradeoffs between heating and cooling costs and other basic needs that affect their food security."[7]

Not content to merely criticize the federal government's methodology, the Heritage Foundation routinely disparages hunger reports by the US Conference of Mayors, even though Heritage usually champions the theory of federalism under which local governments are considered by them to be the most virtuous and competent level of government.[8] Even more hypocritical, these right-wing think tanks dismiss data from soup kitchens and food pantries, even though these agencies are the very faith-based "armies of compassion" that conservatives supposedly champion. The only thing consistent about these ideological policy advocates is that they consistently disregard any hard data that contradicts their preconceived worldviews.

To top it off, such think tanks—and the conservatives who listen to them—often contrast American hunger and poverty with that in the Third World, explaining that we just don't understand how good *our* hungry and poor people have it. They certainly would not want to benchmark the stock market or our military capabilities to the developing world, but they are always willing to let poor people settle for less. They say that because most low-income families in America own air conditioning and cars (ignoring that people often need cars to get to work), they must not really be facing poverty and hunger. Rector once complained that poor people have "color TVs," as if he thought that black-and-white TVs are still sold in America and that the poor should save money by buying them. Rector even complained that people shouldn't be considered poor if they own answering machines.[9]

Note that Rector and company rarely compare hunger and poverty in the US to the levels in Western Europe or Canada. They don't point out that, in a United Nations ranking of twenty-one wealthy nations, the United States was in statistical heat with Great Britain for being last in terms of child welfare, in a study that assessed everything from infant mortality to whether children ate dinner with their parents or were bullied at school. "What they [the United States and Great Britain] have in common are very high levels of inequality, very high levels of child poverty, which is also associated with inequality," said Jonathan Bradshaw, one of the study's researchers. "They don't invest as much in children as continental European countries do," he said, citing the lack of day care services in both countries and poorer health coverage and preventative care for children in the US.[10]

Nor do Rector's allies mention a study written jointly by researchers who work for the US and Canadian governments, which found that the percentage of households who cannot afford an adequate supply of food is far higher in the United States than in Canada—and the difference is particularly severe in families with children. Covering the years 2003 to 2005, the study found that out of all households, 14.1 percent of US adults and 9 percent of Canadian adults suffered from food insecurity.[11] Among households with children, the rate of adult food insecurity in the US was nearly twice that in Canada, and the rate of "severe food insecurity" (the term previously called "hunger" by the US government) among adults was approximately 80 percent higher in the US than in Canada. Food insecurity among children was also substantially higher in the US than in Canada—roughly 70 percent higher for overall child food insecurity and more than 50 percent higher for severe child food insecurity. One might suspect that the reason for these disparities is that America has more poverty and diversity than Canada. Yet the paper found:

The food security status of households is strongly associated with their income, and the national-level differences in food insecurity described above might be thought to result in large part from differences in income distribution between the two countries. Cross-classification of households by food security status and income adequacy, however, suggests that this is not true. Rather, the differences in food insecurity reflect almost entirely differences between the two countries in the prevalence of food insecurity among households with similar cash incomes. Households in the US are, on average, more likely to be food insecure than households in Canada with the same annual income and household size.

In other words, low-income families in the US are far more likely to be food insecure than low-income families in Canada.

When the right-wing think tanks do, on rare occasions, admit the existence of widespread hunger and poverty in the US, they almost always blame it on the hungry and the poor, claiming that they don't work enough hours, or when they do, they don't work hard enough or aren't smart enough. Claims Robert Rector: "There are two main reasons that American children are poor. Their parents don't work much, and their fathers are absent from the home."[12] Having previously blamed poverty on welfare, teenage pregnancy, crack usage, and crime, these institutions are noticeably silent on a big question: Since all those so-called contributors to the problem have decreased in last few decades, why are poverty and hunger still increasing? Also, they never seem to mention that most hungry Americans are in working families.

THE RIGHT'S BIGGEST, FATTEST ARGUMENT AGAINST HUNGER

All their previous arguments having failed, the right-wing think tanks finally hit upon a myth that's working: Americans are too fat to be hungry.

In testimony before Congress in 2003, AEI's Douglas Besharov said:

In the summer of 1967, I saw American starvation and malnutrition up close. As a civil rights worker in the Mississippi Delta, I (literally) carried ill and malnourished black children into hospitals. (The hospitals—without a law student from the North standing in the admitting room and threatening a lawsuit—ordinarily refused to treat poor African Americans.) The children were starving because their families had no money to buy food. Making things worse, many black families were denied welfare, simply because of their race. (I saw mothers with young children who applied for welfare being offered bus tickets to Chicago.) This national disgrace was ended only after sustained media exposure.[13]

Very moving—and smart—testimony indeed. Besharov seeks to inoculate his ultraconservative comments that follow by trying to communicate that he is no racist, that he cares deeply about poor people, and that—decades ago—hunger *was* a huge problem in America. But then Besharov adds the kicker:

But that was thirty-five years ago—before massive expansions of the federal feeding and welfare programs for the poor. . . . Today, instead of hunger, the central nutritional problem facing the poor, indeed all Americans, is not too little food but, rather too much—or at least too many calories.

As effective as his testimony is as propaganda, he leaves out a few very important points. For one, hunger still exists in Mississippi and virtually everywhere else in America (although not as severely as it previously did) and it often coexists with obesity. For another, government officials still frequently deny government benefits to poor people because of their race and social status. And, finally, Besharov supports *slashing* the very government welfare and nutrition programs that he credits with eliminating hunger.

Still, the obesity issue is a compelling argument. "We are feeding the poor as if they are starving, when anyone can see that the real problem for them, like other Americans, is expanding girth," says Besharov.[14] Who can argue with something we all so clearly *see*?

The argument is so compelling that even entities that should know better sometimes buy it. In 2003, and again in 2004, the *New York Times* ran lengthy pieces, claiming to be objective reporting, arguing it was because America was so prosperous that so many people were overweight, and claiming that meant hunger had obviously been eliminated in the US.[15]

Truth be told, too many Americans *are* obese. Fully 34 percent of US adults, and 17 percent of adolescents, are overweight.[16] Yet not only does hunger exist in America despite obesity, and not only are people frequently both obese and food insecure at the same time, but hunger is actually a key *contributor* to the growing obesity problem among low-income Americans. Hunger and obesity are flip sides of the same malnutrition coin.

Some hungry people *do* lose weight. Among the Americans characterized by the USDA as having very low food security (what used to be called "hunger"), 46 percent lose weight some time during the year. But it is even more common for such households to report that they "relied on a few kinds of low-cost foods to feed their children" (96 percent) and "couldn't feed their children balanced meals" (87 percent).[17] An analysis by the Center on Hunger and Poverty at Brandeis University and the Food Research and Action Center found that hunger and obesity not only "pose separate and distinct health risks, but also can coexist in the same household."[18]

Thus, while some of the hungriest and poorest Americans eat so little that they lose weight, many others, with a marginally better ability to get food (either through limited food purchases, meager food stamp allotments, or pantry donations) eat food of such poor nutritional quality that they gain weight.[19]

As demonstrated when I took the Food Stamp Challenge, when people are on a limited budget, the easiest way to fill their bellies is to purchase high-carbohydrate, high-fat, high-sodium foods that are cheaper but more likely to cause obesity. Add the reality that most nutritious types of food aren't even available in many low-income neighborhoods and you have a recipe for dietary failure.

SO HOW *DOES* HUNGER CAUSE OBESITY?

If people can't afford or can't access nutritious food (especially during a time of skyrocketing food prices), they can't eat it. While many people believe that the reason low-income people don't eat more healthfully is that they tend to have less nutritional education (which is, to some degree, true), the primary reason is that they have less money. A formerly middle-class woman who had to face poverty and hunger for the first time as a result of a divorce explained her dilemma in Loretta Schwartz-Nobel's book *Growing Up Empty: The Hunger Epidemic in America*:

> Talking about fresh food might sound trivial under such desperate circumstances, but up until this time I had never ever used canned vegetables in my life. . . . I'm supposed to have a low-fat diet because I have high cholesterol but that's not what was available. When you're poor you take whatever you can get, not just with food, but with everything in life.[20]

When families are forced to accept whatever food pantries or soup kitchens have to give them, they have even fewer nutritional options. While such programs have made great strides in the last few years in giving out more fresh produce and other healthier foods, in general, they are left no choice but to give out the often processed surplus foods donated to them by the food industry and government, which tend to have high amounts of sugar, salt, and fat.

Nutritious foods are frequently more expensive than less nutritious alternatives. In October 2007, a gallon of milk cost $3.84 on average, but two liters of cola were $1.23 and sixteen ounces of alcoholic malt beverages cost $1.13. Potatoes cost $0.52 per pound, while lettuce cost $1.49, broccoli $1.53, and strawberries $2.00.[21] Lean meat is cheaper than fattier meat and whole wheat bread is much more expensive than white bread.

New dietary guidelines recommend that Americans eat nine servings of fruits and vegetables a day, up from five servings in the previous guidelines. One study found that while average Americans spent 15 percent of their food budgets on fruits and vegetables, low-income Americans needed to spend up to 70 percent of their food budgets on fruits and vegetables to meet those new government guidelines.[22]

Poor people often must choose foods that give them the feeling that their stomachs are full for the least possible cost. A national study found that "poverty and food insecurity are associated with lower food expenditures, low fruit and vegetable consumption, and lower-quality diets. . . . The association between poverty and obesity may be mediated, in part, by the low cost of energy-dense foods and may be reinforced by the high palatability of sugar and fat."[23] For example, a survey of Seattle-area supermarkets found that twenty cents spent on cookies would provide the same amount of food energy as ninety-five cents spent on carrots.[24] A parent can quickly and easily feed a large family on a bucket of fried chicken for less than ten dollars, while it would cost far more money, and take far more time, to whip up something healthier from scratch. To keep tummies full, low-income families eat a lot of cheap fast food and processed foods.

FOOD DESERTS IN LOW-INCOME AREAS

Even if people could afford nutritious food, it is often simply unavailable in their neighborhoods. Low-income neighborhoods where it is difficult to find fresh and healthy food are increasingly referred to as "food deserts." In Los Angeles County in 2002, an average supermarket served 18,649 people, while the average supermarket in a low-income neighborhood served 27,986 people. The higher the concentration of poverty within a neighborhood, the fewer supermarkets there were. In zip codes where fewer than 10 percent of households lived below the federal poverty line, there were approximately 2.26 times as many supermarkets per household as there were in zip codes where the number of households living below the federal poverty line exceeded 40 percent. In addition, the higher the concentration of white people in a neighborhood, the greater number of supermarkets.[25]

In neighborhoods without supermarkets, it is corner stores, bodegas, and convenience stores that fill in the gaps. Louisville, Kentucky's *Courier-Journal* notes: "In most of western Louisville and parts of downtown, it's easier to buy a Twinkie than fresh broccoli. A lack of full-service supermarkets, low car ownership and an abundance of fast-food and higher-priced convenience stores are limiting access to fresh fruits and vegetables and nurturing poor eating habits."[26]

In a study of rural Orangeburg County, South Carolina, researchers identified seventy-seven stores in the county, of which only 16 percent were supermarkets and 10 percent were grocery stores. The remaining 74 percent were convenience stores. Low-fat or nonfat milk, apples, high-fiber bread, eggs, and smoked turkey were available in 75 percent to 100 percent of supermarkets and grocery stores versus 4 percent to 29 percent of convenience stores. Just 28 percent of all stores sold any of the fruits or vegetables included in the survey. Convenience stores also tended to charge more for items than did supermarkets.[27]

The lack of supermarkets makes a concrete difference. Areas without a full range of markets are "obesogenic" (obesity producing). Four different studies have demonstrated a positive association between access to food stores and improved dietary choices.[28] A study in four states found that areas with high numbers of supermarkets had lower rates of obesity while areas with higher numbers of convenience stores had higher levels of obesity.[29] Nationwide, for every additional supermarket in a census tract, fruit and vegetable consumption increases by as much as 32 percent.[30]

For people who rely on the Food Stamp Program, the healthiest food choices can be even more difficult to access. Out of the 162,015 retail outlets in America authorized to accept food stamp benefits, only 2,010 are farmers' markets or produce stands. While it's certainly helpful that there are now more than 4,385 farmers' markets in the country—an 18 percent increase since 2004—only 10 percent of them accept food stamp benefits.[31]

The organization I manage, the New York City Coalition Against Hunger, used computer-mapping technology to demonstrate that, like the rest of the nation, low-income neighborhoods in our city lack access to supermarkets, farmers' markets, and other sources of fresh produce and nutritious food. Focusing on the high-poverty neighborhoods of the South Bronx, Central Harlem, and Brownsville, Brooklyn, we found that fresh produce and other nutritious foods are often more difficult to access than more fattening junk foods and restaurant foods.[32] As one example, Community Board District One in the South Bronx has about 90,000 residents, 45 percent of whom are below the poverty line. The district runs about 1.3 miles north to south and 1.5 miles east to west, very long distances if you travel by foot or by public transportation, as most people in the neighborhood do. In 2007, there was not a single supermarket of 2,500 square feet (a common minimal square footage to consider a store a "supermarket") or more in the entire district. Yet convenience stores, bodegas, fast food restaurants, and low-cost sit-down restaurants with limited, mostly unhealthy, menus were plentiful. In just one part of the district, in zip code 10451, there were three McDonald's outlets.

Also in the Bronx, a community food assessment of the Melrose neighborhood, conducted by the food rescue organization City Harvest, found that even the supermarkets in the neighborhood didn't have a full array of nutritious food. Only one supermarket carried all twelve of the basic produce items listed in the USDA's Thrifty Food Plan. Another carried eleven out of twelve, and two local fruit markets each carried eight out of twelve. In addition, the neighborhood residents said they thought the produce sold was of a poor quality.[33]

FAST FOOD AND JUNK FOOD APLENTY

Healthy food choices are further complicated when nutritional information is not available, or is misleading. First of all, sometimes food is labeled as healthy when it's not. Purely as research for this book, I assure you, I bought a tiny, 1.58-ounce bag of the chocolate-covered raisins, Raisinets. To appeal to the health-conscious shopper, the wrapper had a picture of fresh grapes and said, "Natural source of fruit antioxidants." In big print it read "30% LESS FAT," followed by smaller print that said, "THAN OTHER LEADING CHOCOLATE BRANDS." That's like Kuwait bragging it has 30 percent less sand than Saudi Arabia. In even smaller print on the back of the package, the nutrition label stated that the bag contained 190 calories, seventy of which came from fat. It also contained 8.0 grams of fat (12 percent of the entire USDA daily fat allowance) and 5.5 grams of harmful saturated fat (fully 23 percent of the daily allowance). And, yes, they were *delicious*.

In a helpful move to improve nutrition information for consumers, New York City Mayor Michael Bloomberg and his Board of Health now require that restaurants, which previously provided some sort of nutrition information, go one step further and list calorie counts on their menus next to each item. The restaurant industry unsuccessfully tried to block it in court.

Fast food restaurants have other unique ways to make healthy choices more difficult. Here's an interesting Burger King fact: did you know it costs *less* to buy medium fries and a medium soda than to get small fries and a small soda? That's because the "value meals" only come in the medium or large sizes. The cash registers literally won't ring up smaller sizes for the value meals. I wrote to the CEO of Burger King asking him to change this policy, but he never wrote back.

According to nutritional information available at the Burger King corporate Web site in 2007, the nutritional difference between medium and small sizes is massive.[34] A double cheeseburger contains 500 calories and 29 grams of fat, not counting fries and a drink, while a regular, single-patty cheeseburger has 340 calories and 16 grams of fat. Small fries contain 230 calories and 13 grams of fat, and a small Coke has 140 calories. Yet, medium fries have 360 calories and 18 grams of fat and a medium Coke contains 200 calories. Doing the math, a double cheeseburger with small fries and a small Coke equals 870 calories and 42 grams of fat; a double cheeseburger with medium fries and a medium Coke equals 1,060 calories and 47 grams of fat. (Somewhat better, a regular cheeseburger with small fries and a small Coke would be 710 calories and 29 grams of fat.) Given that the USDA recommends that the average adult should eat about 2,000 calories per day, the smaller value meal would comprise 44 percent of that total, while the medium meal would be 53 percent. The king-size value meal comes in at a whopping 75 percent of your total caloric intake for the day. No wonder Burger King doesn't want to post nutritional information.

The food industry spends more than $10 billion per year advertising to children in the United States, and it particularly targets marketing in low-income neighborhoods. The marketing works. A study found that preschool children preferred the taste of food and drinks in McDonald's packaging to the exact same food and drinks in unbranded packaging.[35]

This is not the kind of food Americans need to be eating frequently. Still, advocates often go too far in blaming the food industry and its marketing for society's entire obesity problem. Sweden and Norway banned all TV advertising—including food advertising—aimed at children, but it has not had a dramatic impact upon the child obesity rates in those countries.

Critics of the food industry ignore that, to many of us, burgers and fries simply taste better than steamed tofu and bean sprouts; Pop Tarts taste better than sugar-free, high-fiber cereal; Coke tastes better than water, and so on. Sure, the lower cost of such foods is a key factor, but the yum-factor cannot be discounted.

Of course, the food industry *does* need to be held accountable. It is entirely hypocritical for the industry to expect consumers to take more personal responsibility so long as it actively blocks efforts to give people the nutritional information necessary to exercise such responsibility. People can only eat more responsibly when they have both the money *and* nutritional information.

While it is society's responsibility to fix the problem, parents of all incomes must be held accountable too—to the extent that they are economically able to do so. When it comes to pure junk foods, more parents have to learn to "just say no" (or at least, "not until you've had your vegetables") to their children. Parents themselves also need to eat better in front of their kids, both to live longer and to be better role models. Even if families have to struggle mightily to provide their children healthier foods—whether by scrimping limited funds or taking a bus a few blocks further—few endeavors are more important. Even though it is a sacrifice, it is one worth making for their children's future.

EXTRA WEIGHT STRUGGLES FOR THE FOOD INSECURE

Scientific proof of the link between hunger and obesity continues to grow. One national study found that household and child food insecurity are associated with the risk of being overweight. Child food insecurity is independently associated with the risk of obesity, even after controlling for socioeconomic variables.[36] Another study found that "although a variety of environmental, social, behavioral, or physiologic mechanisms could cause both problems (food insecurity and obesity) independently, an alternative possibility is that hunger and obesity are causally related. [This] report supports this hypothesis."[37] A study of women in California found "obesity was more prevalent in food insecure (31.0%) than in food-secure women (16.2%)."[38] When food-insecure children had access to food, another study found, they ate more and ate faster than other children.[39]

When hungry people are forced to eat at irregular intervals, they frequently overcompensate during the meals they do get by eating portion sizes that are larger than their bodies actually need at that moment. There is also reason to believe that physiological changes may occur to help the body conserve energy when diets are inadequate. The body can compensate for periodic food shortages by becoming more efficient in storing calories as fat.[40]

Topping it off, poor people are less likely to be able to afford gym memberships, have space in their homes in which to work out, or have safe public parks at which they can exercise outdoors. The odds are stacked against them. Some manage to miraculously beat the odds—usually due to luck, extraordinary will, or jobs that require significant physical labor—staying fit despite all those challenges.

Are income-related factors the only reasons for obesity? Of course not. Staying fit is a battle we all face. Plenty of nonpoor Americans are obese. The bottom line is, unless you are one of the rare people genetically blessed with perpetual thinness, if you eat too much food, eat the wrong kinds of food, or burn too few calories, you'll gain weight. Some people, like me, can blame at least some extra weight on bad genes. All my family members (even those who don't eat like hogs) are a little heavy, and even when I successfully trained for and ran the New York City Marathon, I didn't entirely succeed in wiping out my potbelly. (In truth, however, most of the blame for my extra weight must be placed on my addiction to New York's world-class bagels, pizza, and Chinese fried dumplings, and my fondness for snacking and consuming copious amounts of high-calorie beverages.) It's hard enough for people of any income category to keep their weight in check, but the emotional and physical tolls of poverty and food insecurity make the challenges that much harder. Food can be a type of self-medication, no matter your socioeconomic status.

OBESITY KILLS

Poor, middle class, or ultrarich, obesity has a detrimental impact upon human health, increasing the risk for heart disease, stroke, diabetes, and many other serious ailments. But, as with much else, the impact upon low-income people is the most devastating. The link between obesity and diabetes is particularly strong, as the neighborhoods with the highest rates of diabetes are the neighborhoods with the highest rates of obesity and, not coincidentally, the highest rates of poverty and food insecurity. Nutrition-related diabetes has now reached epidemic proportions in the United States.

In New York City, deaths from diabetes skyrocketed by 71 percent between 1990 and 2003. African-American diabetics died at three times the rate of white New Yorkers with the disease, and Hispanic New Yorkers shouldered the greatest increase in death from diabetes since 1990—a rise of 169 percent. Residents of neighborhoods where diabetes was most prevalent—among them East Harlem, the South Bronx, and Brooklyn's Williamsburg and Bushwick—all of which are low-income neighborhoods—died of diabetes at seven times the rate of those in the least-affected parts of the city. They also were hospitalized ten times more than those on the Upper East Side, a wealthy neighborhood. Dr. Shadi Chamany, the head of diabetes prevention and control for the city government, says, "It can be a risk factor if people are more likely to be overweight or obese and less physically active because they live in a particular neighborhood where they don't have access to resources such as parks and nutritious food."[41]

Nationwide, because obesity plays a role in so many serious diseases, it increases health care costs by 36 percent and medication costs by 77 percent. Obesity now costs the country more in health care expenses than smoking.[42]

Even though the stakes are so high, key actors in the system, including the medical profession, remain dangerously ignorant of how obesity, hunger, nutrition, and health interact. Dr. Nevan Scrimshaw, head of the Department of Nutrition and Food Science at the Massachusetts Institute of Technology, said in 1967 that "clinical nutrition is not even taught at most medical schools and is not adequately done in any of them."[43] This remains true today. When I once spoke to a group of second-year students at Mount Sinai School of Medicine in New York, few of them had received extensive training in nutrition. In contrast, agriculture students receive extensive training on how water and soil nutrients affect plants.

Of the hundreds of courses at the Harvard Medical School in 2007, only four dealt with nutrition; out of those, three concerned nutrition in Latin America and one was about pediatric nutrition in the United States. Not one was about the nutrition of adult Americans. Yet the school has three courses on plastic surgery and four on sports medicine. It has twenty-one courses on oncology (cancer) and twenty-seven courses on cardiology and vascular disease.[44] It is curious that medical schools spend so much time on problems like heart disease and cancer, which are frequently caused by poor nutrition, but so little time on nutrition itself. If the medical profession doesn't focus more on nutrition, it is no wonder that the greater society doesn't. We need to change that.

Certainly one huge step toward addressing this spreading obesity epidemic would be to make sure that poor Americans around the country have better access to more affordable, nutritious foods. Far from a reason why we should dismiss hunger, obesity among low-income Americans should only motivate us further to identify and put a stop to it.

CHAPTER 7

DICKENS REVISITED
Life in the New Gilded Age

Some things people can afford, some things people can't.

—New York City Mayor Michael Bloomberg, whose net worth was an estimated $11.5 billion in 2007, commenting on the decision of the Museum of Modern Art to raise its adult entrance fee from $12 to $20, following a major renovation that received $65 million in taxpayer funding[1]

Sometimes I get frustrated when I hear politicians say there are two Americas. I don't believe there are two Americas. . . . There is a model of thought among the Democrats—that the amount of money, the amount of wealth in a nation, is a fixed amount. And that if Bill Gates and Warren Buffet are making a lot of money, that just means somebody else is not able to make as much. That happens to be entirely false.

—Former Massachusetts Governor Mitt Romney, whose net worth was an estimated $350 million in 2007[2]

The last time America had this much inequality of wealth was in 1929.[3] We know what happened after that.

During the 2003–2005 time period, according to the Congressional Budget Office, the amount of *extra* income earned by the wealthiest 1 percent of Americans (on top of their existing income in 2003) exceeded the *total* income of the poorest 20 percent of Americans. In 2005, the total income of the 3 million individuals at the top was roughly equal to the combined income of the 166 million Americans at the bottom.[4] Inequality of wealth is one of the defining features of our age.

CHART 7A

The Poor Stay Poor, the Middle Class Remain Stuck, the Rich Get Richer, and the Very Rich Get Way Richer (Median Household Income, 1973–2006)

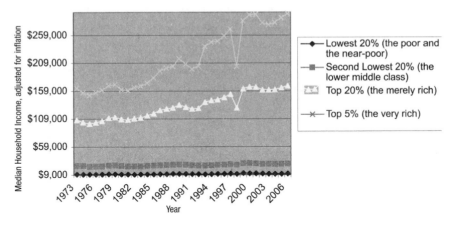

Source: US Census Bureau Current Population Survey

As Chart 7A shows, except for the year 2000, when the Internet bubble burst, massive wealth accumulation at the top has continued unabated for decades, even during times that were tough economically for everyone else. Incomes for the poor, the near-poor, and the lower middle class barely budged.

The extra wealth at the very top was not merely a product of the free market—their taxes had been slashed.[5]

THE EMERGENCE OF THE ULTRARICH

When I was growing up, as far as I knew, America only had two billionaires, J. Paul Getty and Howard Hughes. Today we have more than 400, which means that having a net worth of a billion dollars isn't enough anymore to get you on the *Forbes* list. In just one year between 2006 and 2007, the collective net worth of the nation's top 400 plutocrats rose by $290 billion, to $1.54 trillion. That's more money than the economy of France. Forty-five new billionaires entered the list, more than half of whom got wealthy from hedge funds and private equity.[6] In Chart 7B, I label households in the top 20 percent "merely rich," those in the top five percent "very rich," and those represented on the *Forbes* 400 list as "ultrarich." (I have chosen not to use the term "filthy rich.")

While all of the merely rich and the very rich certainly did far better than

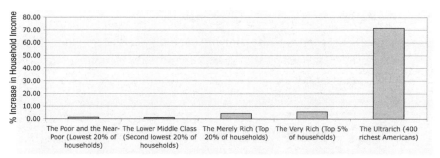

CHART 7B

% Increases in Income in US Households, 2002–2006
(Increases Above the Rate of Inflation)

Sources: US Census Bureau Current Population Survey; *Forbes* magazine; percentage change calculated by author

the poor, the near-poor, and the lower middle class, even the merely rich and the very rich were all left in the dust by the ultrarich. According to my calculations based on Chart 7B, and represented in Chart 7C, between 2002 and 2006, household income increased by 1.38 percent for the poor and the near-poor, 1.08 percent for the lower middle class, 4.38 percent for the merely rich, 5.71 percent for the very rich, and a truly astounding 71.47 percent for the ultrarich.

Even millionaires are starting to grumble about the unfair advantages gained by the new billionaires, many of whom are hedge fund managers. As *Fortune*

CHART 7C

The 400 Richest Americans Have Far More Money than the
23 Million Poorest Households

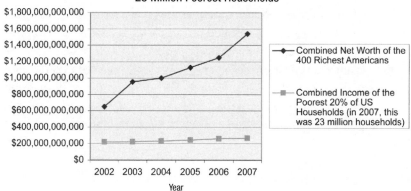

Sources: *Forbes* Magazine; US Census Bureau Current Population Survey

columnist Matt Miller wrote: "Not long ago, an investment banker worth millions told me that he wasn't in his line of work for the money. 'If I was doing this for the money,' he said, with no trace of irony, 'I'd be at a hedge fund.' . . . That [such a statement] is fathomable suggests how debauched our ruling class has become."[7] Of course, given that the gap between the rich and the ultrarich is so massive, the gap between the poor and the ultrarich is astronomical, with the 400 richest people having about seventeen times the combined money of the 23 million poorest families.

NEW YORK CITY: THE EPICENTER OF INEQUALITY

Nowhere is the New Gilded Age more visible than in New York City, which has become the epicenter of the nation's inequality of wealth. According to *Forbes*, the number of billionaires in the city rose from forty-five in 2006 to more than sixty-four in 2007, with their combined total net worth rising from $60.4 billion to $224 billion—a 370 percent increase.[8] In contrast, the 1.7 million city residents living below the federal poverty line earned a combined total of approximately $3.45 billion, about the same amount as the previous year.[9] That means that in 2006, the city's forty-five billionaires had roughly more than seventeen times the money of the 1.7 million poorest, and a year later, in 2007, the city's sixty-four billionaires had about sixty-four times the money of the 1.7 million poorest. The city's wealthiest resident, David Koch, whose net worth rose from $12 billion in 2006 to $17 billion in 2007, had a net worth estimated to be nearly five times the *combined* incomes of all 1.7 million New Yorkers below the poverty line. Meanwhile, fully 1.3 million city residents—including more than 400,000 (one in five) children—lived in food-insecure homes.[10]

In 2005, *New York Magazine* printed figures for what New Yorkers in varied jobs earned. A sampling is on the following page.

These jaw-dropping disparities are not simply the result of differences in skills, work ethics, or luck—they are also the direct result of skewed economic, social, and fiscal policies that make social mobility nearly impossible for the poor and unimaginable growth increasingly possible for the rich.

SALARIES OF SELECT NEW YORKERS, 2005

Edward Lampert, manager, ESL Investments hedge fund.............................$1,020,000,000

Richard Fuld, chairman and CEO, Lehman Brothers $35,257,099

Eric Rosen, first-year assistant district attorney $50,000

Joseph Volpe, general manager, Metropolitan Opera...$713,000

Richard Johnson, gossip columnist, *New York Post*...$300,000

Anna Wintour, editor, *Vogue*...$2,000,000

Sylvana Soto-Ward, assistant to Anna Wintour $40,000

Peter Martins, artistic director, New York City Ballet $619,000

Isiah Thomas, general manager, New York Knicks...$6,700,000

Gregory Burke, private, US Army, stationed in Iraq $18,444

Kevin Sheekey, Bloomberg campaign manager..$270,842

Lori Lyons, garbagewoman...$48,996

Anthony Napolitano, rookie police officer $36,878

Nzue Kohen, cab driver...$37,000

Santiago Segovia, parking attendant...$11,440

Elvin Urena, barber $26,085

Flower, cocaine dealer..$150,000

John Sexton, president, New York University...$740,504

Wol-san Liem, teaching assistant, New York University $19,000

Christina Annunziata, teacher, Bronx public school...$44,000

Herbert Pardes, CEO, New York Presbyterian Hospital $2,327,655

Calvin Klein, consulting creative director, Phillips Van Heusen Corp. $22,200,000

Nivia Nogues, sales assistant, Payless Shoe Source...$15,652

Eddie Santi, pizza server, Famous Famiglia Pizzeria $17,888

Jamal Khandaker, hot dog and pretzel vendor, Broadway and Warren Street $11,200

Mike Kim, Chinese deliveryman, Wang's Restaurant (not including tips) ....$5,200[11]

WHO IS POOR IN THE UNITED STATES?

The fact that wealthy people are getting so much wealthier wouldn't be so troubling if it were not accompanied by the rest of the nation—working
people—facing stagnating wages and surging poverty. In our most recent
Gilded Age, as the ultrarich got ultra richer, hope started vanishing for tens of
millions who toiled hard to reach or stay in the middle class, and, all-too-often,
failed. According to the Census Bureau, between 2000 and 2007 the number
of Americans living below the meager federal poverty line (about $17,000 for
a family of three) increased by more than 5 million people, reaching 37.2 million, a number slightly higher than the number of Americans living in food
insecurity (35.5 million) in 2006. In 2007, 18 percent of all American children
lived in poverty.

The federal government calculates the poverty line utilizing an outdated
method from the 1960s that does not take into account current costs for key
items such as housing, fuel, and health care. This method of measuring poverty
assures that the federal government always undercounts the number of Americans who suffer from economic deprivation. But even if you overlook that
undercounting, the number of people now characterized as poor by the Census
Bureau is massive. America has a far higher rate of poverty than any other
industrialized Western nation.

In 2007, a record number of people—15.6 million Americans—lived in
extreme poverty, meaning that their cash income was less than half of the
poverty line, or less than about $8,500 a year for a three-person family.[12]

Of the 37.2 million Americans living in poverty in 2007, 13.3 million (36
percent) were below the age of eighteen; 3.5 million (9 percent) were above
the age of sixty-five; and 4.2 million (11 percent) were between the ages of
eighteen and sixty-five but were classified by the Social Security Administration as too disabled to work. Thus, 21 million Americans in poverty (56
percent of those in poverty) were either children, of retirement age, or disabled. That meant that about 16.2 million people in poverty (44 percent of
all the people in poverty) were able-bodied and between the ages of eighteen
and sixty-five. Of those 16.2 million able-bodied adults, about 2.7 million (17
percent) worked full time, 6.3 million (39 percent) worked part-time or part
year, and 7.2 million (44 percent) didn't work at all.[13] Those 7 million able-
boded, unemployed people are less than 20 percent of the people in poverty.
Thus, while much of the public still thinks that most poor people are healthy

but unemployed, that describes less than one in five of the people in poverty—and many of those actively are looking for work. Underemployment and low wages are now problems just as troublesome as unemployment, although it is also true that there are still too many able-bodied, low-income people who, by choice or by situation, are not seriously seeking or keeping full-time employment.

While too many senior citizens are poor because they can't afford food, housing, property taxes, health care, and prescription medicine on a fixed income, poverty among American seniors is dramatically less than it used to be because of Social Security and Medicare. About 9 percent of seniors were poor in 2006.

In the same year, the South continued to have the highest poverty rate at 14 percent. The other three regions had poverty rates that were not statistically different from one another: 11.5 percent in the Northeast, 11.2 percent in the Midwest, and 11.6 percent in the West. Twenty-one percent of Hispanics, 8 percent of non-Hispanic whites, 24 percent of African Americans, and 10 percent of Asians were poor in 2006.

WAGES AND EXPENSES

While there seems to be infinite room for advancement for the ultrarich, there is less and less room for poor people to move up the economic ladder. The federal minimum wage has not even come close to rising with inflation over the past few decades. The wage wasn't raised from its measly rate of $5.15 an hour during the entire decade of 1997 to 2007. When the new Democratic Congress in 2007 forced President Bush to sign a measure including an increase, it went up in steps, first going to $5.85 in June of that year, and will eventually reach up to $7.25 by June 2009.[14] Adjusted for inflation, the $5.85 level is still 7 percent less than it was ten years before. Even the $7.25 level will equal only about $15,000 for a year of forty-hour workweeks with no vacation. If a parent with two children earned that much, the family would still be *below* the federal poverty line.

Despite their hard work—frequently at one, two, or more jobs—America's poor must fight an increasingly difficult daily struggle to meet basic needs. Costs for housing, food, medical care, fuel for their homes and cars, child care, and prescription drugs are all skyrocketing. Add to that the extra burden placed on many by the subprime mortgage crisis and you can see why so many lag behind.

Like hunger, poverty defies geographical stereotypes. As an example, according to an article in the *Columbus Dispatch*, in rural, Appalachian Coleville, Ohio, Brian and Melissa Barringer had six jobs between them in 2004, but they were still struggling. Brian, 41, was a jack of all trades, earning $8.55 an hour working at a gas well, a car wash, and a flea market. He also collected used cans for recycling. Melissa, 37, worked as a nurse's aide in a nursing home, earning $8.29 an hour in that job and $5 to $6 an hour in other jobs. Their income totaled $26,000 that year, $4,000 above the federal poverty line at the time. "Despite back-breaking work and hours that are often dawn to dusk, the Barringers barely have enough money to feed and clothe their three boys: Eric, 18; Kyle, 12; and Zachary, 9." They earned too much to qualify for food stamps, so they obtained food from a local food pantry.[15]

Housing has had an especially strong impact on working people's expenses. In 2006, 16 million low-income households either paid more for rent and utilities than the federal government said was affordable or lived in overcrowded or substandard housing. Six million of these households were in especially dire straits; they paid more than *half* of their incomes for rent or utilities or lived in severely substandard conditions. Nearly 2 million poor households were unable to pay their full rent or mortgage at least once in 2006. Nearly 3 million fell behind on their gas or electric bills.[16]

The so-called "Housing Wage," created by the National Low Income Housing Coalition, calculates the full-time hourly wage that a worker would need to earn in order to pay what the federal government estimates to be the Fair Market Rent for a home where that worker lives, while spending no more than 30 percent of that worker's income on housing costs. The 2006 National Housing Wage for a two-bedroom rental unit was $16.31 per hour, more than three times the minimum wage at the time.[17]

Also in 2006, after seven straight years of increases in the number of Americans without health insurance, 47 million Americans—more than one in every seven—were uninsured, including nearly 9 million children. More than 40 million adults—roughly one in five—did not receive at least one type of health care they needed that year (medical, dental, mental health, prescription drugs) because they could not afford it.[18]

Poor people's wages just don't cut it. New York *Daily News* writer Heidi Evans tried living on a minimum-wage income for a week and found the following:

It is impossible to live on $206 a week, or $892 a month, if you like living indoors, or want to put in a full day's work but can't afford to pay a baby-sitter from 3 to 6 p.m. during the school week. Or if you have grown weary of begging and borrowing from every friend, relative and credit card each week just to survive. The basic facts are enough to make a grown person cry. . . . You don't have to be Einstein to see instantly that trying to make ends meet on minimum wage is not about being a better budgeter. You can't squeeze something more from a dollar if you don't have the dollar in the first place. . . . What if Alex loses her winter gloves and hat on the bus? What if she gets strep throat or I get the flu and I have to buy antibiotics? Or the vacuum cleaner breaks? And what about the extras that every child deserves? Instead, there would be the humiliation of showing up at friends' birthday parties without a gift, or having to pass on the class trip because of the $8 the teacher [requested].[19]

Author Barbara Ehrenreich has noted that, in a cruel irony, being poor often forces people to spend *more* than nonpoor people to meet basic needs, such as needing to put up two months rent to obtain an apartment, not having enough storage space to buy food in bulk, or paying more for health care or prescription drugs because you cannot afford insurance.[20] A 2005 study in Philadelphia concluded: "Philadelphia's low-income working families pay higher prices for most everyday goods and services than other households." They paid $500 more for cars and $400 more for auto insurance than people in higher-income households. Their homes were more likely to be over-assessed than homes in higher-income neighborhoods, forcing them to pay higher taxes. Because low-income Philadelphians often do not have bank accounts, they must use one of Philadelphia's 147 check-cashing establishments, which are allowed by state law to charge up to $450 per year to cash checks for a household earning $15,000.[21] Nationwide, low-income families who used tax preparers to obtain Earned Income Tax Credited (EITC) refunds immediately lost $3 billion in 2006 due to tax preparation fees.[22]

The nation's tens of millions of working poor are under compensated, under appreciated, and over stressed, as described by author David K. Shipler in his important 2005 book, *The Working Poor*:

Moving in and out of jobs that demand much work and pay little, many people tread just above the official poverty line. . . . An inconvenience to an affluent family—minor car trouble, a brief illness, disrupted child care—is a crisis to them, for it can threaten their ability to stay employed. They spend everything and save nothing. They are always behind on their bills. They have miniscule bank accounts, or none at all, and so pay more fees and higher interest rates than more secure Americans. . . . When the economy weakens, they slip back towards the precipice. . . . A run-down apartment can exacerbate a child's asthma, which leads to a call for an ambulance, which creates a medical bill that cannot be paid, which ruins a credit record, which hikes the interest rate on an auto loan, which forces the purchase of an unreliable used car, which jeopardizes a mother's punctuality at work, which limits her promotions and earnings capacity, which confines her to poor housing.[23]

Shipler also notes how many working poor families faced hunger, and that parents feel that their inability to feed their children is the ultimate failure.

Barbara Ehrenreich wrote that, in some of the low-paying jobs she held during her research for Nickel and Dimed, employers prohibited employees from eating or even drinking for long stretches of time, withheld first paychecks so employees wouldn't quit suddenly, and required employees to work for hours for which they were not compensated.[24] The New York Times' Steven Greenhouse reported in 2004 that, "experts on compensation say that the illegal doctoring of hourly employees' time records (to reduce the number of hours for which they are paid) is far more prevalent than most Americans believe. Beth Terrell, a Seattle lawyer who has sued Wal-Mart, accusing its managers of doctoring time records, said: 'Many of these employees are making $8 an hour. These employees can scarcely afford to have time deleted. They're barely paying their bills already.'"[25]

Wal-Mart was founded by Sam Walton, and as of 2007, the Walton family still controlled 40 percent of Wal-Mart stock. Two of Sam's heirs, Bill Walton and S. Robson Walton, had a combined net worth of $32.6 billion, according to Forbes. They could certainly afford to pay their employees for the hours they've worked. By 2008, either recognizing the moral bankruptcy of such policies or responding to the public outrage that was starting to harm their bottom line—or both—Wal-Mart started taking steps to end such practices and even improve the health care for its workers, although it still strenuously opposed unionization.

Immigrants, particularly those who crossed into the United States illegally, are often at the very bottom of the nation's economic and social heap, despite their vital importance to our economy. A 2007 study by the Fiscal Policy Institute found that immigrants contribute nearly one-fourth of the economic output of New York State.[26] Yet, according to the Center for New York City Affairs, immigrants in New York City are nearly three times as likely to worry about food or be hungry than the overall population, and one-third of children with immigrant parents live in families that have difficulty affording food. In 1999–2000, 40 percent of legal permanent residents entering New York after 1996 had incomes below the federal poverty line— a rate double that of the city as a whole. By the late 1990s, two-thirds of foreign-born Hispanics in the New York metropolitan area were employed in the bottom one-third of jobs (as defined by job quality and pay) and their median weekly earnings were less than half those of native-born whites. On the whole, foreign-born workers comprised well over half the bottom-tier labor force. More than half of all immigrants in a survey of New York City residents said their net worth was zero or negative, compared to one-third of native-born residents.[27]

While some immigrants are still able to move up to achieve the American dream, the stories abound of those who are not able to do so. In Florida in 2007, migrant farm workers, picking tomatoes ten to twelve hours per day by hand for some of the largest fast-food chains in the world, earned $0.45 for every thirty-two-pound bucket they picked.[28] In New York, in 2004, a Palestinian immigrant named Insesar Museitef commuted four hours a day on a subway to work four hours a day to care for a frail elderly person, earning a total of $28 each day.[29]

Immigrants who come to the US illegally tend to be both invisible and physically at risk. During the California wild fires of 2007, while the wealthy evacuated, immigrant farm workers continued working in a nearby field. Recounted Enrique Morones, who takes food and blankets to the migrant camps: "There were Mercedes and Jaguars pulling out, people evacuating, and the migrants were still working."[30] I witnessed a very similar situation in New York when a restaurant at which I was eating had a kitchen fire so bad that the customers were evacuated and the fire department was called, but the immigrant kitchen staff was expected to stay and work. I don't eat there anymore.

Some of my favorite Chinese restaurants in New York have been accused of insisting their employees make bicycle deliveries in hazardous weather conditions and of paying employees subminimum wages, sometimes as little as $1.75 an hour.[31] Alas, I have to boycott them now, too. A 2004 investigation by the Associated Press found that:

> The jobs that lure Mexican workers to the United States are killing them in a worsening epidemic that is now claiming a victim a day. . . . Though Mexicans often take the most hazardous jobs, they are more likely than others to be killed even when doing similarly risky work. The death rates are greatest in several Southern and Western states, where a Mexican worker is four times more likely to die than the average US-born worker. These accidental deaths are almost always preventable and often gruesome: Workers are impaled, shredded in machinery, buried alive. Some are 15 years old.[32]

If people chose to open their eyes to the existence of such immigrants, they could see them everywhere. In Rockland County, New York, the suburb where I grew up, and in similar towns all over America, large crowds of mostly Hispanic men gather in certain parking lots no matter the weather, waiting to be hired for day labor jobs. Pickup trucks driven by employers pull up and then the drivers select some men out of the crowd. Also in all kinds of weather, Hispanic and other women walk long distances to clean someone else's house, and Haitian and other immigrant women take long bus rides to care for someone else's elderly parents.

AN ENDANGERED MIDDLE CLASS

The middle class is also struggling. You'd never know it from the media's obsession with the rich and famous, but, in 2006, 51 percent of all American households had annual incomes below $50,000 and 81 percent had incomes below $100,000.[33]

Because New York is the inequality-of-wealth capital of America, it is also the shrinking-middle-class capital of America. According to a study by the Brookings Institution released in the summer of 2006, the city had the smallest proportion of middle-class families out of any of the country's metropolitan areas.[34] In a survey conducted of leading New Yorkers by the Drum Major Institute for Public Policy, the respondents said they thought a family of four in New York needed between $75,000 and $135,000 to maintain a middle-class standard of living. Unfortunately, the city's actual median family income is only $49,000.[35]

Housing costs are a central reason why New York's middle class is shrinking. The average price for an apartment in Manhattan in the last quarter of 2007 was $1.4 million, up 18 percent from the previous year, despite the national housing slump. The reason for the increase was the effect of the wealthiest buyers; the number of apartments that sold for $10 million tripled in that year.[36] Such prices have trickle-down impacts throughout the housing market, making even formerly affordable housing unaffordable. In 2005, only 4.6 percent of homes for sale in the city were classified as affordable. According to a study by New York Congressman Anthony Weiner, the percentage of New Yorkers who spent half their paycheck on housing rose from 24 percent in 1999 to 30 percent in 2007.[37]

A typical story is the one of Tom Buscemi, a jewelry merchandiser who made $60,000 a year. His landlord raised the rent of his tiny one-room apartment in Manhattan from $500 to $1,900 per month, forcing him to leave Manhattan.[38]

Wrote Tom Acitelli in the *New York Observer*: "Little wonder the solidly middle class are fleeing the city. Rather than sink over one-third of its monthly income into housing costs—whether through mortgage or through rent—a household making between $40,000 and $60,000 per year generally exits the city, leaving the very wealthy and the working class behind to further stratify the city."[39]

THE RICH *ARE* DIFFERENT THAN YOU AND I

Americans are willing to accept that we have poverty *despite* wealth, but they are loath to consider that we often have poverty *because* of wealth. Because Americans (unlike Europeans) are generally socialized into believing that what's good for rich people is automatically good for everyone, they won't allow themselves to accept the simple truth that, if some become ultrarich in part because the people who work for them—either directly or indirectly—aren't paid enough to support their families, such wealth does indeed cause poverty and hunger.

When one ultrarich family simply must have a Hampton mansion in addition to their penthouse in New York, or if they throw an absurdly expensive party for their eight-year-old, they raise the bar for all their peers, who then believe these are things they too *must* have. It's the new "keeping up with the Joneses"—on steroids.

Even during the recession that deepened in 2008, the ultrarich kept spending madly. While America lost 80,000 jobs in March of that year, Lee Trachman, hedge fund manager, spent roughly $50,000 on a four-day jaunt to Miami for himself and three friends. Reported the *New York Times:*

> The trip was an exercise in luxuriant male bonding. Mr. Trachman, who is 38, and his friends got around by private jet, helicopter, Hummer limousine, Ferraris and Lamborghinis; stayed in V.I.P. rooms at Casa Casuarina, the South Beach hotel that was formerly Gianni Versace's mansion; and played "extreme adventure paintball" with former agents of the federal Drug Enforcement Administration. . . . Some businesses that cater to the superrich report that clients . . . are still splurging on multimillion-dollar Manhattan apartments, custom-built yachts, contemporary art and lavish parties. . . . "When times get tough, the smart spend money," said David Monn, an event planner who is organizing a black-tie party on May 10 for dignitaries and recent purchasers of apartments at the Plaza Hotel; the average price there was $7 million. "Short of our country going on food stamps, I don't think we're doing anything differently."[40]

Personally, I just *love* it when the travails of the ultrarich are jokingly compared to going on food stamps. Can't you hear me laughing?

In 2007, *Forbes* magazine printed the "Cost of Living Extremely Well Index," which lists what the wealthy pay for "crucial" items. I had a little fun with it and added a column comparing the items' costs to the number of weeks or years required to pay for them by someone on a minimum wage salary:

Item on *Forbes'* "Cost of Living Extremely Well Index"	Total Cost of Item	Equivalent in weeks or years of salary worked at the minimum wage
Natural Russian sable coat, Maximilian at Bloomingdale's	$190,000	13 years
Men's custom-made black calf wingtip shoes, John Lobb, London	$4,128	14 weeks
One-year tuition, room, and board at preparatory school, Groton	$39,850	137 weeks
Two Metropolitan Opera season tickets, eight shows, parterre box	$5,440	19 weeks
Caviar, Tsar Imperial Beluga, one kilo, Petrossian, Los Angeles	$7,600	26 weeks
Champagne, Dom Pérignon, case, Sherry-Lehmann, New York	$1,559	5 weeks
Sheets, set of linen lace, Pratesi, queen size	$3,490	12 weeks
Face-lift	$14,500	50 weeks
Motor yacht, Hatteras 80 (with 1550-hp CAT C-30s)	$4,870,000	323 years
Thoroughbred horse, yearling	$323,731	21 years
Olympic-size swimming pool, Mission Pools, Escondido, CA	$1,312,500	87 years
Private Learjet 40, standard equipment, certified, six passengers	$8,750,000	580 years
Private Sikorsky helicopter, S-76C++, with VIP options	$11,000,000	729 years
Hermès purse, "Kelly Bag," calfskin, rigid, 28 centimeters	$6,250	21 weeks

Consequently, if an ultrarich person chose to save $11 million by taking ground transportation rather having their own helicopter, the money saved could allow them to hire 220 additional workers at a middle-class salary of $50,000 each.

The dysfunction of our current system of crony capitalism is based upon the twin assumptions that—in order to be competitive in the world economy—US corporations must award astronomical sums to their corporative executives to achieve optimum performance and must pay as little as they can to their frontline workers in order to hold down costs. Yet exactly the reverse is true: because executives rig the system and then choose to pay themselves arbitrary (but huge) amounts which are far more than the market demands (and necessary only in order to support lifestyles that are beyond extravagant), their companies have less money left over to pay their workers appropriate wages, thereby harming employee morale and dampening worker productivity. It's a sort of "heads I win, tails you lose" approach to management.

As *New York Times* columnist Nicholas D. Kristof has noted: "[Executive] pay is decided by a few board members, often the C.E.O.'s friends, who are perhaps themselves C.E.O.s sympathetic to the argument that $200 million is about right for such hard work. Compensation experts are hired for advice, but they know that the way to drum up business is not to save shareholders money."[41]

Without any meaningful government or self-regulation, executive pay is spiraling out of control. Senator Jim Webb (D-VA), in his response to President Bush's 2007 State of the Union Address, pointed out: "When I graduated from college, the average corporate executive made 209 times what the average worker did. Today, it's nearly 400 times. In other words, it takes the average worker more than a year to make the money his or her boss makes in one day."[42] As if that weren't egregious enough, in 2006, the twenty top hedge fund mangers and private equity shops made more money every ten minutes, on average, than the average worker made for the whole year. But I'm sure it was a very *challenging* ten minutes.[43]

There is ample evidence that executive pay levels often have no relationship to how well executives manage their companies. The Associated Press reported that, in 2008: "As the American economy slowed to a crawl and stockholders watched their money evaporate, CEO pay still chugged to yet more dizzying heights. . . . [Median] compensation of the heads of companies in the Standard & Poor's 500 Index . . . added up to nearly $8.4 million . . . a comfortable gain of about $280,000 from 2006."[44] In 2007, the median wage for workers nationally equaled about $25,000 a year for a forty-hour work week.[45] Thus, merely the one-year *jump* in how much each executive earned equaled the salaries of more than 11 full-time workers.

Government policies fuel this inequality. According to a 2003 report by the Institute for Policy Studies and United for a Fair Economy:

> CEOs at companies with the largest layoffs, most under-funded pensions and the biggest tax breaks were rewarded with bigger

paychecks. . . . At the 30 companies with the greatest shortfall in their employees' pension funds, CEOs made 59 percent more than the median CEO in *Business Week*'s survey. . . . Congress fueled runaway CEO pay and helped US companies avoid paying their fair share of taxes by blocking proposed stock option reforms ten years ago. . . . At the 24 Fortune 500 companies with the most subsidiaries in offshore tax havens, median CEO pay over the 2000 to 2002 period was $26.5 million—87 percent more than the $14.2 million median three-year pay at firms surveyed by *Business Week*.[46]

If executives paid themselves less, they really could pay their workers more. According to airline industry analyst Joe Brancatelli, the United Airlines chairman, president, and CEO, Glenn Tilton, earned 1,000 times what the top-paid United flight attendant took home. Tilton's total compensation package for 2006 was estimated at $39 million. After United flight attendants made several rounds of concessions during the company's bankruptcy, they then ended up with an average salary of about $31,000. New hires made about half that, which means Tilton earned 2,000 times more than the newbies.[47] If those new flight attendants were the sole breadwinners for their children, they likely lived below the poverty line. Some may even have been forced to use food pantries. United had about 26,000 flight attendants that year. Had CEO Tilton decided to pay himself *only* 1 million dollars that year (which would have still paid him more than twice the salary of the president of the United States and more than four times the salary of the US Secretary of Transportation), the $38 million left over could have provided a $1,400 raise to *every one* of his flight attendants, which would equal $116 extra per month, more than enough for an extra bag of groceries. I'll bet *that* would have improved customer service and thereby boosted company profits.

THE SELF-MADE MYTH

Americans have clung to the belief that they themselves—as well as virtually anyone else who has "made it"—have done it on their own, without help from the government. According to polls conducted by the Pew Research Center for the People & the Press, only 34 percent of Americans believed in 2007 that "success is mostly determined by forces outside a person's control."[48]

The classic examples of people who have convinced themselves that they made it on their own are Internet billionaires, who often pride themselves on having succeeded with no help from the government. But that's just not true. The Internet may not have actually been invented by Al Gore, but it certainly was invented by the federal government (with a large push from Al Gore)— taking numerous years and significant tax dollars to do so.

It goes way beyond those who got wealthy off the Internet. *Everyone* in society, no matter how independent they believe they are, depends upon government help to get ahead.

Here's a test. Check any of the following boxes if you have *ever*:

❏ Been born in a hospital even partially subsidized by public funds

❏ Received a vaccine invented by government scientists

❏ Learned the alphabet through *Sesame Street* or any other show on public television

❏ Attended a public elementary, junior, or high school

❏ Received governmental student aid or attended an institution of higher learning that receives government subsidies (which includes virtually every institution in the country)

❏ Driven to work on public roads or traveled to work on public transportation (likewise, if you have ever owned or worked for a business that receives or ships products via public roads, ports, airports, or railways— or uses the US Postal Service)

❏ Had either your personal or business property protected by police officers and/or firefighters

If you checked off *any* of the above, your success has been aided by the government.

While the public thinks of billionaires as the epitome of self-made independence, an average billionaire gets repeated help from taxpayer-supported programs and subsidies every day. Even before the billionaire wakes up in the morning, government-funded trash collectors whisk garbage away from his home to protect both the health and scenic beauty of the neighborhood. When he wakes up and uses his toilet, his waste water is washed away by a government sewer system. When he turns on his tap and brushes his teeth, he uses water that is free from cholera and other diseases thanks to government-run water filtration systems. If he owns a mortgage on the penthouse or townhouse in which he is living, he is likely benefiting from a taxpayer-subsidized mortgage interest deduction. If the billionaire owns factories or real estate, his property is protected by taxpayer-funded police and fire departments, and he likely owns some properties that receive immense tax credits to be located in (or simply fail to move from) certain neighborhoods. When he rides his helicopter to his vacation home (for which he also likely receives a tax break), he takes off from a government-owned heliport and is protected from mid-air collisions by government air traffic controllers.

I do not begrudge billionaires getting government benefits typically available to any American. But, because they own more things and have more property, they need *more* protection and get *larger* tax breaks than average citizens. They can even get extra special benefits—such as farm subsidies for land they own but have never seen—not available to those of us who can't afford to buy land for purely investment purposes. Far from being exemplars of independence, billionaires are often even more dependent on government than the rest of us.

Some billionaires willingly admit how much they owe society, including Warren Buffett, who said, "I personally think that society is responsible for a significant percentage of what I've earned."[49]

WELFARE FOR RICH PEOPLE

While there is much debate about welfare for poor people, there is little discussion of the far more substantial welfare that is doled out to big business and to wealthy individuals through a variety of tax breaks and subsidies.

Again, in New York, the nation's capital for corporate welfare, we see numerous examples of the help the wealthy get from government. State government–created "Empire Zones" give lavish tax breaks to businesses to supposedly stimulate job creation. According to a report from the state comptroller, the zones "are poorly administered, keep inadequate records, and do not hold firms that receive tax breaks accountable for actually producing jobs." While 30 percent of the businesses that received tax breaks met or exceeded their job creation targets, 47 percent created fewer jobs than they promised and 23 percent actually lost jobs.[50] According to a joint report by the Fiscal Policy Institute and Good Jobs First, ten major firms that received other tax breaks supposedly to create or retain jobs showed a collective net loss of approximately 3,000 jobs; companies contributing to this figure used approximately $120 million in subsidies. The agreement the companies signed to get the tax breaks contained no binding commitments to job creation (although most companies can earn additional benefits by increasing jobs). Many agreements contain job retention targets lower than the number of jobs companies actually had at the time they signed their deals. (For example, although Merrill Lynch had 9,693 workers, it signed an agreement to keep only 9,000.) This low-balling allows companies to fire or transfer workers without incurring penalties.

As the New York *Daily News* editorialized: "A state program meant to clean up inner-city blight instead lavishes tax breaks on luxury Manhattan high-rises. . . . Media magnate Barry Diller's new HQ in west Chelsea could reap $158 million in credits, though cleanup expenses are pegged at $18 million. Developer Larry Silverstein's W. 42nd St. apartment tower is in line for $144 million, seven times the cleanup estimate. Of one billion dollars in tax breaks committed so far, state officials reckon barely one-third involves pollution removal; two-thirds is gravy. Meanwhile, inner-city projects that need help go begging."[51] The New York Yankees are able to charge the city for luxury items such as $44 steak dinners, because former Mayor Rudy Giuliani (a huge Yankees fan), on his last day in office, inserted into the city's lease for Yankee Stadium a provision that allows them to deduct all "planning costs" for a new stadium. This new stadium, as well as a new stadium for the Mets, were originally slated to cost taxpayers a combined $1.3 billion.[52] (Both stadiums will have considerably fewer seats than their predecessors, but more luxury sky-boxes and higher ticket prices). In 2008, the Yankees, with the support of Mayor Bloomberg, sought another $400 million in public financing. Talk about foul ball.[53]

The favorite ploy of New York–based corporations is to threaten to move to New Jersey or Connecticut if they don't get bigger subsidies. In 2007, finance giant JP Morgan Chase threatened to transfer their headquarters from Manhattan to Stamford, Connecticut, because they claimed that the $100 million of government funds offered to them to build their new headquarters wasn't enough.[54] I've often been tempted to threaten to move the New York City Coalition Against Hunger to New Jersey unless the city gave us a large subsidy to stay, but given our rough relations with certain city officials, they'd probably pay us to *move*.

TAXES ARE FOR LITTLE PEOPLE

Revenue lost from President George W. Bush's tax cuts could comprise as much as 37 percent of the nation's budget deficit.[55] According to a Congressional Budget Office report, summarized by the *New York Times*, as a result of the Bush tax cuts, families earning more than $1 million a year saw their federal tax rates drop more sharply than any group in the country. Households in the top 1 percent of earnings, which had an average income of $1.25 million, saw their effective individual tax rates drop to 19.6 percent in 2004 from 24.2 percent in 2000. The rate cut for the wealthy families was twice as deep as for middle-income families, translating to an average tax cut of almost $58,000.[56]

At the same time, the Bush administration attempted to eliminate the estate tax, which only affects the very rich, but did not receive approval in Congress. As reported by the *New York Times*, in 2006, the administration "moved to eliminate the jobs of nearly half of the lawyers at the Internal Revenue Service who audit tax returns of some of the wealthiest Americans, specifically those who are subject to gift and estate taxes when they transfer parts of their fortunes to their children and others."[57] Unable to legally end the estate tax, Bush simply fired the people who collected it. Meanwhile, the Bush administration withheld payment of EITC refunds going to 1.6 million working poor families whom the administration claimed had improperly filed for the payments, even though an independent investigator later found that 60 to 80 percent of the families targeted were actually eligible for the refunds.[58]

THE BEST GOVERNING MONEY CAN BUY

So how do wealthy people in America, most of whom are white, convince elected officials to provide massive corporate welfare and tax breaks? That's easy. They buy results with campaign contributions. Of course, by their very nature, campaign contributions are unequal. That's why low-income people, who do not have money to donate, so frequently get shafted.

A 2005 study by the Public Policy and Education Fund of New York found that New York City leads the country in federal campaign contributions, but 93 percent of donations come from majority-white zip codes. One zip code—Manhattan's 10021—is the largest contributor in the country, and it is 84.4 percent white. People in that zip code donated more than twice the amount than did those who lived in the 146 zip codes where more than half the residents were people of color.[59]

Some people, like billionaire Carl Icahn, have so much money that they give to *both* sides of campaigns. According to a campaign finance database—based on federal records—maintained by the Center for Responsive Politics, on one single day, June 30, 2004, Icahn gave $15,000 each to the Democratic Senatorial Campaign Committee *and* the Republican Senatorial Campaign Committee. When you give equal amounts to opposing committees on the same day, what could you possible want other than access? According to New York State records, on August 31, 2006, Icahn donated $30,000 to the Republican candidate for State Attorney General, Jeanine Pirro. But on November 4 of that year, just three days before the election, Icahn donated $25,000 to Andrew Cuomo, the Democratic (and winning) candidate for State Attorney General. It just so happens that Mr. Icahn is a corporate takeover specialist, and the State Attorney General's office has some oversight over business dealings such as his.

Even Mayor Bloomberg, an expert at buying influence, blasted real estate companies for giving identical or nearly identical amounts of campaign donations to the three candidates running to succeed him as mayor, saying: "I happen to think it's a disgrace. I can't think of any reason you'd do it unless you are just trying to hedge your bets and be on the good side of every one of them. And the only reason you'd want to do that is that you think you're going to get something for it."[60]

A 2003 study conducted by United for a Fair Economy found a strong correlation between campaign contributions made by defense contractors and the value of defense contracts awarded to that company. Ninety percent of the difference in contract size can be accounted for by size of contributions. For example, top arms contractor Lockheed Martin was also the top campaign contributor among defense firms. Unsurprisingly, they also found that pay for defense contractor CEOs skyrocketed when the size of their corporate contracts did.[61]

Campaign spending is surely the only thing that keeps alive the country's insane system of crop subsidies, which, between 2000 and 2007, cost American taxpayers an average of $20.3 billion per year. While the public is told that these subsidies are vital to small family farmers, the truth is that most family farmers get no subsidies at all, and those that do usually receive paltry payments. It is the very largest farm operations and corporate agribusinesses that rake in millions in farm welfare, year after year. In 2007, funds went to only one in three farmers and only 6 percent of farms—mostly huge ones—received 70 percent of the money.[62]

It is particularly telling that massive farming operations generally have to fill out far *less* paperwork to get government funding than do recipients of food stamp benefits. Moreover, as Chart 7D shows, crop subsidies dwarf food stamps in both the amount of benefits paid and in how much income and assets you are allowed to have and still qualify for them.

CHART 7D

The Different Requirements for People Who Receive USDA Food Stamp Benefits Versus People Who Own Land and Receive USDA Farm Subsidies (current as of May 2008)

	Food Stamps	Farm Subsidies
Maximum yearly benefit	$11,700 (if the family has 8 people)[63]	Unlimited: largest annual payment to date, $1.031 million[64]
Average yearly benefit	$1,148[65]	$7,501[66]
Maximum income of benefits recipients	$44,952 (if the family has 8 people)[67]	$2.5 million[68]
Maximum assets of benefits recipients	$2,000[69]	No limit (People with assets in the billions of dollars have received farm subsidies for land they own)
Able-bodied recipients without children are required to work	Yes	No
Recipients need to live in the state in which they receive benefits	Yes	No
Recipients may be required to give the government their fingerprints in order to get benefits	Yes	No

In farm subsidies for just the three years between 2003 and 2005, Microsoft billionaire Paul Allen received $30,687; former star basketball player Scottie Pippen got $77,000; Seagram billionaire Edgar Bronfman accepted $17,455; and oil billionaire Aubrey McClendon received $30,050. Said Ken Cook, president of the Environmental Working Group (EWG): "We don't even ask these subsidy guys if they need the money. We just give it to them, no questions asked. . . . If you zoom in on [a subsidy map of] the Upper East Side [of Manhattan], what you see is a whole bunch of beneficiaries. There's not a whole lot of wheat and corn and cotton grown in Central Park."[70]

In fact, in EWG's database of USDA subsidies, fully 593 people and corporations on the tiny island of Manhattan obtained payments between 2003 and 2005. The top Manhattan recipient was Ms. Phyllis Joyner, who received $213,988 over that time for owning land in Virginia that produced wheat, corn, soybeans, cotton, and peanuts.[71] I actually agreed with a statement from the Bush administration (a rare occurrence indeed) when acting Secretary of Agriculture Chuck Conner said in 2007: "Why in the world should tax dollars, collected from middle-income Americans, be going to people off Park Avenue in New York City, some of the highest priced real estate in the world?"

Even the former head of the conservative Farm Bureau, Dean Kleckner, who used to be one of the nation's most vigorous and influential supporters of farm subsidies, wrote in 2007:

I know all about subsidies. For years, I took them myself for my corn and soybean farm. I didn't really enjoy it, but they were available and I rationalized my participation: other industries received payments and tax breaks. . . . Today, it's obvious that we need to transform our public support for farmers. Many of our current subsidies inhibit trade because of their link to commodity prices. By promising to cover losses, the government insulates farmers from market signals that normally would encourage sensible, long-term decisions about what to grow and where to grow it. There's something fundamentally perverse about a system that has farmers hoping for low prices at harvest time—it's like praying for bad weather. But that's precisely what happens, because those low prices mean bigger checks from Washington. Moreover, these practices hurt poor farmers in the developing world who find themselves them struggling to compete.[72]

Crop subsidies have been protested by progressives who detest corporate welfare, as well as conservatives who are against government waste. They've been
opposed by both the Bush administration, which believes they distort free trade,
and some of the most liberal members of Congress, who believe such money
would be better spent fighting hunger. They've been routinely blasted by newspaper editorials. And they've even been routinely opposed by many farmers.

So why in heaven's name do they still exist? You guessed it—campaign contributions.

According to the Center for Responsive Politics, agribusinesses contributed
more than $434 million to federal political campaigns between 1990 and mid-
2008. Also, of the top ten individual recipients of farm subsidies between 2003
and 2005, nine contributed to political campaigns, some quite heavily, with the
vast majority of their money going to the Republican Party (the party of limited government). Given that only 1 percent of the American people donate to
federal political campaigns, it is no coincidence that 90 percent of the top subsidy recipients do. They get what they pay for.

THE AMAZING BUT TRUE TALE OF GOLDMAN SACHS

All the most disturbing facets of our New Gilded Age—excessive executive
compensation, unnecessary corporate welfare, the dominance of campaign
cash, and the control of high government positions by a small band of connected elites—are exemplified by famed investment house Goldman Sachs.

In 2006, reported the *International Herald Tribune*, "Buoyed by massive
gains from trading and investments in leveraged buyouts, Goldman Sachs . . .
announced the biggest profit in Wall Street history. . . . The investment banking company that is the leading adviser in corporate mergers and acquisitions
said it earned $9.34 billion this year. . . . Goldman will set aside $16.5 billion for
salaries, bonuses and benefits, or an average of $622,000 for each employee."[73]
Reporting that some of the company's bigwigs received bonuses of as much as
$100 million on top of their normal salaries, *ABC News* cheekily pointed out
that, for the same $100 million, an executive could: "Provide immunizations
for more than 40,000 impoverished children for a year ($37.5 million), then
throw a birthday party for your daughter and 1 million of her closest friends
($60 million). You'd still have enough to buy a different color Rolls Royce for
each day of the week ($2.5 million)."[74]

The firm experienced a less bountiful year in 2007, but Chairman and CEO Lloyd Blankfein still earned $68.5 million. That year the average earnings of on Aramark food service employee who worked in the Goldman Sachs cafeteria was a measly $21,320. The cafeteria employee would need to work 3,213 years to earn enough to equal Blankfein's 2007 paycheck.[75]

Given the firm's wealth you would think that it not only has enough money to ensure that cafeteria workers in its headquarters earn a living wage, but that it could certainly survive without taxpayer-funded welfare. Think again. After threatening to move the firm's headquarters building (which is only a few decades old) from downtown Manhattan to midtown Manhattan (not even an out-of-state move), New York City government officials agreed to provide the firm up to $1.65 billion in Liberty Bonds, which were made available by the federal government after September 11, 2001, to spur construction projects downtown. The firm was also slated to receive $30 million in cash grants, as well as low-cost electric power and tax breaks.[76]

According to the Center for Responsive Politics's analysis of federal election commission records, Goldman Sachs and its employees were the seventh-largest contributor of federal campaign cash in the nation, donating $26.414 million between 1989 and June 2007. That equaled an average of $978 per employee.

As of June 2008, with five months still to go in the presidential race, Goldman Sachs employees contributed $1.7 million to presidential candidates in the primary campaigns: $601,480 to Barack Obama; $460,100 to Hillary Clinton; $229,675 to Mitt Romney; $171,945 to John McCain; and the rest split between Rudy Giuliani and Christopher Dodd. Add to that untold millions given by Goldman Sachs employees to candidates for governor, US Congress, state legislatures, mayor, and city council.

It is likely that this campaign largesse is the reason a company generating $16.5 billion in compensation ($622,000 per employee) in 2006 was able to con government into giving it $1.68 billion in subsidies for its new headquarters (equaling $62,000 per employee).

Not only do the company's political donations help ensure that elected officials will enact policies highly favorable to the company (corporate welfare, lax government regulation on their industry, lower corporate taxes, etc.) but the donations also help ensure that elected officials will enact policies beneficial to wealthy individuals in general, such as lower income taxes and reductions in estate taxes. Again, big campaign donors get what they pay for.

Blankfein's four immediate predecessors as CEO of Goldman Sachs—Henry Paulson, Jon Corzine, Stephen Friedman, and Robert Rubin—each left the company to serve in high level of government: Paulson as President George W. Bush's secretary of treasury; Corzine as a US senator (later governor of New Jersey); Friedman as chairman of the National Economic Council (NEC) also under Bush; and Rubin as both chairman of the NEC and later treasury secretary under President Bill Clinton. Needless to say, none left the company to work for antihunger groups.

IT'S ABOUT POWER, STUPID

The number one difference between rich and non-rich people is money. Obviously. The number two difference, perhaps less obvious, is power. The rich have it and the non-rich generally don't.

The imbalance in economic power between rich and poor is bad enough, but it's even worse when reinforced by an imbalance in political power that results in increased poverty and hunger. As President Franklin D. Roosevelt said in 1940, "It is an unfortunate human failing that a full pocketbook often groans louder than an empty stomach."[77]

Keeping the power imbalance in place, our political system reinforces both the participation of wealthy people and the *non*participation of low-income people. Wealthy Americans vote regularly and donate to candidates. As a result, elected officials tend to respond to their needs, which reinforces the elites' perception that political activity matters, so they continue it. But poor people can't afford to donate to campaigns, and generally vote less frequently, so they get less attention from elected officials, which reinforces their original, negative perception that politics does not matter—and they participate less.

For instance, according to census data, 10 percent of New Hampshire's households have an annual income below $15,000, compared to 22 percent that have income above $100,000. Yet according to the exit polls conducted in the 2008 New Hampshire primary, only 6 percent of Democratic primary voters and 3 percent of Republican primary voters had incomes below $15,000, while 28 percent of Democratic primary voters and 34 percent of Republican primary voters had salaries in excess of $100,000. This may explain why even John Edwards—who made poverty reduction a centerpiece of his campaign in Iowa and elsewhere—talked a bit less about poverty before the New Hampshire primary.

Republican party leaders, in particular, want to minimize the votes of low-income people, and particularly low-income people of color. They have pushed for voter-identification laws and opposed vote-by-mail laws. Plus, Republican and Democratic political insiders alike have generally opposed serious campaign finance reforms that would reduce the power of money in our political system, thereby giving outsiders more of a shot.

This gap in political participation has demonstrable impacts upon public policies that increase hunger and poverty. Peter Edelman, an aide to Senator Robert Kennedy, described how an inquiry spearheaded by Kennedy in low-income neighborhoods nationwide found both serious hunger and vast differentials in political power:

> In nearly every place [in the nation], especially rural communities, where we found a severe unwillingness to help the poor, we also found, and not always because of ethnic differences, a pocket of feudalism in America: a local power structure committed to perpetuating itself at all costs and unwilling to countenance the slightest improvement in the lives of the excluded, for fear they would gain the confidence and the wherewithal to overturn the status quo at the ballot box. Elected officials, judges, police officers and sheriffs, and local bankers and business people were always ready to use any tool necessary to squash dissidence whenever it appeared.[78]

Such power differentials still cause pernicious results. They are why food stamp applicants get fingerprinted for a few dollars received, but agribusinesses get asked few questions at all before receiving millions. They are why minimum wages aren't raised, as corporations get massive welfare. They are why the rich get further tax reductions, while the poor get further program cuts.

And these disparities are why, if America is to be the land of opportunity again and everyone is to get a decent shot at the future, our first step must be to achieve more equitable political power for all our people, not just the golden few.

WHEN GRASS IS TRAMPLED

It is true that America has always had inequalities in money and power, and has thrived as a result of the economic output of low-wage workers. But we have reached a point now where it is almost impossible for poor Americans and their children to move up the ladder—no matter hard they study, no matter how many hours they work, no matter how diligently they save their money. Even as the productivity of American workers continues to soar, their wages either stay the same or decrease, as their cost of living rockets upwards. Toil is not rewarded.

As an article in the *Christian Science Monitor* put it, economic research "has found that upward mobility has faded; most of the children of rich parents stay rich and the children of the poor remain poor." It quoted Samuel Bowles, an economist at the Santa Fe Institute, saying, "It is actually two or three times as difficult for children of poor families to rise above economic circumstances as economists reckoned in the 1970s and 1980s." Bhashkar Mazumder, a Federal Reserve Bank of Chicago economist, calculated that, on average, fully 60 percent of the income gap between any two people in one generation persists into the next generation. In the 1980s, studies found that only 20 percent of the income gap persisted. We are not the upwardly mobile society we used to be.[79]

There's an old African proverb: "When the elephants fight, it's the grass that loses." While the pachyderms joyfully tussle, sun themselves, preen, procreate, and generally have their way with life, the grass toils all day long at the hard, thankless tasks of photosynthesis, creating the food the elephants need to survive. The only thanks the grass gets is getting trampled on—over and over again. People in poverty are America's grass. They clean our offices, care for our children, box up and ship our new goodies ordered over the Internet, landscape our homes, nurse our sick, and fix our cars. And, yes, they harvest, package, prepare, and serve the very food we require to live. Yet they, too, get trampled on every day. When the elephants (and the donkeys) fight—and their bitter partisanship prevents government action to reduce poverty and hunger—it is low-income Americans who suffer most.

The driving engine of American economic growth and prosperity has always been hope. Hope that you are competing on a level playing field. Hope that your hard work will pay off. Hope that your children will do better than you. In our most recent Gilded Age, as the ultrarich got ultra richer, hope started vanishing for tens of millions who toiled hard to reach or stay in the middle class, and, all-too-often, failed.

A fairer form of capitalism allowed my immigrant grandparents—who came to America in the 1910s and 1920s—to build a better life for their families in New York City through sweat and ambition. But when one New Yorker has five times the money as 1.7 million New Yorkers—many of whom can't afford enough food—the American dream is fundamentally at risk. And when many corporations receive massive government subsidies and government protection against environmental and worker safety lawsuits (often because corporate leaders have traded upon connections, bought-off elected officials, and stacked the legal system), we have moved far away from a true free market system. We have reached a point at which today's crony capitalism must be replaced by the opportunity capitalism of the past that allowed my grandparents to move up and give America the world's largest and most prosperous middle class. Success should not be based on who you know or who your parents are, but upon how well and how hard you work.

Low-income Americans may "work hard and play by the rules," as Bill Clinton used to say, but today they face only two real options: a) live life on a perpetual treadmill, working harder and harder just to break even, or b) get even poorer and hungrier. Such grim options pose a threat to us all. The bottom line is that when most workers believe they can no longer advance, the economy will cease to advance. And economies, like sharks, start to die as soon as they stop moving forward.

People will tolerate performing functions that society deems menial (for poverty wages) on one condition and one condition only: that they or their children have a reasonable opportunity to eventually be rewarded for their hard work, with a real chance to move into the middle class and beyond.

If we don't restore the hope that people can once again move ahead because of their hard work and talents, we are all in serious trouble.

CHAPTER 8

LET THEM EAT SOUND BITES
The Polarized Politics of Welfare Reform

*The irrational tendency of this and every preceding generation to
view the welfare sector as a social aberration to be desegregated
physically and spiritually from the rest of the population has operated to the detriment of both recipients and marginal workers. . . .
America regards the welfare poor as a public nuisance to be regu-
lated by quasi-public measures which include the distribution of
bare survival rations.*

—James Graham, *Enemies of the Poor*, 1971[1]

During the original debate on welfare reform in 1996, both the Left, which
predicted a massive increase in poverty, and the Right, which predicted
that poverty would end after the "culture of entitlement was eliminated"—were
dead wrong.

Here are some truths that many on the Left will rarely admit: In the late
1990s, when the economy was strong, many of the people who left the welfare
rolls obtained jobs—or increased the hours they were working in their preexisting jobs—thereby lifting their incomes and giving them increased pride from
work. The nation's overall poverty rate and the child poverty rate decreased.
Poor people themselves generally supported welfare reform.

Here's the truth that many on the Right will rarely admit: Even when welfare
reform was working most effectively in the late 1990s, some of those who left
welfare for work earned less than they did on public assistance, and people who
remained on the rolls struggled with ever-shrinking benefits. Even as the overall poverty rate decreased, the number of people in extreme poverty increased.
After the economy weakened in 2001, states still kept removing people from

welfare, but fewer and fewer were finding jobs, and more were being pushed into the streets. As a result, the overall poverty rate *and* the extreme poverty rate both surged.

In short, welfare reform has helped more families achieve independence than the Left will acknowledge, but has sent far more families to soup kitchens, food pantries, and homeless shelters than the Right will admit. Moreover, it has actually changed the overall state of poverty in America—for good *or* bad— far *less* than either side will admit.

In truth, the nation has never had a serious assessment of whether welfare reform truly worked, not only in reducing the rolls but in enabling families to achieve economic independence. Politicians and pundits are so busy defending their 1996 positions that neither side is willing to seriously address what went right, what went wrong, and—much more importantly—what still needs to be done.

Welfare is still an incendiary issue, and asking people how they feel about welfare it is like conducting a Rorschach test to determine their views on poverty, race, gender, social programs, and government. That is why the issue of welfare reform is the poster child for American's broken Left/Right debate. As Chart 8A demonstrates, both sides reflexively view the issue, as well as the greater poverty debate, through a prefabricated set of political assumptions. The biggest mistake both sides make about welfare reform is assuming that poor people are incapable of, or unwilling to, work. In reality, many poor people were already working full- and part-time (often secretly) before welfare reform, and others did increase their work as a result of it.

If we first understand why both sides were so wrong about welfare dependency—and are still wrong about the broader issue of poverty—it will be easier to understand why the nation now needs an entirely different, "third-way" approach to actually solve these problems.

HELPING PEOPLE . . . BY CUTTING THEM OFF

Almost as soon as the modern welfare state was created in the 1960s, a backlash began, with conservatives slamming lazy welfare recipients for soaking up tax dollars. While such attacks had an undeniable political appeal (and helped Reagan win the presidency) they also had a downside, reinforcing the image of conservatives as hard-hearted haters of the poor.

CHART 8A
How Conservatives and Liberals See Welfare and Poverty

Conservatives	Liberals
Punish and scapegoat the poor	Patronize and glamorize the poor
Focus on only the rare success stories of people who climb their way out of poverty with no government help	Focus only on the rare people with so many problems they can't move to self-sufficiency, no matter how much government help they get
Provide poor people with marginally less government funding, but never so little they starve in mass numbers	Provide poor people with marginally more government funding, but never enough so they can stand on their own
Overemphasize personal responsibility	Discount personal responsibility
Ignore economics	Overemphasize economics
Believe that poor people are too lazy to work	Believe that poor people are too oppressed to work
People who make poverty policy spend very little—or no—actual time with poor people	People who make poverty policy spend very little—or no—actual time with poor people
Don't really want policies that will substantively reduce the power of the ruling elites over the lives of poor people	Don't really want policies that will substantively reduce the power of the ruling elites over the lives of poor people
Are convinced that their poverty policies are nothing like the Left's	Are convinced that their poverty policies are nothing like the Right's

(Feel free to cut out the above chart and keep it in your wallet for future reference.)

But in the 1980s, conservatives came up with a much more appealing way to sell the slashing of social programs, claiming (with very straight faces) that such slashes were actually good for the people being affected. They even went so far as to claim they were "liberating" poor people, in contrast to liberals who were keeping poor people enslaved by government programs. In 1981, influential conservative theorist George Gilder wrote that conservatives, by cutting social programs, were working to "extend to the poor the freedoms and opportunities," and the "values of families and faith that are indispensable to all wealth and progress."[2]

Rep. Clay Shaw (R-FL), chair of the House Committee on Ways and Means, which is in charge of welfare reform, said that Democrats defend the "last plantation in this country. . . . We [the Republicans] are the ones trying to break the cycle of poverty. No I do not believe it is the Republicans who are cruel. It is the Democrats."[3]

WELFARE AS LIBERALISM RUN AMUCK

While this sentiment might have been manipulative, the old welfare system was not exactly popular elsewhere. Welfare was hated by the low-income people who received it, the social workers who dispensed it, the taxpayers who paid for it, and the Congress who voted for it. Comedian and activist Dick Gregory described in his autobiography how humiliating it was to grow up in a family receiving welfare:

> I wonder how [my mom] kept from teaching us hate when the social worker came around. She was a nasty bitch with a pinched face who said: "We have reason to suspect you are working, Miss Gregory, and you can be sure I'm going to check on you. We don't stand for welfare cheaters."
>
> Momma, a welfare cheater. A criminal who couldn't stand to see her kids go hungry, or grow up in slums and end up mugging people in dark corners. I guess the system didn't want her to get off relief, the way it kept sending social workers around to be sure Momma wasn't trying to make things better.
>
> I remember how that social worker would poke around the house, wrinkling her nose at the coal dust on the chilly linoleum floor, shaking

her head at the bugs crawling over the dirty dishes in the sink. My Momma would have to stand there and make like she was too lazy to keep her own house clean. She could never let on that she spent all day cleaning another woman's house for two dollars and carfare.[4]

My own mother, who was a social worker in the Red Hook section of Brooklyn in the 1940s, told me similar stories of how absurd program rules punished her clients. She often repeated the story of a woman living in a sixth-floor walk-up apartment with her five children, who was forced to get rid of her clothes-washing machine because it was deemed a luxury.

Middle-class taxpayers, including African Americans, likewise loathed the system. When I started my career in community organizing and politics in the 1970s and 1980s, I would frequently canvass door-to-door in the evenings in middle-class neighborhoods to drum up support for varied causes. Often, the people who answered the door, still in their work clothes from their blue-collar jobs, would bring up the issue of welfare. They'd look me in the eyes and ask: "Why should I have to work my tail off to pay for people who won't work?" While I did—and still do—have ready responses to most objections to government social programs, I didn't—and still don't—have a great answer to that one.

In these neighborhoods and beyond, welfare reinforced hateful and racist stereotypes about the poor, and in so doing, hindered advancements of social programs across the board. When Bill Clinton entered the national scene in 1992, he understood this challenge. Having spent more than a decade in Arkansas trying to enact progressive welfare reform policies, as author Jason DeParle put it, Clinton had "a vision of how welfare had poisoned the politics of poverty and race. Welfare cast poor people as shirkers. It discredited government. It aggravated the worst racial stereotypes. It left Democrats looking like the party of giveaways."[5]

Clinton and his allies at the Democratic Leadership Council and Progressive Policy Institute (where I also worked) believed that, if progressives themselves tackled welfare and other excesses of government, they would win back the public trust for a new wave of innovation and progress. They were largely correct.

THE RELATIVELY SMALL DIFFERENCE MADE BY WELFARE REFORM

What exactly did welfare reform do? The 1996 welfare reform law ended the old Aid to Families with Dependent Children (AFDC) program and replaced it with the Temporary Assistance for Needy Families (TANF) program. Unlike benefits under AFDC, benefits under TANF were not entitlements, meaning they had far fewer federal standards and protections, with much greater discretion left in the hands of the states, who received federal welfare funding in the form of TANF block grants. TANF limited people to five years of federal welfare aid, although some states used their own funds to allow people to stay on cash assistance longer.

Most states nudged and pushed large numbers of people off the rolls even before their five years were up, and the strong economy of the late 1990s helped them do so. Consequently, there was a dramatic 68 percent decline nationwide in the number of people receiving federally funded welfare (AFDC or TANF) benefits between August 1996, when President Clinton signed the welfare reform bill into law, and June 2007. The number dropped from 12.2 million people to 3.95 million.[6] Many of those who remained were forced into workfare jobs to earn their benefits.

When most Americans imagine poor people, they imagine people on welfare. Yet, as Chart 8B proves, there has *never* been a time in American history when the majority of people living in poverty were on welfare. In 1960, only 8 percent of poor Americans were on welfare. As a result of welfare expansions prompted by the War on Poverty and the National Welfare Rights movements, the welfare to poverty ratio swelled to 48 percent in 1973, when 10 million peo-

CHART 8B
% of Americans in Poverty on Welfare, 1960–2007

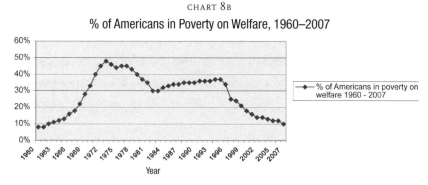

Sources: Poverty data from US Census Bureau "Historical Poverty Tables 1959-2006"; welfare data from US Department of Health and Human Services Office of Family Services; calculations by author

ple were on the rolls. The rate was 37 percent in 1995, the last year before welfare reform, and dropped to 18 percent by 2000, the last year of the Clinton presidency. By 2006, only 10 percent of US poor people were on welfare, slightly above the 1960 rate.

As Chart 8c shows, in 1973, the year that the percentage of people in poverty on welfare reached its peak (48 percent), poverty was at one of its *lowest* points in US history, with 38 percent fewer Americans in poverty than in 2007.

The historical record shows that poverty was at its lowest when the highest

CHART 8C

Americans in Poverty vs. Americans on Welfare, 1960–2007

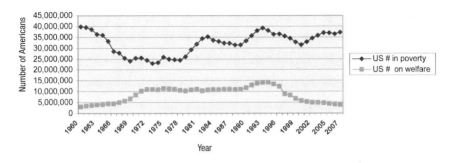

Sources: Poverty statistics from US Census Bureau Current Population Survey; welfare statistics from
US Department of Health and Human Services

proportion of the poverty population received welfare. I'm not arguing that high levels of welfare reduced poverty, since people on welfare are, by definition, poor. But this does prove that a central conservative argument—that high levels of welfare created poverty—is bunk.

Most people assume that welfare reform slashed funding for poor Americans in poverty. It didn't. It *shifted* funding from welfare payments to work-support activities, including Earned Income Tax Credit (EITC) payments. The Clinton pre–welfare reform budget of 1993 dramatically increased funding for EITC, just a few years before welfare reform restricted welfare payments to families. But even welfare reform itself, while it did result in some funding cuts, actually ended up prompting most states to spend their newly unrestricted welfare block grants on other tools (such as expanded child care, transportation support, job training) to help people leave welfare, and, sometimes, escape poverty. As Chart 8D demonstrates, the combined federal spending on welfare and EITC payments was far greater in 2007 than before the reform.

CHART 8D

Federal Spending (in Billions of Dollars) on EITC vs. Welfare (AFDC and TANF) Payments, 1992–2006

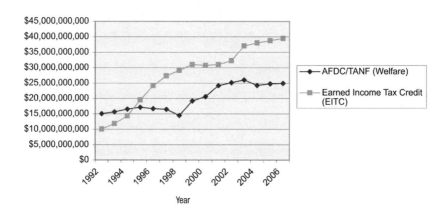

Sources: Tax Policy Center of the Urban Institute and Brookings Institution, based on data from the
Internal Revenue Service and the Budget of the United States

By 1995, EITC spending actually eclipsed welfare spending, and by 2007, EITC spending was significantly greater than welfare spending. By design, the welfare block grant amounts stayed about the same every year. True, some of the states did divert some of their welfare block grant money away from programs that aided poor people (a violation of federal law that was rarely prevented by the federal government). However, some states took progressive additional steps, such as creating state EITC supplements, using both state general funds and welfare block grant funds. Overall though, there was a fundamental shift in government funding away from people staying on welfare to people leaving the rolls.

These large-scale changes, however, didn't result in massive shifts in the day-to-day living conditions of most people on welfare. As Jason DeParle chronicles in his excellent book on welfare reform, *American Dream,* in which he closely follows the lives of three women in Milwaukee who were directly affected by welfare reform, the people he met had long, albeit spotty, work histories. They worked both full and part-time. They worked both on and off the books. They worked before, during, and after the times they were receiving welfare payments. Just because, as part of welfare reform, the government recognized them as working for the first time, it didn't mean that they thought that their lives had changed dramatically. DeParle explains, "As they saw the world, if the (welfare) money was there, they were happy to take it; if not, they would make other plans."[7]

Simply put, the implication by critics that a previously robust and uniform safety net was dismantled by the new law is misleading. While critics note that welfare reform ended welfare as a formal federal entitlement, even before the new law went into effect, state benefit levels varied tremendously. For example, while Alaska paid a mother of two $923 a month, Mississippi gave her $120.

DeParle sums up the reaction of two of the women whose lives he followed, Angie and Jewell:

> The welfare revolution grew from the fear that the poor were mired in a culture of *entitlement*—stuck in a swamp of excessive demands, legal prerogative, and social due. There was certainly a culture of entitlement in American life, but it was scarcely concentrated at the bottom (as anyone following the wave of corporate scandals now knows). What really stands out about Angie and Jewell is how little they felt they were owed. They went through life acting entitled to nothing. Not heat or lights. Not medical care. Not even three daily meals. And they scarcely complained. . . . In ending welfare, the country took away their single largest source of income. They didn't lobby or sue. They didn't march or riot. They made their way against the odds into wearying, underpaid jobs.[8]

Even liberal welfare reform critic Peter Edelman has written that recipients themselves had mixed feelings about the changes, quoting a Chicago woman as saying: "They have gone to the extreme in a negative way, but some of the policies are good policies. I don't necessarily agree with five years. I can live with it but some can't. But it does push you to get going."[9]

In the end, low-income Americans—with their customary but conflicting mix of idealism, fatalism, and realism—understood that some parts of their lives had improved, other parts had worsened, but that, primarily, they continued to get the short end of society's stick. Once again, major decisions regarding their lives were made without any input from them. And as always, they had to hustle to make a living.

SO HOW WELL *HAS* WELFARE REFORM WORKED?

Many of the nation's political, economic, and media elites seem to take it for granted that welfare reform was a smashing, unqualified victory. They generally judge welfare reform based on one outcome and one outcome only—the dramatic reduction in the rolls. Yet judging the success of welfare reform solely by how many people leave welfare is a bit like judging the success of a hospital by how many people leave it—without differentiating between how many people leave it cured, ill, or dead.

Has it worked? Yes and no. Some people fared much better and others much worse. For every welfare recipient who moved into a long-term living wage job, many more moved into short-term jobs that paid too little to support their families, were sanctioned off the rolls without having any employment at all, or continued to struggle on paltry welfare payments. As of 2008, there has yet to be a comprehensive national study of the effectiveness of welfare reform in both boom times and recession. Yet some state studies in past years do offer important clues. For instance, a study conducted in Illinois in 1997 and 1998 found that, of the first 137,000 people to leave welfare as a result of the new law, 55 percent of those who left TANF had job earnings during the quarter in which they left, but those earnings averaged only $10,100 when spread out over a year. The survey also showed a high degree of job instability, with only 37 percent saying they were employed continuously during the six to eight months after exiting welfare.[10]

What are the hard numbers nationwide for the job placement rates and average wages for people leaving during all twelve years since the law was signed? They don't exist.

Government agencies have consistently failed to collect the data that can truly help us understand how well welfare reform worked or didn't work. State and city government studies do not fully account for people who left the public assistance rolls but did not obtain employment. For example, the most significant New York State study on this topic was able to obtain information from only 53 percent of sampled families. The study assumed that, based on

2001 data, the families interviewed had identical outcomes to the 47 percent of families who did not respond. But it is more likely that the families who could be located for interviews had far better financial and employment conditions than those families who were not found by the researchers and therefore did not participate.[11] Furthermore, as of 2007, neither the state of New York, the federal government, nor any major private entity had conducted a comprehensive study of what happened to people who left welfare after 2001, when the economy started worsening.

We know that following 2001, as the welfare rolls continued to decline, the nation suffered soaring poverty, stagnant wages, increasing hunger and food insecurity, and surging homelessness. Common sense would seem to dictate that at least some of those problems were caused by deficiencies in welfare reform, although hard evidence for such a link is limited, mostly because large agencies and institutions with enough resources to fully investigate the issue have neglected to do so.

At least one study has directly connected welfare reform with increasing food insecurity and health problems for children. After controlling for other confounding factors, the study found that children in families whose welfare was terminated or reduced by sanctions were more likely to be food insecure and more likely to be hospitalized the day of an emergency department visit.[12] However, in fairness, the study did not consider the status of families who left the welfare rolls because they obtained employment.

As Chart 8E demonstrates, in the late 1990s, decreases in the welfare caseloads were accompanied by decreases in food insecurity and poverty, but from 2001 to 2006, while the rolls continued to decline, food insecurity and poverty spiked. Supporters of welfare reform often point out that more women entered the

CHART 8E
Increasing Poverty and Hunger—But Decreasing Welfare—in the US, 1998–2006

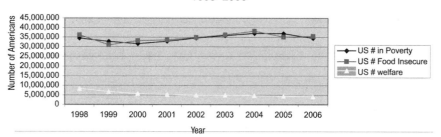

Sources: Poverty data from US Census Bureau; food insecurity data from USDA; welfare caseload data from US HHS

workforce, but they don't seem to consider the possibility that they did so by displacing low-income men, and leaving more children without adequate care.

Supporters of welfare reform tend to say that a job—any job—is better than welfare. They rarely discuss how much people are paid in their new jobs. Consider a Lexington, Ohio, woman whose story was chronicled in the *Columbus Dispatch*: "Nine years ago, Mary Meade left the welfare rolls for work as an aide at a group home for the mentally disabled adults. She's had the same job since, but steady work has not brought self-sufficiency—the stated goal of welfare reform—to the 38-year-old mother of three teens. At $7.68 an hour, Meade's annual salary is about $16,000—$2,850 less than the federal poverty rate for a family of four . . . 'I need to make sure to pay the electric bill this month because I didn't pay it last,' said Meade. 'I rob Peter to pay Paul.'"[13] All this occurred in 2004, before the more severe economic downturn began in 2007, making conditions even worse.

If such cases were common when the economy was stronger, it is fair to wonder how well welfare reform works when subjected to it truest test—how it operates in a recession when living-wage jobs are even scarcer. This concern is especially critical given that welfare reform ended the previous circumstances in which the safety net was counter-cyclical, meaning it expanded when the economy was weak and contracted when the economy was strong. Because funding is now in set block grants, it remains the same size no matter the extent of the current need.

The reality is that states, counties, and cities across America are still removing low-income families from the welfare rolls, but many of those families are increasingly failing to find or keep paid employment.

THE CASE STUDY OF NEW YORK CITY

New York City's Mayors Rudy Giuliani and Michael Bloomberg have taken the lead in trumpeting the myth of the unequivocal success of welfare reform. For many years prior, the city seemed to assume that reductions in the welfare rolls automatically meant increases in self-sufficiency. In his State of the City address in 2004, Mayor Bloomberg said: "The number of New Yorkers receiving public assistance also continued to decline. . . . That's a tribute to our city's commitment to replacing the dependency of welfare with the dignity of work."

Yet according to the Preliminary Mayor's Management Report, for the fiscal year 2004, "Reported job placements for welfare recipients fell during the reporting period, reflecting recent economic trends. . . . The proportion of public assistance participants who left welfare for work and did not return within 180 days declined, and is lower than the target for Fiscal 2004. This downturn is another reflection of economic trends." More recently, the Mayor's Management Report for the fiscal year 2006 stated that "the number of public assistance recipient job placements declined 9.2 percent."

I have repeatedly heard city officials say that, of those public assistance recipients who moved from welfare to work, 88 percent have retained their jobs after three months, and 75 percent have stayed employed after six months. Yet the officials often leave the impression that this means that 75 percent of *all* former welfare recipients have jobs after six months. That claim glosses over the reality that, as reported by *City Limits* magazine in 2006 and never contradicted by city government officials, only 23 percent of New Yorkers who left the welfare rolls reported having jobs at the time of their departure.[14]

Since only 75 percent of that 23 percent reported jobs after six months that meant that only 17 percent of all New Yorkers who left welfare—less than one in five—reported having paid employment six months after they left public assistance.

What happened to the other 83 percent? One possibility is that they had jobs but didn't bother to report them to the city. Another possibility is that they failed to obtain any employment at all, subsequently falling even further into destitution. My anecdotal experience leads me to believe that the first scenario occurred occasionally and the second occurred more frequently, but that most former welfare recipients fell between those extremes, perhaps having some full- or part-time work but not earning enough to entirely support their families. Certainly, given that the number of people forced to use soup kitchens, food pantries, and homeless shelters skyrocketed upward at the time this data was released, there is ample reason to believe that many welfare leavers were *not* achieving economic independence.

Sometimes New York City hides these failures by decreasing its performance targets. For instance, in 2003, the city set a goal of placing 120,000 welfare recipients in jobs, but ended up placing only 70,410, or 58 percent, of the original goal. By decreasing the 2004 goal to only 90,000 job placements, when the city was able to place 82,651 people in jobs, the city produced an appealing but misleading chart showing that they had achieved 92 percent of their placement goal in 2004. By the year 2007, they had lowered their placement goal even further to 80,000, enabling them to claim that, when they placed only 70,286 people in jobs, they had achieved 88 percent of their goal. The city has explained that these reduced job placement rates are a function of the fact that the people remaining on the welfare rolls tend to have more barriers to employment. That is certainly true. But they are supposed to be helping people with such barriers to find employment before pushing them off the dole.

As of 2007, New York City had growing poverty and hunger, and record homelessness. The number of poor New Yorkers increased by 151,000 between 2000 and 2006. Yet during that same time, the number of people receiving public assistance dropped by 241,388. The city claimed that the simultaneous rise in poverty and drop in public assistance recipients is only coincidental. That defies logic.

SHOULD CLINTON HAVE SIGNED THE WELFARE BILL?

It is true that in 2006, the overall national poverty rate, while higher than in 2001, was still lower than when the bill was signed in 1996. This decrease in poverty suggests that welfare reform, on a whole, has worked. But if you look at what has happened to poverty since 1996, it becomes clear that poverty rates didn't drop *because* of welfare reform, but *despite* the bill. The act was not signed until the summer of 1996 and did not take full effect until 1997. Yet, between 1993 and 1997, there was a 25 percent, or a 7.7-million-person decrease in poverty. Between 1997 and 2000, poverty declined by 15 percent, a 4-million-person decrease.[15] In other words, poverty dropped more rapidly before welfare reform than after.

It is unclear why that occurred, but it certainly proves that welfare reform wasn't the key reason for the poverty drop in the 1990s. While President Clinton brought the poverty rate to its lowest point in decades, even at its lowest rate in his presidency (11.3 percent in 2000), it was still slightly higher than the historic low (11.1 percent) in 1973 and still far higher that most industrialized countries. By 2005, the amount by which the average poor person fell below the poverty line—$3,236—was the highest on record. Furthermore, by 2007, as Chart 8F shows, the number of people in severe poverty—earning less than $8,500 a year for a family of three—arrived at 15.6 million, its highest point since the US began tracking that statistic in 1975. While large numbers of people left poverty, those who did not fell even further behind.

CHART 8F

Americans in Severe Poverty Versus Americans on Welfare

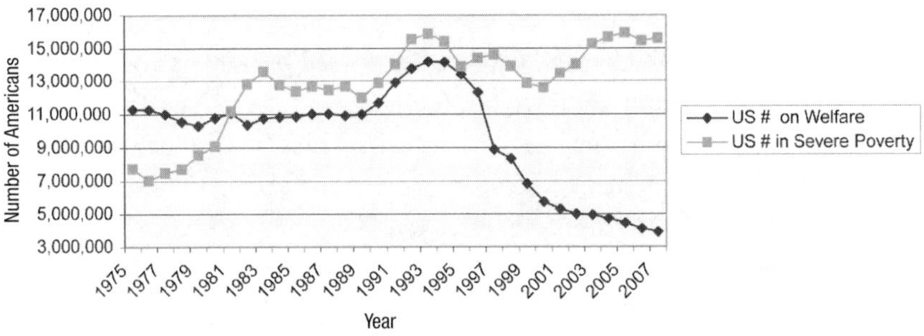

Sources: Welfare Data from US Department of Health and Human Services; Poverty data from US Bureau of the Census, Current Population Survey, Annual Social and Economic Supplements, and from Poverty and Health Statistics Branch/HHES Division US Bureau of the Census, US Department of Commerce, Table 22. Number and Percent of People Below 50 Percent of Poverty Level: 1975 to 2006

Despite all the problems with welfare reform, I still think Bill Clinton was right to sign the bill (after vetoing two earlier, more conservative versions), although it was certainly a close call. Welfare needed to be reformed, and the idea behind the reform—to move people into jobs and financial security—is valid. However, we have not been as successful as we need to be, and the tactics need to be reassessed.

Because the bill was left intentionally vague in many areas, it was a tool that could be used for widely divergent purposes, depending upon how different presidents, states, and localities decided to implement it. While Clinton was in office, he used the device—as well as a strong economy that he bolstered and other antipoverty measures that he created—to reduce the number of people on welfare and also to reduce poverty. It was after Clinton left office that welfare reform strayed most from his original vision and faltered, becoming more punitive, with a higher priority placed on boosting corporate profits for contractors and slashing government social service spending than on cutting poverty.

I think a greater share of the blame should be assigned to the Democrats in Congress who refused to lead on the issue when they had a chance to do so before the Republicans took over Congress in 1994. Fearing that no good could come from discussing welfare reform, they, in effect, conceded the issue entirely to conservatives, resulting in outcomes far more detrimental than they could have originally imagined.

THE LATEST ROUND OF WELFARE REFORM

In December 2005, congressional Republicans enacted the budget reconcilia-
tion bill for fiscal year 2006 by the barest of margins. Vice President Dick
Cheney broke a tie in the Senate, and the bill passed by only a two-vote mar-
gin in the House. Not one Democrat in the House or the Senate voted for it.
The media coverage on the bill's debate and passage focused mostly on large
cuts in Medicaid, student loans, and other programs that benefit low- and middle-income Americans. Largely overlooked, however, was that, because
Congress could not reach enough of a consensus on welfare to pass a stand-
alone reauthorization bill, it threw into this budget bill the most sweeping
changes to hit TANF since President Clinton signed the law in 1996.

The new law in effect increased the percentage of families who are required
to work while receiving public assistance in every state, and imposed new
penalties on states for failing to meet federal requirements. Inexplicably, the
bill limited welfare recipients to only six weeks of training in job searching and
job readiness.

The Congressional Budget Office estimated that the new law would cost
states $8.4 billion over the following five years, but the only significant new
federal funding provided in the law was $200 million per year for increased
child care, all of which would have to be matched by states.

Since states had struggled to meet lower levels of work participation requirements when the economy was far stronger in the late 1990s, it is likely that
many will not be able to meet higher work participation levels in a weaker economy. New York City alone could be forced to pay $200 million a year in
penalties if it does not meet the stricter new work requirements.[16]

These changes will have a dramatic impact upon the millions of Americans—most of whom are children—who currently receive TANF benefits, as
well on many of the tens of millions of other Americans living below the
poverty line. They will have to work even more and get even less help to do so.
Yet the changes were enacted without any hearings on the final provisions. Nor
was there substantial floor debate in either the Senate or the House on these
final provisions.

Leading politicians of both parties—who frequently spoke glowingly about
welfare reform in the late 1990s—now all but ignore the welfare issue in their
public utterances. Democrats are afraid to speak out against more restrictions
on public assistance because they don't want to be labeled "pro-welfare" or be

seen as undoing Bill Clinton's progress. Republicans are afraid to speak out in favor of those restrictions because they don't want their compassion questioned. Both sides are loath to admit there's increasing evidence that welfare reform may not be working as well as previously advertised. After all, to truly fix welfare reform—so that it helps poor people achieve self-sufficiency—would require massive new investments in child care and job training, among other things. Both sides have other priorities.

During the entire presidential primary season of 2008, I never heard the issue of welfare raised. The media have moved on, too. The few people still remaining on welfare—and the many people who left it but are still struggling—can no longer afford to wait for politicians and government officials to offer more than a few good sound bites.

Farewell, welfare reform. We hardly knew you.

CHAPTER 9

THE POVERTY TRAP
Why It Is So Hard to Escape Poverty in America

*We've learned the hard way that you can't fight poverty by duck-
ing its principal causes—that includes not only a lack of
education, but also dependency on government.*

—New York City Mayor Michael Bloomberg, speaking at the Brookings Institution in Washington, DC, to brag about his antipoverty policies, on a day
that the US Census Bureau announced that poverty had increased in New
York City in the years since Bloomberg had been mayor.[1]

*Some people say that if you are poor, it is your own fault. . . . I
don't believe them, and I don't think God believes them either. I
believe that the reason most people are poor is they never got a
decent break.*

—President Lyndon B. Johnson[2]

I'll again make an obvious (but rarely stated) point: the main cause of poverty
is a lack of money. And the main reason poor people lack money is due to
failed government policies and bad economic conditions, not because they are
irresponsible.

Sure, personal responsibility *does* matter, but the biggest missing ingredi-
ent from the debate over personal responsibility is a full discussion of the role
that government policies and economic trends play in encouraging—or dis-
couraging—people from acting responsibly. Take the vital issue of family
structure. Not only are families with two parents in the house far less likely to
live in poverty, they are far less likely to face hunger, having a 10.1 percent rate

of food insecurity (slightly less than the national food insecurity rate for all households) compared to a 30.4 percent rate of food insecurity for female-headed households without a spouse and 17 percent for male-headed households without a spouse.[3] Yet, it is government policies that often discourage people from staying in stable relationships or working full time. If two adults live together or are married, their combined income still makes it more difficult for them to get food stamps, WIC, or many other vital benefits.

This extends far beyond marriage. Under federal and state laws, social service benefits for welfare recipients are generally pegged to resources so minute and incomes so meager that many families lose food, medical, and other benefits when they leave welfare, enter the workforce, and increase their earnings. In many cases, the total value of the benefits lost exceeds the increase in their income. That's worse than living on a treadmill—that's quicksand: the more you struggle, the deeper you sink.

It should be no surprise that such perverse incentives play a significant role in hampering the effectiveness of welfare reform. Why in the world would any sane person want to work more, just to have *less* ability to support his or her family? In the greatest irony of all, it would actually be *irresponsible* for parents to leave welfare for work, if that move left them with less ability to feed, clothe, and house their children.

Here's a very specific example of how government policies discourage families from taking the steps necessary to move toward self-sufficiency. Under 2008 Food Stamp Program operations in most states, if a person was legally disabled or over the age of sixty, his or her household could only have $3,000 in countable resources and still receive food stamp benefits. For all other food stamp households, including large families, the resource limit was a paltry $2,000.

If you had $2,001 in a bank, you lost every penny of your food stamp benefits. There was not even a ramp downward in which your benefits were reduced as your resources increased; there was simply a complete cut-off. What did that mean to actual families? Let's say Family A and Family B were both low-income working families receiving food stamp benefits. Let's also say both families scrimped and saved so well that they miraculously managed to end the year with $2,500 saved. Family A spent that $2,500 on a new high-definition, flat-screen TV. Family B put the money in the bank to save for their children's college educations. Family A kept every penny of their food stamp allotment. Family B lost every penny.

Now, I don't begrudge Family A for buying that flat-screen TV. If they live in a low-income neighborhood, chances are there isn't a movie theater in their neighborhood anymore. There might not even be a public park that's safe to use. Unlike many American families, they can't afford fun vacations to Europe, the Caribbean, or even Disney World. So I don't begrudge any family, no matter how poor, for spending their meager savings on entertainment.

That being said, given the fact that government resources are finite, shouldn't the family that makes an even greater sacrifice of saving for their children's education be rewarded, or at least not punished? After all, helping their children go to college is one major way Family B can give their children the opportunity to enter the middle class.

In 2008, the new Farm Bill made it somewhat easier for families to save money for education and retirement and still receive food stamps, but much more needs to be done in this regard.

Cycles of mutually reinforcing negative events and conditions—usually fueled by failed government and economic policies—often trap people in poverty. Because public transportation is so inadequate in most parts of the country, when poor people's cars break down, they often lose their jobs, making it more difficult for them to fix their cars and get new jobs. Because economic opportunity is so limited in low-income neighborhoods, poverty makes people more likely to steal, and their subsequent prison terms and incarceration records make it more difficult for them to get future jobs other than stealing. Because America's health care system is so broken, poor people are frequently unable to afford adequate treatment for physical and mental health problems, thereby limiting their employment options, and also making it even less likely for them to have jobs that provide adequate health insurance.

Most of the worst damage perpetrated upon poor people is both socially imposed and self-inflicted. For instance, education is woefully inadequate for poor people but also the surest tool to get out of poverty. It is true that most high schools in low-income neighborhoods are underperforming and violence ridden, but it is equally true that people who stick with it and graduate from even the worst schools will, statistically, be far less likely to spend their lives in poverty than those who, through their free will, drop out without graduating.

Yet, even the most seemingly irrational behavior of poor people, when examined more carefully, can have a sort of logic. While researching a book on inner-city poverty, author Adrian Nicole LeBlanc observed that the stepfather of the woman she was studying received a $70,000 check after winning a lawsuit and spent all the money in a matter of months. "That abandon made perfect sense," she wrote. "Holding onto the money placed him in physical danger; he'd also have to field an endless litany of heartbreaking requests from family and friends. Putting it into the bank wasn't practical, because he might lose his disability benefits if the government knew of his assets; for the same reason, he couldn't invest the money legally, which left him especially vulnerable to scams. The smartest thing was for him to treat it like the windfall that it was—like hitting the lottery."[4]

WELFARE DOUBLE STANDARDS

Changes caused by welfare reform further exposed the tremendous double standards the nation has regarding poverty. The federal government now requires public housing authorities across the country to compel their residents to perform community service. Yet rich people who get tax breaks for their vacation homes have no work requirement. Not content with ending welfare benefits for parents without jobs, some elected officials proposed cutting off their children as well, arguing that punishing their children will push their parents to work. Yet the very same elected officials aim to eliminate the estate tax in order to give the children of the very wealthiest a free ride.

There is certainly nothing wrong with the concept that people who receive assistance from the government should have to provide some tangible service to the country. That's one of the reasons that my other great public policy passion, in addition to fighting hunger, is promoting national service programs, like AmeriCorps, which reward people who perform full-time community service with educational and other benefits. (But that's a topic for a whole other book.)

Reciprocal responsibility *should* be a cornerstone of all our public policies. What's wrong with the way the word *responsibility* is used today is that it is *only* applied to poor people. When government largesse is bestowed upon upper-income Americans, little or nothing is required in return.

We say people on welfare are "dependent," as if all the rest of us are somehow entirely independent of government and of each other. Given how—as demonstrated earlier in the book—so much corporate and other welfare goes to rich Americans, that's absurd. If dependency on government were a main cause of poverty, as Bloomberg and others claim, then former executives of

Bear Stearns—which received a massive federal bailout—would be living in homeless shelters (which, for the record, they are *not*).

Because low-income people themselves also frequently buy into that myth, it is often difficult to convince eligible people to accept any government help at all, even benefits such as food stamps that are vital for their family's nutritional needs. I face this problem every day, meeting many hungry New Yorkers, such as the panhandler I mentioned in the prologue, who are too embarrassed to obtain food stamps, who believe they don't deserve the help, or believe (falsely) that, if they accept such help, people even needier than they will be deprived of the benefits.

There is also a double standard in society concerning the importance of a college education. Middle-class and wealthy students are told higher education is essential for our economy and for their future. But for low-income Americans in need of welfare, higher education is often described by conservatives as a "dodge" that helps them avoid real work. As a result, the new welfare requirements passed by Congress in 2005 may actually make it more difficult for welfare recipients to obtain higher-education degrees. Such restrictions are ridiculously counterproductive, and research overwhelmingly proves that programs combining education, training, and work experience are the best way to help low-income people achieve long-term economic self-sufficiency. Indeed, a 2008 report found that Hispanic and African Americans were falling behind whites and Asians in earning college degrees, making it harder for them to enter the middle class or higher. Said Ron Haskins, a former Republican White House staffer who played a leading role in enacting welfare reform: "A growing difference in education levels between income and racial groups, especially in college degrees, implies that mobility will be lower in the future than it is today."[5]

One of the most galling double standards is the one regarding work. The federal work requirement for welfare recipients in 2008 was thirty hours a week, about equal to the number of hours the average working American puts in each week. But when you factor in paid vacation and sick time, which wealthy people generally receive and which low-income workers usually do not, welfare laws and regulations require that low-income Americans work far *more* hours a week than do average Americans.

Perhaps the most outrageous double standard is that the federal government's revised welfare reform regulations, released in 2006, only allowed ten excused absences from work in any twelve-month period, and only two in any given month. In other words, if welfare recipients happen to be sick three days in any month, they are penalized. Given that the federal employees who wrote these regulations have, by law, at least twenty-six sick and vacation days a year available to them (and often many more), limiting low-income Americans to only ten is an appalling act of hypocrisy.

When you consider all the corporate scandals, from Enron to WorldCom to Halliburton to Hewlett-Packard, not to mention all the scandals and confirmed criminal activity in Congress itself, it really is outrageous that Congress has passed new welfare reform rules based on the premise that poor people need to work even *harder* and act even *more* responsibly. Maybe the lawmakers ought to look in the mirror.

A great irony, as Jason DeParle has documented, is how government hired private corporations to administer welfare-to-work programs—supposedly because the private sector was more efficient than government. But many of these companies performed very poorly, wasting vast sums of money, frequently violating conflict-of-interest rules, and sometimes even breaking the law. One contractor spent at least $100,000 on welfare-to-work money buying golf balls, fanny packs, CD-ROMs, mugs, and backpacks to promote the company, in addition to paying more than $2,000 for professional clowns to liven up a company event. This company also spent over 1 million dollars on an advertising campaign, buying ads on billboards and bus stops.[6]

It certainly harms our collective efforts at convincing low-income Americans that the best way to escape poverty is to work hard and follow the rules when so many people at the top are making themselves even wealthier by skirting the rules and avoiding work. Let's just call that the Paris Hilton rule.

I certainly understand—and am viscerally attracted to—the populist impulse to say that, since people at the top of society often act irresponsibly, poor people should be excused if they do the same. After all, if we see limos speeding, we want to speed as well. If everyone else around us seems to be looting during a blackout, what's the big deal if we grab an iPod or two for ourselves? But despite those natural impulses, I think we must all stand up against any message that would drag all of society down to the lowest common denominator. A much better approach would be to require more personal responsibility from *all* Americans. As a moral matter, none of us should be excused from the responsibility to aid the greater good. As a practical matter, a society in which we all race toward greater heights of lawlessness is a society doomed to fail. Thus, for welfare reform to be truly effective—and really, for our society as a whole to be truly effective—all of the nation's rules of behavior need to be fairer and more evenly enforced.

ARE SISTERS DOING IT FOR THEMSELVES? SEXISM AND POVERTY

In 2006, adult women were 41 percent more likely to be poor than adult men. Women who worked outside the home were 36 percent more likely to be poor than men who worked outside the home. While higher education levels reduced poverty for both men and women, educated women were much more likely to be poor than men with the same levels of education.[7]

Considering how hard conservatives worked to remove women from the welfare rolls, it's particularly ironic when they argue that women can't make it in the workforce either, as George Gilder argued:

> Once a family is headed by a woman, it is almost impossible for it to greatly raise its income even if the woman is highly educated and trained and hires day care or domestic help. Family commitments and distractions tend to prevent her from the kind of all-out commitment that is necessary for full earning power. Few women with children make earning money the top priorities in their lives. A married man, on the other hand, is spurred by the claims of family to channel his otherwise disruptive male aggressions into his performance as a provider for a wife and children.[8]

I'm surprised that Gilder didn't go on to explain why men need to club their dinner to death then drag it back into the cave. Women just can't win. Due largely to inequities in divorce laws, divorced women are far more likely to become poor than divorced men. When it comes to raising their children, they are victims of yet another double standard. When a yuppie woman leaves her child with a nanny, she is blasted for leaving the child with a caregiver just to go to work. But a low-income mother is punished for not wanting to leave her children alone in order to go to work. In fact, given that funding for child care did not increase by anything close to the amount necessitated by the change in law, one of the main impacts of welfare reform has been to leave more children unattended. As John Woolman, a Quaker writer, wrote as far back as 1764: "One poor woman, in providing for her family and attending the sick, does as much business as would for the time be suitable employment for three."[9] Shouldn't caring for a small child be considered work by our government? I'd say yes. But under welfare rules, raising a child generally does *not* count as work.

Other government policies also seem to go out of their way to harm women. The collection of child support from absent fathers is failing to help many of the poorest families. In part because the government uses the father's payments largely to recoup welfare costs rather than passing on the money to mothers and children, close to half of the states pass along none of the collected child support to families on welfare.[10] In a vicious cycle, when fathers know their money really isn't going to their children but to the government, they have less incentive to pay.

Just as single female–headed households are more likely to be food insecure, they are also more likely to be poor. In 2006, married-couple families had a poverty rate of 5 percent, compared with 28 percent for female-headed, no-husband-present families, and 13 percent for those with a male householder and no wife present. This leads conservatives such as the Heritage Foundation to flatly declare: "Marriage breakdown causes poverty."[11] But an analysis by researchers affiliated with the Council of Contemporary Families found that "lack of marriage is sometimes a symptom rather than a root cause of poverty, and encouraging people to marry without giving them long term support systems may do more harm than good."[12]

In 2007, according to *Forbes*, out of the seven wealthiest Americans (all white men), only two were in relationships that were their first marriages. Of the other five, one was single, one was widowed, one had one divorce, and two others had three divorces each. Thus, two of the richest men in America had six divorces between them. Perhaps being in stable marriages is *not* what makes rich people rich or poor people poor.

LET'S TALK ABOUT RACE

In the past decade's debate over welfare, as in so many issues in American life, racial stereotypes remained central to the thought processes underlying the debate and at the same time were nearly unspoken in public. I do think it is clear that—whether consciously or unconsciously—conservatives played upon the general, but false, public perception that virtually all welfare recipients were non-white. But just as the nation was always wrong when it equated poverty with welfare, it was also incorrect when it equated welfare with people of color. As Chart 9A demonstrates, only one in twenty-five African Americans and only one in forty Hispanics were on welfare in 2006. Even of those living in poverty, more than 77 percent of African Americans and almost 89 percent of Hispanics were *not* on welfare.

CHART 9A

Race, Poverty, and Welfare

	Likelihood in poverty	Likelihood on welfare	Likelihood of those in poverty to be on welfare
Total Population	1 in 8	1 in 72	1 in 9
White	1 in 10	1 in 181	1 in 18
African American	1 in 4	1 in 25	1 in 6
Hispanic (any race)	1 in 5	1 in 40	1 in 9
Asian	1 in 9	1 in 152	1 in 16

All data from 2005. Calculations by author. Original data sources: Population data from US Census Bureau "Quick Facts," Poverty data from US Census Bureau "Historical Poverty Tables 1959–2006." Welfare data from US Department of Health and Human Services, Office of Family Services, Table 8, Temporary Assistance to Needy Families Active Cases October 2004–September 2005.

Furthermore, nonwhites also disproportionately engage in the most *virtuous* behavior. While African Americans comprise 14 percent of the US population, they comprised 19 percent of the people who volunteer for charities. Hispanics are 15 percent of the population and 14 percent of the volunteers. Asians comprise 5 percent of the population and yet 19 percent of the volunteers.[13] It is clear that while there are many legitimate, non-racist reasons to want to reform welfare, racism always provided additional fuel. People supporting welfare reductions in Wisconsin in the late 1960s called welfare recipients "gorillas." In the 1996 welfare reform debate on the floor of the US House of Representatives, a congressman held up a sign that said DO NOT FEED THE ALLIGATORS.[14] People who write or work on welfare and poverty issues often get e-mails or letters about the topic that are either overtly or subtly racist (frequently peppered with the phrase "these people"). Right-wing blogs on these issues often have racist tinges.

I believe that a key reason the United States never developed a more robust social safety net like those in Western Europe is that Americans falsely believed that most of the people needing help were nonwhite, and thus they did not want to use their tax dollars to support the "others." I don't think it's a coincidence that, as Western Europe has become both more racially diverse and more populated with immigrants over the last few decades, voters in those countries have supported scaling back their social safety nets.

Likewise, in the United States, a surge in immigration—and particularly Hispanic immigration—is fueling more resentment. In arguing against funding social service programs, Heather Mac Donald, of the conservative Manhattan Institute (a group that frequently advised New York City Mayor Rudy Giuliani) wrote: "The explosive growth of the US Hispanic population over the next couple of decades does not bode well for American social stability. Hispanic immigrants bring near-Third World levels of fertility to America, coupled with what were once thought to be First World levels of illegitimacy."[15] (I can't help but note the irony of how many conservatives are outraged when poor people have either abortions *or* too many children.)

Meanwhile, American liberals could not quite allow themselves to grapple with the implications of the reality that, while a bare majority of welfare recipients nationwide were indeed white, the overall percentage of African Americans receiving welfare was far higher than the percentage of white people receiving it. After all, if you acknowledge that people of color disproportionately obtain welfare, as well as acknowledge that they are disproportionately perpetrators (and victims) of violent crime, users of hard drugs, and high school dropouts, that raises very disturbing questions.

Afraid of being called racist or bogged down in liberal guilt, white liberals usually act as if these issues don't exist. However, prominent African Americans, including Senator Barack Obama, *New York Times* columnist Bob Herbert, and comedian Bill Cosby, are starting to raise these issues more pointedly than ever, thus making it OK (sort of) for white people to discuss them.

Just as with the wider behavior-versus-economics debate, the racial debate is multilayered, with economic, social, cultural, and psychological dimensions— and double standards against nonwhite people—all interconnected.

When high-profile African Americans behave badly (such as when rapper Remy Smith, convicted of shooting a friend in an angry tug-of-war with a purse, flew into a rage at her sentencing hearing, lunging at court officers, overturning a garbage can, and shouting at the guards, "Go ahead, lock me up"), people tend to sigh and say, "That's just like black people." But when whites behave just as badly (such as Lindsay Lohan, Eliot Spitzer, Dick Cheney, Britney Spears, Larry Craig, Mel Gibson, polygamists in Texas, half the people in YouTube videos—need I go on?), no one says, "That's just like white people." I look forward to a time—in a less racist future—when, if someone does something truly moronic, people will sigh and say, "That's just like humans."

There is no question that people of color still face significant discrimination in America. Reported the *Wall Street Journal*:

> In a carefully crafted experiment in which college students posing as job applicants visited 350 employers, the white ex-con was called back 17% of the time and the crime-free black applicant 14%. The disadvantage carried by a young black man applying for a job as a dishwasher or a driver is equivalent to forcing a white man to carry an 18-month prison record on his back.[16]

Nonwhites, even those in the upper classes, are routinely stopped and sometimes arrested by law enforcement officers (who, ironically, are increasingly nonwhite) for minor or nonexistent offenses. An African-American *New York Times* reporter detailed how, when covering gang activity in North Carolina, he was arrested, slammed to the hood of a police cruiser, and handcuffed, just for the crime of standing in a neighborhood. When he asked the officer why he was arrested, he was told, "You were loitering."[17] In the course of a lifetime, an African-American man is more likely to go to prison than to graduate college.[18] High rates of incarceration among minorities is one of the reasons that 2.3 million Americans are behind bars, the highest number of prisoners of any nation. African Americans are far more likely than whites to be arrested for drug offenses, although African Americans and whites use drugs at roughly equal rates.[19] But again, the situation is complex, as Harvard Professor Orlando Patterson, who is African American, has noted:

> A tenth of all black men between ages 20 and 53 are in jail or prison; blacks are incarcerated at over eight times the white rate. The effect on black communities is catastrophic: one in three male African Americans in their 30s now has a prison record. . . . Part of the answer is a law enforcement system that unfairly focused on drug offenses or other crimes more likely to be committed by blacks, combined with draconian mandatory sentencing and an absurdly counterproductive

retreat from rehabilitation as an integral method of dealing with offenders. . . . But there is another equally important cause: the simple fact that young black men commit a disproportionate number of crimes, especially violent crimes, which cannot be attributed to judicial biases, racism, or economic hardship. The rate at which blacks commit homicides is seven times that of whites. . . . The circumstances that far too many African Americans face—the lack of parental support and discipline; the requirement that single mothers work regardless of the effect on their children's care; the hypocritical refusal of conservative politicians to put their money where their mouths are on family values; the recourse of male youths to gangs and parental substitutes; the lack of skills among black men for the jobs and pay they want; the hyper-segregation of blacks into impoverished neighborhoods—all interact perversely with the prison system that simply makes hardened criminals and spits out angry men who are unemployable, unreformable, unmarriageable, closing a vicious cycle.[20]

While the African-American middle class is slowly growing over time, it is even harder for African Americans to stay in the middle class than whites. According to a study by the Pew Charitable Trusts as summarized by the *Washington Post*:

Nearly half of African Americans born to middle-income parents in the late 1960s plunged into poverty or near-poverty as adults. Overall, family incomes have risen for both blacks and whites over the past three decades. But in a society where the privileges of class and income most often perpetuate themselves from generation to generation, black Americans have had more difficulty than whites in transmitting those benefits to their children. Forty-five percent of black children whose parents were solidly middle-class in 1968—a stratum with a median income of $55,600 in inflation-adjusted dollars—grew up to be among the lowest fifth of the nation's earners, with a median family income of $23,100. Only 16 percent of whites experienced similar downward mobility. At the same time, 48 percent of black children whose parents were in an economic bracket with a median family income of $41,700 sank into the lowest income group.[21]

In fact, incomes among African-American men have declined over the last few decades after taking into account inflation.[22]

Although the degree of racial segregation in the United States has declined somewhat in the last few decades, African Americans in every large northern city are still more segregated than any one group of people of European ancestry has ever been in any American city.[23]

I would argue that racism, the denial of economic opportunities, and the legacy of slavery's forced breakup of African-American families created and perpetuated many of these problems. While white racism is decreasing with each generation, all those forces continue to work against nonwhite people. Perhaps most insidiously, the collective weight of these forces has, over decades, ingrained significant anger in many African Americans, adding further obstacles to achieving their dreams. As Senator Barack Obama said in his famous speech on race on March 18, 2008:

> That anger is not always productive; indeed, all too often it distracts attention from solving real problems; it keeps us from squarely facing our own complicity in our condition, and prevents the African-American community from forging the alliances it needs to bring about real change. But the anger is real; it is powerful; and to simply wish it away, to condemn it without understanding its roots, only serves to widen the chasm of misunderstanding that exists between the races.[24]

Sometimes such anger leads nonwhites to be just as racist as whites, further widening the gulf between both sides. Yet there is some hope. According to polls conducted by the Pew Research Center for the People & the Press, the thinking of blacks and whites has narrowed over the years on contentious issues such as affirmative action and interracial dating. But the gap has actually increased on economics. About half of African Americans say success in life is largely determined by forces outside of one's control, compared with 31 percent of whites. A decade ago, the racial differences in views of personal empowerment were much narrower. Fewer than 40 percent of African Americans and 31 percent of whites said that success was mostly the result of external forces.[25]

In a speech on Father's Day in 2008, Obama went even further:

> If we are honest with ourselves, we'll admit that what too many fathers also are is missing—missing from too many lives and too many homes.

They have abandoned their responsibilities, acting like boys instead of men. And the foundations of our families are weaker because of it. You and I know how true this is in the African-American community. We know that more than half of all black children live in single-parent households, a number that has doubled—doubled—since we were children. We know the statistics—that children who grow up without a father are five times more likely to live in poverty and commit crime, nine times more likely to drop out of schools, and twenty times more likely to end up in prison. They are more likely to have behavioral problems, or run away from home or become teenage parents themselves. And the foundations of our community are weaker because of it. How many times in the last year has this city [Chicago] lost a child at the hands of another child? How many times have our hearts stopped in the middle of the night with the sound of a gunshot or a siren? How many teenagers have we seen hanging around on street corners when they should be sitting in a classroom? How many are sitting in prison when they should be working, or at least looking for a job? How many in this generation are we willing to lose to poverty or violence or addiction? How many? Yes, we need more cops on the street. Yes, we need fewer guns in the hands of people who shouldn't have them. Yes, we need more money for our schools, and more outstanding teachers in the classroom, and more after-school programs for our children. Yes, we need more jobs and more job training and more opportunity in our communities. But we also need families to raise our children. We need fathers to realize that responsibility does not end at conception. We need them to realize that what makes you a man is not the ability to have a child—it's the courage to raise one.[26]

Rev. Jesse Jackson, Sr., famously responded to this speech by decrying Obama for "talking down to black people" and for focusing on personal, rather than governmental, responsibility. Jackson ignored the reality that Obama's speech won rapturous applause from a mostly black crowd and that it contained calls for both government *and* individuals to take more responsibility for social problems. Obama was absolutely right. We need *everyone* to take more responsibility. Just because lousy social and economic conditions are an *explanation* for self-destructive behavior (and should be corrected), they shouldn't be an *excuse* for such behavior.

Don't get me wrong. I think people of all incomes and races can be their own worst enemies. (I'd be my own worst enemy if there wasn't so much competition for the title.) I believe that all human beings have competing strands within their personalities that are deeply responsible and self-sacrificing *as well as* deeply irresponsible and selfish.

But, when wealthy people are irresponsible, they are more likely to shaft people they don't know, many of whom are poor. When poor people are irresponsible, they tend to shaft themselves and other poor people.

CONNECTIONS MATTER

Reading the alumni magazine for Columbia College, the expensive institution from which I graduated, I noticed that, when former fellow students announced their marriages in the publication and included photos of other alumni attending their wedding, the people in the picture looked a whole lot like them. The white students tended to have white guests, the African Americans tended to have African-American guests, and the Asian Americans tended to have Asian-American guests. Bonds formed in early in life often have lasting implications because they frequently mold social and business networks that can benefit people for life.

People in low-income neighborhoods also network, but in very different ways, as sociologist Sudhir Alladi Venkatesh found in Chicago:

> The seemingly random collection of men and woman in the community—young and old, professional and destitute—were nearly all linked together in a vast, invisible web that girded their neighborhood. . . . Through it the local doctors received home-cooked meals from the stay-at-home [mom] down the block; a prostitute got free groceries by offering her services to a local grocer; a police officer overlooks minor transgressions in exchange for information from a gang member.[27]

Alford Young studied the lives of very low-income, marginalized African-American men in Chicago. He concluded that not only did they lack income and assets, they lacked social capital and what he called "family-based capital": the connections, networks, and knowledge—as well as the confidence that comes with them—that are provided by associations with family, friends, and colleagues that have such assets. He detailed how their lack of such capital harmed their ability to obtain good jobs:

> The myriad ways and manners in which these men approached work prospects must be understood as part of their repertoire of responses to the challenges of being in poverty. . . . Included in this repertoire was the general sentiment that jobs were not available (as evidenced by so many of their peers being out of work) so that there were none to seek. . . . Much of their interaction was with individuals who were not attached to networks that could either produce or inform them about employment options.[28]

A study in Hartford, Connecticut, found that social capital, both at the household and community levels, can even decrease the risk of hunger. Reciprocity among neighbors was particularly helpful. Having family and friends that can share extra food with you, tell you how to apply for food stamps, or drive you to the food pantry can make the difference between being hungry and having enough food to eat.[29]

So we've seen that race, gender, economics, and a lack of social connectedness—spurred on by government policies that are either inadequate, patronizing, outdated, or downright hostile—all conspire to trap people in poverty and hunger. In response, continuing an ominous cycle, too many people engage in harmful behavior that only strengthens the traps.

Yet, at this point in our history, the debate over whether self-destructive behavior of poor people (and particularly of poor people of color) is caused by economics and racism, or by irresponsibility and culture, does little but distract from what we need to do to fix the problems. No matter the reasons we have such problems today, we all need to work together to fix them. As we'll see later in the book, the way to break the cycle once and for all is to take on all parts of the problem at once—with government, families, neighborhood institutions, businesses, and individuals each playing vital roles.

Some say we can accomplish all of that without significant new expenditures of money. That's absurd. Since the fundamental feature of poverty is a lack of money, trying to fight poverty without money is like trying to fight a drought without water. But however much such efforts cost, the amount won't come anything close to the dismal cost of doing nothing.

CHAPTER 10

THE CHARITY MYTH

There is a big difference between the guy with food stamps and the organizations that I donate my time, money, and energy to. The guy with the food stamps took my money at the point of a gun, he obtained it by force. I had no choice in the matter. The charities and the people they support received my money and efforts of my own free will and desire to help. . . . They receive zero government dollars.

—Anonymous posting on the Web site of an upstate New York newspaper, in response to an article on food stamp benefits

Americans love charities almost as much as they hate government. The irate person who posted the quote cited above encapsulates how many Americans feel, but he ignores two vital points. First, the food stamp recipients did not take his money at the point of a gun; they legally received aid allocated to them by government officials who were democratically elected to represent his community. Second, I can virtually guarantee that the charity of which he speaks receives at least some of their food—and possibly even money—from government.

Most Americans hold tight to the myth that neighbor-to-neighbor generosity and compassion is the best support system for those in need. But trying to end hunger with food drives is like trying to fill the Grand Canyon with a teaspoon. Because local charities cannot possibly feed 35.5 million people adequately, and because their efforts rarely enable people to become self-reliant, this belief that charity does it better than government only ensures hunger will persist in America.

Permit me to use the evolution of firefighting in America as a parable to explain why our current method for addressing hunger is so archaic. Before the mid-1800s, the most common way of fighting fires in the nation's cities and towns was bucket brigades comprised of volunteers. When a fire was spotted, the cry of "throw out your buckets" would be sounded, and a bucket brigade would be formed, two lines of people stretching from the town well to the fire, delivering sixty gallons of water per minute. Such brigades epitomized the very best of the fledgling nation, representing the kind of voluntary community associations that foreign observers such as Alexis de Tocqueville said made the United States so different from old Europe. But they almost always failed to extinguish the fires and cities were reduced to cinders.

Today, urban fires no longer destroy entire cities or towns. What changed? Government—yes, government—took effective actions to prevent fires and limit their damage. Buckets were replaced by modern fire trucks (which now deliver up to 1,000 gallons of water per minute); untrained volunteers were replaced by professional, full-time government firefighters; and fire safety codes were enacted by local lawmakers to make buildings safer.[1]

When it comes to fighting hunger, America has moved away from coordinated, guaranteed, government antipoverty programs of proven effectiveness and has instead increasingly returned to reliance on social service bucket brigades—volunteer-run food pantries and soup kitchens.

In the decades since the 1980s, as the federal antipoverty safety net eroded and wages lost their purchasing power, the number of charitable antihunger agencies exploded. In 1980, there were only a few hundred of these agencies, mostly soup kitchens on the "skid rows" of large cities. Today, there are more than 40,000 feeding organizations across urban, suburban, and rural areas of the nation—with roughly two-thirds being food pantries that serve families.

Rather than using modern sorting machines, these charities typically sort their food donations by hand, one can at a time. Rather than being staffed by trained social service professionals paid to work regular business hours, they are usually run by untrained volunteers available to provide food only a few times a month when they have no other obligations. And rather than serving as a last resort—in other words, secondary to more serious government hunger-prevention efforts such as boosting the minimum wage or hiking food stamp benefits—these agencies have increasingly become the nation's first line of defense against hunger.

Unfortunately, these grassroots feeding programs have one other similarity with the original bucket brigades—they are mostly failing to solve the problem.

While the unpaid volunteers and underpaid staff who run these agencies engage in inspiring efforts every day—and while they do supplement government programs enough to prevent Americans from starving (certainly a vital role)—they have not—and cannot—end hunger in America. In fact, after 2001, as the number of people using these agencies skyrocketed, so did the number of Americans facing hunger and food insecurity.

HUNGER CHARITY AID BECOMES A CLICHÉ

Nowadays, the nation's charitable events have become blurred in the minds of Americans so much so that the specifics of individual causes have become almost indistinguishable from one another. Once outside the entrance to a ritzy fundraising event for a hunger relief organization in New York City, I overheard this exchange between two tuxedo-clad attendees:

Attendee One: "So what's this event for, anyway?"
Attendee Two: "It's that hunger thing."
Attendee One: "Oh, yeah."

Efforts to fight hunger have become so widespread and so ingrained in American society—and so unquestioned—that they have become the ultimate cliché. It's been this way at least since Hands Across America in 1986, an event during which approximately 7 million people (including, in separate locations, President Ronald Reagan, Speaker of the US House of Representatives Tip O'Neill, Liza Minnelli, Yoko Ono, Brooke Shields . . . and me) held hands in a human chain for fifteen minutes along a path across the continental United States in order to raise money to wipe out hunger and homelessness. Intended to raise $50 million, and sponsored by Coca-Cola and Citibank, the event reportedly cost $17 million to stage but raised only $20 million. Hunger and homelessness kept growing following the event, but those continuing problems received much less media attention than the celebrities holding hands for fifteen minutes.

Today, there are almost as many charitable ways to fight hunger as there are hungry Americans. A food bank's annual "Check Out Hunger" campaign at Price Chopper stores "provides shoppers with a quick and easy way to help feed the hungry" by buying donation coupons worth two, three, or five dollars. A part-

nership between Share Our Strength and Clos du Bois Wines encourages consumers to host holiday parties to help feed the hungry. Leaders of hunger relief
organizations (myself included) ring in the trading day at major stock exchanges
to mark National Hunger Awareness Day. In 2007, Tim Janus (a Wall Street
trader by day and a member of a competitive eating league in his free time) ate
a ten-pound turkey, four pounds of mashed potatoes, three pounds of cranberry
sauce, two and a half pounds of green beans, and a pumpkin pie within one fif-
teen-minute span to "raise awareness of [New York City's] truly hungry."

There's more: Private cooking lessons from celebrity chefs are auctioned
online to "raise funds to stop hunger." Boy Scouts and letter carriers around
the nation come to your door to pick up donated foods. Antihunger messages
are "wrapped around the wrists of over 1 million adults in the trendiest clubs
and music venues." Gwyneth Paltrow, Michael Stipe, and Mike Myers design
custom lunchboxes to be auctioned off to fight hunger. Safari Club members
donate the venison they kill to local food banks.

Note the similarities in all these efforts. They use language that implies they
will actually end hunger in America, when they will barely dent the problem.
They say it is "quick" or "easy" to make a significant difference. Antihunger
promotions often imply that, if you donate a few cans, "none of your neighbors
will go hungry," when the reality is that, even if people donated truckloads of
food, plenty of their neighbors would still go hungry. But none of them ask the
question that should be at the center of it all: if we need to raise money to make
sure Americans have enough food to eat, isn't the government failing in some
fundamental way?

Part of the problem is that nonprofit hunger organizations across the
nation—including the New York City Coalition Against Hunger—depend heavily upon such charitable donations to support our vital work. We've come to
learn that talking too much about the role of government can decrease donations and that the most effective fundraising strategies give potential donors
the clear impression that the only thing standing between a family and hunger
is their donation to our organization.

MAKING THE DONOR AND THE VOLUNTEER FEEL GOOD

Keeping a charity alive is sometimes more about making the donors and the
volunteers feel good about themselves than it is about accomplishing concrete

tasks that will reduce hunger and poverty. One holiday event I attended even gave gift bags to the prominent people who volunteered, as if they needed a reward for their one hour spent serving turkeys in front of cameras.

The majority of people who donate and volunteer to fight hunger—especially those who volunteer for countless hours over many decades to run pantries and kitchens—are some of the most generous, good-hearted, and uplifting people I have ever met. They are the backbone of the charitable feeding system.

Likewise, most celebrities who lend their star power to a good cause are well intentioned, and their support can be helpful for fundraising and publicity. Yet there are also troubling aspects to celebrity participation in antihunger events. A typical holiday news story, headlined CELEBS SERVE HOLIDAY MEALS TO THE HOMELESS, reported that, "Kirk Douglas, Harrison Ford, and other celebrities 'shared the Thanksgiving spirit' by serving hot meals to homeless people on skid row." In a press release issued by the mission, Kirk Douglas noted the effect on celebrities: "Their involvement will help their souls as much as the guests being served."[2] I am concerned that a charity would equate the desire for celebrities to feel good about themselves during the holidays with people's need for food and shelter.

Volunteer efforts are often based on the assumption that they will meet the full needs of every hungry person, when the fact is, the manner in which many people volunteer—infrequently, for just a few hours, or performing only manual tasks—actually does relatively little to end hunger. For example, business executives organizing community service days for their employees often request that feeding organizations place large groups of highly skilled professional employees together for just a few hours to perform manual labor during prime business hours in just one location, which must be near the corporation's headquarters in the central business district of the city. When we respond that it would be much more beneficial to place smaller groups in higher-need (but more distant) neighborhoods in order to use their employees' professional skills to mentor agencies over time on challenging tasks such as bookkeeping or strategic planning, they still usually insist that their employees volunteer as a large group, near downtown, just once, to carry out manual tasks such as serving soup or putting cans in pantry bags.

HOW THE EMERGENCY FOOD ASSISTANCE SYSTEM WORKS

Nationwide, there is a three-level system of charitable food distribution. At the grassroots level, more than 40,000 food pantries, soup kitchens, homeless shelters, senior centers, and battered women's shelters directly distribute food to low-income people in their communities. Many of these agencies are based within religious organizations (usually churches, but sometimes mosques, synagogues, or temples), and are usually run on shoestring budgets entirely by volunteers, many of whom are senior citizens who have been with those agencies for decades.

Most, but not all, of these frontline agencies receive much of their food from two types of local entities, which are essentially nonprofit wholesalers of charitable food: food banks (which provide mostly canned, boxed, and frozen foods) and food rescue organizations (which provide mostly perishable and prepared foods). In many cities, both functions are combined into one agency, since the local food bank also performs the city's food rescue functions.

While most food bank founders thought they were providing a temporary response to the new hunger needs of the Reagan era, these agencies have increasingly become institutionalized. Food bank warehouses, generally massive and expensive to run, are the ultimate example of the institutionalization of hunger. For example, in 2007, an editorial in the *Boston Globe* entitled "A Fortress Against Hunger," reported that the Greater Boston Food Bank was doubling its original capacity by building a new 110,000-square-foot home.[3]

Most, but not all, food banks and food rescue organizations belong to the national Feeding America organization (formerly America's Second Harvest), which has more than 200 affiliates and serves all fifty states, Puerto Rico, and the District of Columbia. It is now one of America's largest charities. A few other national organizations, such as Feed the Children, and many unaffiliated large and small local groups, also provide charitable food in low-income neighborhoods.

Many of these agencies obtain federally funded commodities, such as peanut butter and canned vegetables, through The Emergency Food Assistance Program (TEFAP), administered by the USDA, and receive limited operating funds from the Emergency Food and Shelter National Board Program, administered by the Federal Emergency Management Agency (FEMA). Many states and cities also provide extra funding.

Additionally, this nation has an incredible number of informal feeding programs. In just one example I learned from reading the *New York Times*, every night at around 9:30 P.M., a man named Jorge Muñoz arrives in his white pickup truck at a Queens intersection populated by a large crowd of immigrant day laborers, and he serves them free supper such as chicken and rice. Muñoz used to be hungry himself and finances this feeding program out of the $600 a week he earns driving a school bus.[4]

One Saturday morning, I was en route to a soup kitchen on the Lower East Side of Manhattan when I stumbled upon a line of people being fed by a religious group in Tompkins Square Park. The program was not on the New York City Coalition Against Hunger's list of feeding programs, which we try to maintain as the most comprehensive such list in the city. On my way back from the soup kitchen a few hours later, again walking through the same park, I stumbled upon yet another feeding line, sponsored by completely a different group, and also not on our list.

These lines represented both the best and the worst of the country's charitable response to hunger. The people running them were incredibly generous, taking it upon themselves to feed masses of strangers on their own dime. But on the negative side, both lines forced people to wait outside in the cold for long periods of time, and one of the lines provided them horribly nonnutritious fast food and sugared drinks. Neither operation coordinated with other feeding agencies in the neighborhood nor helped the people receiving food to access any services that could help them achieve self-sufficiency.

Such situations always evoke a very mixed feeling for me. I am thrilled that good-hearted people are helping, but dismayed that the way in which they do perpetuates a failing system. As long as there is a need, it is of course a good thing that people have access to food. And I try to remind myself that putting a Band-Aid on a problem is better than bleeding to death. But ultimately, the best solution for hungry Americans would be for the government to ensure that they never go hungry in the first place. The charitable food system is not getting us any closer to this goal—in fact, in many cases, rather than challenge the government to take on these responsibilities—charities compensate for its failures by trying to do the job themselves.

WHAT'S WRONG WITH THE EMERGENCY FOOD SYSTEM

Food prices, increasing an average of 36 percent from 2000 to 2007, significantly diminished the amount of food being provided to food banks and food pantries nationwide under the USDA's TEFAP. Combined with a nearly 80 percent reduction in federal bonus commodities (such as cheese and canned vegetables) during the same period, emergency food providers across the US increasingly failed to meet local hunger needs.[5]

More and more, food pantries and soup kitchens nationwide are forced to ration food because they don't have enough resources to meet the growing demand.

Because these small programs don't have enough food, money, and staff to fully feed all the people who come to their doors, many are forced to choose between three appalling options: reducing their hours of operation, limiting portion sizes, and/or turning away hungry people at the door. In 2007, at least half of the programs in New York City had no choice but to use one or more of these methods to ration food.

In early 2007, while performing client/customer intake at one of the city's largest pantries, I was personally forced to turn away a hungry person seeking food for the first time in my career.

Part of my job that day was to check the records of clients to see if they had previously received food that month. If they had, I was supposed to tell them—politely but firmly—that they would have to wait until the following month to get more food from the charity. The intake database eventually informed me that an elderly woman I was assisting had already received food there earlier in the month. Even though she reminded me of my mother, who was then eighty-three, I had to tell her that I could not give her food.

Turning her away was necessary to make sure everyone in the community received a fair amount of food. But, as hardened as I am by decades of antipoverty work, I still had to strain to hold back tears. Despite having fought hunger for so many years, I had to face the hard reality that our efforts fell short for this woman, on this day.

The fact is that pantries, despite the tireless work of volunteers, have their failings. Sociologist Janet Poppendieck, in her seminal book about the emergency food system called *Sweet Charity*, listed what she called the "Seven Deadly 'ins'" of the network: insufficiency (not enough food); inappropriateness (people don't get to pick what is best for their families); nutritional inadequacy (too much high-sugar, high-sodium, high-fat junk food); instability (feeding agencies can't always predict when they will be open and when they will run out of food); inaccessibility (particularly in rural areas, or for seniors and people with disabilities or without cars, the agencies can be very hard to get to); inefficiency (the agencies require a massive, three-tier system just to give out free food); and indignity (at even the best-run agencies, it is usually degrading to obtain emergency food).[6]

All these problems concern me but perhaps the worst is the insufficiency, because the average amount of food given out by a pantry is generally dwarfed by the amount of food a family could be getting if it were enrolled in the Food Stamp Program. For example, in 2007, a family who got food from the South Texas Food Bank based in Laredo generally received fifty dollars' worth of groceries per month. Compare that with the average household food stamp benefits of $239 in Texas that year.[7]

On the receiving end, the many faults of this charitable system become even clearer. In her time living on low-wage work for *Nickel and Dimed*, Barbara Ehrenreich was forced to obtain charitable food, often in humiliating ways. At one agency, she was grilled as to why she needed food if she had a job. She was sent across town to get food, leaving Ehrenreich to wonder: "Why this assumption that the hungry are free all day to drive around visiting 'community action centers' and charitable agencies?" Another agency gave her a food voucher for a local store in which her dinner choices were:

> limited to any two of the following: one box spaghetti noodles, one jar spaghetti sauce, one can of vegetables, one can of baked beans, one pound of hamburger, a box of Hamburger Helper, or a box of Tuna Helper. No fresh fruit or vegetables, no chicken or cheese, and, oddly, no tuna to help out with. For breakfast I can have cereal and milk or juice. . . . Bottom line: $7.02 worth of food acquired in seventy minutes of calling and driving, minus $2.80 for the phone calls—which ends up being equivalent to a wage of $3.63 an hour.[8]

WHY CHARITIES CAN'T SOLVE THE PROBLEM

Charities cannot take the lead role in ending hunger. Even with a dramatic expansion of charitable food distribution efforts, these charities couldn't even come close to meeting the needs of all hungry Americans. In 2002, America's Second Harvest (now called Feeding America) distributed about 1.8 billion pounds of food. Despite the reality that preexisting industry donors were scaling back their donations due to changes in the industry, America's Second Harvest nevertheless set daunting goals to further increase their poundage. Effective and insistent at convincing donors of the moral imperative and practical need to fight hunger, they achieved incredibly impressive results in fundraising and scrambling to find new sources of food. By 2006, their network was able to deliver 2.1 billion pounds of food, which meant they were able to achieve a 17 percent increase over three years, or about a 6 percent increase per year. Using their rough formula that 1.5 pounds of donated food equals a meal, that means they helped provide an astounding 1.4 billion meals per year, certainly a massive number. But there are 35.5 million food-insecure Americans, so that 1.4 billion meals number breaks down to an average of only thirty-nine meals per person provided for an entire year. If a person were to eat three meals a day for one year, that would equal 1,095 meals. Thus, the massive, heroic work of the entire charitable network would only provide 39 out of the 1,095 meals, or about 3.6 percent, that a hungry American would need each year.

The public is often led to believe that, when charitable food is used as a substitute for a government safety net, all the local food needs are met, even though people who receive charitable food only get a small fraction of what they should be getting through a government program. Some conservatives even believe that more Americans going to food pantries is a *good* thing. In the late 1990s, I attended a regional food bank conference at which Congressman Jack Kingston (R-GA), then a member of the House Appropriations Subcommittee on Agriculture that funds USDA antihunger programs, praised the food bank directors for feeding a record number of people and told them to keep up the good work. There were a few quiet gasps in the audience, but no one had the nerve to set the congressman straight on the reality that the increased need for their services was a bad thing, demonstrating increased poverty in their communities. The fact is, charity is doing the government's job, and unsuccessfully. Still, politicians can shirk responsibility and look good at the same time by supporting and praising them.

In New York City in 2007, the city government proudly spent about $14 million of its own money funding local food pantries and soup kitchens, but continued to quietly place barriers in the way of food stamp participation, thereby denying low-income New Yorkers more than $400 million in federally funded food stamp benefits. That's a true hunger "bait and switch."

Certainly, charities should fill in the gaps when government safety nets aren't enough, and we should do everything possible to make sure these charities receive the public and private support they need to fill those gaps. But, the only way to *really* solve this problem is for government to bolster economic advancement and fill the holes in its safety net programs.

WHY GOVERNMENT IS MORE EFFICIENT THAN FOOD CHARITIES

When the American people were asked in 2007: "How much of the time do you think you can trust the government in Washington to do what is right?" only 36 percent answered "just about always or most of the time."[9] Due to that belief, many people falsely assume that charities provide more food than government, and that they provide it more efficiently and economically. Perhaps if they knew the truth—that government feeds more people and does so more cost-effectively than charities—they surely would feel differently about government's ability to do the right thing.

First, it's vital to note that much of the food distributed by charities was paid for by government in the first place. In 2007, America's Second Harvest distributed about 494 million pounds of federal government food, which comprised about 24 percent of the network's total. Many food banks also get food and money from state and local governments, resulting in a situation where some food banks obtain fully half their resources from government. Likewise, when companies and private individuals donate to feeding charities, they often get tax deductions, further costing public revenues. Thus, much of the food distributed by charities is just as much a government subsidy as food stamp benefits.

Second, because charities create a system of food distribution that is in addition—and parallel—to the existing commercial food distribution system, they have to spend additional money on overhead. When a national food manufacturer donates food to a national organization, which then ships it to a local food bank, which, in turn, trucks it to local food pantries, such logistics often involve two or three sets of trucks and fuel costs, two or three sets of warehouses, and two or three sets of administrative and fundraising staffs. Dick Gabel, one of the pioneers of the food banking system, once told me that the emergency food system is the "most inefficient system in the world. I should know. I helped create it."

While it is often a great burden to enroll in the Food Stamp Program, once someone receives the benefits, it is usually relatively easy to use them, espe-cially since paper coupons have long ago been replaced by easy-to-use EBT cards. The government merely transfers the money electronically onto EBT cards and then, at virtually no additional cost to the government other than the benefits themselves, recipients are able to use the money solely for food. That's why the vast majority of money in the Food Stamp Program goes to food, not to administrative overhead. In the fiscal year 2007, out of total Food Stamp Program costs of $33.0 billion, the federal government spent $30.3 billion on benefits and only $2.6 billion on administrative overhead.[10] While the federal government pays for 100 percent of benefits, state and localities paid roughly 50 percent of the administrative costs, which means that they spent approxi-mately $2.6 billion as their share of the overhead. Thus, out of the $35.6 billion spent by all levels of government on the Food Stamp Program, $30.3 billion went directly to food benefits. Consequently, 85 percent of all spending went directly to benefits and only 15 percent went to administrative overhead. If the government reduced many of the unnecessary barriers to application and recer-tification, the overhead costs would be even lower.

In contrast, some food banks have overhead rates of up to 20 percent. When you add in the overhead of a national organization that distributes to food banks as well as the overhead for local community-based pantries and kitchens that directly feed people, the total overhead for the entire system—from original donation to final distribution—is far greater than 20 percent.

Case closed: The Food Stamp Program is more cost-efficient than charities.

HOW FOOD CHARITIES BUY INTO—AND PERPETUATE—
THE MYTH OF THEIR SUPERIORITY

Unfortunately, many feeding charities unconsciously—and sometimes delib-erately—feed the false impression that they are more effective and efficient than government. Often, they even have themselves convinced that's true.

Feeding America has said in fundraising materials that "every $1 you give provides 16 meals for families in need."[11] Many local food banks and food res-cue organizations make similar claims. While such statements can be considered technically true, they gloss over the reality that much of the food provided—as well as much of their transportation costs—is subsidized by gov-ernment funds. Thus, a more accurate (but less appealing to donors) way to describe the costs would be: "Because your tax dollars have already enabled the government to buy much of our food and transport it to our warehouse, each additional private donation of a dollar that you provide will help us move enough food from our warehouse to pantries and kitchens to provide sixteen meals for families."

A feeding charity in New York claimed in its newsletter that a five-dollar donation "provides four children and their families with lunch for a week." That equals only seven cents a meal, which couldn't possibly be even close to the full costs of collecting and serving full meals to both adults and children. Such claims matter because, if people believe that ending hunger is as easy as giving just five bucks to an ultraefficient charity that leaves government in the dust, why would they ever support government policies that spend their tax dollars to tackle the problem?

Some charities operate as if government aid is intrinsically bad. One time I received an urgent e-mail—as part of a mass solicitation list—from a feeding charity in New Jersey that said they were short of summer meals for children and were searching for people to literally donate lunch bags full of food and to physically bring them to a distribution site. In response, I sent the director of the program an e-mail indicating that I had great news: there was a federal program—the USDA Summer Food Service Program—that would provide reimbursements for every meal. I explained that this meant that they would never have to worry about getting haphazard individual donations of food (some of which might be unsafe or nonnutritious) ever again in order to feed children during the summer months. I assumed that the director would be overjoyed, but she wrote back: "Traditionally we have not taken or requested federal funding. We have a large group of volunteers who are happy to 'give back' by providing lunches." She then made a perfunctory request for me to send her information on how she could get the government funding. I sent her a detailed response giving her clear instructions on how to apply for the food aid, including the points of contact in her state, and explained how relatively easy it was to get help. I also pointed out that since she received donations from tax-exempt foundations and from people taking individual tax deductions, she was already getting governmental help, so there was no reason to reject a program specifically designed to feed kids a nutritious lunch. She never responded. A few weeks later, I received another urgent mass e-mail from her again stating that they were running short of food and requesting an immediate donation.

It is also problematic that many food charities go out of their way in their marketing materials to all but ignore that poverty, inequality of wealth, and failed government policies are responsible for hunger. They are far more likely to highlight the latest Boy Scout food drive or fundraising dinner than the latest poverty statistics or legislative debate on job training programs. Even when they do discuss statistical increases in hunger, they are more likely to use the media coverage they get in conjunction with those numbers to call for more private donations to their agencies, rather than for more government leadership on the safety net or for greater business leadership on wages.

WHAT VOLUNTEERS THINK ABOUT HUNGER

In the fall of 2007, on a trip to St. Paul, Minnesota, I visited a Loaves and Fishes soup kitchen, one of the organization's eight feeding program sites in the Twin Cities area. In 2006, they served 313,348 meals, averaging 1,740 each night, and gave out 1.3 million pounds of food (an average $2.84 per meal) on a total yearly operating budget of $989,455. The compassion, effectiveness, and commitment of their staff and volunteers was truly moving.

At least 270 volunteer teams provided an estimated 110,000 volunteer hours of service in 2006. The agency gives out an eight-page volunteer handbook to the people who help, complete with very detailed guidelines on what to wear and how to perform each necessary volunteer task. But the handbook included no explanation of why people are hungry or poor and no request that volunteers contact elected officials regarding poverty or hunger policies. Such a lack of focus on the broader policy issues is typical of feeding programs nationwide.

Even though St. Paul is one of the most liberal cities in one of the most liberal Midwestern states, the volunteers I met that night, arranged by a local church, assumed that many people who were eating there were lazy and weren't trying hard enough to find well-paying jobs. One told me, "I don't know why people are coming here when the economy is so good," although the volunteer next to him did add that "wages are too low." They believed that government programs rewarded laziness and suggested that the Food Stamp Program have work requirements and time limits; they were surprised when I told them the program already had both. One volunteer complained that food stamp recipients spent all the money on shrimp (at least they didn't say lobster) and other fancy food that was better than his family could afford. One volunteer told me that he had "more faith in church than government" to fight hunger. Such attitudes and beliefs are typical of volunteers nationwide.

THE MISTAKEN HALO FOR NONPROFIT GROUPS

When I worked for the government I was derided as a bureaucrat, but when I moved to the nonprofit sector I was lauded as a saint, even though I performed nearly identical work in both roles. People simply assume that nonprofit work is more laudable than government work.

Yet I have seen firsthand that nonprofit groups (even those that are faith-based) often have the same problems with turf battles, bureaucracy, waste, and inefficiency as government. Nonprofit groups can even be outright corrupt. National studies have found that more than half of all charity employees have witnessed ethical lapses and that $40 billion was stolen from nonprofit groups in 2006, equaling 13 percent of the $300 billion given to charities that year.[12] If that much theft in government were exposed, it would create a firestorm. Yet charities tend to get a free pass from the media, government regulators, and the public based on the false assumption that anyone who works for a "non-profit" group is by definition a do-gooder, even if such work is very well compensated.

A colleague of mine, Robert Egger, once took a leave of absence from the DC Central Kitchen—a pioneering food rescue/job training program that he founded—to serve as acting head of the United Way of the National Capital Area, in an effort to help it recover from a highly damaging fiscal scandal. When he set his United Way salary at $85,000 annually ($30,000 more than his job at DC Central Kitchen, (colleagues running other United Way chapters nationwide, whose average salaries exceeded $200,000, grumbled that he made them look bad by taking such a low salary.[13]

In 2006, Philippe de Montebello, director of the Metropolitan Museum of Art—which is legally a nonprofit group and which received $18 million in government funding that year—was provided a compensation package of $4.557 million. In 2005, Columbia University—which received $603 million in government funding that year—paid Dr. David N. Silvers, a clinical professor of dermatology, $3.7 million. The John F. Kennedy Center for the Performing Arts—which received $40 million in government funding—paid conductor Leonard Slotkin $1.2 million and President Michael M. Kaiser $1.0 million.[14]

I'm sure these people work very hard and do a fine job. I am merely pointing out that the line between the for-profit, nonprofit, and public sectors is not as clear as most people think, and the public should end its knee-jerk preference for anything with the "nonprofit" label.

SHOULD FOOD PANTRIES, SOUP KITCHENS, AND FOOD BANKS STILL EXIST?

Janet Poppendieck argues that food pantries and soup kitchens have the net effect of increasing hunger:

> My argument, in short, is that this massive charitable endeavor serves to relieve pressure for more fundamental solutions. It works pervasively on the cultural level by serving as a sort of "moral safety valve"; it reduces the discomfort evoked by visible destitution in our midst by creating the illusion of effective action and offering us myriad ways of participating in it. It creates a culture of charity that normalizes destitution and legitimates personal generosity as a response to major social and economic dislocation.
>
> It works at the political level, as well, by making it easier for government to shed its responsibility for the poor, reassuring policymakers and voters alike that no one will starve. By harnessing a wealth of volunteer effort and donations, it makes private programs appear cheaper and more cost effective than their public counterparts, thus reinforcing an ideology of voluntarism that obscures the fundamental destruction of rights. And, because food programs are logistically demanding, their maintenance absorbs the attention and energy of many of the people most concerned about the poor, distracting them from the larger issues of distributional politics. It is not an accident that poverty grows deeper as our charitable responses to it multiply.[15]

Similarly, Mark Winne, a long-time antihunger advocate and service provider, wrote:

> My experience of 25 years in food banking has led me to conclude that co-dependency within the system is multifaceted and troubling. As a

system that depends on donated goods, it must curry favor with the nation's food industry, which often regards food banks as a waste-management tool. As an operation that must sort through billions of pounds of damaged and partially salvageable food, it requires an army of volunteers who themselves are dependent on the carefully nurtured belief that they are "doing good" by "feeding the hungry." And as a charity that lives from one multimillion-dollar capital campaign to the next . . . it must maintain a ready supply of well-heeled philanthropists and captains of industry to raise the dollars and public awareness necessary to make the next warehouse expansion possible.

The ability of food banks to attract volunteers and to raise money approaches that of major hospitals and universities. While none of this is inherently wrong, it does distract the public and policymakers from the task of harnessing the political will needed to end hunger in the United States.[16]

I agree with much of what Poppendieck and Winne argue, but I strongly disagree with their conclusion that the emergency food assistance system makes the problem worse. They assume that there is a set amount of energy that exists among people who fight hunger, and that if they are distracted by charity, they won't focus on advocacy. But there is no fixed amount of antihunger energy. If many people now engaged in charitable antihunger work no longer were, they would likely be engaged in some other sort of charitable work helping seniors, people with disabilities, etc. Often the personality and outlook of a charitable service provider is very different from that of a policy advocate. There is no evidence that large numbers of service providers would all of a sudden become advocates if they weren't "distracted" by their charitable feeding work.

And importantly, when antihunger service providers *do* engage in public policy advocacy (and an increasing number do, especially since the Feeding America network has stepped up to the plate and has made advocacy a much higher priority nationwide), they have more credibility with elected officials and the media than mere advocates. When these charitable food providers are able to illustrate public policy points with their personal experiences feeding the hungry, they become the most effective advocates of all.

Because millions of Americans, most of whom are *not* low-income, volunteer at pantries and kitchens nationwide, they are able to learn about poverty firsthand. American society is so segregated—by both income and race—that if people didn't see poverty through their work at feeding agencies, they would *never* see it. Thus, while Poppendieck claims that the agencies provide a "moral safety valve" to relieve guilt, I believe that the reverse is true: they are the only places most nonpoor Americans are forced to face poverty because they are the only place that most Americans directly confront it.

Poppendieck and Winne, harking back to the old radicals, seem to assume that, if these charitable programs didn't exist, the situation would be so bad that the people would rise up and demand social justice. I don't think that's likely. It's certainly true, as I argue throughout the book, that meaningful progress can only be achieved if low-income people build a mass political movement. But they are less likely to have the energy to build such a movement if they are hungrier. And shutting down pantries and kitchens would eliminate some of the best potential centers for organizing such a movement. Thus, if charitable feeding groups vanished overnight, additional suffering by poor people would be a far more likely outcome than a progressive revolt.

Furthermore, many grassroots feeding programs are increasingly involved in improving the nutritional content of their food, enabling people to apply for food stamps and other benefits on-site, connecting people with job training and education programs, etc. Much more progress is needed, but it's a start.

Perhaps most importantly, people can't eat hope. As long as wages aren't high enough and the safety net isn't robust enough to provide people all the food they need, grassroots feeding programs must remain as the last defense against starvation. So, yes, these agencies still need to exist. The emergency food assistance system is indeed inefficient, costly, humiliating, and distracting. But if you rely upon it to feed yourself or your family, it's a lot better than simply the promise of better government programs and policies down the line.

RELIGION AND HUNGER

Another key factor in the nation's response to hunger is religion. Many religious denominations put their ideals into action in an honorable way—and even make great sacrifices to provide space, food, money, and volunteer time to sponsor feeding charities. However, many of these organizations also teach their congregations (either consciously or subconsciously) that hunger is an inevitable part of both human history and God's will and—while it should be ameliorated with charitable acts—it can't really be eliminated.

As James Graham wrote in 1970: "It is too cynical to suggest that church-men *want* to believe that the bulk of reliefers are moral delinquents, because to admit to economic causes would betray the startling contrast between Chris-tian rhetoric and reality, between the comfortable circumstances of the great mass of believers and the innocents on the AFDC [welfare] roll."[17]

Further complicating the matter are some religious traditions that teach that suffering is noble and that the mere act of giving makes one holier. Such beliefs further reinforce society's predilection to support charity over government, and while they may encourage service providers to feed hungry people, they do not necessarily help the poor achieve economic self-sufficiency.

In addition, many of these agencies uncomfortably mix proselytizing with providing food and shelter, and often believe that the need to repair one's soul is far more important than the need for meals and a roof overhead. The late Joan Kroc, heiress to the McDonald's fortune, left more than $1.5 billion to the Salvation Army upon her death, one of the largest gifts ever to one organiza-tion in the history of philanthropy. During an interview with W. Todd Bassett, the head of the Salvation Army, Deborah Solomon of the *New York Times* said that the gift "could be a tremendous boon at a time when the federal govern-ment has made so many cuts in aid to the poor and the homeless." Bassett responded: "Well, the community centers that will be built as a result of Joan Kroc will not do social services like feeding or housing. Rather, they are for edu-cational and recreational activities, for character building. We provide activities that relate to the holistic person—body, mind, soul and spirit."[18] One mission in New York has a sign, directed at its clients, that says: WORRY ABOUT NOTHING, PRAY ABOUT EVERYTHING.

Because many of these agencies believe they are acting on the direct instruc-tion of God, they are sometimes dismissive of government regulations and paperwork requirements that cover their work and ensure that the government money they are getting is properly used. Some also oppose helping people get food stamps, believing that such programs somehow promote more depend-ency than going to a food charity, demonstrating their belief that there is no need for a strong government role in feeding people, while overlooking how much of their own food and funding is from government. When someone says one of those things to me, I go out on a limb and cite Christ (always a bit dicey for a Jew), who said, "Render unto Caesar what is Caesar's," explaining my view that the phrase means that secular and religious work should coexist, that reli-gious people also need to deal with the real-life problems on Earth here and now, and that religious service providers should work with government when it is appropriate to do so. Sometimes I'm able to convince people, but not often.

THE FABRICATED DISCRIMINATION AGAINST THE FAITH-BASED "ARMIES OF COMPASSION"

A few days before Thanksgiving 2007, President George W. Bush visited a food bank in Virginia, and, wearing a full business suit, moved some boxes around the warehouse for the cameras. Later that day he said, "As we count our many blessings, I encourage Americans to give back. . . . Our nation's greatest strength is the decency and compassion of our people."[19] Urging Americans to donate their private funds to food banks nationwide, the president conveniently ignored how his administration had slashed their food supplies.

Supposedly to prove his commitment to "compassionate conservatism," Bush has trumpeted the strength of charity in the US and promoted and protected faith-based programs. In his 2003 State of the Union Address, he said: "Religious charities of every creed are doing some of the most vital work in our country—mentoring children, feeding the hungry, taking the hand of the lonely. Yet government has often denied social service grants and contracts to these groups, just because they have a cross or Star of David or crescent on the wall."

When it comes to antihunger work, the implication that faith-based organizations can't get government support is completely fabricated. In New York City, according to a 2002 survey of food pantries and soup kitchens conducted by the New York City Coalition Against Hunger, faith-based feeding agencies were actually *more* likely than secular agencies to receive food and funding from all three levels (federal, state, and city) of government. The largest soup kitchen in New York City is based at the Holy Apostles Episcopal Church in the Chelsea neighborhood of Manhattan. The food is distributed in the main sanctuary of the church, right in front of very large religious symbols. The program receives significant federal, state, and local funding and has never once been asked to take down their religious ornaments in order to receive government funding.

Traditionally, there have been two, and only two, unique restrictions placed on religious organizations that receive government aid: one, they can't use government money to discriminate; and two, they can't use government money to proselytize.

Thus, the *only* reason to change the law, as President Bush wanted (but failed) to do, was to allow religious organizations to use our tax dollars to discriminate and proselytize, which would clearly be unconstitutional. Outrageously, when the president was unable to get such changes through Congress, he made them through executive orders that directed federal agencies to take the exact steps that Congress refused to authorize.

His one new program—the Compassion Capital Fund—aided mostly right-wing religious groups with ties to his administration, although, in fairness, even some of the most conservative groups end up using the funds for useful poverty-fighting purposes. Ironically, the organization I run received a dollop of that money for our work with faith-based pantries and kitchens. Still, the vast majority of funding for the initiative has simply transferred from other existing programs—and lax oversight of the fund has made it nearly impossible to judge its effectiveness.

The absence of serious new funding provided more fuel to cynics, myself included, who believed that the initiative was more about shoring up Bush's evangelical political base than it was about fighting poverty. The first head of Bush's faith-based office, John Dilulio, quit in disgust, admitting that the initiative was more about politics than results and saying the White House was run by "Mayberry Machiavellis." Another top aide in that office, David Kuo, later resigned, making similar comments.

Just because Bush hijacked the concept doesn't mean the entire idea of building better partnerships between faith-based and secular nonprofit groups is intrinsically a bad one. In fact, as I'll argue later in the book, Al Gore, Barack Obama, and others were correct when they proposed their own faith-based initiatives that would both respect the Constitution and advance progressive goals.

HOW THE WEALTHY "REGIFT"

Another big influence over charities are those who donate big money. Donors are an essential part of keeping these charities alive, and they hold a lot of power over how the money is spent, and therefore help determine the focus of the each nonprofit's effort.

I'll admit up front that, when it comes to describing the role of donors, I may pull my punches a bit. After all, I run a nonprofit group that desperately needs their money. So while I want to slaughter sacred cows, I do need their milk. But I'll still let the reader in on a secret: not all donors are highly sensible or entirely altruistic.

Hotel tycoon Leona Helmsley left $12 million in her will for her eight-year-old Maltese dog, Trouble. If that amount weren't staggering enough, she also bequeathed $8 billion—yes, *billion*—for the care and welfare of dogs overall. As law professor Ray D. Madoff has pointed out, because the money was given through a charitable foundation, it was never subject to taxes, so "her $8 billion donation for dogs is really a gift of $4.4 billion from her and $3.6 billion from you and me."[20] Since at least a portion of this bequest can be considered public money, shouldn't the public have a say as to whether the money should be better spent, let's say, on basic housing for the more than 100,000 human beings who slept in New York City homeless shelters in 2007, rather than on platinum doghouses studded with diamonds?

When billionaires receive massive tax cuts, farm subsidies, or other government subsidies, then make ostentatious shows of being generous philanthropists, they are merely regifting with *our* money.

Many nonprofit organizations, including the one I run, rely heavily upon private foundations. The best ones support unpopular causes such as fighting poverty, and provide funding with a minimal amount of paperwork and strings. (Note to the foundations who support the New York City Coalition Against Hunger: Thank you, thank you, thank you. Please ignore the bad things I am about to say about *other* foundations.) But many more foundations are obsessed with the new and different, at the expense of old and effective (yet underfunded) efforts. Some give mostly to massive cultural institutions, universities, and hospitals that already have plenty of money. And some are so secretive that you have to be a detective to figure out how they give out money. Other foundations are hardly more than tax shelters for wealthy families, and give out little or no money.

The large foundations that do give out large sums of money are increasingly shying away from funding any sort of policy advocacy or community organizing work that could be considered controversial. Many are thoroughly "establishment institutions." In 2006, foundation CEOs were 94 percent white, and foundation board members were 88 percent white.[21] Most foundation board members are wealthy. It only follows that foundations tend to prefer treating the symptoms of a problem (for example, funding food pantries and soup kitchens) rather than dealing with the underlying causes (for example, funding efforts to advocate for a higher minimum wage).

Even progressives in the nonprofit field, so beaten down by decades of policy defeats, seem to have conceded that foundations should no longer focus on trying to get government to do the right thing. Writing in the *Chronicle of Philanthropy*, Gar Alperovitz, Steve Dubb, and Ted Howard argue that since "it has been long clear that government is not going to expand its effort," it is foundations that have to take the lead in funding new approaches to curb poverty.[22] To be sure, that is a capitulation destined to become a self-fulfilling prophesy. After all, if you no longer insist that government do the right thing, it never will.

THE ROLE OF CORPORATE DONORS

Many business leaders whose corporations donate food and money to feeding charities, and who personally sit on the boards of such groups, simultaneously hire lobbyists to oppose increasing the minimum wage and to derail government efforts to take other steps that could actually end hunger. In fact, the two industries that provide the biggest direct donations to food banks and food rescue organizations—the supermarket and the restaurant industries—are the two most opposed to minimum wage increases. While a few brave food banks, such as the Oregon Food Bank and the Food Bank for New York City, advocate for minimum wage increases anyway, the vast majority of charitable feeding programs remain silent on this vital issue.

Because the food industry and agribusinesses give so heavily to feeding organizations (one food bank even had its new warehouse named after the agribusiness giant Cargill), these charities rarely speak out against the continued corporate agribusiness welfare distributed through the Farm Bill (which totals in the tens of billions of dollars each year), even though eliminating such subsidies is the most obvious way to obtain extra funding for antihunger programs.

Throughout history, less-than-savory characters and companies have used charitable donations to gloss over their less charitable acts. Reacting to a holiday food donation by Boss Tweed, the corrupt boss of the Tammany Hall political machine, the *New York Times* opined: "When a man can plunder the public at a rate of $75,000 or $80,000 a day, it does not cost him much to give a few thousand dollars to the poor."[23] Brutal Chicago mobster Al Capone sponsored a soup kitchen in Chicago that provided, on Christmas in 1930, "turkey, cranberry sauce, and a full Christmas dinner, as well as a tree."[24] The *Chicago Tribune* wrote: "Now it seems that Mr. Alfonse Capone has started a free soup kitchen in Chicago and [is] feeding a couple of thousand homeless people every day at an expense of something like twenty-one dollars a week. . . . And just when we were going to reprove Mr. Capone quite sharply for expediting the demise of rival gangsters, we are confronted with the picture of hungry men netting three meals a day at his free kitchen. It is indeed most embarrassing."[25]

Modern America's corporate givers don't generally murder their opponents, but their records aren't perfectly clean either, and they still use charity as a shield. FreshDirect, a New York–based company that delivers groceries ordered over the Internet to people's homes, wrote customers a letter in response to unfavorable publicity that it had allegedly fired undocumented immigrant workers as a way to bust a union. The letter defended its labor polices but then included the boast: "We are one of the biggest feeders of NY's needy, having donated over 1 million pounds of fresh quality food" to a local feeding charity.[26]

Some of the nation's leading corporate sponsors of antihunger efforts engage in corporate conduct that likely increases hunger. As Tyson Foods said on its Web site in 2007: "Since we joined the fight against hunger in 2000, Tyson Foods has partnered with several national organizations . . . to help make a difference where we can. Through these partnerships, Tyson Foods has donated more than 50 million pounds of chicken, beef or pork—enough for approximately 200 million meals—to food banks and agencies serving local communities around the country."[27] Many of Tyson's employees are immigrants and work in slaughterhouses, some of the most dangerous workplaces in the nation, yet the company has consistently tried to bust their unions.[28] In a Tyson packing plant in Pasco, Washington, according to the US Department of Labor's Occupational Safety and Health Administration (OSHA), the rate of injury and illness at the facility is more than two and a half times the national average for meatpacking plants and more than twice that of meatpacking facilities with a thousand or more workers. The company also worked hard to "jettison the union, Teamsters Local 556, that has represented meatpacking workers there for more than 25 years . . . workers at the plant voted to decertify the union under a cloud of allegations of dirty tricks, labor law violations, and union busting."[29] In 2006, Tyson workers at its beef packing plant in Holcomb, Kansas, charged that they were illegally required to work "off the clock" and were denied overtime wages.[30] If such companies paid their workers better and supported rather than busted labor unions, those actions would likely do far more to reduce hunger in America than would their charitable contributions.

What saddens me most is that national feeding charities not only tend to decline raising broader issues with Tyson, but they even actively promote Tyson as a particularly praiseworthy donor. (Note to any Tyson executives reading this book: should you decide to support unions, reduce on-the-job deaths, increase wages, *and* make a large donation to the New York City Coalition Against Hunger, I would be more than happy to accept your generosity and take the above paragraphs out of the second edition—as well as the movie version—of this book.)

Some of the corporate charitable responses seem to be more about advertising the donor company than solving a pressing social need. For instance, Tide laundry detergent created "Loads of Hope," a mobile laundry facility to help people clean their clothing after natural disasters. You can go to their Web site and buy a T-shirt to support the efforts. The only thing on the T-shirt is a big Tide logo.

It's clear that charity—not matter how vast or small—cannot substitute for systematic, progressive social change that would reduce poverty and inequality nationwide. We need to advocate for fundamental change that includes living-wage jobs and a robust safety net. I guarantee that would do a lot more good than buying another T-shirt with a corporate logo.

CHAPTER 11

HOW MEDIA IGNORES HUNGER (EXCEPT DURING HOLIDAYS AND HURRICANES)

I don't know which is worse, a press that is censored, or one that doesn't need to be.

—Abbie Hoffman, activist

When I watch TV over my dinner at night, I see a world in which almost everyone makes $15 an hour or more . . . so it's easy for a fast-food worker or a nurse's aide to conclude that she is an anomaly—the only one, or almost the only one, who hasn't been invited to the party.

—Barbara Ehrenreich, author of *Nickel and Dimed*[1]

When, in 2003, the media trumpeted news that the national economy had just expanded by 7.2 percent, it reminded me of the exchange in Woody Allen's *Annie Hall,* in which a young Alvie Singer says he is depressed because the "universe is expanding." Alvie's mother responds: "What has the universe got to do with it? You're here in Brooklyn! Brooklyn is not expanding!"

You would have been hard-pressed in 2003 to find evidence that the economy was expanding in either Brooklyn (where I live), the rest of New York City, or anywhere in America. Unemployment and underemployment were high, wages for most workers were flat, and the number of people forced to utilize food pantries and soup kitchens was soaring.

It made more sense to me when, in the same week, the federal government released the annual USDA food insecurity statistics, which showed that the number of Americans who faced the threat of hunger in 2002 rose by 13 percent.

Which of these two statistics was more meaningful?

Well, the expanding economy hadn't yet created one single new job that wasn't offset by the loss of at least one existing job. And meanwhile, the increase in hunger left a total of 34.9 million Americans that year without a steady, secure source of food—the third year in a row that food insecurity in America grew. The statistic on the expanding economy covered only three months, but the hunger statistic covered a whole year.

Hmm, that's a tough call.

So, which statistic received more attention from the media? The expanding economy, of course. Neither CBS, NBC, ABC, the *New York Times*, nor the *Washington Post* reported on the hunger study.

HUNGER IN AMERICA? NOT ON THE EVENING NEWS

For much of the modern media age—before the relatively recent rise of cable TV and the Internet—the single greatest sign of whether an issue had permeated the consciousness of the American people was whether it was covered on the national network evening TV news shows. Chart 11A shows all the stand-alone national network TV news stories that focused on the issue of domestic hunger from 1969 through 2006.

CHART 11A
Network TV News Stories on US Hunger, 1969–2006

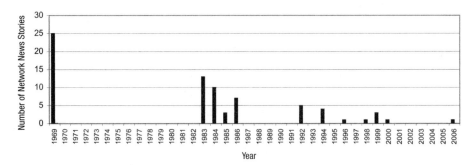

Source: Vanderbilt Television News Archives

This chart vividly demonstrates the pack mentality of media coverage, in that an issue gets a great amount of media coverage when an issue is, in the judgment of the media, "hot," but virtually no coverage the rest of the time, even when, from a substantive standpoint, the issue is still vital to tens of millions of Americans. Coverage surged in 1969, when Congress held a major hunger hearing and President Nixon sponsored a hunger conference, and then plummeted to virtually nothing in most of the years since. Out of the seventy-seven network news stories over this thirty-seven-year time period, twenty-five were in 1969, thirteen were in 1983, and ten were in 1984 (during the latter two years, there were major controversies over Reagan hunger policies). While these three years constituted only 8 percent of the years in that time period, they had a whopping 62 percent of the hunger stories. In contrast, in twenty-seven out of the thirty-seven years, there was not a single network news story on hunger. There was not one story in the fourteen years between 1969 and 1983, despite the fact that this period had the greatest concentrated growth in federal antihunger programs in US history. There was not a single story in 1987, the first full year of national welfare reform implementation. And there was not one story in the first five years of George W. Bush's administration, despite the very significant hunger increases during that time.

To be sure, there were still occasional flashes of journalistic courage. On the evening of February 25, 1985, John Chancellor reported on *NBC Nightly News* that 25 million Americans were hungry and that the problem was getting worse. Chancellor, obviously moved by the extent of hunger, warned that the "veneer of civilization seems to have worn very thin."[2]

But as the years went by, even the few times the media did cover the issue, it stopped assuming that it was government's role to solve the problem, unlike the assumptions in the 1960s media coverage. In the 1960s, the media's direct or implicit question was, "How can a country this wealthy let children go hungry?" By the Reagan era and for many subsequent years, the implicit question asked by the media became, "Why are all these undeserving people getting benefits with our tax dollars?" Those changing attitudes influenced—and were influenced by—the changing attitudes of elected officials and the public.

In a 2007 study of network evening news broadcasts over more than three years, the media watchdog group Fairness and Accuracy in Reporting (FAIR) found the following in a study of weeknight news broadcasts on CBS, NBC, and ABC:

During the more than three years studied, there were just 58 stories about poverty on the three network newscasts, including just 191 quoted sources. For perspective, a FAIR study of network newscasts found that in just one year (2001), the three networks included a total of 14,632 sources. Assuming that the nightly news still features a like number of sources per year, that would amount to some 46,000 sources over the 38 months of FAIR's study, making sources appearing in poverty stories just 0.4 percent of overall sources. . . . Driving home poverty's low rank as a news priority is the fact that fewer nightly news segments were dedicated to it than to millionaire pop star Michael Jackson. During a study period that saw 58 stories about poverty, the three network programs dedicated 69 stories to Jackson's legal woes. Of the three networks, only NBC aired more stories on poverty than on Michael Jackson (25 to 24). Moreover, in 2005, the year that saw the Katrina disaster and the culmination of Jackson's rather less consequential trial, the networks deemed the pop star's legal problems twice as newsworthy as the economic plight of tens of millions of poor citizens, running 44 stories on Michael Jackson to 22 for poverty.[3]

When I am most troubled with this disparity, I console myself with the memory that, once upon a time, Michael Jackson gave the world *Thriller*.

In 2008, in response to the recession and soaring food prices, the mainstream media did again start reporting on rising hunger. But they seemed obsessed with highlighting stories of individual middle-class families, who formerly donated food to pantries, but who had lost jobs and now needed help from such programs, even though, in truth, such occurrences were relatively rare. The media didn't seem nearly as interested in the reality that millions of Americans who were previously poor and hungry had become poorer and hungrier.

WHAT WE CAN LEARN FROM THE SUNDAY *NEW YORK TIMES*

To understand to whom America's most elite media is oriented, you need to look no further than the legendary Sunday *New York Times*. Let's examine a typical Sunday for the newspaper: September 23, 2007.

The wedding section for that day featured couples that were virtually all white, all graduates of elite undergraduate and graduate institutions, and all professionals. None of the couples featured so much as one partner with a blue-collar job. However, one person described their profession as a "risk advisor specializing in boat and yacht sales." (I *wish* I was making this up.)

The fashion section in the back of that day's *New York Times Magazine* featured clothing for the ultrarich, including dresses with prices up to $7,500; shirts costing $790; scarves priced at $375; and jackets at the bargain-basement price of $950. It also included, as it does every Sunday, a section entitled "luxury homes and estates." Of the eleven listings that included both a photo and an asking price, the average price was $3.8 million. (Such *Times Magazine* real estate listings are *in addition to* the massive numbers of luxury listings in the separate *Times* Sunday real estate section.)

The *Times*—like much of society in today's Gilded Age—is beset by glaring paradoxes. For instance, on October 15, 2007, the paper ran a probing and insightful news story on African famine, but the article was surrounded by ads for the following products: Chanel J 12 GMT watch ($8,500); a Louis Vuitton Duomo in Damier canvas bag ($1,200); a pair of Gucci men's boots ($850); TAG Heuer Aquaracer Steel and Gold 18K watch with diamonds ($3,000); a piece of Cartier diamond-crusted jewelry (price not listed—clearly falls into the "if-you-gotta-ask . . ." category); a Tiffany & Co. watch with all sorts of diamonds (no price listed); a Saks Fifth Avenue Tevrow+Chase dress ($445); Mikimoto pearls and gold ($3,980); Brooks Brothers made-to-measure suits (at least $900 each); and a Steuben Glass "Our Town" with a photo of the New York skyline etched into it ($8,500).[4]

My all-time favorite ad in the *Times*, for a private jet, posed the question: "How cool would it be to fly to Palm Beach in your own private jet?" My answer: *very* cool.

Hard to imagine that the *Times* doesn't focus more on the lives of low-income Americans, huh?

News executives sometimes piously insist that such ads geared toward the rich don't affect who or what they cover, but just as any good reporter would roll his or her eyes when politicians say that campaign contributions don't affect their voting record, we should roll our eyes when the media denies the influence of advertisers.

Add to that bias the extreme consolidation of ownership of local and national news media by just a handful of giant corporations and the problem is magnified. While most American cities previously had at least two competing daily newspapers, with one or more owned locally, most cities now only have one daily newspaper, usually owned by a major national chain. In New York City, the two leading news radio stations, WCBS and WINS, are now both owned by the *same* company. Consequently, all mainstream media are reporting on— or *failing* to report on—the same issues.

In addition to these influences on the news, those delivering the news themselves are often out of touch with working-class life. In 2006, the median income nationwide for a person who worked full time was $42,742 for men and $32,905 for women.[5] In contrast, in 2006, the minimum salary for a reporter at the *Boston Globe* with at least five years' experience was $84,577.[6] In 2007, local TV news directors made an average of $84,900 (with the highest salary $300,000), while local assistant news directors earned $67,500 (the highest earned $200,000). Local news anchors on the other hand, made an average of $72,400 (with the top anchor earning $1.2 million) and local weathercasters made an average of $62,700 (with a maximum of $500,000). Local sports anchors even averaged $52,300 (with the highest-paid receiving $400,000).[7] Of course, people who worked for national networks, or worked as editors and publishers, earned far more.

Like everything else in New York, media salaries are also higher. As of 2001 the *Times* reporters' salaries started at $70,720 and peaked after decades of work at around $120,000. Columnists earned from $150,000 to $350,000.[8] In 2005, Bill Keller, executive editor of the *Times*, earned $650,000, and Will Shortz, the crossword puzzle editor, earned $90,000. Over at the far-right-wing *New York Post*, which both denies that hunger exists in New York and loses millions of dollars a year, Editor in Chief Col Allen earned $600,000, and Page Six gossip columnist Richard Johnson earned $300,000.[9] In fairness, as I pointed out in the previous chapter, nonprofit executives often earn large salaries too.

IGNORING POVERTY AND HUNGER

Given that the media caters to the advertisers of luxury products, and further given that people employed in the media mostly earn well above poverty wages, it is not surprising that the media usually overlooks poverty and hunger. To be sure, there are exceptions to the rule, such as the compelling series on hunger by the *Columbus Dispatch*, the *Pittsburgh Post-Gazette*, and the *Dallas Morning News*, as well as hard-hitting features on NPR and PBS and in the excellent print stories cited in this book. But, most of the mainstream media simply ignore these issues, except for obligatory holiday stories that make it seem as though charity will solve the problem.

Assignment editors just don't seem to take these issues seriously. Loretta Schwartz-Nobel recalled that early in her writing career, as an intern at *Philadelphia* magazine, when she suggested to her editor that she write a story on the local hunger problem, "He laughed and said there was no hunger in our city, that the only problem was that people in Philadelphia were eating too much."[10]

In November 2007, when the Bush administration belatedly released the annual federal hunger numbers, Associated Press and Reuters ran detailed stories on this major development, but not a syllable on the subject was printed in either the *Washington Post* or the *New York Times*. Of course, I e-mailed detailed letters complaining to editors at both the *Times* and the *Post*—pointing out that the issue directly affected tens of millions of Americans—but never received a response from either.

Few if any of the major national media outlets maintain a "poverty beat," even though 37.2 million Americans live in poverty. In contrast, the major media collectively have hundreds of reporters on business, sports, and entertainment beats.

In coverage of other topics, the closer to home an event occurs, the more news coverage it attracts. That's certainly true for natural disasters and terrorist attacks. But this is not the case for hunger and poverty issues, where some of the media elite are actually *more* likely to cover international poverty and hunger than those same conditions locally. Perhaps the reason is that international poverty is always *someone else's* fault, but if we take an honest look at domestic poverty and hunger, they might prove to be *our* fault.

You can often find a focus on domestic issues including hunger on the editorial and op-ed pages of papers like the *Times,* however this coverage is egregiously lacking in their news coverage. The Metro section of the *New York Times* provides relatively little reporting on the daily conditions of low-income people. While the local hunger issue receives better coverage in the more working class–oriented *Daily News*—and massive coverage in Spanish-language publications such as *El Diario* and *Hoy*—I consistently have to battle to see hunger reporting in the *Times*. If readers of the *Times* used that newspaper as their only source of information, they would likely know more about poverty in New Orleans—which the *Times* covered significantly post–Hurricane Katrina—than they would about poverty in New York.

In November 2007 alone, the *Times* Metro section ran eight different stories (totaling 7,794 words) by reporter Carol Vogel on a series of high-end art auctions in which 389 paintings sold for a total of $2.65 billion.[11] The same month, the New York City Coalition Against Hunger released its 2007 hunger study. Our announcement's event was attended by the New York City Council Speaker, the second most powerful elected official in the city, as well as by high-ranking representatives of the mayor's office. The study's release generated significant coverage in the city's electronic and print media. It was even picked up by foreign services and featured in newspapers and magazines in more than a dozen countries, including *Der Spiegel*, Germany's equivalent of *Time* magazine). The BBC World Service ran an interview with me about the study. So how many words of coverage did it garner in the *New York Times* print edition? Ninety-six. No, that's not a typo. Ninety-six words, for an annual study about 1.3 million hungry people in the paper's backyard.

In March 2008, the *Times* assigned thirty-two different reporters to cover the Governor Eliot Spitzer prostitution scandal, but did not assign even one reporter to cover an oversight hearing of the City Council held on the same day, which discussed the budgets for three large city agencies that collectively manage all child protection, Medicaid, hunger, homeless services, and welfare programs that support millions of New Yorkers. In contrast, *Daily News* did cover the hearing, reporting how the council was opposing the mayor's proposal to slash funding for pantries and kitchens.

Oddly, in 2007, the *Times* started a habit of posting lengthy stories about local hunger—carefully reported by good reporters—on its Web site, but not printing them in its paper. The Web site ran a story on June 12, 2008, about a major study by the Food Bank for New York City, and ran one on July 15, 2008, about new city government figures on rising pantry and kitchen use. Even though the latter story was featured by the rival *Metro New York* newspaper as a banner headline on its front page, not a word about either story made it into print in the *Times*. I am singling out the *Times* not only because it is the most influential and widely respected newspaper on the planet, but because if a publication such as the *Times*, dedicated to excellence and inclined to publish liberal-leaning editorials and op-eds, is disinclined to print stories on domestic hunger and poverty, other media outlets naturally follow suit.

PRESIDENTIAL CAMPAIGNS

The reporting on the 2008 presidential campaign provides an example of how the major media don't just cover up the existence of hunger and poverty, but also hide the fact that the public actually *does* care about those issues.

In more than twenty debates during the Democratic primary season, poverty, hunger, homelessness, and low-wage work were barely raised by media moderators, even after both John Edwards and Barack Obama raised the issue. In a poll conducted by the *New York Times* and CBS News in December 2007, when citizens in the early voting states of Iowa and New Hampshire were asked which issues mattered to them most, poverty, hunger, and homelessness weren't even listed as choices.[12] If the poll had simply asked an open-ended question, and few voters volunteered those issues, then I'd have no complaint. But the poll actually provided a list of twenty issues and didn't include poverty or related issues. Right after the poll was conducted, the *Times* ran a front-page, above-the-fold graphic that listed the issues most important to voters in Iowa and New Hampshire, but of course, since poverty was not on the list of questions, it was not on the graphic of answers.

But a CNN national poll, conducted just a week before the *Times*/CBS poll, asked voters to rank issue importance and *did* include poverty as an option. Here's what it found:

Issue	Importance to Americans in determining their vote for President
Economy	82%
The situation in Iraq	80%
Health care	76%
Terrorism	76%
The situation in Iran	73%
Gas prices	67%
Poverty and homelessness	65%
Taxes	63%
Illegal immigration	61%
Global warming	48%
Abortion	46%
Gun policy	46%
Policies toward gays and lesbians	27%

226 Section I—The Problem

More Americans chose poverty and homelessness as pressing issues than they chose taxes, illegal immigration, abortion, gun policy, or global warming.[13] Yet the media coverage told us far more about the candidates' positions on immigration, abortion, gun control, and global warming than it did on poverty and homelessness.

CLASS BIASES IN REPORTING

In 2004, Brent Cunningham wrote in the *Columbia Journalism Review* that "today's journalists are more isolated than ever from the lives of poor and working-class Americans." It shows. *Washington Post* columnist E. J. Dionne told the *Review*: "I actually think there's structural bias in the media against the poor. Newspapers are built to cover the wealthy and famous much more than they are built to cover the working class and the poor."[14]

In the rare instances in which reporters raise the topic of welfare, they particularly expose their bias. In a 2000 Republican presidential debate, CNN reporter Judy Woodruff asked the following question of a religious conservative candidate, former ambassador Alan Keyes:

Mr. Ambassador, a central target of your campaign has been what you called the moral crisis gripping this country. And yet . . . over the last six, seven, eight years, the abortion rate is down, teen pregnancy rate is down, welfare rolls are down, violent crime rate is down. Now, granted, none of these are acceptable. They're all too high. But my question is, given all of these trends, are you prepared to give the current administration some credit for these very clear improvements?[15]

On what did Woodruff base her judgment when she expressed that the welfare rolls—which had just been slashed—were "too high." What level would she claim is "acceptable"? Also, notice how welfare is equated with violent crime, a common juxtaposition in the media.

In a 2006 piece on Mayor Bloomberg in the *New York Times Magazine*, Jonathan Mahler wrote: "Nor is there much doubt that by virtually every measure, New York is a better place to live and work than when Bloomberg first took office—crime is down, the welfare rolls are shrinking, the city is experiencing a historic boom in construction."[16] Again, the welfare drop is equated to the crime drop, and the city apparently improved under "virtually ever measure" during a time when poverty, homelessness, and hunger all increased in New York City.

And that's the mainstream media. Then there is the right-wing media—Fox News, the *Wall Street Journal* editorial page (although not their news coverage, which was excellent and fair, at least before Rupert Murdoch bought the paper), the *Washington Times, New York Post,* much of talk radio, and countless conservative blogs. In the extraordinarily rare instances that poverty issues are ever covered in any of these outlets, it is usually to report on some sort of alleged fraud or crime committed by poor people.

The rabid *New York Post,* which doesn't even observe the traditional practice of separating its news coverage from its editorializing, takes the cake. The news staff at *New York Post* almost uniformly ignores poverty or hunger-related news, and the editorials proclaim things like: "There is no hunger crisis in New York City. None whatsoever." In an editorial blasting a bipartisan group of city officials for taking a few small steps to address hunger, a *New York Post* writer managed to—in just a few paragraphs—distort the amount of money people can make and still get food stamps, mischaracterize USDA food security data, falsely equate food stamps with welfare, and imply that any poor person who needs government help is likely engaged in fraud.[17] The language the *Post* uses regarding low-income people is consistently vicious and dehumanizing; a writer once once implied that anyone hungry in New York was either a drug addict or mentally ill. I have written to their editorial board multiple times challenging them either to meet with me or to visit a food pantry, but they have never responded. Have you detected a pattern yet?

THE MEDIA'S FIXATION ON CHARITY AND FEEL-GOOD (AND FEEL-BAD) STORIES

When the media does cover domestic hunger stories, usually around the holidays, they almost never include any discussion of the government's role in creating or solving the problem. During their staple Thanksgiving and Christmas newscasts in late 2005, both CBS and NBC ran stories on food banks running short of donations, without explaining or even asking why.

I have often stressed in interviews that more private donations are not the best answer to the problem and that changes in government policies are far more important, only for the final media reports to leave out both points entirely. Holiday charity stories in the mainstream media go to such great lengths to ignore broader governmental and societal implications that they are often indistinguishable from those run by the right-wing media.

As an example, since 1912, the *New York Times* has run an annual series, mostly around the holidays, called the "Neediest Cases," to detail hard luck stories of individuals and to raise money for charities that help them. In one such story in 2007, headlined "Defeating Hunger and Homelessness, Step by Step," a man lost his job because he suffered from depression and then became homeless.[18] A social service agency taught him "budgeting and discipline" and the Neediest Cases Fund provided him $250 for a winter coat and other warm clothing. The 679-word story did not include a single mention of government's role related to solving such problems. It highlighted only his neediness and that he was prompted to improve his personal behavior. The story neglected to observe that there were tens of thousands of New Yorkers homeless, making it very unlikely that donors could really "defeat" the problem by helping only one person do it "one step at a time."

Yet that identical phrase is used by the media, as well as many charities, year after year. A Brooklyn newspaper ran a headline over a photo of New York Jets football players serving Thanksgiving meals alongside a nun: TACKLING HUNGER, ONE TURKEY AT A TIME.[19] The reason the media use that phrase is that they—and the American people—have been fooled into thinking that social problems are just so unsolvable that the best we can hope for is to chip away at the problem one person at a time. The phrase is meant to make the situation feel less hopeless, but I think it usually has the reverse effect.

Another key theme is that, no matter how down-and-out recipients of holiday help are, they are supposed to be darn grateful for the charity they receive twice a year. For example, next to a photo of Mayor Bloomberg serving a turkey, *Daily News* ran a headline: WON'T SQUAWK OVER TURKEY; MINUS FAMILIES, GLITZ AND COMFORTS, MANY AT RESCUE MISSIONS STILL SAY THEY ARE THANKFUL.[20]

Perhaps the best example of how the charity mindset has taken over media coverage of hunger is a series that ran on CBS' *The Early Show* during a full week in April 2008 titled, "Facing Hunger, Feeding America." I was grateful that the show invited staff from the New York City Coalition Against Hunger to stand out on the show's plaza one morning with a banner, thereby briefly advertising our organization to the nation. They even did a live mini-interview with two of our employees, but it was so brief that our folks weren't able to even touch upon the governmental causes of—or solutions to—hunger. Even more frustratingly, the one actual news story about hunger that CBS ran during the series barely mentioned the government's role, even though Congress was in the midst of debating a Farm Bill with major implications for hunger. During a whole week touting their "hunger" coverage, the show mentioned food stamps only once, in passing. Rather, the prime focus of the week was *The Early Show's* nationwide food drive. Each day, food companies—receiving lengthy and glowing on-screen marketing time for their companies—would come on the show and announce their "generous" donations. The show gave great credit to Tyson Foods for donating $65,000 worth of meat to the show's food drive, but according to my calculations, Tyson had at least $500 million in sales that week alone, meaning that the donation equaled less than 1/1,800 of what Tyson earned. The total national contributions by six major national companies equaled $172,527 for the week.[21] That sure sounds impressive, but CBS chair Leslie Moonves—who received a 29 percent pay hike that year despite declining profits—earned about $36.89 million that year, or about $709,000 per week. In other words, his weekly pay equaled about four times the entire food donation from all the national corporations combined. Moreover, the Food Stamp Program spent about $694 million on benefits that week, meaning that the charitable effort—so lauded by the show—provided less than 1/4,000th of the food value that the Food Stamp Program—virtually ignored by the show—provided that week.

WHAT THE CONTEMPORARY MEDIA REALLY CARES ABOUT

From April through June 2008, the *Times* Metro section devoted seven lengthy stories—taking up a whopping 6,356 words—to the trial of Uma Thurman's stalker. Since the media now seems to be obsessed with such things, as well as with young blonde women abducted while on Caribbean vacations and celebrity drunk-driving arrests, I thought I'd provide a handy-dandy guide in Chart 11B on the likelihood of certain occurrences—that are routinely covered by the media—happening to you:

What are the Odds for Americans Each Year?

There were an estimated total of 299,398,484 people living in the US in 2006, according to the US Census Bureau (Annual Estimates of the Population for the United States, Regions, States, and for Puerto Rico: April 1, 2000, to July 1, 2006.)

Category	Number of Americans Afflicted	Likelihood of suffering under this category in the US
People murdered in the US, 2006	17,034 (FBI Uniform Crime Report, 2006)	1 in 17,576
People murdered by foreign terrorists on US soil, 2001	About 2,800 (*New York Times*)	1 in 103,860
People murdered by foreign terrorists on US soil, 2007	0	0
People killed in plane crashes in the US, 2006	114 (Aircraft Crashes Record Office, 2006)	1 in 2,626,302
People killed in car and motorcycle crashes in the US, 2006	36,002 (National Highway Traffic Safety Administration, 2006)	1 in 8,316
Blonde teenage girls from the US missing in Aruba	1 (wall-to-wall coverage in US media)	1 in 299,398,484
People *injured* by shark attacks in US waters, 2005	38 (University of Florida, 2005)	1 in 7,878,907
People *killed* by shark attacks in US waters, 2005	1 (University of Florida, 2005)	1 in 299,398,484
Americans who lived in households that suffered from food insecurity, 2006	35,515,000 (USDA, 2006)	1 in 8
Americans forced to get emergency food from charities, 2005	25,300,000 (America's Second Harvest, 2005)	1 in 12
Americans who lived in poverty, 2005	36,460,000 (US Census Bureau, 2006)	1 in 8
Former pop stars named Britney Spears	1 (any tabloid you can find)	1 in 299,398,484

Here's a question that answers itself: Which of those occurrences obtained more media coverage?

WHEN THE MEDIA DID COVER HUNGER AND POVERTY IN AMERICA

This kind of media negligence has not always been the case. In the years 1968 and 1969 the media did focus intensively on hunger and poverty, earning two different news Emmy Awards for hunger reporting. The Emmy for "Outstanding Achievement Within Regularly Scheduled News Programs" went to *The Huntley-Brinkley Report* (NBC) for "Coverage of Hunger in the United States." The Emmy for "Outstanding News Documentary Program Achievements" went to *CBS News Hour: Hunger in America,* which was one of the most daring and influential television documentaries of all time.

Broadcast on May 21, 1968, *Hunger in America* was the work of TV journalism's historical all-stars—directed by Edward R. Murrow, produced by Fred Friendly (the guy played by George Clooney in the movie, *Good Night, and Good Luck*), and narrated by Charles Kuralt. The show took ten months to produce, and was broadcast for an hour in prime time.

The show opened with a long, unflinching close-up shot of a premature baby literally dying on screen. Then the narration kicked in: "This baby is dying of starvation. He was an American. Now he's dead." The show pulled no punches. It said 30 million Americans were poor, and 10 million were hungry, and blamed the problems squarely on government inaction and racism. It even told the story of an eleven-year-old girl who had to engage in prostitution to be able to afford food. Its images were searing, and its language both outraged and poetic, with lines like this: "Dessert and meat were like a star. Able to be seen, unable to be reached."

The show contained segments on four distinct populations: Mexican Americans in San Antonio, Texas; rural whites in Loudoun County, Virginia; Navajo in Arizona; and African Americans in Hale County, Alabama.

It broadcast a white county commissioner in Texas saying that hunger among local Mexicans was a good thing because society needed inequality of wealth to function: "If you don't have that condition, you'll never have Indians and chiefs. And you've got to have a chief." Then, in an odd jump, he blamed the hungry for their own plight: "You'll always have hunger because men just aren't worth a dime."

The show featured Dr. Jean Van Dusen, describing in painstaking detail, the malnutrition found on the Navajo reservation, and pointing out that some people had to walk twenty-five miles to get government commodities. It showed film of rows of small lumps of dirt in Tuba City, Arizona, and explained: "These little short mounds are for little short caskets."

While the media today won't usually go near the issues of inequality of wealth and class, this show reveled in those issues. Most strikingly, the program laid the problem directly at the door of failing USDA programs, explaining how food stamps were too expensive to buy, how local officials created practices to deny food access, and how the USDA failed to spend much of the antihunger funding available to it. Kuralt editorialized that "prayer is not what a man wants when he is hungry . . . a hard time earning means a hard time eating." He said that, "the Department of Agriculture protects farmers, not consumers, especially not destitute consumers" and called for moving food programs to the Department of Heath and Human Services. He closed by saying, "In this country, the most basic need must become the most basic human right."

The Lyndon B. Johnson administration and Secretary of Agriculture Orville Freeman were outraged. Freeman called it "shabby journalism" and contacted Frank Stanton, then-president of CBS, demanding equal time. Here's the telegram that Stanton shot back to Freeman:

Dear Mr. Secretary: Your letter to me on May 27 requesting "equal time" to reply to allegations contained in CBS Reports' "Hunger in America" was received in the mail only this morning although released to the press on Monday. Pending an opportunity to make a complete study of your charges, I would like to make four points. First, no issue of "equal time" is involved since such an obligation can only arise under Section 315 of the Communications Act relating to candidates for public office. Second, we acknowledge an obligation to make a reasonable effort to present contrasting viewpoints on controversial issues of public importance on an overall basis. We will continue to provide news coverage of the differing views on the issue of hunger. Third, the thrust of your complaint does not appear to be concerned so much with the existence of any significant inaccuracies in our reporting of the issue as it is with your feeling that any blame for the inadequacy in meeting the problem of hunger in America should have been attributed to inaction by Congress or by local governments and not to the Department of Agriculture. But the issue of hunger in America transcends the superficial issue of assessing blame for its continued existence. Fourth, the purpose of the broadcast was to report to people the fact that hunger is a problem in America not that most Americans are well fed. Finally, just as your colleagues in the Department of Agriculture are properly jealous of their reputations so our journalists at CBS News are proud of their profession and seriously concerned about intemperate attacks on their honesty and integrity. "Hunger in America" was a hard hitting job of investigatory reporting with respect to a critical and shameful national problem. Unless it is established that the report was in significant respects erroneous, it is my purpose to stand by those who researched and produced it.

Frank Stanton, President
Columbia Broadcasting System Inc."[22]

I think that was a pitch-perfect response—a great combination of facts and "screw you, buddy." The truth that a network president would never broadcast such a show today—nor defend it against self-serving attacks in such a steadfast way—is exactly what's wrong with the modern-day media.

But the attacks against the CBS report continued. Jamie Whitten, the powerful and reactionary chair of the House Appropriations Subcommittee on Agriculture, actually asked the FBI to investigate the validity of the documentary, which the FBI proceeded to do in a tragicomic manner. FBI agents in suits grilled cowering Mexican Americans as to what they said to the producers. An agent even interrogated one of the show's cameramen about the exact location of a scrawny dog featured in the show. The aim was more to intimidate than to find the truth.[23]

Conservatives howled that the whole show was a fake, that it was fraudulent to broadcast the child dying, since the child was born prematurely. They ignored that malnutrition was a key cause of premature birth. Reed Irvine, who went on to create the right-wing media watchdog group Accuracy in the Media, credited this outrage over the show with launching his career.

But others who watched had an entirely different reaction. Congressman Charles E. Bennett of Florida wrote to CBS stating that he had introduced antihunger legislation in response to the show. "I want to congratulate you on this program. I was greatly disturbed and shocked by it, and I want to thank you for bring this matter to the public's attention."[24]

Senator George McGovern recalled: "It was 1968 and I remember saying, 'Why are they looking at hunger in the United States?'" McGovern was riveted by a young boy who told CBS that he was "ashamed" that he did not have enough money to buy food at school. "I said to my family that was watching the documentary with me, 'You know, it's not that little boy who should be ashamed, it's George McGovern, a United States Senator, a member of the Committee on Agriculture.'"[25] McGovern also took action, and his outrage— coupled with the shock and anger of other members of Congress and many of the American people—directly led to the enactment of the modern nutrition assistance safety net that has done so much to reduce hunger in America.

So, the media *does* matter—and it can matter for the better. Let's hope that, post-Katrina, with our nation in an economic downturn, food prices soaring, and a new administration in the White House, the media pendulum is swinging back to focus on poverty and hunger.

SECTION II

THE SOLUTION

CHAPTER 12

HERE IT IS: THE PLAN TO END DOMESTIC HUNGER

The country demands bold, persistent experimentation. It is common sense to take a method and try it. If it fails, admit it frankly and try another. But above all, try something. The millions who are in want will not stand idly by silently forever while the things to satisfy their needs are within easy reach.

—President Franklin D. Roosevelt, 1932[1]

A very good president put the US on a trajectory to the moon. A truly great president would end hunger in America.

The next president and Congress should transcend petty partisanship and unite all Americans to solve one of our most harmful and needless problems. They should jointly set a goal of ending hunger among children and seniors within five years, as a down payment on a ten-year goal of ending all hunger in America.

To accomplish that goal, the nation must put serious resources behind a comprehensive food security continuum that will reinvent the federal nutrition safety net to make it both more generous and less bureaucratic; make school meals universal regardless of family income; provide incentives for states to reduce hunger; launch a truly meaningful faith- and community-based initiative; empower more food pantries and soup kitchens to help their customers to achieve self-sufficiency; join with the business community to make all full-time salaries start at a living wage; and (as outlined in the next chapter) bolster community food production and marketing.

MODERNIZING AND EXPANDING THE FEDERAL NUTRITION SAFETY NET

The quickest and easiest way to end most hunger in America—with one bold action—would be to entirely reinvent the existing system by combining all existing federal programs (food stamps, WIC, commodities, etc.) into one larger, but more efficient, entity.

Today, even if all the nation's food charities somehow accomplished the Herculean task of doubling their food distribution (increasing such efforts by 100 percent), this feat would barely dent the nation's hunger problem, merely reducing the number of food-insecure Americans by 2 million—from 35.5 million to about 33 million. In contrast, if the US government increased the size of the federal nutrition safety net by only 10 percent, 8.5 million Americans would no longer be food insecure. A mere 20 percent safety net increase would nearly cut hunger in the United States in half. And a 41 percent increase would entirely eliminate food insecurity in America, ensuring—finally—that every child, adult, and senior citizen in the nation had enough to eat.

This measure would be easy and affordable. We can end all food insecurity in America for just the cost of what the federal government spends on a year of agribusiness subsidies, three months of war in Iraq, or 6 percent of President George W. Bush's tax cuts. The investment would repay the nation many times over through increased educational performance, reduced health care spending, and increased worker productivity.

Of course, if wages were significantly boosted and community food production was dramatically increased, the federal safety net wouldn't need to take on all the burden of ending domestic hunger itself. But until those other goals are achieved, federal nutrition programs are the fastest and most efficient way to make America hunger-free.

To win public support for a massive expansion of these government programs, they must be reformed and modernized. As I explained in Chapter Four, the current safety net is a confusing array of programs, each of which have different eligibility requirements, application procedures, and physical locations at which people need to apply. There is a far better way. I have proposed combining all these programs into one streamlined, seamless entitlement program available to all families at 185 percent of the poverty line or below (meaning any family of three with a yearly income below $32,500 would be eligible). My colleague, Thomas Z. Freedman, suggested calling this the "American Family Food, Opportunity, and Responsibility" (AFFORd) program. More low-income Americans would be eligible for this program than the existing, separate programs—and eligibility determination and application processes would be dramatically simplified.

There would be one short, universal federal application for AFFORd benefits, which Americans could complete online or during a visit to any office that administers any part of the program. Not only would this significantly increase the amount of nutrition provided to low-income families, it would reduce government paperwork and bureaucracy. AFFORd applications would also tie into annual tax forms, and families who qualify for the Earned Income Tax Credit (EITC) would automatically receive AFFORd benefits if they have incomes below 185 percent of poverty. Any legal immigrant who would otherwise be eligible based on income would be eligible for the program. Families with low incomes would be allowed to save money for their futures and not immediately lose benefits, allowing them to eventually enter the middle class and no longer need benefits at all.

Not only would this program be far easier for low-income families to access, it would also be far easier for the federal, state, and local governments to administer. Right now, each level of government has separate offices to administer all of the overlapping programs. The money saved through the administrative consolidation would be pumped right back into feeding hungry families.

The new program would still allow women and children in the WIC program to get the extra special nutritional and medical help that has made that program so successful, but families would generally have a lot more flexibility in how to use the AFFORd benefits than they do in using the benefits under the current nutrition programs. AFFORd benefits could be used for hot and prepared foods, as well as at farmers' markets, Community Supported Agriculture (CSA) projects (in which people buy shares in local farms), fruit and vegetable carts, and farm stands.

The program would reach far more people than the current Food Stamp Program does and would especially help working families struggling just above the poverty line. Raising eligibility levels to 185 percent of the poverty line (from the current 130 percent in the Food Stamp Program) would increase by 29.8 million, or 57 percent, the number of people eligible for this new program who are not now eligible for food stamps. Such a program would not only significantly reduce hunger, it would be such a large wage supplement that it could help the nation decrease the number of people living in poverty conditions as well.

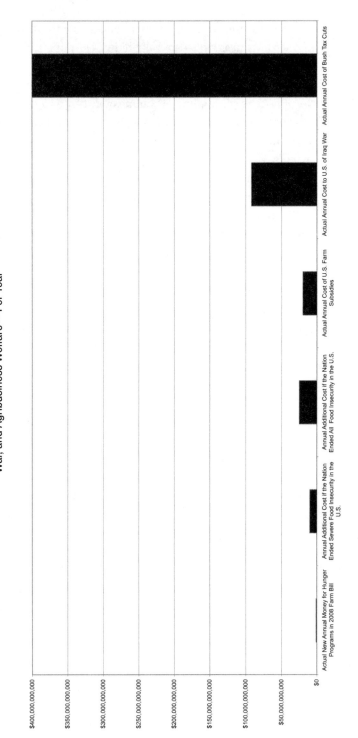

CHART 12A

The Cost of Ending Hunger/Very Low Food Insecurity and of Ending All Food Insecurity vs. the Costs of Tax Cuts, War, and Agribusiness Welfare—Per Year

EVEN BETTER NEWS: IT'S QUITE AFFORDABLE TO END FOOD INSECURITY IN AMERICA

According to the same 2006 USDA report that indicated there were 35.5 million food-insecure Americans, of which 11.1 million lived in households with "very low food security" (hunger), food-insecure people spent an average of thirteen dollars per person per week less on food purchases than did people who were food secure.[2] Multiplying thirteen dollars by fifty-two weeks by 35.5 million people, I calculate that, if Americans with low food security had an additional $24 billion in food purchasing power annually, they would no longer go without enough food. But what about a smaller goal of just ending hunger for the very worst off? The same USDA report also stated that people with "very low food security" (hunger) spent an average of $13.50 per person per week less on food purchases than did people who had enough to eat. Multiplying $13.50 by fifty-two weeks by 11.1 million people with hunger/very low food security, I calculate that, if hungry Americans had an additional $7.8 billion per year in food purchasing power annually, they would no longer suffer from hunger.

Given how hard it was for me to live on an average food stamp allotment of just $28.30 for one week, an extra thirteen dollars might not sound like a lot of money. But since, with careful shopping and cooking help, I was able to marginally scrape by on the $28.30, the extra thirteen dollars really could make the difference between a nutritious and a nonnutritious week, especially given the increased food prices since then. Besides, in 2006, there were about 9 million more food-insecure people than people enrolled in the Food Stamp Program. My calculations assume that all of those 9 million who received no food stamp benefits at all would obtain an extra thirteen dollars a week through the efforts outlined above. Of course, $24 billion is only a rough estimate, because some people would need more than the thirteen dollars and others would need less, but I came up with the number as an object lesson to prove just how affordable it would be to end hunger and food insecurity in America.

That $24 billion number sure *sounds* like a like of money (and it's certainly a bit more than I have in my bank account), but compared to the great amount of wealth concentrated at the very top of our society, it's a drop in the bucket. In 2007, $24 billion represented only 9 percent of the combined net worth of the top ten wealthiest people in America ($217 billion) and only 2 percent of the combined net worth of the *Forbes* list of the 400 richest Americans ($1.54 trillion—yes, trillion). The smaller $7.8 billion amount necessary to eliminate the most severe form of food insecurity in America equaled only 13 percent of Bill Gates's net worth, only 4 percent of the top ten Americans' wealth, and only about 0.5 percent of the collected wealth of the *Forbes* Top 400.

Notice that I said $24 billion in "food purchasing power," which is not quite the same as saying $24 billion in new federal spending. I would be more than happy if wages were increased so much that those dollars alone provided the nation's lowest-wage workers with that much additional food purchasing power. But, the federal budget of course *could* afford to spend $24 billion more fighting hunger— it is simply a matter of priorities. As Chart 12A shows, that $24 billion equals only about 6 percent of the annual cost of President George W. Bush's annual tax cuts, a little more than one quarter of the annual cost of the war in Iraq, or just a little more than what the nation now spends on crop subsidies.

The chart also shows just how little money antihunger advocates settle for before declaring victory. In May 2008, Congress passed a new Farm Bill, over-riding a veto from President Bush. The new law left crop subsidies mostly intact and provided an extra $10 billion for nutrition programs over the subsequent ten years, equaling an extra 1 billion dollars per year. Yet that 1 billion dollars (which equaled only fifty-four cents a week extra for every food insecure person in America), didn't come close to ending hunger in America; it is a number so small that, when compared to other forms of federal spending on Chart 12A, it barely even registered.

If the Bush tax cuts were maintained and put fully into effect, their annual cost, not including additional interest on the national debt, would total about $400 billion per year, sixteen times the cost of ending food insecurity.[3] While Americans have been conned into believing that higher taxes on the wealthy cripple economic growth, long-term economic growth in Western Europe, where taxes on the wealthy are far higher than in the US, has proven that's just not true. Chart 12B shows that the US has the 28th lowest tax burden out of thirty countries, mostly because our taxes on the wealthy are so much less, as a percentage, than taxes on the rest of the world's wealthy. These other nations understand that when higher taxes fund infrastructure, education, and health, then productivity is improved and economic growth is boosted.

I am *not* arguing that low-income and middle-class Americans are under-taxed. When you factor in payroll and sales taxes, most poor and middle-income Americans are *overtaxed*. It is the wealthy in America who are under-taxed and who, if they were taxed at an appropriate rate (as they *used* to be), could easily pay for ending food insecurity and hunger in America.

CHART 12B

Total Taxes as a Percentage of National Gross Domestic Product, 2004

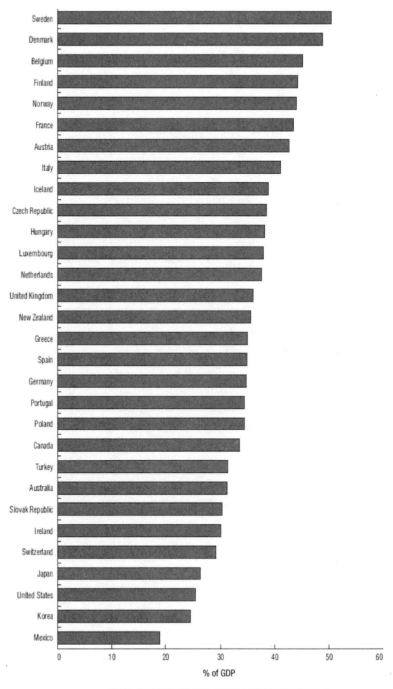

% of GDP

Source: Organization for Economic Cooperation and Development

CHART 12C
Federal Spending on Major Domestic Nutrition Programs vs. Military Spending, 1980–2006 (adjusted for inflation)

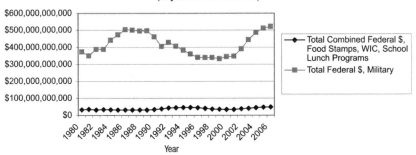

The first five years of war in Iraq cost US taxpayers $448 billion, which averaged $89 billion per year.[4] Consequently, we could entirely end food insecurity in the US for only 27 percent of the annual cost of the Iraq war—or for an amount which equals funding for just three months of combat.

As demonstrated earlier in the book, money for federal nutrition programs has increased slightly faster than the rate of inflation, but Chart 12c puts the issue into fuller perspective by showing how increased nutrition assistance funding was dwarfed by increases in military spending.

Yes, we need a strong military to protect us against real threats to our security. But still—call me crazy—I think feeding all Americans would do more to improve our national security and long-term strength than invading and occupying a nation that couldn't seriously harm us or spending billions on weapons systems needed by no one except campaign-donating defense contractors.

I also return to the topic of crop subsidies, because the coexistence of this colossal corporate welfare with a grossly underfunded hunger safety net exemplifies everything wrong with our current political system. Between 2000 and 2007, US crop subsidies cost the American taxpayer an average of $20.3 billion per year. Given that these corporate handouts increase hunger overseas, provide tax dollars to wealthy Americans who don't need them, and are opposed by many family farmers (who don't get them), it would make sense that some of this money be redirected into food aid.

Thus, there are clearly at least three pots of money available to the federal government to fully fund a plan to end hunger in America. But it will take a great deal of political capital to free up any of those closely guarded pots for that purpose.

UNIVERSAL, IN-CLASSROOM, SCHOOL BREAKFASTS

Another way to dramatically reduce hunger in America—and particularly child hunger—is to ensure that free school meals are available to all children, regardless of income.

As detailed in Chapter Four, because school breakfasts are hampered by both stigma and logistical hurdles, few eligible children receive them. The best way to reverse that trend is for the new president and Congress to agree to provide universal school breakfast to all children free of charge, and to do so directly in first-period classrooms. Both universal and in-classroom breakfasts have already proven their success in select school districts nationwide. For instance, in Newark, New Jersey—where both are utilized—the district has a 94 percent breakfast participation rate. When I visited Newark to check out the effort for myself, I was thrilled to find elementary school student breakfast monitors cheerfully delivering breakfasts to all their peers. I also learned of a local high school in which the number of breakfasts served increased literally tenfold after the meals were provided in classrooms.

In 2008, New York City launched a pilot project to try out in-classroom breakfasts in a number of schools. While I have obviously been very critical of Mayor Bloomberg in this book, I must point out that, on school meal issues, his administration has been excellent. They've improved the nutritional quality of school meals and greatly expanded participation through some innovative initiatives. At one pilot site I visited, Public School 68 in the Bronx, every student ate breakfast together during their first-period class. The pilot is working better than anyone could have anticipated. The school's principal told me that, before the pilot, an average of fifty kids came to school late every day, so many that she had to assign extra staff to write out late slips. When they started serving breakfast in their classrooms, kids came in early just for the meals, and now only about five kids a day are late—a 900 percent decrease in tardiness. The principal also told me that absenteeism and visits to school nurses also dropped, and in the afternoons, kids fell asleep in the classrooms less frequently. This is obviously not only good nutrition policy but also good education policy.

Given that most school districts must now have a complex system in place to collect forms and data on the income of each student's parents to determine the eligibility of each child for either free, reduced-price, or full-cost meals, when a district adopts a universal breakfast or lunch policy, not only does it reduce the stigma faced by children and thereby increase participation, it also reduces the paperwork and bureaucracy, saving the school district time and money. When kids eat breakfast in a classroom instead of a lunchroom that is a hallway or two away, they have more time to focus on their studies and are protected from the stigma of having to leave their friends to go to a special breakfast room "for the poor kids."

Given that textbooks are widely understood to be a critical educational tool, public school districts typically lend them out free of charge to all students. The time is ripe for the nation to view school meals in the same way. Free breakfast and lunch should be universal in all classrooms around the country.

Access to summer meals for children also needs to be simplified and expanded. In July 2006, only 18 percent of low-income children who received school lunches received summer meals, according to the Food Research and Action Center (FRAC). That means that 78 percent of kids who received government food support during the school year failed to also get it in the summer, when their caloric needs are likely even higher. After-school snacks and supper programs also have similarly low participation rates.

To increase participation in both summer and after-school feeding programs, the president and Congress need to ease eligibility rules, increase reimbursement rates for program sponsors, and reduce the paperwork necessary to be a sponsor. All those improvements, as well as a move to universal in-classroom breakfasts, could be accomplished through the next Child Nutrition Reauthorization Bill, scheduled to be considered by Congress in 2009.

THE ROLE OF THE STATES

Another way to fight hunger is to reward states that succeed in reducing their rates of hunger and food insecurity. Given that federal law places most of the authority for actually administering federal nutrition assistance programs with the states, their role is crucial. Currently, the federal government monetarily punishes states for food stamp "error rates," or the number of paperwork mistakes that states make. In recent years, the USDA has also given some limited rewards for states that improve food stamp access, but, still, the funding is based mostly on measuring the success of administrative processes, not necessarily on how well the states do in reducing hunger.

I propose creating a special program to reward states that do the best job in actually reducing hunger and food insecurity, moving beyond bonuses for mere process improvements.

Here is how it could work: Every three years, the USDA would provide monetary bonuses of up to 10 million dollars each to ten states, with the amount of money provided being proportional to the size of their populations. Five of the states would be those that had the greatest reduction in the three-year averages for their USDA-measured food insecurity rates. However, since food insecurity is often dependent on factors other than food programs (such as poverty), the other five awards would be given to states that had the most success in reducing food insecurity relative to their poverty line. In addition, a special additional bonus could be awarded to any state that demonstrates it has ended child hunger. States would then be required to use those bonuses to expand and improve existing antihunger and antipoverty programs. Such incentives would draw attention to truly effective antihunger programs, which would serve as models for other states. The program would focus on quantifying success with published numbers every year, and sharing research on what works.

A PROGRESSIVE FAITH-BASED AND COMMUNITY INITIATIVE

Another aspect of government spending that is in need of reform is the ongoing issue of federal faith-based initiatives. President George W. Bush turned his own faith-based initiative into mere political window dressing. In addition, when he failed to convince Congress to pass the Charity Aid, Recovery and Empowerment Act that would have allow faith-based organizations to use federal funds to proselytize and discriminate, he went around Congress by signing executive orders to try to achieve those ends through federal agencies. In reaction, some Democrats wanted to shut the whole effort down entirely, which is a shame, because Bush *was* correct about a central point—government should help to increase the involvement of churches, synagogues, mosques, and temples in tackling America's most pressing social problems. Not a penny of government money should be used to proselytize or discriminate. But their often-excellent work, which strengthens and enables communities and is rooted within them, would be a most powerful tool for alleviating hunger.

In fact, long before George W. Bush became president, many federal agencies had already begun efforts to partner with religious groups. For example, the USDA Community Food Security Initiative, which I ran—and which was, absurdly, opposed by the Republican Congress and ended by the Bush administration—worked closely with both faith-based and secular groups throughout the country to fight hunger and strengthen neighborhoods. Providing such organizations with technical assistance, national publicity, staff support, and (when Congress let us) limited seed money, we began to see increases and improvements in their services. It is no wonder that Vice President Gore, when running for president in 2000, proposed expanding such efforts.

Forging such partnerships isn't easy. It can't be done on just "a wing and a prayer." And it can't be accomplished solely by leaders using the bully pulpit to encourage citizens to donate and volunteer more either. If the government wants these groups to substantially increase their services, then the government must provide them with a substantial increase in resources—including direct funding, technical assistance, staff support, and surplus property and real estate.

Government should allow nonprofit groups—as well as state, local, and tribal government agencies—to compete equally with faith-based organizations for the right to aid local social services. Not all faith-based organizations are effective, and not all effective grassroots social service organizations are faith-based. No single faith-based organization should automatically be granted a monopoly over any service area or task. Since Republicans keep telling us that competition always improves services, they should particularly embrace this suggestion.

Government should also overhaul its procedures for running programs and awarding funds by modernizing procedures for federal grants, cooperative agreements, contracting, and financial management in order to meet the unique needs of nonprofit groups. Most government grant management systems are the worst of both worlds: they require a mountain of paperwork but do little to ensure that grantees use the money well and run their programs effectively. These systems should be entirely revamped to make tracking performance more important than checking the right boxes on the paperwork.

It is always vital to make clear that such nonprofit efforts are intended to supplement—not replace—a strong federal government safety net. Most faith-based organizations—already reeling under the additional burdens placed upon them by welfare reform and bad economic conditions—are barely able to keep up with their current caseloads. They would be the first to tell the federal government to strengthen—not cut—core federal programs that provide low-income families with food, child care, housing, and health care. We must again ensure that government does what it does best (providing a basic safety net, ensuring equal rights and equal protection in programs, guaranteeing uniform coverage of benefits, etc.), so that faith-based and secular nonprofit groups would be freed up to do what they do (providing individual attention to people, building a sense of community, and rapidly responding to changing conditions, etc.).

In July 2008, Barack Obama proposed a faith-based social services plan that embraced virtually all of the above principles, including an equal role for secular organizations and a strict prohibition on proselytizing and discriminating with federal monies.[5] Yet he was roundly excoriated by the Left and the Net Roots, who claimed he was shredding the Constitution. Even the *New York Times* editorial board, which had previously editorialized in favor of more government funding for pantries and kitchens (the vast majority of which are faith-based), fumed that Obama's proposal "violates the separation of church and state."[6]

Such reactions are mostly a knee-jerk aversion to anything merely associated with George W. Bush. But that's counterproductive. If a stopped clock can be right twice a day, so can Bush. Moreover, it's hypocritical for progressives to automatically oppose the involvement of religious groups in the public sphere when they embraced—rightfully so—the efforts of the Reverends Dr. Martin Luther King, Jr., William Sloane Coffin, and Jesse Jackson, Sr., to connect religious imperatives with public policy. After all, the Civil Rights Movement was, at its core, a faith-based initiative.

So the debate shouldn't be over whether religious groups should be involved in the fight against hunger. They already are, up to their necks. The real debate should be over whether they can obtain serious resources needed to do so more effectively.

Religious organizations are already doing more than their part to fight hunger, but they could do even more if they used their resources and influence both to fight for better public policies and to provide technical assistance to struggling pantries and kitchens who are trying to provide self-sufficiency-boosting social services beyond food. For example, the Episcopal Diocese of New York, the Trinity Church Grants Program, the Cathedral Church of Saint John the Divine, and the New York City Coalition Against Hunger came together to launch the Feed the Solution initiative in 2004, which combined public policy advocacy work with technical assistance provision to build the capacities of Episcopal-run feeding programs.

Religious leaders make particularly compelling advocates. They have a unique ability to describe the limits of their charitable efforts and the moral imperative for government agencies to take the lead in solving problems. For those reasons, the Feed the Solution initiative helped us achieve a number of significant public policy victories at the city and the state levels while helping local feeding agencies better serve their clients. It provided an effective model for how other religious denominations can make a difference.

THE ROLE OF FOOD PANTRIES AND SOUP KITCHENS

Kitchens and pantries should do more to provide their customers with more choices, less stigma, and more power. In New York City, the West Side Campaign Against Hunger (WSCAH) was among a few food pantries nationwide that pioneered an entirely new "supermarket-style, customer choice model" of providing food. At most pantries, people are given a preselected bag of food—the same as every other bag of food no matter what they or their family actually need. But in the customer choice system, people are allotted a certain number of points and then they may "shop," choosing as many items (which are also coded on a points basis, with meats usually having the highest point value and produce the lowest) as they can purchase with their points, thereby being able to choose items that best meet the needs of their families. WSCAH goes to great lengths to empower its customers, who volunteer to conduct many of the tasks needed to run the pantry and who also serve on its board. Such customer choice pantries cost more money, need more space, and utilize more staff time than regular pantries, but they are well worth the extra effort. More pantries nationwide should adopt this model.

Because most grassroots pantries and kitchens are tiny and entirely volunteer-run, it is not realistic to expect that all of them will automatically become all-purpose social service agencies. But every feeding program should engage in at least a little advocacy for improved public policies and should consistently make it clear that charity never could—and never should—replace government. It is also reasonable to ask every feeding agency in America to take at least one other step to bolster the self-sufficiency of their clients/customers, by helping them to obtain government nutrition assistance and/or antipoverty benefits; engage in local food production or marketing activities; increase their nutritional knowledge; gain job skills; or otherwise advance their economic and job security. Food banks and food rescue groups should encourage their member pantries and kitchens to do all those things.

Many pantries and kitchens have already done just that. In 2000, just before I joined the group as executive director, the New York City Coalition Against Hunger launched the pioneering Emergency Food Action Center to provide technical assistance to help pantries and kitchen provide additional, non-food, services. Partially as a result of that work, many more feeding agencies are enabling their clients/customers to obtain federal EITC payments and WIC benefits. Others are starting Customer Advisory Boards to better enable their clients to play leadership roles in the operations of the feeding program and in government advocacy efforts. Some launched after-school and summer feeding programs for children. Still others started community gardens.

The Coalition also helped start a pilot project to help people apply online for food stamp benefits on-site at a few pantries and kitchens. This involves physically scanning in all their required documents at the location, and, for some, enabling them to avoid entirely a time-consuming and often-humiliating visit to a government office in order to get their food stamp benefits. Out of the first groups of people processed through this new and innovative system, more than 75 percent received food stamps, which is a far higher percentage than for any other food stamp outreach project with which I am familiar.

Across the nation, pantries and kitchens are empowering the people they help with more than just food. One food pantry in Milwaukee, operated by a local hospital, has a special clinic to help people prevent and treat high blood pressure, diabetes, and other ailments. The director of the program, Bill Solberg, said, "We're taking a window of opportunity approach. We know we can see these people once a month."[7]

Perhaps the most exciting project that the organization I manage has helped initiate is an effort that connected pantries and kitchens in Harlem and Queens and enables them to collectively bring fresh produce from a small upstate New York organic farm into the neighborhoods. Some of the produce was distributed free through the pantries and kitchens, some of it was purchased by low-income residents using scholarship funds or food stamp benefits, and the remainder was bought at market prices by middle-class people in the neighborhood.

Willie Sutton, the famous bank robber, was once asked why he robbed banks. He responded, "That's where the money is." When asked why the organization I head uses food pantries and soup kitchens as prime places at which to provide social services and self-sufficiency aid, I say, "That's where the poor and hungry people are." For that reason, I always tell government officials and private donors that one of the best places to pilot a new antipoverty initiative is at a feeding program. But these tiny, strapped agencies will need far greater resources to do so.

THE BUSINESS COMMUNITY

In addition to bolstering the nutritional safety net, the president and Congress must also stand up to the business community. It is high time.

First and foremost, businesses should be pressured to ensure that their workers—as well as the workers of their contractors, including the contractors that hire people to clean or guard their offices at night—are paid living wages, provided full benefits, are guaranteed safe working conditions, are allowed to bargain collectively, and are given paid family and medical leave, as well as vacation and sick leave. Investing in workers will both reduce workers' hunger (and that of their families) and boost their long-term productivity. American businesses should also make a commitment to keeping as many jobs as possible in the United States.

The business community should certainly donate money and food to anti-hunger and antipoverty organizations, but when they do so, they should do it on top of—*not instead of*—providing adequate compensation to their workers.

Businesses should also be challenged to limit the disparity between what their highest-paid executives and their lowest-paid workers earn. A few decades ago, CEOs made 209 times what the average worker made, which was already a far higher ratio than in most of the world's major industrialized nations. In 2007, CEOs made at least 400 times as much. I propose that CEOs voluntarily limit their compensation to no more than one hundred times that of their lowest paid workers. Thus, in a company at which the lowest-paid worker earned $20,000 a year, the CEO could still earn $2 million, which he or she might not think is much, but is actually five times what the president of the United States makes. Currently, business leaders are rewarded with higher salaries for limiting worker wages and downsizing payrolls. But if a CEO voluntary pegged his or her pay to no more than one hundred times the pay of their lowest-paid workers, that would give the tangible incentive to actually raise worker pay. Thus, in the example above, if the CEO raised minimum salaries of his or her workers to $40,000, then she or he could raise their own salary to $4 million. Besides, the 1-to-100 pay ratio that I propose is far more generous than the ratio at more progressive companies like Ben & Jerry's, where, in 2001, the highest-ranking executive earned only sixteen times the salary of the lowest-paid employee.

Business executives should take all those steps voluntarily, out of patriotism and a sense of common good. But if they don't, the government should step in. In 2008, the Netherlands was up in arms about large payouts to corporate leaders, even though executive pay there was 25 percent less than in the US. As a result, the Dutch finance minister sent a bill to their parliament limiting executive windfalls.[8] The US should consider similar measures. The US should also increase minimum wage levels; require that companies and organizations getting government grants and contracts pay their employees living wages; and end tax breaks that encourage companies to downsize or outsource jobs while increasing executive pay. Furthermore, businesses should stop hiding behind their trade associations and lobbyists who work effectively on their behalf to oppose such measures.

The business community should also design job training and job apprenticeship programs that promise living wage, career-ladder jobs to people who successfully complete such programs.

More businesses should encourage their employees to volunteer at antihunger and antipoverty charities. But when they do, they should also move beyond the common practice of encouraging large groups of employees to volunteer just once or a few times a year in large group events. Rather, businesses should widely encourage employees with professional expertise (in accounting, law, public relations, technology, marketing, etc.) to volunteer, either on company time or their private time, in the most effective way possible, working on their own or in very small groups to "adopt" a nonprofit agency and to apply their professional skills to help that agency build its long-term capacities.

WHY THE AMERICAN PEOPLE WOULD EMBRACE THIS PLAN

Public opinion polling seems to indicate that, if a president proposed to end hunger in the way I have outlined, the proposal would likely garner broad, bipartisan support from average Americans. A bipartisan poll in 2007 examined what the pollsters called "Do Right Voters"—people who "urgently wanted policy action to solve problems like hunger and poverty"—and found 46 percent of the people in the category were Democrats, 27 percent were Republicans, and 16 percent were Independents. Of course, the Do Right Voters were far more likely to be in households with lower income levels.[9]

A 2007 survey by the polling firm Peter D. Hart Research Associates on behalf of antihunger groups found that 78 percent of voters think hunger is a problem in America, 57 percent feel that the government is spending too little on antihunger programs, and 81 percent believe food stamps are important. Seventy-nine percent said they would increase the minimum monthly food stamp benefit (which was then $10), but when they were told most of the people who would get that benefit were elderly or disabled, that number shot up to 90 percent. Yet when they were read arguments in support of increasing food stamp benefits (that current benefits don't keep up with rising costs) alongside language opposing such a move (that food stamps were meant to simply supplement other food spending and that the government can't afford this extra spending), support dropped to 66 percent.[10]

These results don't mean that Americans necessarily share the view of advocates that expanding the Food Stamp Program is the single best way to fight hunger. When people are asked an open-ended question about how to end hunger in America, they often pick private charity and local government as the top entities to solve the problem, followed by state government and then, as a last resort, the federal government. In other words, without being given details of the status quo—in which federal programs provide the most significant funding and local programs the least—voters have a hazy idea that they prefer a situation that is almost exactly the reverse of today's reality.

Polling also shows that "even voters who strongly believe in helping the poor and hungry will balk at increasing programs they view to be ineffective." Also, when voters were asked to evaluate government's response to hunger, 46 percent said, "The government is not making a big effort to reduce hunger" while 33 percent said, "Government is making a big effort to fight hunger, but it is not working." Only 14 percent thought, "The government is making a big effort to reduce hunger, and it is working." Voters across the political spectrum also strongly believed that federal nutrition assistance programs should promote self-sufficiency.[11]

People hold complex and sometimes conflicting opinions regarding poverty policies, as evidenced by detailed annual polling conducted by the Pew

Research Center for the People & the Press.[12] In 2007, Pew found that 69 percent of all Americans, 83 percent of Republicans, and 60 percent of Democrats believe that poor people have become too dependent on government programs. Notably, reported Pew, 63 percent of those who say the poor are too dependent also believe that the government has a responsibility to take care of people who cannot take care of themselves. And nearly half of those who say the poor have become too dependent on the government (48 percent) also agree with the statement: "The government should help more needy people even if it means going deeper in debt." Who ever said human beings were consistent?

The single most popular policy prescription continues to be ensuring that work pays. Fully 93 percent of Democrats, 85 percent of Independents, and even 69 percent of Republicans told Pew in 2007 that they favored raising the minimum wage. Even three quarters of small business owners supported raising the minimum wage, which is particularly striking because the organizations that purport to represent small businesses usually oppose such wage hikes.

What do these polling numbers tell us? First, it's clear that we need to do a better job of telling the story of how existing federal nutrition assistance programs *are* working, and how they promote work and strengthen families by enabling parents to feed their children while staying employed.

Second, these polls tell us that the American people would only support an expansion of federal nutrition programs if they were reformed and modernized, exactly what my plan would do. Also, by giving more aid to struggling working families just above the poverty line, my plan is perfectly in line with the nation's desire to promote work. It is also clear that the public would widely support my calls to provide more meaningful aid to nonprofit groups and to pressure big businesses to pay living wages.

WHO WOULD OPPOSE THIS PLAN, AND WHY

My plan would run into a buzz saw of opposition from a wide range of special interests. Conservative fiscal watchdogs would oppose an increase in social spending. Liberal groups would object to increased aid to faith-based agencies. Business organizations would fight efforts to raise wages. Agribusinesses and their campaign-donor lobbyists would defend crop subsidies. Many wealthy Americans—who also give heavily to campaigns—would object to having their taxes raised.

Even many of the people who work for national hunger groups, including people who are personal friends of mine (and with whom I agree on 99 percent of the issues)—are critical of the plan—particularly the part about combining existing federal nutrition assistance programs into one new streamlined program.

A few antihunger advocates and service providers who oppose my reforms likely do so because they are afraid of angering the agribusinesses that fund their organizations and that help get Congress to fund food stamps as parts of Farm Bills. A few others may fear—either consciously or not—that restoring the role of government would reduce the role of nonprofits and thus possibly put them out of work.

However, there is one very valid, progressive criticism that some fellow advocates have of my plan: if all nutrition programs were combined, it might make it easier for future conservative political leaders to cut them all at once. The worry is that my plan sounds too much like "block grants," a term used by conservatives to justify slashing programs under the guise of merely combining them. There is certainly great validity to that fear, but I believe it overlooks that old adage that the best defense is a strong offense, and that, if keeping the programs separate makes it difficult to decrease all their funding at once, keeping them apart also makes it more difficult to increase their funding all at once.

Some friends who oppose my proposal have said, "Why fix what's not broken, Joel? The only major thing wrong with our existing nutrition assistance programs is that they are underfunded." Fair enough. As I've hammered home throughout this book, it is true that programs such as food stamps, WIC, and school lunches have nearly wiped out large-scale starvation in America, a vital accomplishment that should not be understated—and, if they were significantly expanded, they could further decrease hunger.

But while these programs have reduced severe hunger, they have not ended hunger, and they have barely dented *poverty*. Thus, it's not that these programs aren't working—as many conservatives falsely charge—it's that they were never really designed to significantly reduce the poverty that causes hunger in the first place.

Plus, as I have demonstrated in Chapter Four, the existing safety net reaches far too few people and has not adequately adapted as recipients evolved from being on welfare to entering the workforce. As I've said earlier, any system in which a third of those eligible don't receive the help they need is broken. The time is long overdue for major reforms of these nutrition programs, most enacted more than thirty to forty years ago.

What is the Best Way to End Hunger in the US?

In 2006, there were:

> **35.5 million** food-insecure Americans

If we were to...

We would have...

Double the nation's *charitable* food distribution system

> **32 million** food-insecure Americans

Or, if we were to...

We would have...

Increase the *federal* nutrition assistance programs by **10%**

> **26.7 million** food-insecure Americans

Increase the *federal* nutrition assistance programs by **20%**

> **18.2 million** food-insecure Americans

Increase the *federal* nutrition assistance programs by **40%**

> **0.7 million** food-insecure Americans

Increase the *federal* nutrition assistance programs by **41%**

> **ZERO** food-insecure Americans

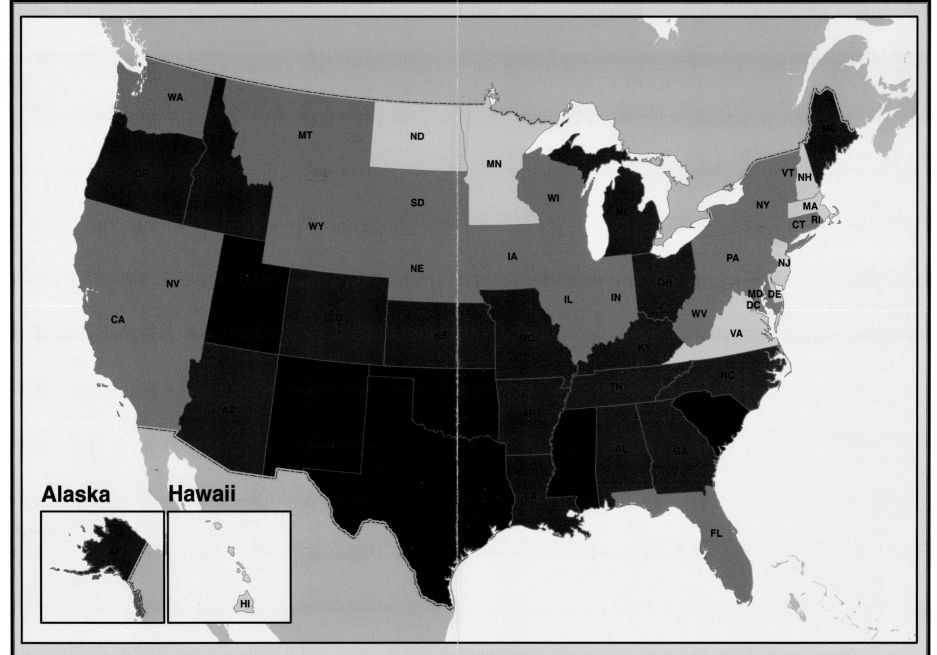

Alaska   Hawaii

% of Population with Food Insecurity, by State

Food Insecurity in the United States of America, 2006

Source: "Household Food Security in the United States, 2006,"
United States Department of Agriculture, November 2007.

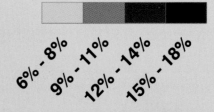

6% - 8%   9% - 11%   12% - 14%   15% - 18%

I want to once again emphasize that an inefficient, somewhat outdated, and patronizing safety net is far better than no safety net at all. Without the system in place, America really could experience mass malnutrition for the first time since the Depression.

Conservatives offer nothing but less government (less government for *low-income people* that is). But traditional liberals have offered little more than the same generally underperforming government, albeit with less incompetent management and a bit more funding.

In a nation that has zillions of choices when it comes to items such as water (tap vs. bottled, flavored vs. unflavored, sugared vs. nonsugared, even caffeinated vs. decaffeinated, etc.), why must our policy choices be so limited?

I vote for a better choice: a forward-thinking middle ground that achieves massive change but uses mainstream values and common-sense approaches to achieve that change. That's my plan.

To enact it, we'll need both a massive grassroots movement and serious national leadership. There is no time to waste. After all, we all want to be able to, once again, sleep at night.

CHAPTER 13

BOLSTERING COMMUNITY FOOD PRODUCTION AND MARKETING

Cultivators of the earth are the most valuable citizens. They are the most vigorous, the most independent, the most virtuous, and they are tied to their country and wedded to its liberty and interests by the most lasting bands.

—Thomas Jefferson[1]

Amid the tightly packed row houses of North Philadelphia, a pioneering urban farm is providing fresh local food for a community that often lacks it, and making money in the process. Greensgrow, a one-acre plot of raised beds and greenhouses on the site of a former steel-galvanizing factory, is turning a profit by selling its own vegetables and herbs, as well as a range of produce from local growers. . . . The farm, in the low-income Kensington section . . . also makes it own honey—marketed as "Honey from the Hood."

—New York Times, May 20, 2008[2]

In the spring of 2008, the *New York Times* ran a series of articles and op-eds featuring high-profile food activists who argued that the recent spike in food prices could be a good thing. In an article titled, "Some Good News on Food Prices," Michael Pollan, sustainable food guru and author of popular books *In Defense of Food* and *The Omnivore's Dilemma*, said, "Higher food prices level the playing field for sustainable food that doesn't rely on fossil fuels."[3] In other words, he predicted that, because processed, mass-produced foods would become just as expensive as organic, locally produced foods, consumers would

259

make better food choices. But even if nonorganic processed foods did become as expensive as organic foods (which, as of mid-2008, had not come even close to happening), Pollan still cavalierly overlooks the reality that price hikes on either type of food place severe pressure on struggling families.

Similarly, food activist Dan Barber opined: "If financially pinched Americans opt for the cheapest (and the least healthful) foods rather than cook their own, the food industry will continue to reach for the lowest common denominator. But it is possible to nudge the revolution along—for instance, by changing how we measure the value of food. If we stop calculating the cost per quantity and begin considering the cost per nutrient value, the demand for higher-quality food would rise."[4] Note his claim that poor people purposely "opt" to eat low-quality food.

Asked by a reporter what families should do if they cannot afford enough food as a result of the price hikes, organic foods diva and celebrity chef Alice Waters, whose restaurant in Berkeley, California, charges between fifty-five and eighty-five dollars per person for dinner, said families should "make a sacrifice on the cell phone or the third pair of Nike shoes."[5] Pollan, Barber, and Waters alike seem oblivious to the harsh truth that, for many Americans, rising food prices threaten their ability to afford food at all. Even though most food activists are well intentioned and understandably disturbed by the trend of increasing domination by just a handful of massive food conglomerates, they often display glaring class bias. The growing community food security movement in America is a much-needed force that aims to aid small farmers and promote organic or sustainable food, but I hope that they can join with the antihunger movement in making the needs of the lowest-income Americans central to any proposed solutions.

FAMILY FARMERS: AN ENDANGERED SPECIES

It is worth considering one of the most pronounced trends in modern America that has inspired community food production organizing—the accelerating consolidation and corporate control of the entities that grow, process, transport, and sell our foods. Given the trouble our world has gotten into because oil—which, arguably, is not absolutely vital for human survival—is controlled by just a few colossal companies, imagine what calamities await us when the same is true for food. We're fast heading in that direction.

In 1990, 72 percent of all US beef was packed by the top four firms; by 2003, 84 percent of beef was packed by the same four companies. Between 1982 and 2004, the amount of flour milled by the top four companies rose from 40 percent to 63 percent. The percentage of pork packed by the top four firms nearly doubled between 1987 and 2003, raising their control to 63 percent of the market.[6]

With smaller competitors shoved out of the way, massive processors and distributors snare an ever-increasing share of the food economy's dollars, and are free to pay small farmers less and less for their product. In 2007, out of a $4.00 gallon of milk, dairy farmers received $1.60; out of a pound of bread that retailed from $2.49, farmers got $0.10; out of two pounds of lettuce that retailed for $1.79 cents, farmers received $0.28; and out of one pound of sirloin steak that sold for $7.99, farmers got $0.94.[7] The future of family farming in America is grim. According to the USDA, American farmers are more than four times as likely to be above the age of sixty-five as below the age of thirty-four. About 27 percent of farm operators report their age as sixty-five years and older, compared to only 7 percent of self-employed workers in other industries. Average farms were about three times as large in 2002 as in 1835. Small farms tend to make so little income today that households operating small farms typically receive substantial off-farm income. For households operating limited-resource or retirement farms, more than half of their off-farm income comes from unearned sources—such as Social Security, pensions, dividends, interest, and rent—reflecting the advanced age of those operators.[8]

Small farmers are continuously exposed to greater financial risk than people in virtually any other industry: if there is frost, hail, an infestation of insects, or too much or too little heat or rain, they can lose all of their crops. If food prices—which fluctuate more wildly than prices for most other things—plummet, farmers can lose their entire income for the year, and go further into debt. It is obvious why so many farmers need a second (and often third) source of income to survive. Also, in a trend that should alarm everyone, the nation's farmland is rapidly being devoured, transforming into condominium developments, golf courses, and shopping malls.

Independent grocery stores are also disappearing. As Chart 13A shows, in just the thirteen-year period between 1987 and 2000, there was a tremendous consolidation in the grocery industry. Today most supermarkets are owned by a handful of chains, which are more likely to close stores in low-income communities and neighborhoods. While consumer prices sometimes drop in the

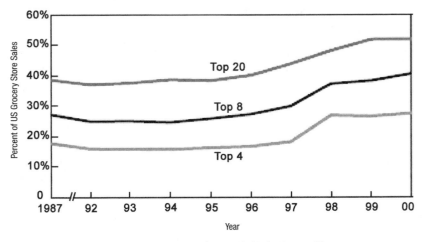

CHART 13A
Consolidation Has Contributed to Increased Shares of Grocery Store Sales
by the Largest 4, 8, and 20 Retailers

Source: USDA Economic Research Service, *Food Review*, Summer/Fall 2002

fevered competition that leads up to consolidation, after other competition is driven out of business, prices often again increase.

The fortunes of farmers and consumers are wholly dependent upon each other. Farmers need strong consumers in order to remain economically healthy. Consumers need strong farmers to remain physically healthy, which of course, affects their economic health as well. The problem is that these connections are increasingly frayed.

People who work on these intersecting issues like to use the term "food systems," a wonkish phrase that basically encompasses the entire interlocking web of food production, processing, distribution, and consumption—from farm to fork. Today's food systems are dysfunctional, particularly in urban neighborhoods and rural towns with high poverty rates. Too many neighborhoods bear high costs of buying food, but don't benefit from the income and economic growth associated with producing, processing, and selling food. Neighborhood residents have to rely too much on their local bodegas (small corner grocery stores that carry a very limited selection of foods) or convenience stores, where it's usually easier to buy cigarettes, beer, and potato chips than whole-grain bread or fresh produce.

GRASSROOTS FOOD ACTIVISTS FIGHT BACK: THE GROWTH OF THE COMMUNITY FOOD SECURITY MOVEMENT

Community food security work, at its best, can bring new supermarkets into inner city neighborhoods; develop and mentor new farmers; promote nutrition education; establish new farmers' markets in low-income neighborhoods; launch urban farms; and start food-related small businesses. Generally, but not always, such projects use sustainable and organic growing methods. The Community Food Security Coalition—the national organization most associated with this crusade—says that the movement's goals are to "Ensure access to affordable, nutritious, and culturally appropriate food for all people at all times . . . develop self-reliance among all communities in obtaining their food and to create a system of growing, manufacturing, processing, making available, and selling food that is regionally based and grounded in the principles of justice, democracy, and sustainability."

Exciting and innovative food security projects abound. I even visited one, in the basement of a building on the urban campus at Brooklyn College, in which a professor was experimenting with ways to help low-income people farm their own edible fish.

One of the hallmarks of the community food security movement is creating ways through which small agricultural producers can market directly to consumers, cutting out profit-sapping intermediaries. One popular way of doing this is creating Community Supported Agriculture (CSA) farms that enable consumers to provide up-front cash to purchase shares of that year's output from the farm. The shareholders then receive a portion of what the farm produces each week over the growing season. This reduces the risk for the farmer and provides fresh, delicious, and sometimes competitively priced, food for the shareholders.

Other popular methods of direct marketing are increasing nationwide: farmers' markets, online sales of farm products, and farm stands. Much work has also gone into helping farmers directly sell their products to school systems and other large institutions, earning money that can potentially dwarf their combined income from all other sources.

THE CLASS BIAS OF SOME FOOD ACTIVISTS

While the local and sustainable food ethos has been taking on new converts daily and its growth is encouraging, as Alice Waters's earlier comments illustrate, the movement—while idealistic in its belief that all food should be nutritious, organically grown, and delicious—too-often demonstrates a pronounced class bias. Some of these advocates—as well as their brethren in the related "slow foods" crusade—even imply that one must purchase food that is both local and organic; grow your own food in gardens; reject any food that is processed; refuse to shop at chain supermarkets; spurn food from major manufacturers; scorn all fast food; and cook all your meals from scratch, preferably very slowly. These assertions often ignore the reality that people in poverty rarely have the time and money to do all those things. Perhaps the most egregious example of this attitude is the assertion that increasing food prices are a good thing because they deter people from buying junk food.

It's worth examining all those assumptions. While the official USDA distinction between foods that are organic and nonorganic is a bit fuzzy, most people take it as an article of faith that organic food is automatically healthier for humans than its nonorganic counterparts. Yet, while some studies show that organic food *may* be marginally healthier, the Mayo Clinic declared: "No conclusive evidence shows that organic food is more nutritious than is conventionally grown food. . . . Some people buy organic food to limit their exposure to [pesticide] residues. Most experts agree, however, that the amount of pesticides found on fruits and vegetables poses a very small health risk."[9]

Don't get me wrong, there are plenty of good environmental reasons to buy organic food, and, if the crops are actually grown by small farmers who pay their workers a living wage, there are also excellent social justice reasons to do so. I buy organic food whenever I can (much of it from a glorious farmers' market down the street from where I live), but I can *afford* to do so. The point is that many families *can't* afford to shop that way because organic produce is almost always more expensive than the nonorganic kind. People who give the impression that it's better to have no fruit or vegetables at all than it is to have nonorganic produce are doing low-income families a grave disservice. After all, there are mountains of scientific evidence that people who eat large amounts of fresh fruits and vegetables (whether organic or nonorganic) are likely to significantly reduce their risks of diabetes, obesity, heart disease, cancer, and stroke. In contrast, most scientific studies indicate that, if people eat nonorganic produce throughout their lives, the trace pesticides on their fruits *may* very slightly increase their chances of getting cancer down the line, especially if produce is not washed before eating. Less than perfect produce is *far* healthier than no produce at all.

There is also an obsession among food activists for food that is locally grown. Certainly, it is better to purchase food grown as close to home as possible. Such food tends to be fresher and, of course, less fuel is used to transport it. But writer Sarah Murray has made the point that some food grown farther away could potentially be *more* environmentally friendly than food grown much closer—if the food at the further distance was grown in a way that was less environmentally harmful than was the local food.[10] Additionally, local food is just as likely to be harvested by exploited immigrant farm workers as food grown somewhere else. Simply being local doesn't mean a farm is a social justice utopia. After all, the worst-polluting, labor-abusing behemoth farm operations are "local" *somewhere.*

Plus, we must remember that the international food distribution system, for all its vast faults, does have certain benefits, including consumer health benefits. When people in frigid northern cities in the dead of winter can buy fresh fruit from Florida or Chile, it is good for both their bodies and their spirits. Also, given how many Americans are immigrants, the international food system does play a helpful role by allowing people to eat foods from their homelands. In contrast, if you live in the northern United States and are a Caribbean immigrant following the strict dictates of buy-local advocates, you'd never be able to have plantains or coconuts again, which would be a pretty big denial of your heritage. Some of the most extreme food advocates forget that good nutrition and sustainable living should be about independent choices and overall balance.

While increasing the consumption of organic and locally grown foods are important goals, too many community food security advocates act like they are the *only* goals. Sometimes they even scoff at the notion that lower food prices could ever be a good thing, believing that would automatically mean the environment was harmed and small farmers were shafted. Even if all those things were the case, we can't ignore the fact that lower food prices *are* better for low- and middle-income Americans, and that the most nutritious food is often the most expensive food. As Raj Patel wrote in his book *Stuffed and Starved,* "To be able to go on a culinary odyssey in the first place, and to be truly at liberty to savor food . . . the majority of people need that passport to all other freedoms— money."[11]

While there are many good reasons to slam Wal-Mart, we must keep in mind that their lower prices *do* provide genuine relief to struggling families. It is no wonder then that, according to the Pew Center for the People & the Press, two thirds of working-class Democrats have a favorable view of Wal-Mart compared with only 45 percent in the professional class.

GROWING OUR OWN FOOD: THE POLITICS OF COMMUNITY GARDENS

When I worked at the USDA, I briefly led the federal government's efforts to expand community gardens. The nonprofit organization I now run provides AmeriCorps national service participants to aid community gardens. I no doubt agree it would be helpful if more poor communities were able to grow more of their own food. Food-producing community gardens improve diets by increasing fruit and vegetable consumption, reduce crime by turning empty lots into safe spaces, teach people about nutrition in a hands-on manner, and generally improve the community spirit in neighborhoods in which they are located.

But we need to be mindful of how impractical community gardens are as a mass response to hunger and poor nutrition. In a 2008 essay, Michael Pollan wrote that everyone should be "growing some—even just a little—of your own food. Rip out your lawn, if you have one, and if you don't—if you live in a high-rise, or have a yard shrouded in shade—look into getting a plot in a community garden." He then said that getting your equipment and tools should not involve "too many drives to the garden center."[12] Pollan seems to assume that everyone has a car and lives somewhere where there even *is* a garden center. Surely, those who have the ability and desire to do so should grow more of their own food. But the suggestion that *everyone* should participate in a community garden is absurd. Pollan places the burden of gardening on all individuals themselves, glossing over the reality that most poor people don't have control of land, and that remaining plots of urban garden land are often already fully used. He also overlooks the fact that poor people don't have money for garden tools, seeds, water, etc. He seems to assume that massive amounts of extra land and supplies will somehow magically appear for anyone who wants to garden.

Mark Winne is one of the founders of the Community Food Security Coalition, and one of the strongest, most consistent voices for ensuring that community food security work always meets the needs of low-income people. Because he founded so many community gardens, he knows their benefits—and their limitations—

better than anyone. In his 2008 book, *Closing the Food Gap*, Winne wrote: "Having witnessed many sincere but ultimately failed attempts to transform dirt, water, and seed into food, I tend to look somewhat askance at those who suggest that more of us, if not all of us, should 'grow their own.' . . . Claims of self-reliance come precariously close to self-righteous pontificating."[13]

In a piece on community gardens in Albany, New York, Marlene Kennedy, the business editor for the *Times Union*, wrote: "Rather than working hard to increase participation in food and nutrition assistance programs, why not try to reduce the need for such aid? Instead of spreading the word about food stamps and the urban poor, why not give them a way to grow their own food?" Her article quoted Matthew Schueler, education center planner for the Capital District Community Gardens, as saying: "Access to food stamps does not imply access to healthy food. What our food programs may need more than expansion is an adaptation to the reality of the movement. Our food policy is killing more people with empty calories than by withholding meals."[14] Doesn't that sound almost exactly like what the far Right says about poor people?

These arguments fail to consider that food stamps promote self-sufficiency by helping people stay in the workforce and by giving them increased purchasing power to support their families. Perhaps the most preposterous argument is that people should work in a community garden *instead* of getting food stamps. Albany has a thriving community garden scene, and, as of 2008, had nineteen community gardens, including a total of 379 plots. Generously assuming that each plot provided enough produce for a family of four, the gardens could theoretically have helped feed up to 1,500 people—at least during the handful of months that food could be harvested in Albany's short growing season. Yet at the same time, Albany had a population of 89,000, of which 30,000 (27 percent) lived in poverty.[15] That means that no more than 5 percent of the poverty population, or no more than 2 percent of the entire population of the city, could possibly have gotten food from the gardens. Let's say, for the sake of further argument, that each and every garden plot was phenomenally productive, creating $100 worth of produce each over the course of a season, that would have generated almost $40,000 worth of produce. Compare that to the Food Stamp Program, which spent more than $15 million in Albany that year, more than 370 times the value of the garden food. Even if the number and productivity of gardens were dramatically increased, they still would not even scratch the surface of the nation's true food needs. Saying that seasonal gardens should replace a year-round government safety net is ridiculous and counterproductive.

It is also wrong to imply, as some food security advocates do, that the Food Stamp Program increases obesity by giving low-income Americans extra funds to purchase what the advocates deem food of substandard nutritional quality. A major USDA study published in 2007 found no significant difference between the body mass index of food stamp recipients and equally poor people who did not receive food stamps.[16]

Such thinking also leads some food advocates to propose that the government limit the items that people can purchase with food stamps—an idea also popular with the Right—or place a so-called "fat tax" on junk food. While well intentioned, such policies would be a big mistake—both patronizing and a waste of time and money. With billions of dollars at stake, the battle to define junk food would be epic, with nutrition experts pitted against food-industry lobbyists, slugging it out one food item at a time. Are Raisinets junk food or fruit? Junk food, you say? Then how about a caramel apple? What about a Fig Newton? Banana chocolate chip muffins? There would be protracted battles every year as new products were introduced and as the ingredients of existing products changed, requiring a massive federal bureaucracy to continuously make such determinations. Such a policy would also place a great burden on food stores to keep their lists of acceptable products updated. Other advocates want to ban fast food restaurants from low-income neighborhoods entirely.

Yet micromanaging the lives of poor people—or anybody, for that matter—is patronizing and usually backfires. A far better strategy than limiting food choice with food stamps, banning fast food, or passing a "fat tax" is to increase the average benefit amount of food stamps so people can afford to buy the healthiest foods—which most food stamp recipients desperately want to do.

Another challenge facing the community food security movement is that its overall scale is still so tiny. Many community food security projects are small, boutique efforts through which yuppies have been able to pay sky-high prices for small amounts of pristine, organic greens—but they haven't fed masses of people. Some in the movement even resist ramping up the size and scope of their projects, as if that would be selling out the "small is beautiful" ethos. But unless such efforts grow dramatically, the movement won't come even close to significantly challenging the dominant, corporate-run food system.

One of the largest and most innovative community food security groups in the nation, Growing Power in Milwaukee, is planning a ten-story glass building that will grow fish, fruit, herbs, and vegetables that supposedly will provide enough food for 10,000 people. That would be a truly remarkable accomplishment, and those 10,000 people would surely lead healthier and happier lives because of it. But Milwaukee has a population of about 600,000, so even one of the largest such projects planned in the nation would feed less than 2 percent of the population of its own hometown. Yes, we need to expand such efforts nationwide, but until we do, we shouldn't scoff at people who still need to get their food through the dominant food outlets—mainstream supermarkets, restaurants, and convenience stores.

THE LINK BETWEEN FOOD SECURITY AND ANTIHUNGER WORK

Despite all my reservations about how some community food security work is carried out or communicated, I *do* think that local food production and marketing should play a much greater role in our fight against hunger. Such work *is* empowering to all people involved—but especially to low-income people.

Just as I rebuke food security advocates who are disdainful of the need to make food affordable and to fight hunger, I must also chide my colleagues in traditional hunger organizations for too frequently looking down their noses at the community food security movement just because most of the projects are still small-scale. If antihunger advocates agree that such projects are helpful but believe their scale is too small to make a meaningful difference, the most logical response should be to help them expand. The bottom line is that the continuing rhetorical and philosophical fights between community food security and antihunger advocates are both silly and counterproductive. If they can't even agree with each other, they'll never be able to make the changes necessary society-wide. Both sides need to embrace the reality that we are all in this together.

As Chart 13B demonstrates, for a community to have good nutrition, three things need to happen: food must be affordable; food must be physically available; and individuals and families must have enough education to know how to eat better and regularly choose to perform the extra work necessary to do so. If you don't have all three legs of this table, the table will collapse. Yet all too often, projects only focus on one of the three. Many provide nutrition education, lecturing people that they should eat better, but neither make food more available nor more affordable and are therefore destined to fail. Sometimes, food is brought into low-income neighborhoods, but at prices too high for most people to afford. That won't work either. The *only* way to truly succeed is to focus on all three aspects of this problem at once.

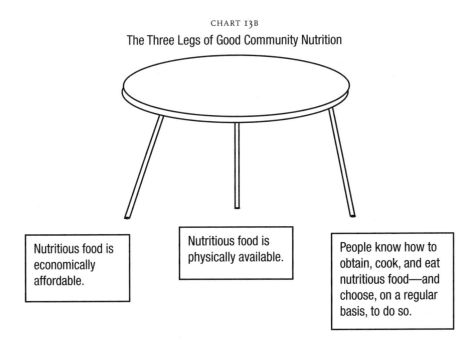

CHART 13B

CHART 13B
The Three Legs of Good Community Nutrition

Nutritious food is economically affordable.

Nutritious food is physically available.

People know how to obtain, cook, and eat nutritious food—and choose, on a regular basis, to do so.

Once food is affordable and available, and people are properly educated on how to obtain and prepare it in a time-efficient manner with equipment they already have in their homes, I think it's perfectly fair to focus on the need for parents (including even the lowest-income parents) to take personal responsibility for feeding themselves and their children more nutritiously. If society does its job, so should parents.

To achieve all those objectives, we all need to do a better job at educating the public on the central role that food should play in community development and antipoverty efforts. The former chair of the House Committee on Agriculture, Congressman Kika de la Garza (D-TX), used to quiz audiences with a riddle: "When does a nuclear submarine need to rise out of the water?" People would guess it would rise when it needed air, but he explained that it could turn the water into oxygen. Others would guess it would rise when it ran out of fuel, but he would then explain that the nuclear fuel would last for years. When no one could guess, he'd answer the riddle: "When it ran out of food."

Given that food is a basic human need, it is amazing that people almost always failed to figure out his riddle. More broadly, it is amazing how often food is over-looked in so many vital policy discussions, as well as in pop culture. For example, the earliest version of the classic computer game SimCity enabled you to design an entire city. While the game could help you decide where a city would have a football stadium or a museum, it didn't allow you to consider where food stores or markets would be. Likewise, for most of US history, real-life professional urban and other planners usually ignored food issues in their grand schemes.

We need an entirely different mindset. Food should be a central organizing tool of neighborhood development, uniting communities through community gardens, farmers' markets, nutrition education, supermarkets, food coopera-tives, and food-related small businesses. Community gardens can reclaim empty lots from drug-pushers. Food businesses can create jobs and raise com-munity income. Farmers' markets can give neighborhoods central gathering spaces and nurture a feeling of the "public commons" that is so often lost in today's society.

A NEW FOOD SECURITY PUBLIC POLICY AGENDA

For fundamental change to occur in food security and hunger issues, govern-ment must be a key player. In the late 1990s, when Secretary of Agriculture Dan Glickman launched the USDA Community Food Security Initiative and placed me in charge of it, most community food security adherents were highly skeptical, worrying that we were simply trying to co-opt the movement for nefarious ends. By the time the Bush administration took office and summar-ily ended the effort we had only just begun a few years earlier, I hoped we had won over most of the doubters with our work, which gave out million of dollars in Community Food Project grants each year to aid food security efforts, named Coordinators of Community Food Security in all fifty states, boosted commu-nity gardens, and ramped up technical assistance efforts to such projects.

The newly elected president should re-launch such an initiative immediately and work with Congress to give it serious resources. The president and Con-gress should also work together to more fully integrate these efforts with the USDA nutrition assistance programs. One way to accomplish this would be to dramatically expand the ability for WIC and food stamp participants to use their benefits at farm stands, farmers' markets, CSAs, and street vendors that sell fruit and vegetables.

State and local governments can launch similar community food security initiatives. One effective way to aid such efforts is to start state and city food policy councils in order to plan and coordinate state food policies across agency lines. Many states and localities already have them and those that don't should create them.

All levels of government should increase their funding for nonprofit groups running effective community food security projects.

The president and Congress must end corporate agriculture welfare, and focus resources on aiding truly struggling small farmers, particularly those growing fresh fruits and vegetables. The federal government should also better protect drinking water by increasing aid for conservation measures on small farms.

The president and Congress—as well as states, localities, and tribal governments—should shift procurement rules to make it easier for school districts, public hospitals, prisons, and all other public institutions to purchase food directly from small farmers. Also, more of the food commodities purchased by the government for soup kitchens and food pantries should be purchased directly from small farmers.

All levels of government should also use a combination of tax breaks, grants, land swaps, and other innovative efforts to preserve farmland. Localities must preserve new and existing land for farmers' markets and urban farms and gardens. Local governments should require all large real estate development projects to include plans for food, including rooftop gardens and greenhouses; affordable supermarkets, staffed by employees paid a living wage; and farmers' markets in public spaces.

Since the big money in agriculture is made from processing, all levels of government will want to support the creation of local and regional processing facilities.

Government can also do a much better job at encouraging new supermarkets in low-income neighborhoods and at preventing existing food stores from going out of business. A study conducted by the City of New York found that "The city is vastly underserved by local grocery stores. NYC has the potential to capture approximately $1 billion in grocery spending lost to suburbs."[17]

Pennsylvania has provided a model of how the nation can bring more food stores to underserved areas. The Food Trust, a Philadelphia-based nonprofit group, formed a public-private partnership in collaboration with other organizations and the State of Pennsylvania, to create the Pennsylvania Fresh Food Financing Initiative, which gives supermarkets a secure source of funding, as well as technical assistance, to locate in low-income areas. The initiative was well funded—with $120 million in combined governmental and private money in 2008—and committed resources to fifty supermarket projects in Philadelphia, Pittsburgh, Eddystone, Gettysburg, and other cities and towns across Pennsylvania.[18]

As critical as I have been of New York City Mayor Michael Bloomberg on food stamp and antipoverty issues, I must be equally effusive in my praise for him on food quality issues. At the urging of advocates, he appointed the city's first-ever food policy coordinator. The city launched a "Healthy Bodegas Initiative" to help small food stores increase the availability of fresh produce and low-fat milk. The city created a "Health Bucks" program to give low-income New Yorkers more purchasing power at farmers' markets. In 2008, Bloomberg, as well as City Council Speaker Christine Quinn, put their full weight behind a controversial (yet courageous) proposal to create a "Green Carts" program to place fresh fruit and vegetable vendors in underserved neighborhoods. The local food industry bitterly opposed that effort, hiring lobbyists to make two central claims, which just happened to contradict each other: one, that low-income people were too ignorant to know that they needed to buy fresh produce, so the initiative would fail due to lagging sales; and two, that the competition from the Green Carts would be so great that it would put existing food stores out of business. As I write this book, the initiative is in its beginning stages, so it's too early to tell whether it will work or not, but it's certainly worth a try.

Nonprofit groups should also do more to combine antihunger work and community food security work. They should make a greater effort to place CSAs and farmers' market projects in low-income areas, and they should make this fresh food affordable to everyone by providing low-income people with scholarships and also by accepting food stamp and WIC benefits.

In addition, whenever possible, more food banks, food rescue organizations, soup kitchens, and food pantries should sponsor their own farms, gardens, farmers' markets, and CSAs. In the low-income New York neighborhood of Red Hook, Brooklyn, a model program run by the nonprofit group Added Value sponsors a farm and a farmers' market, hiring neighborhood youths to work the farm and staff the market, all the while teaching them about farming, nutrition, and entrepreneurship. This model could be replicated across the nation.

America will never fulfill Thomas Jefferson's professed dream of being a nation of nothing but yeoman farmers. But if we collectively take the steps suggested above, at least we won't have a day when all our food comes from Exxon.

CHAPTER 14

A NEW WAR ON POVERTY

*What does it profit a man to be able to eat at an integrated lunch
counter if he doesn't earn enough money to buy a hamburger?*
—Rev. Dr. Martin Luther King, Jr., 1968[1]

I t's relatively easy to end hunger in America. If the nation increased and modernized the already-existing safety net and took all the other basic steps I have proposed, we'd finally wipe out this egregious problem. But even if we ended hunger as we know it, if poverty continued to increase in America, not only would people continue to suffer, but taxpayers would need to continually pump more money into the safety net to prevent hunger from returning. Consequently, in order to truly make the American dream attainable for all those willing to work for it, the country must make the eradication of hunger just the first step in a broader effort to slash domestic poverty.

Poverty in America hurts everyone. As harmful as the $90 billion cost to our economy resulting from hunger among adults and children is, the $500 billion cost to our nation as a result of childhood poverty is even worse, equivalent to 4 percent of the US gross domestic product (GDP), according to a study by the Center for American Progress. This reduces productivity and economic output by about 1.3 percent of the GDP, raises the cost of law enforcement and prisons by 1.3 percent of the GDP, and raises health expenditures and reduces the economic value of good health by 1.2 percent of the GDP.[2] Ultimately, America's high poverty rate hampers its ability to compete in the world economy. It is in the best interest of the country to invest in its citizens, and therefore its own future.

AN ASPIRATION EMPOWERMENT AGENDA

If we want to see real change, we need an entirely new framework for address-ing domestic poverty. While our leaders still choose sides—and boldly declare that either faltering economics or personal irresponsibility alone are responsi-ble for poverty—the American people know that we need to move beyond such false choices. The public knows that increased government support, economic growth, community involvement, *and* a focus on personal responsibility are *all* needed to solve the problem. While the citizenry is ready to move forward based on common sense answers, our leaders are stuck in a partisan and ideological time warp.

To make matters worse, neither conservatives nor liberals spend significant time interacting with poor people. It is no wonder that neither side has advanced a serious plan to empower low-income American families to accom-plish their primary goal: to be able to enter—and stay in—the middle class, and have a serious expectation that each subsequent generation has a real shot of moving further up the economic ladder.

The nation must move beyond our current stalemate in poverty politics by enacting an "Aspiration Empowerment Agenda" that gives all families the opportunity to advance their dreams through hard work and responsible choices. Rather than focus only on those rare stories of poor people who climb their way out of poverty against all odds or those rare people with so many prob-lems they can't move to self-sufficiency no matter how much help they get, this clearheaded new approach would focus on the majority of folks who could climb out of poverty with some help.

The Aspiration Empowerment Agenda would provide an array of govern-ment-funded benefits and work supports at levels sufficient enough to enable low-income people to develop assets and move out of poverty. It would empha-size the importance of personal responsibility for *all* members of society, including the rich, but also design public policies that reward—not punish—low-income people for positive behavior. This new empowerment-centered agenda would create economic pathways for upward mobility—and reverse a trend that is ensnaring more and more working people into poverty.

We need to empower low-income families to end debt and move from owing to owning. New efforts would help low-income families achieve their dreams by learning, earning, and saving their way out of poverty. The agenda is both revolutionary in its ambition and mainstream in its values. The goal is to overhaul all our programs and policies in order to give low-income families the tools they need to achieve a middle-class lifestyle—with a good job, a safe place to live, and a hopeful future for their kids and grandkids.

MOVING FROM OWING TO OWNING

While the most obvious difference between poor Americans and the rest is that they earn less income, in actuality a far bigger difference is that they *own* less and have miniscule financial assets. Wealth inequality outstrips income inequality by large margins. According to Citizens for Tax Justice, in 2004, the wealthiest 1 percent of Americans owned 33.4 percent of the nation's wealth, up from 30.4 percent in 1989. The wealthiest 5 percent owned 55.5 percent of the wealth in 2004. The poorest 50 percent collectively owned 2.5 percent of the wealth in 2004, down from 3.0 percent in 1989.[3] The gap in ownership by race is even vaster.

The government has long encouraged asset development for the middle and upper classes through tax incentives. According to the New America Foundation, the federal government spends over $300 billion per year on asset-building activities. But approximately 90 percent of those benefits go to individuals earning more than $50,000 annually.

All federal and state social programs should be reformed to make it easier for recipients to save their money so they can pay for a down payment on a first home, start a business, pay for higher education for their children, or build a retirement account. This can be done by eliminating provisions that automatically kick people out of such programs when they save money.

One embodiment of the assets growth idea is the Individual Development Account (IDA) program, created in the 1990s by an ideological odd couple: then-President Bill Clinton and then-chair of the House Committee on the Budget, archconservative John Kasich. These accounts allow low-income families to match their own savings with funds from government and private sector sources in order to save for job training, home ownership, or business start-ups. Such accounts are often coupled with financial education. IDAs are still only available in small pilot locations and have been further hampered because too few people in poverty had even minimal disposable incomes that they could save. Furthermore, even though IDA projects are very labor-intensive to run, most money for IDA projects that goes through nonprofit groups is set aside for the benefits themselves, with little or no administrative funding going to the organizations. To truly expand into a universally available benefit for people in poverty (as we should), the government needs to both increase the matching funds and also provide more realistic support to the entities that operate such efforts.

Surely, programs like the IDA, which promote both personal responsibility and economic opportunity, should be supported by liberals, conservatives, and moderates alike as bold new steps to finally stem the growing tide of poverty. Likewise for the idea of "Kids Accounts"—which have already been created in the United Kingdom—through which every child born in the nation automatically receives a savings account with a small deposit in it, and is provided with long-term incentives (with extra incentives for low-income families) to save more for education, job training, home purchases, or retirement.

An assets agenda would also ensure greater availability of low-cost banking services, as well as crack down on payday loans, high-fee check-cashing facilities, and other financial services that rip off poor people. This plan should also dramatically ramp up governmental and private efforts to provide micro-loans to start very small businesses. Helping someone open his or her own shoe shine stand, for example, or to start a sidewalk business to sell ethnic food delicacies, can help people enter the economic mainstream and perhaps later expand their efforts by hiring employees to aid them.

WAGES AND WORK

One major caveat about such an assets agenda is that it will only work in the context of broader economic and poverty policies that increase what people earn and decrease what they pay for basic necessities. For instance, if a family earns $20,000 per year in salaries but pays $24,000 in rent, not only won't they be able to develop assets, they will go into debt. Thus, lower costs and higher wages for people in poverty are an absolute prerequisite for assets building.

To reduce costs, the nation must enable all Americans to obtain health care, housing, and child care that is both affordable and high quality. Once the nation has accomplished that very simple task, we can turn to the issue of wages.

It is often said that the "best social program is a job." I agree with that adage, but would modify it to say: "The best social program is a job that provides people with wages and benefits sufficient enough to ensure at least a bare middle-class existence." We need to design all our antipoverty plans to create good jobs and ensure low-income Americans have the tools to get them and keep them.

The New Hope initiative in Milwaukee in the mid-1990s (before welfare reform) required low-income people to commit to full-time work, and in exchange provided them with a package of benefits that included wage supplements, health insurance, child care, and short-term community service jobs for those unable to find private sector jobs. According to the Hamilton Project of the Brookings Institution, New Hope "functioned as a social contract rather than as a welfare program." For participants, it increased their employment by 5 percent, decreased their poverty by 8 percent and improved the classroom achievements of their children. We need new national policies on supporting work that are equally comprehensive.

We must continue to raise the federal minimum wage and index it to inflation annually. If Congress and the president don't agree to that, we should insist that, every time they raise their own salaries, they must also substantially raise the federal minimum wage.

We also need to significantly expand the federal Earned Income Tax Credit (EITC) program, increasing the number of eligible working parents, increasing the payments available to parents who contribute to their children's welfare through child support payments, and also increasing benefits for families with three or more children. We should also increase EITC payments to childless adults, which would particularly aid low-income men, the most overlooked population in America.

State governments should also raise state minimum wages and index those to inflation and create new—or expand existing—state EITC programs.

We need more public/private partnerships to increase EITC redemption, as well as to reduce the absurdly high fees that many low-income people pay for tax preparation. All levels of government must work together to streamline and combine applications for vital work supports, providing one-stop-shopping that enables low-income working families to more easily access child care, health insurance, and food benefits.

JOB READINESS, TRAINING, AND PLACEMENT

Government and the private sector must do a better job of working together to ensure that people are ready to enter and stay in the workforce, have the skills and education necessary to do so, and then are placed in actual, living-wage jobs that meet their training and skill levels. And training must be more appropriately matched with actual workforce needs. While we school far too many people for hair stylist and auto repair jobs that have fewer current opportunities, we don't educate nearly enough people for the vital professions of nursing and teacher's aides, which are in desperate need of more workers.

Career ladders for upward mobility are crucial. I support Barack Obama's plan to invest 1 billion dollars over five years in transitional jobs and career pathway programs that implement proven methods of helping low-income Americans succeed in the workforce.[4]

America also needs more apprenticeships, which are common in Europe for many professions in the business sector, but exist in the US mostly in skilled, unionized trades. While we need college to be more affordable and available, it will never be right for everyone, and apprenticeships can be an important tool of upward mobility for people without college degrees. For example, a person who begins his career as a hotel clerk could, through apprenticeships, train to someday enter hotel management.

Given that many unemployed and underemployed poor people live in inner cities, though the fastest job growth has been in suburbs and exurbs, we need to increase government programs that help people make a reverse commute or otherwise get to their jobs. Of course, we should also focus on bringing more jobs to the neighborhoods in which poor people already live.

We must make elementary and secondary education work again, ensuring that everyone who earns a high school degree has the skills necessary to attend college, should he or she wish to do so. While obtaining a college degree is no guarantee that you won't live in poverty, statistically, it's darn close. You just don't see many people with college degrees in line at food pantries. Making higher education more broadly available is vital for our future economic competitiveness. Hillary Clinton was correct to propose both creating a $3,500 tuition tax credit—which, in 2007, would have equaled more than 50 percent of the cost of annual tuition at the average public institution—and increasing Pell grants (which offer partial payment for college, with no repayment required) in order to unlock the doors to higher education for millions of Americans.

We should also greatly expand the AmeriCorps national service program, and significantly increase the educational award that it provides, to ensure that if someone performs two years of full-time community service work, virtually all of their college education would be paid for by a combination of government and private, including university, matching funds.

FINISHING THE JOB ON WELFARE REFORM

As detailed in Chapter Eight, America never really completed reforming welfare. We need to finish the job. Welfare reform should itself be reformed to have three equally important goals: one, further reducing the welfare rolls; two, ensuring that people leaving welfare—as well as people who previously left— have long-term, living-wage jobs, and are better able to support their family off welfare than on; and, three, reducing poverty for both children and adults.

Heather Boushey of the Economic Policy Institute found that women leaving welfare were far more likely to stay employed after leaving welfare if they had child care in professional centers and received subsidies for it; a high school degree; and a starting job that provided relatively good wages and health insurance.[5] Based on that study and my other experiences, here are some basic things we should do to make welfare reform work better:

- Focus more on the wage levels of the recipients' first jobs. The first decade or so of welfare reform was obsessed with getting people a job—any job— without worrying too much if they earned wages above the poverty line. The next wave of welfare reform should ensure that the jobs are living-wage jobs, either because the starting salary is high enough or because the workers receive enough wage supplements to put them above the poverty line.
- Enable welfare recipients to combine more access to immediate work with more access to education and training programs. Research proves that approaches that mix work with education and training are the most effective.
- The federal, state, county, and city governments should coordinate a nationwide plan to create more living-wage jobs in areas of high unemployment and give employers more incentives to hire and retain former welfare recipients.
- Job training program design should be improved by asking businesses that are hiring welfare leavers to offer concrete suggestions on the types of training needed and by requiring job training contracts to be based on real performance rather than on political favoritism.

■ Welfare leavers should automatically be able to receive the tools they need to obtain and keep jobs, including child care, wage supports, tax refunds, transportation help, health care, and nutrition assistance.

RESTORING THE AMERICAN DREAM

All four of my grandparents, as well as my mother, were born outside America, in poverty. They came to America for freedom. The freedom to practice their own religion—or not. The freedom from the fear of Cossacks riding into town to slaughter their families. And yes, the freedom to make a fair day's wages for a fair day's work.

It wasn't easy. They risked their lives to get here. Both of my father's parents worked in garment industry sweatshops for paltry wages, until the unions they helped organize raised their pay and improved their working conditions. My mother's father started out selling dry goods door-to-door, until he saved enough money to buy his first parking garage, and then saved even more money to buy a mini-chain of parking garages. Those garages paid for my mother to become the first person in her family to go to college, and—because my grandparents saved far more than they ever spent—ultimately paid for much of my Ivy League college tuition. My father fought in World War II, and then used the GI Bill to become the first person in his family to go to college.

Why did my grandparents and parents risk so much, work so hard, and sacrifice so consistently? Because, even as they were bending over white-hot sewing machines or knocking on their thousandth unresponsive door, they knew—just knew—that the America of their dreams would ultimately reward them and their offspring.

The very name "America" became an ideal for the world.

But we've lost that. Our growing poverty crushes hope and squanders dreams.

America must once again live up to those ideals by restoring pathways of mobility and returning to the land of my grandparents' dreams.

CHAPTER 15

HOW ALL OF US (INCLUDING *YOU*) CAN END HUNGER IN AMERICA

A grandfather is pensively sitting on the couch. His grandchild asks him, "Grandfather, you look so worried, what's the matter?" The grandfather answers, "I have two dogs that are fighting in my heart." The child asks, "What are the names of these dogs, Grandpa?" He responds, "Their names are hate and love." The child looks up anxiously. "Grandpa, who do you think is going to win?" The grandfather answers: "The one that I feed."

—Sufi parable[1]

The American people have already taken the first steps. They've sorted cans in church basements and served meals in community meeting rooms. They've voted for referendums to raise the state minimum wages. And they've begun demanding that their candidates for public office deliver change—real change.

But that's just the beginning. In order to end hunger and slash poverty, the nation must build a strong grassroots antipoverty movement with low-income Americans making up key portions of both its leadership and its membership. And Americans of all incomes must first be convinced that the nation can once again solve big problems.

According to the Pew Research Center for the People & the Press, from 2002 to 2007, the percentage of Americans who agreed that "Americans can always find a way to solve large problems" dropped from 74 percent to an anemic 58 percent.[2] So we shouldn't be shocked that many Americans think we can't end domestic hunger.

When I speak in public, the first thing I do is to try to get my audience to overcome this hurdle by taking them back to a time when the country *did* solve big problems. My best example is how the US ended yellow fever, cholera, and malaria within our borders, all of which used to be deadly mass killers in America.

In 1795, yellow fever killed 732 people in New York City, or about one out of every sixty-eight people. (As a point of comparison, when the AIDS death rate in New York was at its highest in the mid-1990s, it killed about one out of every 1,000 residents).[3] In New York City in 1832, cholera killed one hundred people every day in July, with the year's death toll equaling 3,500 people, about one in fifty-seven of the city's residents. If the same proportion of New York City residents died today, that would equal 112,000 deaths per year. Malaria infected US presidents from Washington to Lincoln. During the American Civil War, malaria accounted for 1,316,000 illnesses and 10,000 deaths. An estimated 50 percent of the white soldiers and 80 percent of the African-American soldiers contracted the disease.[4]

The public believed that all these diseases were simply a natural part of existence and that there was nothing that mere mortals could do stop them, leaving it up to private charities to do the best they could to marginally ease the horrible but inevitable suffering. Today, those three diseases are still rampant in many parts of the developing world. Yet these diseases no longer exist in the US. Why? Because the US government wiped them out. Yes, the *government* solved major problems facing the country.

Since cholera was found to be caused by dirty water, government authorities devoted vast sums of money and a massive effort to create public works projects to bring fresh water into—and remove waste water from—US cities. They also created and enforced a wide variety of sanitary and public health laws. As for yellow fever, scientists, led by American Army General Walter Reed, discovered that the disease was caused by mosquitoes, then sent public health officials to destroy mosquito breeding grounds, clean local water supplies, and fumigate.

During World War II, in 1947, the National Malaria Eradication Program, a cooperative effort by state and local governmental health agencies and the US Public Health Service, conducted more than 4.6 million anti-mosquito spray applications, and, within a few years, the US was declared "free of malaria." That effort launched the modern US Centers for Disease Control and Prevention.[5]

What does this have to do with hunger? A lot. The beliefs held by the American public about those diseases—that they were inevitable and unstoppable and that the best humans could do was apply a little charity to slightly reduce the misery—were almost identical to the beliefs that Americans hold today about hunger.

Considering that most Americans today believe that the government can't do something as simple as deliver trailer homes to disaster areas (and, under President George W. Bush, it *couldn't*), successful governmental interventions may be hard to imagine. But they have worked in the past, and they will work now—if we give the government a significant push in the right direction. Hunger *can* be eliminated, but only if Americans band together to demand that their government once again solves big problems.

THE ANTIHUNGER MOVEMENT NEEDS TO REFORM ITSELF

Before we can recruit mass numbers of the American public to join our cause, the US domestic antihunger movement must first reform itself. In previous chapters, I explained why it is vital for the movement to wean itself off dependence on financial and political support from multinational agribusinesses. But it must also be far more aggressive in trying to get straight answers from people campaigning for public office and in holding elected officials accountable for their actions (and nonactions).

In 2004, even though poverty and hunger had increased in each of the previous four years, those issues were virtually ignored in the presidential race, and advocates did little to force the candidates to address them. In 2008, partially because of a number of the Democratic presidential candidates' long-time interest on poverty issues, and partially because of the increased media attention on poverty post-Katrina, the candidates talked much more about poverty than did the candidates in the 2004 race. John Edwards, Barack Obama, and Hillary Clinton each issued statements about hunger during Thanksgiving week of 2007. Edwards released a significant plan on hunger, Obama released a lengthy statement about the need for a strong Farm Bill, but, interestingly, Clinton focused almost exclusively on encouraging her supporters to aid local antihunger charities. Later in the primary campaign—too late to change the outcome of it—Clinton actually offered a plan to end child hunger in the US by 2012, focusing on the need for universal school meals, as I and many others had proposed.

Significantly, also in the 2006 primary campaign, Republican Mike Huckabee also started talking about poverty and hunger, bragging in debates and TV appearances that he was the only Republican "talking about hunger." Yet, on his campaign Web site, under the eighteen "issues" listed, not one specifically addressed poverty or hunger. Huckabee did promise to enact significant tax cuts for all Americans, including "rich" ones. Not only that, in the years that Huckabee served as governor of Arkansas, the state was actually tied for the second-highest increase in food insecurity. Thus, the candidate who bragged about "talking" about hunger not only had no plan to reduce it, but he also stood for tax cuts that could increase it, and was demonstrably responsible for increasing hunger in his own home state. And no one ever called him on it.

It would be nice if politicians cared in their hearts about our issue, but that's not what motivates them to get things done. They take action when unions, environmental groups, religious organizations—or other groups with money, troops, or media—demand it. We need to build an antihunger movement with clout that politicians will fear, not only when they are running for office, but when they are in it.

A perfect example of the problem is the Hunger Free Communities Act of 2005. It had very modest goals—creating a small antihunger grant program of $50 million and committing the nation to cutting hunger in half by 2010— while providing virtually none of the resources to reach that noble benchmark. Many nonprofit groups and activists (including me) thought the bill was mostly symbolic. Still, the national groups supporting it were happy that it obtained dozens of cosponsors, many of whom were Republicans. But it never even reached the floor of either the House or the Senate for a vote.

Yet a big hunger vote *did* come to the floor of the House that same year—a budget bill that would have removed more than 200,000 people from the Food Stamp Program. While virtually all Democrats voted against the budget, most Republicans voted for it, including most of the Republicans who had cosponsored the Hunger Free Communities Act, many of whom prided themselves on being moderates. That's right, the very people who sponsored a mostly symbolic antihunger bill turned around and voted for a highly meaningful bill that would have concretely increased hunger. The *New York Times* published an editorial, "Profiles in Pusillanimity," slamming these members of Congress as "spineless."[6]

How did hunger advocates react to this betrayal? Did we threaten to withhold future campaign donations to the offenders? No, because we didn't have any donations to withhold. Did we at least act like other grassroots interest groups, holding press conferences to name names and to denounce the people who sold us out? Nope. Did our leaders at least bawl them out in private? I don't think they even did that. As far as I know, the national groups did little to nothing to try to make the members of Congress who voted against us pay for their actions. When I suggested that some of the national groups take a more aggressive approach, I was politely dismissed. In fact, some of groups held press conferences with the same elected officials in the weeks and months *after* the budget vote, still thanking them profusely for their leadership on the Hunger Free Communities Act, which never got off the ground. When advocates act that way, I can only assume elected officials must think we're suckers.

All movements, including the antihunger cause, need to continually reform themselves in order to be effective. A good analogy is that of the labor unions, which lost their way when the leaders started getting rich enough to act like management. Only when they started reforming themselves, when progressive unions recently broke away from the AFL-CIO, did they start truly organizing new immigrant workers and reenergizing the movement.

Even many employees with national antihunger groups, as well as leaders of state and local organizations, agree privately that the hunger and poverty crusade needs to be reformed and reinvigorated. Virtually all of us agree that, if we are to achieve the kinds of advances that the movement won in the 1970s and 1980s, we must once again build a broad-based national coalition.

HOW TO BUILD A MASS ANTIHUNGER AND ANTIPOVERTY MOVEMENT

No social movement in history has won major gains without leadership from people who benefit most from that change. While it was certainly crucial that white people were involved in the civil rights crusade and that men were involved in the women's rights cause, neither would have had such rapid and far-reaching success had not the people most affected served in the key leadership roles, fighting hard for their own advancement and for that of their own children.

Yet today some antihunger leaders still believe that, if we simply do enough to stoke the guilt and prompt the conscience of middle- and upper-income America, the nation will magically wake up to the reality and provide enough resources to end hunger. That won't happen. History proves that significant progress will only occur when low-income people insist on creating and using political power on their own behalf.

While low-income people don't have a lot of money to donate to political campaigns, they do have compelling numbers on their side. In 2007, the entire combined memberships of labor unions, the National Rifle Association (NRA), MoveOn.org, and the Christian Coalition equaled about 23.9 million people, only about two thirds of the 35.5 million people living in food insecurity. If hungry Americans organized themselves into a powerful political force, they could immediately have a dramatic impact upon hunger and poverty policies.

The sad reality is that America doesn't really have a national antipoverty movement today, and hasn't truly had one since the demise of the Poor People's Campaign shortly after the assassination of Dr. King. Some of the old-line antipoverty organizations that still exist have been bought-off by donors and politically entrenched allies, so much so that they have mostly lost both their effectiveness and their street credibility. A few have even become downright corrupt. There have been some cutting-edge grassroots antipoverty organizations that have arisen over the last few decades, but few have expanded enough to make much of an impact beyond their home neighborhoods and cities.

Ironically, some of the most dynamic antipoverty organizations, based in Washington, DC, perform effective policy research work and do an admirable job lobbying Capitol Hill, but don't really have a nationwide, grassroots network behind them. Imagine the impact they'd make if they did. I hope that such national groups will evolve from being mostly policy and research institutions into forceful umbrella groups for grassroots community organizations, including some of the smaller innovative neighborhood-based antipoverty organizations that have sprung up in recent times. National groups should more actively solicit the involvement of grassroots organizations as formal affiliates, who would give the national associations more credibility. They could also provide direct technical assistance to small groups on how to raise money, create and deliver a message, lobby elected officials, utilize up-to-date technologies, etc. To do so will require significant extra funding, but I believe donors could be rallied around the prospect of enacting more fundamental and lasting progress.

Part of the challenge is that low-income people face the cycle of political disempowerment outlined earlier in the book. It is *tough* to break that cycle. Another challenge is that low-income and hungry people don't *want* to think of themselves as poor and hungry. In contrast, most African Americans are proud to be African Americans, environmentalists are proud to be environmentalists, gay and lesbian people are proud to be gay and lesbian, etc. Yet the greatest goal of low-income and hungry people is usually to *escape* their condition. It's darn hard to organize among individuals whose top goal is to no longer be a part of the group being organized.

It's also true that hunger nonprofits, the New York City Coalition Against Hunger included, don't do nearly as good a job as we should to reach out and draw in hungry people to participate in our advocacy activities. I attend hunger conference after hunger conference—including those in cities, such as Washington, DC, and Philadelphia, with very large nonwhite and low-income populations—and the vast majority of participants are upper-middle-class white people. I have nothing against upper-middle-class white people (especially since I am one), but we simply must broaden the team if we want to have any hope of winning.

To truly empower Americans in poverty, I believe that we must realistically understand the challenges faced by low-income neighborhoods and families. We must value reality and results over rhetoric and ideology. We must prove to low-income Americans that making the political system more responsive to their needs can concretely improve their living conditions. And we must also focus on not just stoking people's fears, but on enabling them to realize their aspirations. Appendix B gives very specific organizing tips to activists on how to accomplish those goals.

Encouraging low-income people to speak for themselves is key. It is vital that they be recruited and trained to testify before government hearings and speak to the press. We must implement concrete mechanisms to ensure that low-income people are able to attend antihunger and antipoverty conferences, meetings, workshops, and technical assistance and professional development courses. To make this a realistic option, organizations will likely need to provide scholarships, free transportation, and, when meetings are out of town, lodging for people to participate. Groups can hold meetings at night or on weekends when working people are available. We advocates must also practice what we preach and take active steps to diversify boards, staffs, and even donors.

In New York, the group I lead has begun—in partnership with a handful of the most visionary food pantries and soup kitchens—to establish Customer Action Boards (CABs) at those agencies. (We use the term "customers" because we feel that the usual term, "clients," denotes passive recipients of services, exactly the kind of mentality we want to move beyond.) The purpose of these CABs is to develop the leadership skills of people who use pantries and kitchens, first working with them to make improvements in the way the feed-

ing program is managed, and then helping them advocate to government officials for broader public policy improvements. Such CABs are very
labor-intensive to organize and maintain—especially because once people
become independent and no longer need the feeding programs, they may not
come back for CAB meetings. The groups can also be costly, as we've found
that you may need to pay stipends, cover transportation, and provide food to
compensate participants for missed work, or for day care costs incurred so they
can attend meetings. Despite all those challenges, I think every food bank and
antihunger organization in the country should initiate programs to specifically
engage the customers of pantries and kitchens. Given that 25 million Americans use these agencies, this is a great way to start a mass movement.

LEADERSHIP MATTERS

Poverty in the United States is far from static and unchangeable. As Chart 15A
shows, in the more than four decades in which poverty data has been kept by
the federal government, poverty has gone up every time Republican presidents
have been in power and gone down every time Democrats have been in power,
with the only exception being the one-term Carter administration, during which
efforts to tamp down inflation resulted in rising unemployment and poverty.
This stark trend is no coincidence. All told, since 1960, whenever Democrats
controlled the White House, there was a net decrease in poverty of 16.6 million Americans, but when the Republicans controlled the White House, there

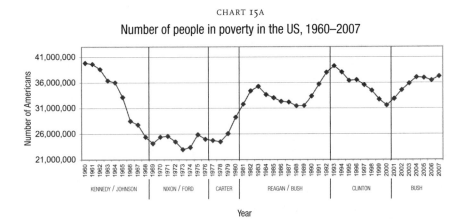

CHART 15A
Number of people in poverty in the US, 1960–2007

was a net increase in poverty of 14.9 million Americans. Presidents Kennedy, Johnson, and Clinton dramatically decreased poverty, while Reagan and the two Bushes dramatically increased it. Leadership *does* matter.

In the early 2008 presidential primary season, the media exaggerated slight disagreements in emphasis between Senators Clinton and Obama over whether it was President Johnson or Dr. Martin Luther King, Jr., who was most responsible for the passage of civil rights laws in the 1960s. But the reality is that both sides were responsible. It is absolutely true that the laws could never have been passed had Johnson not used his considerable legislative skills to marshal them through Congress—and then thrown his prestige and political career on the line by signing them into law. But it is equally true that, had the civil rights crusades not swung public opinion so dramatically in favor of racial progress, such bills never would have even made it onto the agenda of both a Congress and a president.

It takes broad social movements pressing elected officials for progress and building public support for the agendas of those elected officials who support the improvements *as well as* forward-thinking elected officials willing to fight for change. After all, in order to move, a car needs both gas and a driver. For social progress to occur, we need to apply grassroots political pressure and encourage mounting media agitation to fuel the advancements—but we also need progressive and effective political leaders to steadily drive the improvements.

In 2009, the new president will have the perfect opportunity to be a truly great leader. As I finish writing this book in the summer of 2008, I don't yet know whether Senator Barack Obama or Senator John McCain will be the next president. But both candidates have a chance to be great, and to make good on each of their key campaign promises, by making the United States hunger-free.

Obama would be the first president in history to have grown up in a family that received food stamps. He started his career as an antipoverty organizer, and when he was in the Illinois State Senate, he authored the law that gave state tax credits to low-income working families. During his primary campaign for president, he proposed a concrete plan to halve domestic poverty in ten years and offered specific ways to reduce child hunger.[7]

McCain routinely voted as senator for cuts in antipoverty and antihunger programs and, as a presidential candidate, continued to back large tax cuts for the wealthy, which would make it more difficult to fund social programs. However, during his primary campaign, McCain pledged to be a different kind of Republican. He toured parts of the country with deep pockets of poverty, and

292 Section II—The Solution

even said he would "make the eradication of poverty a top priority of the McCain administration."[8]

Despite their very different backgrounds and records, either a President Obama or a President McCain could use the issue of domestic hunger as a test case to prove they are serious about carrying out the pledges that were central to their campaigns.

For Obama, his core promise was to transcend partisanship in order to bring Americans together to solve big problems. There's no better issue than domestic hunger through which he can prove he is able carry out that pledge. After all, the nation achieved its greatest progress in slashing malnutrition at the time in our history of the greatest bipartisan cooperation on the issue of hunger—during the late 1960s to mid-1970s, when a broad coalition led by Democratic Senator George McGovern and his Republican colleague, Bob Dole, created the modern nutrition safety net. Yet to achieve that goal, Obama would need to take on those in his own party who would value revenge against the Republicans over progress for the nation.

McCain's core promise was that he would go against his party's orthodoxies to take on special interests in order to advance the broader public interest. For him, too, there's no better issue than domestic hunger through which to prove he's serious about that pledge. After all, the most sensible way to find extra funding for USDA antihunger programs is to eliminate the USDA crop subsidy programs that provide tens of billions of dollars each year in corporate welfare to massive agribusinesses. Yet to achieve that goal, McCain would need to take on those in his own party, as well as key Democrats, who depend mightily on the hundreds of millions of dollars in campaign donations showered on them by agribusinesses and their lobbyists.

In short, for either Obama or McCain, the issue of hunger provides a golden opportunity to truly lead and do it well. For while it does indeed take a village to raise a child, it takes a leader to get the village to do so.

BUT, IN THE END, IT'S UP TO *YOU*

While I work to end hunger each and every day, ultimately it's up to each of us as individuals to feed the solution to domestic hunger. You and everyone you know.

Sure, individuals could volunteer at a feeding charity. And that is noble work indeed. But many pantries and kitchens need relatively few volunteers throughout the year for manual tasks like serving soup or packing cans—which can easily be performed by kids as young as thirteen—and most agencies usually don't need large groups of professionals to perform manual tasks involved in feeding people. It would help the agencies much more if people could help with long-term professional tasks related to their personal skill set—accounting, working on computers, public relations, fundraising, graphic design, or even organizing other volunteers.

More people need to donate to—and volunteer with—organizations (such as the New York City Coalition Against Hunger and other groups listed in Appendix A) that focus on working to enact governmental and economic policies that reduce both hunger and the poverty that causes hunger. Such organizations can provide citizens with the training and ammunition they need to write letters to the editor, call in to talk radio shows, contact elected officials, post on blogs, organize people who have already committed to ending hunger, and most importantly—persuade the people who have not (yet) made that commitment.

When businesses brag about their charitable donations, customers should research how they treat their workers. If they treat their workers poorly, people should contact them to let them know that they appreciate their donations to charities, but would appreciate it even more if they paid their workers enough so these same workers wouldn't need to *use* such charities.

So much can be accomplished if people all over the country increase what their congregations or civic groups are doing, advertise the cause and the issues on their Facebook or MySpace pages, contact the print and electronic media and ask them to cover poverty and hunger more, raise money for advocacy efforts, and generally speak out.

Individual citizens can contact elected officials, candidates, and their staffs. Over and over again. And pressure them to support specific proposals on how to end hunger. Ask them to be very concrete about how they will pay for their proposals, particularly if they have already promised more tax cuts for the rich. Make them promise not only to sponsor antihunger and antipoverty legislation, but to exercise their leadership to allow those bills to have straight-up-or-down votes in committee and on the floor. Monitor whether any of their earmark funding goes to antihunger or antipoverty programs or whether they only go to pork barrel projects affiliated with campaign donors and well-heeled lobbyists. Watch them like a hawk on close budget votes, which are often the ones that matter most. Praise them in public when they do the right thing and come down on them like a ton of bricks (peacefully and politely, of course) when they don't.

Popular movements emerge from the daily struggles of thousands of citizens. Progress is never easy, but as we've seen with the end of cholera, yellow fever, and malaria, if government has the will, it has the way. If enough people push for change, then the government can solve big problems. We are at a moment in US history during which we must expect and demand real change. It is simply not acceptable to have hungry people amid such skyrocketing wealth. We must start feeding the solution.

FROM THE INEVITABLE TO THE UNTHINKABLE

A school official in the Bronx recently told me that he saw a small child rummaging through a trash bin outside his school for extra food. Can we really allow that in America?

What seemed inevitable in one age is unthinkable in other another. Take slavery. Or child labor. When we look back into our country's history, we can't allow ourselves to imagine how bad things really were. We ask ourselves, can we truly remember that America used to be so barbaric that it was acceptable to buy and sell human beings?

Can we imagine that the country was so heartless that "breaker boys" as young as the age of six often worked in anthracite coal mines separating slate rock from coal, for fourteen to sixteen hours a day, six days a weeks, frequently losing fingers or dying from black lung—all for just a few cents per month?

No, of course, we can't imagine it.

It is my hope that the same will happen with the idea of hunger after is it eliminated in America, a decade or two from now.

Someday we'll ask ourselves, can we imagine a time when America was so stonyhearted that it forced working families to seek food from charities just to survive? A time when the nation was so cavalier that it forced elderly cancer patients to choose between food and medication? A time when the nation was so divided that it had hundreds of billionaires but tens of millions of people facing hunger? A time when the country was so asleep that it didn't see school children scavenging through garbage bins to eat?

I hope that, in twenty years, our answer to all those questions will be, no, we can't imagine it.

HUNGER AND POVERTY-FIGHTING RESOURCES

US ANTIHUNGER/COMMUNITY FOOD SECURITY ORGANIZATIONS

All the groups below perform vital functions fighting hunger and poverty. While some of the organizations might find some points of disagreement with this book, and while I may not always agree with every one of their policy prescriptions or tactics, the broader point remains that we are all in this together and that it will take all of us working as a world community to build the movement needed to end hunger and reduce poverty. I urge you to obtain information from and offer your money and assistance to any or all of the organizations listed below.

Of course, I'd be remiss in my duties as a nonprofit organization's executive director if I did not shamelessly plug our group, the **New York City Coalition Against Hunger.** The coalition is an nonprofit umbrella group that represents the more than 1,200 soup kitchens and food pantries in New York City and the more than 1.3 million low-income New Yorkers who are forced to use them. The coalition works to both meet the immediate food needs of low-income New Yorkers and enact innovative solutions to help them move "beyond the soup kitchen" to self-sufficiency. Specifically, the coalition conducts advocacy, research, and communications work to improve the public and economic policies that create hunger; enables low-income New Yorkers to obtain fresh, affordable produce from organic farms; recruits and places both long- and short-term volunteers with pantries and kitchens; helps people enroll in federal nutrition and antipoverty programs; provides technical assistance and technology help to pantries and kitchens; and develops a new generation of leaders through AmeriCorps programs. The coalition's comprehensive Web site enables people to make a tax-deductible donation, volunteer their time, and contact their elected officials to urge support of current public policy priorities.

> New York City Coalition Against Hunger
> 16 Beaver Street, 3rd Floor
> New York, NY 10004
> Phone: (212) 825-0028
> Fax: (212) 825-0267
> E-mail: info@nyccah.org
> Web site: http://www.nyccah.org

■ **The Alliance to End Hunger** engages diverse institutions in building the public will to end hunger. The organization builds strategic partnerships to work for a world free from hunger; political commitment to ensure that our leaders do what it takes to end hunger; and global connections with the International Alliance Against Hunger and others to help achieve the United Nations' first Millennium Development Goal: cutting the number of hungry people in half by 2015.

> Alliance to End Hunger
> c/o Bread for the World Institute
> 50 F Street, NW #500
> Washington, DC 20001
> Phone: (202) 639-9400 x178
> Web site: http://www.alliancetoendhunger.org

■ **Feeding America** (formerly America's Second Harvest—The Nation's Food Bank Network) provides emergency and supplemental food to low-income Americans through a nationwide network of member food banks and food rescue organizations. You can find more information about their agencies throughout the United States—all of which need donations of money, food, and volunteer time—by going to the Feeding America Web site.

> Feeding America
> 35 E. Wacker Dr., #2000
> Chicago, IL 60601
> Phone: (800) 771-2303
> Phone: (312) 263-2303
> Web site: http://www.feedingamerica.org

■ **The Center on Hunger and Poverty** promotes policies that improve the lives of low-income children and families. Center activities include research and policy analysis, public education initiatives, and assistance to policy makers and organizations across the country on poverty- and hunger-related issues.

> Center on Hunger and Poverty
> Institute on Assets and Social Policy (IASP)
> The Heller School for Social Policy and Management
> Brandeis University, Mailstop 077
> Waltham, MA 02454
> Phone: (781) 736-8885
> Fax: (781) 736-3925
> Web site: http://www.centeronhunger.org

■ **The Community Food Security Coalition** is a North American organization of social and economic justice, environmental, nutrition, sustainable agriculture, community development, labor, antipoverty, antihunger, and other groups. The coalition has 325 organizational members in forty-one states, four Canadian provinces, and the District of Columbia. They are dedicated to building strong, sustainable, and local and regional food systems that ensure access to affordable, nutritious, and culturally appropriate food to all people at all times. They seek to develop self-reliance among all communities in obtaining their food and to create a system of growing, manufacturing, processing, making available, and selling food that is regionally based and grounded in the principles of justice, democracy, and sustainability.

> Community Food Security Coalition
> 3830 SE Division Street
> Portland, OR 97202
> Phone: (503) 954-2970
> Web site: http://www.foodsecurity.org

■ **The Congressional Hunger Center** (CHC) is a nonprofit antihunger training organization founded by former Rep. Tony Hall and is located in Washington, DC. Members of Congress Rep. Jo Ann Emerson (R-MO) and Rep. James P. McGovern (D-MA) are the cochairs of the CHC board of directors and exemplify the group's bipartisan approach to ending hunger. CHC places "Hunger Fellows" with antihunger and antipoverty organizations throughout the nation and the world.

Congressional Hunger Center
Hall of the States Building
400 North Capitol Street, NW, Suite G100
Washington, DC 20001
Phone: (202) 547-7022
Fax: (202) 547-7575
Web site: http://www.hungercenter.org

■ **The Food Research and Action Center** (FRAC) is a leading national nonprofit organization working to improve public policies and public/private partnerships to eradicate hunger and undernutrition in the United States. FRAC works with hundreds of national, state, and local nonprofit organizations, public agencies, and corporations to address hunger and its root cause: poverty. FRAC's Web site often has updated "action alerts" explaining how people can contact their US senators and US representatives about pending hunger legislation and funding.

Food Research and Action Center
1875 Connecticut Avenue, NW, Suite 540
Washington, DC 20009
Phone: (202) 986-2200
Web site: http://www.frac.org

■ **Mazon: A Jewish Response to Hunger** allocates donations from the Jewish community to prevent and alleviate hunger among people of all faiths and backgrounds. Mazon provides for people who are hungry while at the same time advocating for other ways to end hunger and its causes.

Mazon: A Jewish Response to Hunger
1990 South Bundy Drive, Suite 260
Los Angeles, CA 90025
Phone: (310) 442-0020
Fax: (310) 442-0030
Web site: http://www.mazon.org

■ **Share Our Strength** is a national organization that works hard to make sure no kid in America grows up hungry. They weave together a net of community groups, activists and food programs to catch children at risk of hunger and surround them with nutritious food where they live, learn and play. They work with the culinary industry to create engaging, pioneering programs like Share Our Strength's Taste of the Nation, Share Our Strength's Great American Bake Sale, Share Our Strength's A Tasteful Pursuit, Share Our Strength's Great American Dine Out, and Share Our Strength's Operation Frontline.

Share Our Strength
1730 M Street, NW, Suite 700
Washintgon, DC 20036
Phone: (800) 969-4767
Web site: http://www.strength.org/

■ **WHY** (World Hunger Year) is a leading advocate for innovative, community-based solutions to alleviate hunger and poverty. WHY challenges society to confront these problems by advancing models that create self-reliance, economic justice, and equal access to nutritious and affordable food. WHY uses its extensive contacts to create networking opportunities for grassroots organizations. For thousands of organizations WHY has helped raise more than $6 million, initiated countless media connections, and facilitated meetings with policy makers. It also runs the only centralized, nationwide database of innovative organizations working on food, nutrition, and agriculture issues across the country.

WHY
505 Eighth Avenue, Suite 2100
New York, NY 10018
Phone: (800) 5-HUNGRY
Web site: http://www.worldhungeryear.org

US ANTIPOVERTY/ASSETS DEVELOPMENT ORGANIZATIONS

■ **The Center on Budget and Policy Priorities** is one of the nation's premier policy organizations working at the federal and state levels on fiscal policy and public programs that affect low- and moderate-income families and individuals.

Center on Budget and Policy Priorities
820 First Street, NE, Suite 510
Washington, DC 20002
Phone: (202) 408-1080
Fax: (202) 408-1056
Web site: http://www.cbpp.org

■ **The CFED** (Corporation for Enterprise Development) expands economic opportunity by helping Americans start and grow businesses, go to college, own a home, and save for their own and their children's economic futures. They identify promising ideas, test and refine them in communities to find out what works, craft policies and products to help good ideas reach scale, and develop partnerships to promote lasting change. They bring together community practice, public policy, and private markets in new and effective ways to achieve greater economic impact.

> CFED
> 1200 G Street, NW, Suite 400
> Washington, DC 20005
> Phone: (202) 408-9788
> Web site: http://www.cfed.org

■ **The Mobility Agenda** is dedicated to advancing a long-term vision for a fairer, more inclusive, and sustainable world. Their current work focuses on identifying and promoting new ideas for better jobs while stimulating and shaping a dialogue to build public support for strengthening the labor market to benefit our economy, workers, and communities.

> The Mobility Agenda
> 1707 L Street, NW, Suite 750
> Washington, DC 20036
> Phone: (202) 730-9372
> Web site: http://www.mobilityagenda.org

■ **The New America Foundation** seeks to bring exceptionally promising new voices and new ideas to the fore of our nation's public discourse. Relying on a venture capital approach, the foundation invests in outstanding individuals and policy solutions that transcend the conventional political spectrum. Through its fellowships and issue-specific programs, the foundation sponsors a wide range of research, writing, conferences, and public outreach on the most important global and domestic issues of our time. Of particular interest is their Assets Building Program.

> New America Foundation
> 1630 Connecticut Avenue, NW, 7th Floor
> Washington, DC 20009
> Phone: (202) 986-2700
> Fax: (202) 986-3696
> Web site: http://www.newamerica.net

■ **The Progressive Policy Institute** (PPI) is a research and education institute that is a project of the Third Way Foundation Inc., a nonprofit corporation. PPI's mission is to define and promote a new progressive politics for America in the twenty-first century. Through its research, policies, and perspectives, the institute is fashioning a new governing philosophy and an agenda for public innovation geared to the Information Age. PPI has pioneered policies on national service, individual development accounts, and EITC expansion.

> PPI
> 600 Pennsylvania Avenue, SE, Suite 400
> Washington, DC 20003
> Phone: (202) 547-0001
> Fax: (202) 544-5014
> Web site: http://www.ppionline.org

■ **United for a Fair Economy** raises awareness that concentrated wealth and power undermine the economy, corrupt democracy, deepen the racial divide, and tear communities apart. They support and help build social movements for greater equality. They accomplish these goals through participatory education; media outreach; research; the Responsible Wealth Project; and cross-class, cross-race networking opportunities.

> United for a Fair Economy
> 29 Winter Street
> Boston, MA 02108
> Phone: (617) 423-2148
> Fax: (617) 423-0191
> Web site: http://www.faireconomy.org

INTERNATIONAL ANTIHUNGER/ANTIPOVERTY ORGANIZATIONS

■ **Friends of the World Food Program** is a US-based nonprofit organization dedicated to building support for the United Nations World Food Program (WFP) and other hunger relief efforts. Their mission is to: increase awareness about global hunger issues; mobilize support for hunger relief programs and activities; and generate resources for WFP operations and other activities that alleviate hunger. They have played a vital role in supporting the expansion of the George McGovern-Robert Dole International Food for Education and Child Nutrition Program, which sets up school meals programs in developing nations.

> Friends of the World Food Program
> 1819 L Street, NW, Suite 900
> Washington, DC 20036
> Phone: (202) 530-1694
> Fax: (202) 530-1698
> Web site: http://www.friendsofwfp.org

■ **Kiva Microfunds** is the world's first person-to-person micro-lending Web site, empowering individuals to lend directly to an entrepreneur in the developing world. By combining microfinance with the Internet, Kiva is creating a global community of people connected through lending. Kiva predicts that this will have facilitated loans totaling $100 million by 2010.

> Kiva Microfunds
> 3180 18th Street, Suite 201
> San Francisco, CA 94110
> Web site: http;//www.kiva.org

■ **Oxfam International** is a confederation of thirteen organizations working together with over 3,000 partners in more than one hundred countries to find lasting solutions to poverty and injustice. With many of the causes of poverty global in nature, the thirteen affiliate members of Oxfam International believe they can achieve greater impact through their collective efforts. Oxfam International seeks increased worldwide public understanding that economic and social justice are crucial to sustainable development. They strive to be a global campaigning force promoting the awareness and motivation that comes with global citizenship while seeking to shift public opinion in order to make equity the same priority as economic growth.

> Oxfam America
> 226 Causeway Street, 5th Floor
> Boston, MA 02114-2206
> Phone: (800) 77-OXFAM
> Phone (617) 482-1211
> Fax: (617) 728-2594
> Web site: http://www.oxfam.org

REVISED RULES FOR RADICAL CENTRISTS
Tips for Activists on How to Organize and Craft Messages for
Successful Advocacy Campaigns

To win any political fight, people must do three things: neutralize the opposition, mobilize those who already agree with them, and convince those who don't. Yet many progressive advocates today believe that they have to engage in only the first and the second, and outright ignore the need to persuade people who do not agree with them. If we want to win a mandate for governing once again (in order to accomplish such vital goals as ending hunger and slashing poverty), we'll have to learn how to chew gum and walk at the same time—in other words, to simultaneously energize our base and persuade undecided Americans.

TAKING ON THE RIGHT

It is dangerous to underestimate the fervor of the far Right in America. Many liberal people I know think that John Kerry lost the 2004 election because he wasn't liberal enough. Yet a *Washington Post*-ABC poll conducted in the first week of March 2004 found that 33 percent of voters thought Kerry was "too liberal" and only 6 percent thought he was "too conservative." Thirty-three percent thought Bush was "too conservative" but a startling 14 percent thought Bush was "too liberal," almost three times the number who thought Kerry "too conservative." That's right, one out of eight American voters were such hardcore conservatives they believed that George W. Bush was too *liberal*. That's what we're up against. And it's time poverty advocates dealt with this reality.

Whenever hunger and poverty issues are discussed, these rabid right wingers (some of whom have clearly racist tendencies) pop up on talk radio and on blogs. Their vehemence is exceeded only by their ignorance. One blogger in New York City posted this comment: "I hope they've ended the practice of food stamps acceptance at fast food outlets." In truth, food stamps have never been accepted at fast food outlets.

Progressives cannot just sit back and assume such comments are so outrageous that we won't even dignify them with a response. If something asserted by the Right is simply ignored by advocates, people will actually start to believe it and then it will become conventional wisdom—as has happened with the issue of obesity. We must call in to every radio station, respond to every blog, and counter every letter to the editor. This is a fight in the trenches of social change. And truth and openness won't win out over lies and ignorance unless we fight back. When we do fight back, we should do so in defense of our mainstream values, such as rewarding work, strengthening families, aiding our elderly—all the time highlighting how all those goals are accomplished when we fight hunger and poverty.

WINNING THE MIDDLE

Even as we battle the Right, we must never forget that most Americans are moderates at heart. In 2007, Pew found that in Iowa, the early Democratic caucus state with the most liberal voters, fully 44 percent of Democrats called themselves "moderate" and 23 percent called themselves "conservative." In South Carolina, the early Republican primary state with the most conservative voters, 29 percent of Republicans called themselves "moderate or liberal."[1] Though the liberal base drives the Democratic Party in their primaries and blogs and the conservative base drives the Republican Party in theirs, it is the people in the middle who decide general elections and issue campaigns.

While progressives should certainly maintain the moral clarity and focused outrage that represented the best of the 1960s, it is vital for us to also embrace the language and realities of our contemporary times.

While people hold differing (and often contradictory) views about policy specifics, the American people tend to share bedrock values, such as the importance of work, life, faith, competition, responsibility, ambition, community, choices, family (in the broadest sense), and opportunity. Poverty progressives should talk more about those values—not in a hollow, half-hearted way that gives the impression we are faking it just to win conservative votes—but in a full-throated, passionate voice that is able to convince people that those values are *our* values, because they *are* our values. In order to take back our country, first we need to take back our language.

When the public already agrees with us fully, such as on the importance of rewarding work, we should press forward more aggressively. At every possible opportunity, we should use ballot measures and/or legislative drives to enact higher living wage and minimum wage laws, and to raise the value of the federal Earned Income Tax Credit and the state and local wage supplements. The public clearly agrees that nobody working full time should be poor. Many conservatives who stand in the way of enabling the nation to accomplish the goal of a living wage should be pummeled (verbally, not physically)—not only by advocates but by political opponents and the media.

Working to convince people who have yet to be convinced is *not* about selling out and finding the lowest common denominator. It is about bringing people together to find common ground that reinforces both idealism and mutual self-interest.

Being mainstream does *not* mean being tepid. Progressives should embrace "radical moderation," in which we achieve fundamental, massive social change based on mainstream values. Yes, the American people do want wholesale change in order to improve the lives of themselves and their neighborhoods, but they want that change to be accomplished in a way that reinforces their core values.

COMMUNICATING ABOUT POVERTY AND HUNGER

Given that most Americans are not poor, communicating with them about poverty issues is a particularly tricky task. The toughest challenge is to mobilize low-income people without causing a backlash among everyone else. If we energize low-income people but create a backlash against such mobilization, that will only set us back as it did in the Nixon and the Reagan years. Conversely, if we make some headway in increasing goodwill among the general public without poor people fully engaging in the process, it is unlikely that meaningful, large-scale action will result. Yes, it's really tough to do these two things at once—but we must.

To achieve that difficult balance, it is vital to convince middle-class Americans that the necessary steps to help people climb out of poverty—improving education, ensuring adequate health care, making housing affordable, increasing job security, improving neighborhood safety, etc.—are the very same steps that they need to take to remain in the middle class. The middle class needs to know people in poverty are their allies, not their competitors or antagonists.

Once again, the single most compelling message is collective self-interest. "Do Right Voters" respond both to moral arguments that fighting hunger is the ethical and religiously appropriate thing to do *and* also to practical arguments that fighting hunger will improve the long-term development and learning of children and reduce societal crime and violence.[2]

Further building upon the theme of self-interest, the Web sites Inclusionist.org and the MobilityAgenda.org (a project of the Center for Economic Policy and Research) have started to make the argument that we should move beyond the discussion about ending poverty to talking about a new vision for the nation that includes all Americans in the success—or the failure—of the economy. They argue that asking voters to have sympathy for the poor is not nearly as effective as explaining that inequality and lack of opportunity stand in the way of building a "strong economy and good-paying jobs for all our workers." Their key message is that our goal should be to ensure that "everyone has what they need to be a participant and contributor to our economy" because our "communities and our nation are stronger when everyone can work and participate" fully in society.[3] Or, as Bill Clinton repeated throughout his career, if the US wants to be competitive in the world economy, "We don't have a person to waste."

Advocates need to learn to engage in professional message development and media outreach. Too many activists still think getting mainstream media coverage is somehow too self-promoting, yet they wouldn't think twice about standing on a corner for a month handing out flyers. That's shortsighted. If you can get a positive story on the local evening TV news or in the major local newspaper, that's the equivalent of having ten people handing out your flyer for a year. The New York City Coalition Against Hunger aggressively seeks media coverage and has been highly successful in doing so, which has had the concrete impact of prompting local elected officials to focus much more on the hunger issue than they otherwise would have.

In major urban areas where there are significant non–English language media outlets, we need to do a better job of reaching out to them. Unlike the mainstream media, to which you have to sell the idea that poverty is worth covering, many of the editors for these alternative media already know that.

Activists also must respond to breaking news quickly enough to be included in the same day's ever-changing news cycles. For instance, if the Census Bureau releases new poverty numbers in the morning, activists should put out a press release in response no later than that afternoon. If they do the typical thing—hold a series of committee meetings over the course of a week to decide how to respond—the news will be stale and they won't receive coverage.

It can also help to use humor to simultaneously reinforce our main messages and go against stereotypes that activists take themselves too seriously. One group very effective in doing this is "Billionaires for Bush," which shows up outside of Republican events in tuxedos and evening gowns in order to "thank" the event attendees for all their policies, which aid billionaires and harm poor people.

Some groups use humor only for shock value, such as having outrageous props covered with blood, showing off dead bodies, or using images that compare their opponents to Nazis. That only turns people off. A much more effective way to use humor is to show people that you can actually laugh at yourself at the same time you reinforce your basic message. On the next page, check out the press release I distributed one April Fool's Day. Note that we make fun of ourselves, by gently parodying how activists are outraged by everything. Yet we still used the release to reinforce our main two points about increasing poverty and hunger in New York.

NURTURING ALLIES

To win over undecided voters who swing elections and public policy debates, we need to highlight our commonalties and become allies with their allies.

One place to start is with religious leaders and congregations. We shouldn't just be organizing with the same five liberal priests, rabbis, imams, and ministers who already attend every rally and meeting we sponsor. We should also seek out leaders of conservative congregations, who are increasingly focusing on the issue of poverty. As just one example, Evangelical Christian leader Bill Hybels, senior pastor of the Willow Creek Community Church outside of Chicago (the second largest church in America), said in 2007, "If the poor are being neglected by the government in some way, then you have to stand up for the poor."[4] While progressives have often sparred with evangelicals over culture politics, I believe there is a unique opportunity for us to unite with evangelicals in opposition to the worst aspects of modern pop culture. Conservatives may worry that

For Immediate Release:

April 1, 2007

Contact: Joel Berg, (212) 825-0028, ext. 204

jberg@nyccah.org

Everything Perfect – and Getting Better, Advocates Say

Urge Elected Officials to Do *Less* Since City is "Problem-Free"

The New York City Coalition Against Hunger, an umbrella group for the city's more than 1,200 soup kitchens and food pantries, announced today that not only was everything perfect in the city, things were, in fact, getting substantially better.

According to a comprehensive new study released today by the Coalition, the "perfection index" for the city had increased by a whopping 485% in just the month of March alone. Citing these findings, the Coalition urged the city's largest corporations to pay the people who clean their offices at night even less.

Said Joel Berg, the Coalition's executive director, "It turns out the *New York Post* was right all along – there are no serious problems impacting poor people in New York City. Since the city is entirely problem-free, we now urge all our elected officials at the Federal, State, and City levels to do *less*, and we formally apologize to them if we ever criticized them for not doing more."

The Coalition also announced that, because it was so ecstatically happy at the state of affairs in the city, it would no longer use any of the following words in press releases or in testimony before the City Council: "outraged," "disappointed," "flabbergasted," "flummoxed," "lied to," "angered," "troubled," "aghast," "indignant," "slack-jawed," or "fatoozled."

The Coalition indicated that it had commissioned a new study to find alternative adjectives to use to express its pleasure with the status quo. The entire staff of the Coalition has also been enrolled in a special re-training program to learn new, non-outraged, facial expressions.

Continued Berg, "Because the city has solved all its problems, we are going to take this Sunday – and the entire month of April – off work. True, the number of families forced to use city homeless shelters is at the highest level in history, one in six New Yorkers live in households that can't afford enough food, and the City is still removing families from the welfare rolls before they have jobs – but just imagine the problems we'd have if our elected officials hadn't done everything perfectly."

###

pop culture promotes sex and violence, but poverty advocates should worry that it promotes nihilism and materialism. Both sides should work together toward enabling our society to better stress an ethic of community and a belief that each life has meaning and purpose; one of the best ways to instill this is to have people work together to fight hunger and poverty.

Poverty progressives should also seek out alliances with forward-thinking business leaders. Business heads can provide powerful testimony on behalf of the effectiveness of social programs. In 1991, five corporate executives testified before the House Budget Committee in support of the WIC program, releasing a joint statement: "We're convinced that WIC . . . can make an important contribution to ensuring that the nation's education objectives are met, and that in turn, we have the productive workforce we need." Robert C. Winters, chairman and chief executive officer of the Prudential Insurance Company of America, said, "We should invest our health care dollars where they will do the most good. That means in prevention. We need to start preparing our children today so they can lead productive and meaningful lives tomorrow." I guarantee that such testimony carried far more weight than the opinions of hundreds of advocates. Business leaders with the most common sense understand that our nation's economic health is based on the broader success of society.

Find allies wherever you can, even if they agree with you on just one issue. For instance, when I worked for the Clinton administration, the White House was in a knockdown, drag-out fight to the death with the National Rifle Association (NRA) over a ban on assault weapons and other issues related to gun control. Yet I still managed to work with the NRA to jointly promote the "Hunters for the Hungry Program," through which hunters donated meat to food banks nationwide. Working with them didn't mean that we agreed with each other on guns, but it did mean we could transcend our differences when it came to feeding hungry Americans. The most successful advocates frequently form unusual alliances on varied issues, knowing that, in politics, neither friends nor enemies are permanent.

POWER TO THE PEOPLE . . . TWENTY-FIRST CENTURY STYLE

Unfortunately, many progressive activists—most of whom are extraordinarily well meaning and with whom I usually agree on the issues—are too often stuck in a tactical time warp. They still spend much of their time shouting through a bullhorn, raising a fist, marching behind a frayed cloth banner, parading with giant puppets, or drumming loudly on cans. I certainly sympathize with their anger, but it is often self-defeating. Rather than connecting with undecided people on their issue, such images only reinforce negative stereotypes of the protesters.

I, for one, never understood the popular chant: "The people united will never be defeated." Our causes are defeated all the time. So, does that chant mean that we were never united in the first place? Or that we were never people? Plus, that phrase is incredibly alienating to many because it implies that anyone who does not agree with you on any particular cause is not part of "the people," and that, perhaps, they are instead a form of plant life.

Other activists insult the very government officials from whom they are seeking support, such as one group in New York whose members shouted down a commissioner at a public meeting and then issued a press release to brag about it. They later protested social service cuts, claiming the cuts would make it impossible for people to pay for their electricity bills, by dropping off lightbulbs at the offices of elected officials—including some who are usually allies—and saying, "We won't be needing these, but maybe you can get a bright idea about how to create a budget without balancing it on our backs!" Organizers like these are often better at making enemies than winning substantive victories. And while they may garner some news stories, if the coverage makes them look hostile or silly, that only sets the cause further back.

Some organizers still cling to the fantasy that large numbers of poor Americans will "rise up and take to the streets" to seize power by force or by threat. A favorite organizing stunt is showing up at someone's office unannounced and demanding a meeting. One antipoverty group did that to Senator Clinton, and even proudly put in their press release that Clinton's staff called them "unprofessional." I just don't see how that kind of attention helps anyone. Besides, "getting a meeting" isn't the panacea to which these groups, often obsessed with process, should aspire. It is merely a first step and does no good if you aren't respected when you get to the table.

I also think we need to move beyond narrow identity politics. Constant arguments over which group is the most oppressed help no one.

It's time for advocates to get real. We should focus on substantive issues that matter to real people, right in our neighborhoods. Jobs. Shelter. Food. Health and child care. Wages. And rather than merely support abstract goals like "everyone should have a right to food and housing" advocates should focus on fighting for very specific measures, such as making food stamp benefits generous, passing a living wage ordinance, or making Section 8 housing vouchers more available.

It's certainly important to focus on planetary issues like world peace and global suffering, but it is just as important—and often far harder—to get people to focus on problems in their own hometowns, especially when the blame for those problems might be closer than is comfortable. When a problem exists across the globe, it's easier to blame than when it's in our own backyards. Author Nick Kotz described how Ralph Abernathy, who led the Poor People's Campaign in the wake of Dr. King's assassination, lamented how white northerners, sympathetic when southern Negroes were violently attacked for sitting at lunch counters, had notably less sympathy when Negroes tried to dramatize the extent of poverty and hunger nationwide, saying: "It was easy enough to blame a southerner for barring his restaurant door . . . but who was the northern white man to blame for nationwide hunger, except himself, and who would have had to pay for the cure?"[5] It is clear that, as hard as it is to achieve victories closer to home, it's even harder to have credibility on the world stage if you can't even fix the problems in your very own house.

Progressives must nurture traditional on-the-ground organizing at the grassroots level, and must also bring more diversity to the Net Roots movement. The 2007 Daily Kos conference of bloggers and net-roots activists were mostly white, and more male than female. Wrote an attendee: "Only a handful of the 1,500 conventioneers—bloggers, policy experts, party activists—are African American, Latino, or Asian. Of about 100 scheduled panels and workshops, less than half a dozen dealt directly with women or minority issues."[6] And few dealt with poverty issues. More diverse activists and antipoverty organizers need to start their own blogs (see the New York City Hunger Blog at http://www.nyc-cah.org) and get invited (or invite themselves) to meetings of bloggers to ensure that poverty issues are discussed.

TIPS FOR CONVINCING ELECTED OFFICIALS

In trying to convince elected officials or the public to support key antihunger and antipoverty initiatives, I suggest you follow these guidelines that I have developed over my years of experience:

- Determine one basic message of what you want and repeat it over and over (and over) again. Just because you have delivered your message to officials at different times and in different ways, do not expect that they or their staff have heard it or remember it. Given that they receive so many brief and conflicting messages, repetition is vital in getting your point across.

- **Demonstrate significant community-based support.** Constantly demonstrate to elected officials that you represent numerous groups, institutions, and people in your community. Always reinforce that you are not just giving your personal opinion, but that many other voters in their district share your beliefs. Encourage these groups, institutions, and people to contact elected officials directly to echo your policy message.

- **Know how the system works.** Know which level—federal, state, or municipal—you should target, and what hurdles your policy initiatives must clear to be enacted. Remember that different committees and subcommittees will also need to take action to implement your policy goal. Know not just elected officials, but also their personal and committee staffs—who often do the *real* work and make major decisions.

- **Have specific policy goals and realistic strategies.** Don't seek a "moral victory." Seek a realistic way for government to take a specific action to directly improve the lives of the people you represent. Decide what goals you want to accomplish and at which level of government. Then figure out exactly which elected official you will need to vote for the action, and develop an individualized strategy to get them to vote your way or to persuade their colleagues to do likewise. Ask elected officials to take actions that are difficult but not politically impossible.

- **Know your facts.** For instance, if you volunteer with a food pantry or soup kitchen, have as much information as you can about how many people it feeds, how its need has been increasing, how many of the people it feeds are children and senior citizens, how many work but still cannot afford to feed their families, etc. Never make up information or exaggerate; let the powerful truth speak for itself.

- **Keep it simple.** Use language that everyone understands, even if they are not experts on your issue. Don't use lots of abbreviations or technical terms. Every communication you have—by phone, or in person, or in writing—should have one basic message: there is an important problem in your community and you are asking the elected official to take a specific, governmental action to solve that problem.

- Have it in writing . . . and in pictures. Always have at your fingertips a one-page fact sheet that describes both the problem you want solved and specifically what actions you want the elected official to take in order to fix it. Leave this fact sheet wherever you go, even if the people you came to visit were out. Whenever possible, also have relevant photographs and easy-to-understand charts and graphs.

- Get elected officials and their staffs to visit. Invite elected officials and their staffs to visit antihunger programs. They can obtain media coverage for the visits or put a photograph of it in their newsletters. Touring your site not only helps them better understand the problems you are up against, but it usually solidifies their commitment to helping your program.

- Avoid confrontational tactics whenever possible. You will almost always get better results meeting with government officials face-to-face rather than picketing against them. Save confrontational tactics as a last resort for when there is no other way to get the attention of the officials you are targeting. Rarely make political threats, and only do so if you are absolutely convinced you can make good on them.

- Repeat your basic message over and over (and over) again. (See the first item.)

ACKNOWLEDGMENTS

If I properly thanked everyone who has helped, inspired, and informed me over the last fifteen years that I have worked on hunger issues, this acknowledgments section would be longer than the entire book. That being said, I want to issue a blanket thanks to all the low-income and hungry people who have taken the time over the years to share their stories and ideas with me. I also want to thank the incredibly idealistic and dedicated people who volunteer at—and work for, often at wages not much higher than volunteering—nonprofit soup kitchens, food pantries, food rescue organizations, food banks, and advocacy organizations nationwide, for providing input and insight, and more importantly, for the incredible service they provide to the country. I especially want to thank my wonderful colleagues at other New York City antihunger, antipoverty, and food security organizations, whose names are too numerous to mention.

I also want to warmly thank the staff, board, volunteers, donors, and partners of the New York City Coalition Against Hunger—past and present—who empowered the organization not only to help meet the direct food needs of hungry New Yorkers, but to ask broader questions about poverty and hunger in America, such as those in this book.

I also want to thank many of the dedicated public servants I met at the US Department of Agriculture, whom I directly worked with during my eight years there and many of whom I still work closely with in my current job. I especially want to thank current and former USDA employees James Coyle, Ronald de Munbrun, David Gibson, Donna Hines, and Mark Nord. They and others taught me how best to make government work. I also want to thank many excellent public employees at the state and city levels who work on antihunger and antipoverty problems. While it is fashionable today—even for liberals—to deride public employees as bureaucrats (and while some public employees are far better than others), I think we all need to do a better job of recognizing how talented and dedicated many of these folks are, and that many chose lower-paying government jobs over high private sector salaries solely because they believe in serving the public. I also have to thank two other public servants: President Bill Clinton, for giving me the honor of serving the American people in his administration, and my previous boss, Secretary of Agriculture Dan Glickman, for his unswerving commitment to reducing hunger, not only in the US but worldwide.

Beyond those wide thanks, I do have to especially express my gratitude for a number of people who went above and beyond the call of duty with their friendship and collegiality to help me with this book, and the work that went into it.

I am eternally indebted to my partner, Lori Azim, who has not only been an extraordinarily insightful and helpful editor, proofreader, ideas-bouncer, and credibility gauge at every step of the process of conceiving and writing this book, but she deserves extra special credit and pity for often having been the first person suffering through my early morning (post-newspaper-reading) rants that ended up being key sections of this book. This book couldn't have happened without her.

Tremendous thanks to Crystal Yakacki, my editor at Seven Stories Press, for championing this project and providing feedback that improved the work at every step of the process. I also thank everyone of Seven Stories Press for having the courage to print the kinds of progressive, challenging works few other publishers will touch.

Amazing thanks to Jonathan Eig, an accomplished author and a long-time friend, for extraordinarily detailed and helpful editing and feedback on many drafts, despite being absurdly busy writing his own excellent books and raising a family.

Thanks also to Sarah Lazin, literary agent extraordinaire, for walking me through the process of getting a book published, and bringing focus to my early book outlines.

I am indebted to the previous research, work, and writing on hunger and poverty of Bill Ayres, Ray Boshara, Dr. J. Larry Brown, Edward Cooney, Jason DeParle, J. C. Dwyer, Peter Edelman, Peter K. Eisinger, Sandie Knapp, Nick Kotz, Janet Poppendieck, Michael Sherraden, David Shipler, Jennifer Tescher, Ellen Vollinger, Margy Waller, Mark Winne, Thomas Z. Freedman, and many others.

I am also grateful to the Columbia University Libraries for providing me with the master's thesis of Frances Perkins; to the Southern Historical Collection, Manuscripts Department, Wilson Library, University of North Carolina at Chapel Hill, for selecting and sending to me materials from the papers of Dr. Raymond Wheeler; and to the staff at the Keel Center at the Cornell University School of Industrial and Labor Relations for sending me a transcript from the Triangle Shirtwaist Factory fire trial.

I also want to thank the Center for Responsive Politics and the Environmental Working Group for their vitally important and user-friendly online databases of federal campaign finances and federal farm subsidies, respectively.

Of course, I have to thank Bruce Springsteen, for three reasons. One, at every one of his concerts, he asks audience members to donate to local anti-hunger groups (including the one I manage). Two, his lyrics speak for the downtrodden and dispossessed more powerfully than just about any artist alive today. And three, he's the *Boss*.

As I mentioned before, some of the people and organizations listed above may disagree with small or large sections of the book. Of course, any mistakes, misinterpretations, conclusions, and controversial claims are entirely my responsibility.

NOTES

Epigraphs

1. Robert Rector, "How Poor Are America's Poor? Examining the 'Plague' of Poverty in America," *Heritage Foundation Backgrounder*, no. 2064 (Washington, DC: August 27, 2007).
2. Editorials, *New York Post*, "Gotham's Latest Non-Crisis," December 30, 2006, and "John Vliet Spitzer," June 6, 2007.
3. Chico Marx, as the character "Chicolini," *Duck Soup*, Paramount Pictures, 1933.

INTRODUCTION. Hunger Amidst Plenty: A Problem as American as Apple Pie

1. President Richard M. Nixon, "Special Message to Congress Recommending a Program to End Hunger in America" (May 6, 1969), Nixon Presidential Papers, Richard Nixon Presidential Library and Museum.
2. US Department of State, Bureau of African Affairs, *Background Note: Mali* (October 2007).
3. United Nations Food and Agriculture Organization, *The State of Food Insecurity in the World, 2006*: 34.
4. US Department of Agriculture, Economic Research Service, *Household Food Security in the United States 2006*, by Mark Nord, Margaret Andrews, and Steven Carlson (Economic Research Report No. ERR-49, November 2007).
5. Ibid.
6. America's Second Harvest, "Food Bank Survey Points to Critical Shortage of Food, Urgency of Farm Bill and Immediate Need for $100 Million in Emergency Federal Funding," press release (May 1, 2008), http://www.secondharvest.org/news_room/2008_press_releases/050208.html (accessed August 2, 2008).
7. America's Second Harvest, *Hunger in America 2006* (Chicago, IL), February 23, 2006, http://www.hungerinamerica.org/ (accessed August 2, 2008). According to the organization, "The study provides authoritative, comprehensive, and statistically valid data on the national charitable response to hunger and the people served by private hunger relief agencies. Through 52,000 face-to-face client interviews and 30,000 surveys of local charitable agencies, *Hunger in America 2006* chronicles the nature and incidence of demand for emergency food assistance. There are two main data sources for *Hunger in America 2006*: client data and agency data, which were collected in early 2005. The client data was amassed through face-to-face interviews with randomly-selected recipients at emergency feeding sites across the country. Over 52,000 individuals offered to share their stories with us, including the circumstances of what led them to the pantry, kitchen or shelter at which they were interviewed. Their generosity makes it possible for us to better understand who seeks emergency food assistance and why. Secondly, we asked participating Network Members to mail surveys to each of their

member agencies, yielding over 30,000 nationwide. The agency surveys provide information on the services available to low-income Americans, their needs and their stability. *Hunger in America 2006* is the independent research conducted on behalf of America's Second Harvest— The Nation's Food Bank Network by Mathematica Policy Research, Inc. (MPR), a leading social policy research firm based in Princeton, NJ. In addition, all aspects of the study were overseen by an independent review team: the Technical Advisory Group (TAG). The TAG is comprised of noted social scientists, including demographers, nutritionists, academics and statisticians, who reviewed everything from the survey instruments to the analysis plan to the final results."

8. Joseph Glauber, Chief Economist, US Department of Agriculture, testimony before the Joint Economic Committee, 110th Cong., 2nd sess. (May 1, 2008).

9. Adam Drewnowsky and Pablo Monsivais, "The Rising Costs of Low-Energy-Density Foods," *Journal of the American Dietetic Association* 107 (December 2007): 2071-2076.

10. See note 8 above.

11. Loretta Schwartz-Nobel, *Growing Up Empty: The Hunger Epidemic in America* (New York: HarperCollins, 2002), 87 and 89.

12. Ibid., 144 and 189.

13. US Department of Agriculture, Food and Nutrition Service, Office of Analysis, Nutrition, and Evaluation, *Characteristics of Food Stamp Households: Fiscal Year 2005* (Report No. FSP-06-CHAR, September 2006).

14. President Ronald Reagan, Memorandum for Edwin Meese III (August 2, 1983): "I am deeply concerned about the extent to which we have a problem that should not exist in this great and wealthy country. That is the problem of hunger. America is literally the breadbasket of the world. We produce and export more food than any other nation. Our farms are the envy of the world. Yet, I have seen reports in the press in past weeks of Americans going hungry. I am deeply concerned by these stories, because I know the suffering that each of these incidents represents . . . I am fully committed to feeding the poor people of this Nation. No child, senior citizen, deserted mother or invalid should have to go hungry in America—not only because we are a land of plenty, but because federal law guarantees that our plenty is to be shared with those in true need . . . If even one American child is forced to go to bed hungry at night, or if one senior citizen is denied the dignity of proper nutrition, that is a national tragedy."

15. Senate, Senator Elizabeth Dole of North Carolina speaking on the floor of the US Senate, 108th Cong., 1st sess., *Congressional Record* (June 5, 2003), 149, pt. 82. In her maiden speech, she said: "Indeed, every religion, not just Christianity, calls on us to feed the hungry. Jewish tradition promises that feeding the hungry will not go unrewarded. Fasting is one of the pillars of faith of Islam, and is a way to share the conditions of the hungry poor while purifying the spirit and humbling the flesh. Compassion or Karuna is one of the key virtues of Buddhism. So, you see, this issue cuts across religious lines too. Mr. President, I speak today on behalf of the millions of families who are vulnerable, who have no voice . . . Mr. President, in my lifetime, I have seen Americans split the atom, abolish Jim Crow, eliminate the scourge of polio, win the Cold War, plant our flag on the surface of the moon, map the human genetic code and belatedly recognize the talents of women, minorities, the disabled and others once relegated to the shadows. Already, a large group of citizens have joined what I believe will become an army of volunteers and advocates. Today, I invite all of my colleagues to join me in this endeavor . . . let us recommit ourselves to the goal of eradicating hunger. Committed individuals can make a world of difference . . . even, I might say, a different world." In subsequent years, she voted for budget cuts in nutrition programs.

16. Senator George McGovern, from the introduction to Nick Kotz, *Let Them Eat Promises: The Politics of Hunger in America* (Garden City, New York: Anchor Books, 1968): xiv.

Section I — THE PROBLEM

CHAPTER 1. **Who is Hungry in America? The Politics of Measuring Hunger**

1. Joseph Stalin to Winston Churchill (1944), as quoted in Ann Fremantle, "Unwritten Pages at the End of the Diary," *New York Times* (September 28, 1958), BR3.
2. Phil McGraw, "Seven Steps to Breaking Your Addiction," http://www.drphil.com/articles/article/173 (accessed December 30, 2007).
3. *Hunger U.S.A.: A Report by the Citizens' Board of Inquiry in Hunger and Malnutrition in the United States* (Washington, DC: New Community Press, 1968), 41 and 42.
4. Nick Kotz, *Let Them Eat Promises: The Politics of Hunger in America* (Garden City, New York: Anchor Books, 1968), 80.
5. Ibid., 59.
6. Ibid., 243.
7. Ibid., 217.
8. Ibid., 186.
9. Larry J. Brown and H. R. Pfizer, *Living Hungry in America* (New York: Macmillan Publishing Company, 1987), xii.
10. Cheryl A. Wehler, "Community Childhood Hunger Identification Project: A Survey of Childhood Hunger in the United States," Food Research and Action Center, Inc. (Washington, DC: July 1995).
11. US Department of Agriculture, Economic Research Service, *Household Food Security in the United States 2006,"* by Mark Nord, Margaret Andrews, and Steven Carlson (Economic Research Report No. ERR-49, November 2007), iv.
12. Ibid., 4 and 7.
13. Ibid.
14. Melissa G. Pardue, Robert Rector, and Kirk A. Johnson, "Mayors' Claims of Growing Hunger Appear Once Again Wildly Exaggerated," Heritage Foundation *WebMemo #620* (December 13, 2004).
15. According to the US Census Bureau American Community Survey, 299 million people lived in the United States in 2006. According to the Federal Bureau of Investigation report, "Crime in the United States 2006," 17,034 Americans were murdered in 2006. By multiplying 299 million people by 365 days of the year, then dividing that by 17,034, the author determined that the average American's chances of being murdered on any given day were 6.4 million to one.
16. See note 11, 9.
17. Ibid., 6.
18. Ibid., iv.
19. Ibid., 8 and 7.
20. Michael Harrington, *The Other America: Poverty in the United States* (New York: Touchtone, 1997), 176.
21. See note 11, 10.
22. Ibid., 10.
23. Ibid., 10.
24. Ibid., 25.
25. US Department of Agriculture, Economic Research Service, *What Factors Account for State-to-State Differences in Food Security*, by Judi Bartfeld, Rachel Dunifon, Mark Nord, and Steve Carlson (Economic Information Bulletin Number 209, November 2006).
26. See note 11, 9.
27. Daily Census, New York City Department of Homeless Services, December 27, 2007.

28. Jason DeParle, *American Dream: Three Women, Ten Kids, and a Nation's Drive to End Welfare* (New York: Penguin Books, 2004), 287 and 288.

29. Barbara Ehrenreich, *Nickel and Dimed: On (Not) Getting By in America* (New York: Henry Holt and Company, 2001), 78.

30. US Department of Agriculture, Economic Research Service, *The Emergency Food Assistance System—Findings from the Provider Survey, Volume II: Final Report*, by James Ohls, Fazana Saleem-Ismail, Rhoda Cohen, Brenda Cox, and Laura Tiehen (Food Assistance and Nutrition Research Report No. FANRR16-2, October 2002).

31. America's Second Harvest, *Hunger in America 2006* (Chicago, IL: February 23, 2006), http://www.hungerinamerica.org/, (accessed August 2, 2008).

32. The emergency food users data is from *Hunger in America 2006* (see note 30), Tables 4.2.1, 5.5.1, 5.3.2, and 5.7.1. The demographic data is from US Census, American Community Survey 2005, General Demographic Characteristics, 2005, Selected Social Characteristics 2005, Selected Economic Characteristics 2005.

33. Ibid., 7.

34. New York City Coalition Against Hunger, "Rising Food Lines, Sinking Economy: Increase in NYC Hunger is Early Proof of Economic Slow-Down," (annual survey), November 2007.

35. Rhonda Amon, "Interfaith Effort to Fight Hunger on Long Island," *Newsday* (New York), September 25, 2007. "Hunger at the Holidays," editorial, *New York Times*, December 16, 2007, Long Island edition.

36. Denisa R. Superville, Jan Barry, and Jason Tsai, "Holiday Dinner's Over, but not Chronic Hunger," *Record* (Bergen County, New Jersey), November 23, 2007, A1.

37. Regional Food Bank of Northeastern New York, Agency List, February 2007.

38. Christina Jeng, "Feasts Served Up for Hundreds," *Journal News* (Lower Hudson Valley, New York), November 23, 2007, A1.

39. Bill Michelmore, "News Neediest: North Tonawanda Food Pantry Has Steady Flow of Helpers," *Buffalo News*, December 19, 2007.

40. Editorial, "Many Wichitans Living on the Edge," *Wichita Eagle*, October 24, 2007. Roy Wenzl, "A Growing Hunger," *Wichita Eagle*, October 21, 2007.

41. Katie Zezima, "Food Banks in a Squeeze Tighten Belts," *New York Times*, November 30, 2007, A1.

42. Leonard Doyle, "Plight of the Huddled Masses: A Hard Time for Thanksgiving," *Independent* (London), November 23, 2007.

43. Shawn Powers, "Community Voices," *Anchorage Daily News*, August 30, 2007.

44. Alex Johnson, "Economy Takes Harsh Toll on Relief Agencies," MSNBC, April 21, 2008, http://www.msnbc.msn.com/id/24186951/ (accessed on August 2, 2008).

45. US Department of Agriculture, Department of Public Affairs, "Glickman Releases State-by-State Food Insecurity Rankings, Announces Significant New Steps to Fight Hunger," press release 0414.99 (October 14, 1999).

46. Ibid.

47. "Carrying the Burden: Bridging the Food Security Gap in the Texas Capital," *Austin Chronicle*, April 28, 2000.

48. Ibid.

49. Fiscal Year 2000 Agriculture Appropriations Bill (as passed by the US House of Representatives), 106th Cong., 1st sess., H.R. 1906.

50. See note 27, 95.

51. See note 11.

52. Elizabeth Williamson, "Some Americans Lack Food, but USDA Won't Call Them Hungry," *Washington Post*, November 16, 2006, A1.

CHAPTER 2. **How Hunger Costs *All* of Us**

1. Deborah Frank, Director, Grow Clinic for Children at Boston Medical Center, and Principal Investigator, Children's Nutrition Sentinel Nutrition Assessment Program, testimony before the Committee on Agriculture, Nutrition, and Forestry, US Senate, 107th Cong., 1st sess. (July 19, 2001).

2. The Sodexo Foundation, in partnership with the Public Welfare Foundation and the Spunk Fund, Inc., *The Economic Cost Of Domestic Hunger: Estimated Annual Burden to the United States*, by J. Larry Brown, Donald Shepard, Timothy Martin, John Orwat, June 5, 2007.

3. Nutrition-Cognition National Advisory Committee, *Statement on the Link Between Nutrition and Cognitive Development in Children,"* 1998.

4. See note 1.

5. Loretta Schwartz Nobel, *Growing Up Empty: The Hunger Epidemic in America* (New York: HarperCollins, 2002), 144.

6. See note 3.

7. J. Larry Brown, *The Consequences of Hunger and Food Insecurity for Children: Evidence from Recent Scientific Studies*, Center on Hunger and Poverty, Brandeis University, June 2002.

8. John T. Cook, Deborah Frank, Carol Berkowitz, Maureen Black, Patrick H Casey, Diana B. Cutss, Alan F. Meyers, Nieves Zaldivar, Anne Salicky, Suzette Levenson, Tim Herrn, and Mark Nord, "Food Insecurity Is Associated with Adverse Health Incomes among Human Infants and Toddlers," *Journal of Nutrition* 134 (June 2004): 1432-1438.

9. *Katherine Alaimo, Christine M. Olson, and Edward A. Frongillo Jr,* "Food Insufficiency and American School-Aged Children's Cognitive, Academic, and Psychosocial Development," *Journal of Pediatrics* 108 No. 1 (July 2001): 44-53.

10. *Carol L. Connell, Kristi L. Lofton, Kathy Yadrick, and Timothy A. Rehner,* "Children's Experiences of Food Insecurity Can Assist in Understanding Its Effect on Their Well-Being," *Journal of Nutrition* 135 (July 2005): 1683-1690.

11. Ronald E. Kleinman, J. Michael Murphy, Michelle Little, Maria Pagano, Cheryl A. Wehler, Kenneth Regal, and Michael S. Jellinek, "Hunger in Children in the United States: Potential Behavioral and Emotional Correlates," *Journal of Pediatrics* 101, no. 1 (January 1998): E3.

12. Patrick H. Casey, Kitty L. Szeto, James M. Robbins, Janice E. Stuff, Carol Connell, Jeffery M. Gossett, and Pippa M. Simpson, "Child Health-Related Quality of Life and Household Food Security," *Archives Pediatric Adolescent Medicine*, 159 (2005): 51-56.

13. Katherine Alaimo, Christine M. Olson and Edward A. Frongillo, "Family Food Insufficiency, but Not Low Family Income, Is Positively Associated with Dysthymia and Suicide Symptoms in Adolescents," *Journal of Nutrition*, 132 (2002): 719-725.

14. *Jacinta Bronte-Tinkew, Martha Zaslow, Randolph Capps, Allison Horowitz, and Michelle McNamara,* "Food Insecurity Works through Depression, Parenting, and Infant Feeding to Influence Overweight and Health in Toddlers," *Journal of Nutrition*, 137 (September 2007): 2160-2165.

15. Robert C. Whitaker, Shannon M. Phillips, and Sean M. Orzol, "Food Insecurity and the Risks of Depression and Anxiety in Mothers and Behavior Problems in their Preschool-Aged Children," *Journal of Pediatrics*, 118, no. 3 (September 2006):. e859-e868.

16. Joy Margheim and Mike Leachman, *Empty Cupboards, Empty Feelings*, Oregon Center for Public Policy, November 28, 2007.

17. Andrew S. London and Ellen K. Scott, "Food Security Stability and Change Among Low-Income Urban Women," Joint Center for Poverty Research, Working Paper 354, May 19, 2005.

18. America's Second Harvest, *Hunger in America 2006* (Chicago, IL), February 23, 2006, http://www.hungerinamerica.org/ (accessed August 2, 2008).

19. United Nations Food and Agriculture Organization, World Food Summit Focus on the Issues, "Banking for the Poor," June 2002.

20. See note 17.

21. US Department of Agriculture, Economic Research Service, *Household Food Security in the United States 2006*, by Mark Nord, Margaret Andrews, and Steven Carlson (Economic Research Report No. ERR-49, November 2007).

22. Leigh Ann Simmons, Susan C. Modesitt, Amanda C. Brody, Allison B. Leggin, "Food Insecurity Among Cancer Patients in Kentucky: A Pilot Study," *Journal of Oncology Practice*, 2, No. 6 (November 2006): 274-279.

23. Nick Kotz, *Let Them Eat Promises: The Politics of Hunger in America* (Garden City, New York: Anchor Books, 1968), 39.

CHAPTER 3. **Why Brother (and Sister) *Still* Can't Spare a Dime: A Short History of Domestic Hunger**

1. Frances Perkins, "A Study in of Malnutrition in 107 Children from Public School 51," (submitted in partial fulfillment of the requirements for the degree of Master of Arts in the Faculty of Political Science, Columbia University, April 15, 1910), Chapter III, 17.

2. George McGovern, Robert Dole, and Donald E. Messer, *Ending Hunger Now* (Minneapolis: Fortress Press, 2005), 55.

3. Peter Eisinger, *Toward an End to Hunger in America* (Washington, DC: The Brookings Institution Press, 1988), citing Leo Marx, *The Machine in the Garden* (London: Oxford University Press, 1964).

4. Christine Kinealy, *This Great Calamity: The Irish Famine 1845–52* (Dublin: Gill & Macmillan Ltd, 1994).

5. Ibid., 40.

6. Ibid., 118.

7. Diane Cardwell, "A City Hall Feeling Its Way in a Renewed Battle on Poverty," *New York Times*, April 19, 2006.

8. Christopher Gray, "Streetscapes: The Municipal Lodging House; A 1909 Home for the Homeless," *New York Times*, November 22, 1991.

9. Theodore Dreiser, *Sister Carrie* (1900; The Pennsylvania Edition), (Philadelphia: University of Pennsylvania Press, 1981), 472.

10. Robert Hunter, *Poverty* (New York: The Macmillan Company, 1904).

11. John Spargo, *The Bitter Cry of Children* (London: Macmillan and Company: 1909), 77.

12. Ibid., 5.

13. Ibid., 76.

14. Ibid., 68 and 73.

15. Ibid., 64.

16. See note 1.

17. Janet Poppendieck, *Breadlines Knee-Deep in Wheat* (New Brunswick: Rutgers University Press, 1986): X, 17, 27, and 31.

18. Ibid., 18.

19. Ibid., 25 and 21.

20. Ibid., 28 and 31.

21. Ibid., X and XII.

22. Ibid., 46 (citing President Herbert Hoover's Address to the Welfare and Relief Mobilization Conference, Public Papers of the Presidents, Herbert Hoover, 1932–1933 (Washington, DC: US Government Printing Office, 1976).

23. Ibid., 50–53 (citing Public Papers of the Presidents, Herbert Hoover, 1931 (Washington, DC: US Government Printing Office, 1976).

24. Ibid., 771 and 772 (citing President Herbert Hoover, News Conference of November 6, 1932 from Public Papers of the Presidents, Herbert Hoover, 1931 (Washington, DC: US Government Printing Office, 1976).

25. Ibid., 24.

26. Marion Nestle, "Hunger in America: A Matter of Policy," *Social Research* 66 (Spring 1999), 257–282.
27. See note 17, X, 17, 27, 31, 62, and 63.
28. Ibid., 33, 46, and 47.
29. Ibid., 74 and 67.
30. Ibid., 80 (citing President Franklin Delano Roosevelt's "Annual Message to Congress," January 4, 1934, Public Papers and Addresses: 19 and 20).
31. US Department of Agriculture, Food and Nutrition Service, *A Short History of the Food Stamp Program* (last modified February 8, 2008), http://www.fns.usda.gov/fsp/rules/Legislation/about_fsp.htm (accessed December 28, 2006).
32. George McGovern, *The Third Freedom: Ending Hunger in Our Time* (New York: Simon and Schuster, 2001), 30.
33. David W. Kirkpatrick, "The WWII GI Bill: Exhibit A for School Choice," US Freedom Foundation, February 8, 2007 (citing Josh Hammond and James Morrison, *The Stuff Americans Are Made Of* [New York: Macmillan, 1996]: 290).
34. US Department of Veterans Affairs, "GI-Bill History," (reviewed/updated July 22, 2008), http://www.gibill.va.gov/GI_Bill_Info/history.htm (accessed January 3, 2008).
35. Ibid.
36. Nick Kotz, *Let Them Eat Promises: The Politics of Hunger in America* (Garden City, New York: Anchor Books, 1968), 40.
37. Senator John F. Kennedy, opening statement, September 26, 1960 presidential debate, John F. Kennedy Presidential Library and Museum.
38. See note 17, 243.
39. Peter Edelman, *Searching for America's Heart: RFK and the Renewal of Hope* (New York: Houghton Mifflin Company, 2001), 52.
40. See note 36, 2.
41. See note 29, 52.
42. Raymond M. Wheeler, "Hungry Children: Special Report," Southern Regional Council (1967), 4–6.
43. Ibid. (field report of Dr. Raymond M. Wheeler's Mississippi Trip to Humphreys and Leflore Counties), 12 and 13.
44. Raymond Wheeler Papers (#4366), 1967, Southern Historical Collection, Manuscripts Department, Wilson Library, University of North Carolina at Chapel Hill.
45. See note 36, 9.
46. Ibid., 24 and 25.
47. Ibid., 44.
48. Ibid., 43.
49. *Hunger U.S.A.: A Report by the Citizens' Board of Inquiry in Hunger and Malnutrition in the United States* (Washington, DC: New Community Press, 1968), 4.
50. Ibid., 9-17.
51. Ronald N. de Munbrun, "Hunger in America: The Hunger Lobby and the Effectiveness of its Problem Recognition Efforts," May 26, 1998 (a paper presented in partial fulfillment for requirements of Journalism 768, Media-centric Politics, University of Maryland).
52. See note 36, 22, 205, and 209.
53. Ibid, 205 and 209.
54. President Richard M. Nixon, "Special Message to Congress Recommending a Program to End Hunger in America," (May 6, 1969) Nixon Presidential Papers, Richard Nixon Presidential Library and Museum.
55. See note 32.
56. See note 36, 22.
57. See note 31.
58. Ibid.

59. US Department of Agriculture, Food and Nutrition Service, federal nutrition assistance program participation data, 1969 and 1979, http://www.fns.usda.gov/fns/data.htm, (accessed on August 3, 2008).

60. Nick Kotz, "Hunger in America: The Federal Response," Field Foundation (New York), 1979.

61. Janet Poppendieck, *Sweet Charity: Emergency Food and the End of Entitlement* (New York: Penguin Books, 1998), 87.

62. Larry J. Brown and H.R. Pizer, *Living Hungry in America* (New York: Macmillan Publishing Company, 1987), 2, 24, 47, 51, 56, 66, 161, and 163.

63. President William Jefferson Clinton, remarks at the Signing of the Agricultural Research, Extension and Education Reform Act of 1998, June 23, 1998.

64. US Secretary of Agriculture Dan Glickman, remarks at the Summit on Food Recovery and Gleaning, September 15, 1997.

65. President William Jefferson Clinton, videotaped remarks for the National Summit on Community Food Security, October 14, 1999.

66. US Department of Agriculture, Economic Research Service, *Household Food Security in the United States 2006*, by Mark Nord, Margaret Andrews, and Steven Carlson (Economic Research Report No. ERR-49, November 2007).

67. Dorothy Rosenbaum, "President's Budget Would Cut Food for Over 420,000 Low-Income Seniors," Center for Budget and Policy Priorities Paper, February 14, 2006.

68. US Department of Agriculture, Office of Public Affairs, "Secretary Schafer, Deputy Secretary Conner Conference Call with Reporters: Announcement of a New Farm Bill from Congress,"press release No. 0123.08, May 9, 2008, http://www.usda.gov/wps/portal/!ut/p/_s.7_0_A/7_0_1OB?contentidonly=true&contentid=2008/05/0123.xml (accessed August 3, 2008).

CHAPTER 4. **The Tattered (But Still Existing) Federal Hunger Safety Net**

1. US Department of Agriculture, Food and Nutrition Service, "The Business Case for Increasing Food Stamp Program Participation," December 2007 (updated February 1, 2008), http://www.fns.usda.gov/fsp/outreach/business-case.htm (accessed August 3, 2008).

2. US Department of Agriculture, Economic Research Service, *Seniors' Views of the Food Stamp Program and Ways To Improve Participation—Focus Group Findings in Washington State: Final Report*, by Vivian Gabor, Susan Schreiber Williams, Hilary Bellamy, and Brooke Layne Hardison, (E-FAN No. 02-012, June 2002).

3. *Kirang Kim and Edward A. Frongillo*, "Participation in Food Assistance Programs Modifies the Relation of Food Insecurity with Weight and Depression in Elders," *Journal of Nutrition* 137 (April 2007): 1005-1010.

4. "Food Stamps as Medicine," Children's Sentinel Nutrition Assessment Program, February 2007.

5. US Department of Agriculture, Food and Nutrition Service, Office of Analysis, Nutrition, and Analysis, *Dynamics of Food Stamp Participation, 2001-2003*, November 2007.

6. Ibid.

7. US Department of Agriculture, Food and Nutrition Service, Office of Analysis, Nutrition, and Evaluation, *Characteristics on Food Stamp Households: Fiscal Year 2005* (Report No. FSP-06-CHAR), September 2006.

8. Peter Eisinger, *Toward an End to Hunger in America* (Washington, DC: Brookings Institution Press, 1988), 37.

9. Laura Kelans, "Food stamps not going to all eligible in state," *Arkansas Democrat-Gazette*, August 19, 2007.

10. America's Second Harvest, *Hunger in America 2006* (Chicago, IL), February 23, 2006, http://www.hungerinamerica.org/, (accessed August 2, 2008), Table 7.1.1, "Use of Food Stamp Program."

11. US Department of Agriculture, Food and Nutrition Service, *State Food Stamp Participation Rates in 2005,* by Karen Cunnyngham, Laura A Castner, and Allen L. Schirm, Mathematica Policy Research Inc., October 2007.

12. Food Research and Action Center, *Food Stamps Access in Urban America: A City-By-City Snapshot,* October 2007.

13. Oregon Hunger Relief Task Force, *2005 Oregon Food Stamp Participation at the County Level,* http://oregonhunger.org/images/stories/documents/OHRTF_FS_counties.pdf (accessed August 3, 2008).

14. US Department of Agriculture, Economic Research Service, *Characteristics of Low-Income Households With Very Low Food Security,* by Mark Nord (Economic Information Bulletin Number 25 May 2007).

15. See note 10.

16. Ibid., Table 7.2.1, "Reasons Why Clients Never Applied for the Food Stamp Program"; Table 7.3.1, "Reasons Why Clients Or Their Households Are Not Currently Receiving Food Stamps, For Those Who Have Applied."

17. Deborah Frank, Director, Grow Clinic for Children at Boston Medical Center, and Principal Investigator, Children's Nutrition Sentinel Nutrition Assessment Program, testimony before the Committee on Agriculture, Nutrition, and Forestry, US Senate, 107th Cong., 1st sess., (July 19, 2001).

18. Jason DeParle, *American Dream: Three Women, Ten Kids, and a Nation's Drive to End Welfare* (New York: Penguin Books, 2004), 290.

19. See note 14.

20. Rebecca Widom and Olivia Arvizo Martinez, "Keeping Food on the Table: Challenges to Food Stamps Retention in New York City," Urban Justice Center, September 2007.

21. Dick Gregory, with Robert Lipsyte, *Nigger: an Autobiography* (New York: E. P Dutton, 1964), 30.

22. J. Michael Murphy, Maria E. Pagano, Joan Nachmani, Peter Sperling, Shirley Kane, Ronald E. Kleinman, "The Relationship of School Breakfast to Psychosocial and Academic Functioning: Cross-sectional and Longitudinal Observations in an Inner-City School Sample," *Archives of Pediatric Adolescence Medicine* 158 (1998): 899-907.

23. *Foodlinks America Newsletter,* December 7, 2007, http://tefapalliance.org/blog/archives/date/2007/12/ (accessed on August 3, 2008)

24. Nick Kotz, *Let Them Eat Promises: The Politics of Hunger in America* (Garden City, New York: Anchor Books, 1968), 163.

25. Carol Pogash, "Free Lunch Isn't Cool. So Some Students Go Hungry," *New York Times,* March 1, 2008, A1.

26. Food Research and Action Center, *School Breakfast Scorecard 2007,* December 2007.

27. Associate Press, "House Overrides Bush veto on Farm Bill," May 21, 2008.

CHAPTER 5. **Let Them Eat Ramen Noodles: One Week Living on $28.30 of Food**

1. Eric Gioia, New York City Council Member, interview by Jay DeDapper, W-NBC4 TV program "New Forum," May 13, 2007.

2. US Department of Agriculture, Food and Nutrition Service, *Food Stamp Program Participation and Costs,* as of November 30, 2007.

3. Food Research and Action Center, "Food Stamp Program Frequently Asked Questions," http://www.frac.org/html/federal_food_programs/programs/fsp_faq.html (accessed August 3, 2008).

4. US Department of Agriculture, Economic Research Service, *Household Food Security in the United States 2006,* by Mark Nord, Margaret Andrews, and Steven Carlson, (Economic Research Report No. ERR-49, November 2007), 22 and 23.

5. The calories and nutrients for what I ate were estimated by using the retail nutrition tracking software, Diet Power, which can be found at http://www.dietpower.com.
6. John Branston and Mary Cashiola, "The Food Stamps Challenge: Two *Flyer* Staffers to eat for a week on $22.47," *Memphis Flyer*, June 26, 2007.
7. Food Research and Action Center, "MI Food Stamp Challengers: Federal Nutrition Programs Update," September 7, 2007.
8. Ryan Powers, "TSA Confiscates Congressman's Last Meal During Food Stamp Challenge," Think Progress, May 21, 2007, http://thinkprogress.org/2007/05/21/food-stamp/ (accessed August 3, 2008).
9. The nutritional goals are from the 2005 federal dietary guidelines for Americans, (see http://www.health.gov/dietaryguidelines/). In these guidelines, the federal government recommends that the average person consume less than 2,300 mg per day of sodium or the equivalent to one teaspoon of salt (special high-risk groups advised to consume much less). It is also recommended that most Americans keep their fat intake between 20 and 35 percent of total daily calories, with less than 10 percent from saturated fat. In addition, the government recommends consuming at least 14 grams of fiber per 1,000 calories.

CHAPTER 6. **Are Americans Hungry—Or Fat?**

1. Robert Rector, "Food Stamp Program is Outdated," (commentary), The Heritage Foundation, August 29, 2003. Robert Rector and David Muhlhausen, "Is There a Hunger Crisis in America?" *Intellectual Ammunition*, The Heartland Institute, November 1, 1999.
2. Naomi Schalit, "Retired Workers, Vets, Children Faces of Hunger," *Kennebec* (Maine) *Journal*, July 23, 2007.
3. The Heritage Foundation and American Enterprise Institute revenues and executive salaries were obtained from Form 990s filed with the IRS. Household income of food pantry and soup kitchen users were obtained from America's Second Harvest, *Hunger in America 2006* (Chicago, IL), February 23, 2006, http://www.hungerinamerica.org/ (accessed August 2, 2008),
4. Mark Green and Gail MacColl, *Reagan's Reign of Error* (New York: Pantheon, 1987), quoting *Economist*, January 14, 1984.
5. See note 1, "Is There a Hunger Crisis in America?"
6. Douglas J. Besharov, the Joseph J. and Violet Jacobs Scholar in Social Welfare Studies, American Enterprise Institute, "Growing Overweight and Obesity in America: The Potential Role of Federal Nutrition Programs," testimony before the Committee on Agriculture, Nutrition, and Forestry, US Senate, 108th Cong., 1st sess. (April 3, 2003).
7. US Department of Agriculture, Economic Research Service, *Keeping Warm, Keeping Cool, Keeping Food on the Table: Seasonal Food Insecurity and the Costs of Heating and Cooling*, by Mark Nord, July 2003.
8. Cheryl Weitzstein, "Hunger Survey Lambasted for Lack of Scientific Base," *Washington Times*, January 6, 2004. Melissa G. Pardue, Robert E. Rector, and Kirk A. Johnson, *Mayors' Claims of Growing Hunger Appear Wildly Exaggerated*, (Backgrounder #1711), The Heritage Foundation, December 15, 2003.
9. Robert Rector, *How Poor Are America's Poor? Examining the "Plague" of Poverty in America*, (Backgrounder No. 2064), The Heritage Foundation, August 27, 2007: 2, 7, and 9.
10. Associated Press, "US, Britain Ranked Last in Child Welfare," January 14, 2007.
11. US Department of Agriculture, Economic Research Service and Food and Nutrition Service, and Health Canada, Office of Nutrition Policy and Promotion, *Food Insecurity in Canada and the United States: An International Comparison*, by Mark Nord (Economic Research Service), Michelle Hooper (Health Canada), and Heather Hopwood (Food and Nutrition Service), (paper presented at the 19th IUHPE World Conference on Health Promotion and Education, Vancouver, British Columbia, Canada, June 11–15, 2007.) The views expressed in this conference

paper are those of the authors and may not be attributed to the US Department of Agriculture, the US Economic Research Service, the US Food and Nutrition Service, or Health Canada.

12. See note 9, 2.

13. See note 6.

14. See note 6.

15. Leslie Kaufman, "Are The Poor Suffering From Hunger Anymore?" *New York Times*, February 23, 2003. Greg Easterbrook, "All This Progress Is Killing Us, Bite by Bite," *New York Times*, March 13, 2004.

16. Adult obesity statistic from Centers for Disease Control and Prevention, National Center for Health Statistics, "New CDC Study Finds No Increase in Obesity Among Adults; But levels Still High," press release (November 28, 2007). Adolescent obesity statistic from Centers for Disease Control and Prevention, "Childhood Overweight," http://www.cdc.gov/nccdphp/dnpa/obesity/childhood/index.ht (updated May 21, 2008).

17. US Department of Agriculture, Economic Research Service, *Household Food Security in the United States 2006*, by Mark Nord, Margaret Andrews, and Steven Carlson, (Economic Research Report No. ERR-49, 66 pp, November 2007): 44.

18. Food Research and Action Center and The Center on Hunger and Poverty at Brandeis University, *The Paradox of Hunger and Obesity in America*, July 14, 2002.

19. US Department of Agriculture, Economic Research Service, "Food Insecurity Statistics Shed Light on Hardships Households Face in Meeting Their Food Needs," by Mark Nord and Mark Prell, *Amber Waves*, June 2007.

20. Loretta Schwartz Nobel, *Growing Up Empty: The Hunger Epidemic in America* (New York: HarperCollins, 2002), 45.

21. US Bureau of Labor Statistics, Consumer Price Index, "CPI Detailed Report," October 2007: 109 and 110.

22. Dina Cassady, Karen M. Jetter, and Jennifer Culp, "Is Price a Barrier to Eating More Fruits and Vegetables for Low Income Families?" *Journal of the American Dietetic Association* 107, (October 19, 2007).

23. Associated Press, "High-Calorie Foods a Bargain for the Poor," February 2, 2004.

24. Adam Drewnowski and S. E. Specter, "Poverty and Obesity: The Role of Energy Density and Energy Costs," *American Journal of Clinical Nutrition* 79 (2004).

25. Amanda Shaffer and Robert Gottlieb, "The Persistence Of L.A.'s Grocery Gap: The Need For a New Food Policy and Approach to Market Development," Center for Food and Justice, Urban and Environmental Policy Institute, Occidental College, May 28, 2002.

26. Chris Kenning, "Lack of Healthy Food Causing Health Concerns," *Louisville Courier-Journal*, November 25, 2007.

27. Angela D. Liese, Kristina E. Weiss, Dolores Pluto, Emily Smith, and Andrew Lawson, "Food Types, Availability, and Costs of Food in a Rural Environment," *Journal of the American Dietetic Association* 107 (November 2007): 1916-1923.

28. Jennifer L. Black and James Macinko, "Neighborhoods and Obesity," *Nutrition Reviews* 66 (February 1, 2008): 2-20.

29. Kimberly Morland, Ana V. Diez Roux and Steve Wing, "Supermarkets, Other Food Stores, and Obesity: The Atherosclerosis Risk in Communities Study," *American Journal of Preventative Medicine* 30 (April 2006).

30. US Department of Agriculture, Agricultural Research Service, *Low-Income Households' Expenditures on Fruits and Vegetables*, by Noel Blisard, Hayden Stewart, and Dean Jolliffe, (Report No. SAER8233, May 2004). Tracie McMillan, "Putting the Cart Before the Market," *City Limits Weekly*, December 24, 2007.

31. US Department of Agriculture, Food and Nutrition Service, Benefit Redemption Division, "Annual Report for Fiscal Year 2006." Farmers' market data from US Department of Agriculture, Agricultural Market Service, "Farmers Markets" http://www.ams.usda.gov/

farmersmarkets/facts.htm (updated April 3, 2008) (accessed August 3, 2008). Percentage of farmers' markets that accept food stamps was calculated by the author.

32. New York City Coalition Against Hunger, *Food Access in Low-Income New York: Poverty and Food resources in Three NYC Community Districts*, by Ben Bakelaar, J. C. Dwyer, Syane Roy, and Malik Jones-Robinson, November 10, 2006, http://www.nyccah.org/files/map_report.pdf (accessed August 3, 2008).

33. City Harvest (New York City), *The Melrose Community Food Assessment*, February 2007.

34. Burger King, "Big Book of Nutrition Facts," http://www.bk.com/#menu=3,-1,-1 (accessed August 3, 2008).

35. "Fast-Food Branding Influences Kid's Choices," *Child Health News*, August 7, 2007.

36. Patrick H. Casey, Pippa M. Simpson, Jeffrey M. Gossett, Margaret L. Bogle, Catherine M. Champagne, Carol Connell, David Harsha, Beverly McCabe-Sellers, James M. Robbins, Janice E. Stuff, and Judith Weber, "The Association of Child and Household Food Insecurity With Childhood Overweight Status," *Journal of Pediatrics* 118 (November 2006): e1406-e1413.

37. William H. Dietz "Does Hunger Cause Obesity?" *Journal of Pediatrics* 95 (May 1995): 766-767.

38. Elizabeth J. Adams, Laurence Grummer-Strawn, and Gilberto Chavez, "Food Insecurity Is Associated with Increased Risk of Obesity in California Women," *Journal of Nutrition* 133 (April 2003): 1070-1074.

39. Carol L. Connell, Kristi L. Lofton, Kathy Yadrick, and Timothy A. Rehner, "Children's Experiences of Food Insecurity Can Assist in Understanding Its Effect on Their Well-Being," Journal of Nutrition, 135:1683-1690, July 2005.

40. G.M. Warldlaw and P.M, Insel, *Perspectives in Nutrition* Third Edition (New York: WCB/McGraw Hill 1998).

41. Jordan Lite, "City Stalked by Diabetes," *Daily News*, July 25, 2007.

42. R. Sturm, "The Effects of Obesity, Smoking, and Drinking on Medical Problems," *Health Affairs* 21 (May-June 2002): 245-0253.

43. Nick Kotz, *Let Them Eat Promises: The Politics of Hunger in America* (Garden City, New York: Anchor Books, 1968), 103.

44. Harvard Medical School, Course Catalogue, December 2007, http://www.medcatalog.harvard.edu/ (accessed December 2007).

CHAPTER 7. **Dickens Revisited: Life in the New Gilded Age**

1. Mayor Michael Bloomberg's net worth estimated in "Forbes 400 Richest Americans," *Forbes*, September 20, 2007. Mayor Bloomberg quote, as well as reporting on taxpayer subsidies to the Museum of Modern Art cited in Michael Saul, "Mike: If Tix Too Pricey, Stay HOMA," *New York Daily News*, September 28, 2004.

2. David Leonhardt, "2 Candidates, 2 Fortunes, 2 Views of Health," *New York Times*, December 23, 2007, A1.

3. Joint Committee on Taxation, "Estimates of Federal Tax Expenditures for Fiscal Years 2004-2008," 108th Cong., 1st sess., December 22, 2003.

4. David Cay Johnston, "Report Says That the Rich Are Getting Richer Faster, Much Faster," *New York Times*, December 15, 2007.

5. Ibid.

6. Matthew Miller, ed., "The Forbes 400," *Forbes*, September 20, 2007.

7. Matthew Miller, "Revolt of the Fairly Rich," *Fortune*, October 26, 2006 (posted on CNN.com).

8. See note 6.

9. Total approximate earnings of New York City residents living in poverty compiled by author using US Census poverty and earnings data.

10. Food insecurity data for 2006, calculated by the New York City Coalition Against Hunger from raw federal data from the US Department of Agriculture.

11. Kate Pickert, ed., "Who Makes How Much," *New York Magazine*, September 18, 2005.

12. US Census Bureau, "Income, Poverty, and Health Insurance Coverage in the United States: 2007" (Report P60-235).

13. Data calculated by the author from US Census, "2007 Current Population Survey" and 2007 disability data from the US Social Security Administration.

14. US Department of Labor, Employment Standards Administration, "History of Federal Minimum Wage Rates Under the Fair Labor Standards Act, 1938–2007," http://www.dol.gov/ESA/minwage/chart.htm (accessed August 3, 2008).

15. Catherine Candisky and Alan Johnson, "A Life Scraping By—the Plight of the Working Poor," *Columbus Dispatch*, June 8, 2004.

16. See note 12.

17. Danilo Pelletiere, Keith Wardrip, and Sheila Crowley, "Out of Reach 2006," National Low-Income Housing Coalition, December 12, 2006.

18. See note 12.

19. Heidi Evans, "My Week Living on the Minimum Wage," *Daily News*, February 7, 2004.

20. Barbara Ehrenreich, *Nickel and Dimed: On (Not) Getting By in America* (New York: Henry Holt and Company, 2001), 27.

21. Bruce Katz, *The Price is Wrong: Getting the Market Right for Working Families in Philadelphia*, The Brookings Institution, Metropolitan Policy Program, April 2005.

22. The Children's Defense Fund, "Keeping What They Earned: The High Cost of Tax Preparation and Refund Anticipation Loans in New York," April 2008.

23. David K. Shipler, *The Working Poor: Invisible in America* (New York: Alfred A. Knopf, 2005), 4 and 11.

24. See note 20.

25. Steven Greenhouse, "Workers Assail Night Lock-Ins by Wal-Mart," *New York Times Magazine*, January 18, 2003.

26. Patrick McGeehan, "Immigrants Pull Weight in Economy, Study Finds," *New York Times*, November 27, 2007, B5.

27. Andrew White, Sharon Lerner, Mia Lipsit and Coco McPherson, "Hardship In Many Languages: Immigrant Families and Children in NYC," Center for New York City Affairs Project on Immigrant Families and Children, Milano Graduate School, New School University, January 2005.

28. Eric Schlosser, "Penny Foolish," op-ed, *New York Times*, November, 28, 2007.

29. Joseph Berger, "4 Hour Trek Across New York for 4 Hours of Work, and $28," *New York Times*, May 6, 2004.

30. Randall C. Archibald and Will Carless, "Glare of Fires Pulls Migrants from Shadows," *New York Times*, October 27, 2007.

31. Jennifer Gonnerman, "For $1.75 an Hour," *New York Magazine*, August 13, 2007.

32. Justin Pritchard, "AP: Mexican Worker Deaths Rise Sharply," Associated Press, March 14, 2004.

33. US Census Bureau, "Income, Poverty and Health Insurance Coverage in the United States, 2006," Table A-1, 29.

34. Alan Berube, "The Middle Class Is Missing, " op-ed, *Daily News*, July 8, 2006.

35. The Drum Major Institute for Public Policy, *Saving Our Middle Class: A Survey of New York's Leaders*, April 2007.

36. Christine Haughney, "Apartment Prices in Manhattan Defy National Real Estate Slide," *New York Times*, January 3, 2008.

37. Marlene Naanes, "Report: Rent a Burden for Some NYers," *AM New York*, April 30, 2008.

38. Judith Messina, "Unaffordable NY: Tough Choices at $150,000," *Crain's New York Business*, January 5, 2008.

39. Tom Acitelli, "Census Shows Middle Class Flight from New York," *New York Observer*, September 19, 2007.

40. Christine Haughney and Eric Konigsberg, "Despite Tough Times, Ultrarich Keep Spending," *New York Times*, April 14, 2008.
41. Nicholas D. Kristof, "Millions for Moochers," op-ed, *New York Times*, March 6, 2004.
42. Senator Jim Webb (D-VA), response to President Bush's State of the Union speech, January 24, 2007.
43. Michael Brush, "Is a CEO Worth 364 Times the Average Joe?" MSN Money, September 5, 2007.
44. Associated Press, "CEO Pay Rises Despite Slow Economy," June 15, 2008.
45. Patrick McGeehan, "Minimum Wage Increases Faster Than Median Wage," *New York Times*, July 11, 2008.
46. Sarah Anderson, John Cavanagh, Chris Hartman, and Scott Klinger, *Executive Excess 2003*, Institute for Policy Studies and United for a Fair Economy, August 28, 2003.
47. Joe Brancatelli, "The Axis of Airline Execs," Portfolio.com, August 9, 2007.
48. Pew Research Center for the People & the Press, "Trends in Political Values and Core Attitudes: 1987–2007," March 22, 2007: 15.
49. Responsible Wealth, a Project of United for a Fair Economy, "Forbes 400 Richest Americans: They Didn't Do it Alone," press release, September 24, 2004.
50. Office of New York State Comptroller Alan G. Hevesi, press release, March 9, 2004.
51. Editorial, "The rich clean up," *New York Daily News*, August 13, 2007.
52. Patrick Arden and Tiffany Kilfeather, "Dinner, on the City's Tab," *Metro New York*, October 4, 2007, 2.
53. Patrick Arden, "Yankees Hit a Nerve with $400M Request," *Metro New York*, June 13, 2008.
54. Charles V. Bagli, "Chase Says It Will Move to Stamford if City Balks," *New York Times*, April 25, 2007.
55. Editorial, "The Tax Debate That Isn't," *New York Times*, December 13, 2007.
56. Edmund L. Andrews, "Tax Cuts Offer Most for Very Rich, Study Says," *New York Times*, January 8, 2007.
57. David Cay Johnston, "I.R.S. to Cut Tax Auditors," *New York Times*. July 23, 2006.
58. John Alexander Burton, "War of Poverty Redefined: The Administration's Approach to Curing the EITC Is to Kill the Patient," Center for American Progress, February 23, 2006, (web-only) http://www.prospect.org/cs/articles?articleId=11204 (accessed August 3, 2008).
59. Public Policy and Education Fund of New York, "The Color of Money in New York: Federal Campaign Contributions and Race," January 13, 2004.
60. Ray Rivera, "Mayor Accuses Realty Firms of Seeking Undue Influence," *New York Times*, February 8, 2008.
61. United for a Fair Economy, "CEOs at Defense Contractors Earn 45% More, Study Finds: Campaign Contributions Tied to Bigger Contracts," press release, April 28, 2003.
62. Editorial, "Feeding Our Hungry with the Farm Bill," *Kennebec Journal*, November 6, 2007.
63. The US Department of Agriculture Food and Nutrition Service Web site for "Applicants and Recipients," states that the maximum monthly food stamps benefit in fiscal year 2008 was $975, which the author calculated to be $11,700 for a year. Technically, families with more than eight children can receive higher benefits, but less than one percent of all food stamps households have more than eight people. http://www.fns.usda.gov/fsp/applicant_recipients/ (accessed August 3, 2008).
64. The Environmental Working Group's database of crop subsidy recipients, compiled from US Department of Agriculture data, indicates that Mr. Maurice Wilder of Wray, Colorado, received $3,092,631, which was the highest amount of farm subsidies going to any individual during the period 2003-2005. The author calculated the annual average payment to Mr. Wilder to be $1,030,877 per year. http://farm.ewg.org/sites/farmbill2007/person1614.php?custnumber=003014976 (accessed August 3, 2008).
65. The US Department of Agriculture Food and Nutrition Service document, "Food Stamp Program Participation and Costs, Data as of November 30, 2007," indicates that the average

monthly benefit in Fiscal Year 2007 was $95.64, which the author calculated to total $1,148 per year.

66. The Environmental Working Group's database of crop subsidy recipients (see note 64) indicates that between 2003 and 2005, a total of 1,544,132 people received $34,752,000,000, which the author calculated to equal $7,501 per person per year.

67. See note 63. The US Department of Agriculture states that, in fiscal year 2008, a household with eight people can earn up to $3,746 per month in gross income and receive food stamps benefits, which the author calculated to be an annual benefit of $44,952. The very rare household with more than eight people can earn more income and yet still receive food stamps.

68. US Department of Agriculture, Economic Research Service, *Effects of Reducing the Income Cap on Eligibility for Farm Program Payments*, by Ron L. Durst, September 2007.

69. See note 63. The US Department of Agriculture states that, in 2008, households may have up to $2,000 in countable resources, such as a bank account. Households may have up to $3,000 in countable resources if one member of the household is disabled or age sixty or older.

70. Adam Lisberg, "$10B Farm Aid for Rich Is No Urban Legend," *Daily News*, June 17, 2007.

71. Environmental Working Group, Farm Bill 2007 Policy Analysis Database, http://farm.ewg .org/sites/farmbill2007/person1614.php?custnumber=001102913&summlevel=address (accessed August 3, 2008).

72. Dean Kleckner, "Today's Harvest of Shame," (op-ed) *New York Times*, October 15, 2007.

73. John Holusha, "Goldman Sachs Profit Is a Wall Street Record: And for Employees an Average $622,000," *International Herald Tribune*, December 12, 2006.

74. Mary Kathryn Burke and Elizabeth Kolleeny, "What to Do with Your Goldman Sachs Bonus," ABC News, December 13, 2006.

75. Patrick Arden, "This Food Fight Pits Rich Against the Poor," *Metro New York*, March 6, 2008.

76. Charles V. Bagli, "Despite Its Jersey City Tower, Goldman Sachs Commits to One in Lower Manhattan," *New York Times*, April 17, 2004.

77. Franklin D. Roosevelt, Campaign Address in Brooklyn, New York, November 1, 1940, The American Presidency Project, University of California-Santa Barbara, www.presidency.ucsb .edu (accessed August 3, 2008).

78. Peter Edelman, *Searching for America's Heart: RFK and the Renewal of Hope* (New York: Houghton Mifflin Company, 2001): 55–56.

79. David R. Francis, "Upward Mobility in Real Decline, Studies Charge," *Christian Science Monitor*, January 27, 2003.

CHAPTER 8. **Let Them Eat Sound Bites: The Polarized Politics of Welfare Reform**

1. James Graham, *Enemies of the Poor* (New York: Vintage Books, 1971), 4.

2. George Gilder, *Wealth and Poverty* (New York: Basic Books, 1981), xi and xii.

3. Jason DeParle, *American Dream: Three Women, Ten Kids, and a Nation's Drive to End Welfare* (New York, Penguin Books Ltd., 2004), 130–136.

4. Dick Gregory, with Robert Lipsyte, *Nigger: an Autobiography* (New York: E. P Dutton, 1964), 28.

5. See note 3, 150.

6. US Department of Health and Human Services, Administration for Children and Families, Office of Family Assistance, AFDC and TANF Caseload Statistics.

7. See note 3, 156.

8. Ibid., 330.

9. Peter Edelman, *Searching for America's Heart: RFK and the Renewal of Hope* (New York: Houghton Mifflin Company, 2001), 162.

10. Craig Chamberlain, "Illinois Study Shows Mixed Results for People Leaving Welfare Rolls," University of Illinois at Urbana-Champaign News Bureau, October 1, 2000.

11. New York State Office of Temporary and Disability Assistance, *Leaving Welfare: Post-TANF Experiences of New York State Families*, June 2002.
12. John T. Cook, Deborah A. Frank, Carol Berkowitz, Maureen M. Black, Patrick H. Casey, Diana B. Cutts, Alan F. Meyers, Nieves Zaldivar, Anne Skalicky, Suzette Levenson, and Tim Heeren, "Welfare Reform and the Health of Young Children," *Archives of Pediatric Adolescent Medicine* 156 (2002): 678-684.
13. Catherine Candinsky and Alan Johnson, "Getting Off Welfare No Guarantee of Success," *Columbus Dispatch*, June 11, 2004.
14. Cassi Feldman, "Dissecting Welfare Stats: Former Clients 'Disappear,' " *City Limits Weekly* #531, April 17, 2006.
15. US Census Bureau, "Income, Poverty, and Health Insurance Coverage in the United States: 2006," Report P60-233.
16. New York City Independent Budget Office, "New Welfare Rules Could Be Costly for City," Fiscal Brief, July 2007.

CHAPTER 9. **The Poverty Trap: Why It Is So Hard to Escape Poverty in America**

1. "Mayor Bloomberg Addresses The Brookings Center on Children and Families 'Briefing On The Census Poverty Report'," Washington, DC, August 28, 2007, http://www.mikebloomberg.com/en/issues/reducing_poverty/mayor_bloomberg_addresses_the_brookings_center_on_children_and_families_briefing_on_the_census_povert.htm (accessed August 3, 2008).
2. President Lyndon B. Johnson, *My Hope for America* (New York: Random House, 1964).
3. US Department of Agriculture, Economic Research Service, *Household Food Security in the United States 2006*, by Mark Nord, Margaret Andrews, and Steven Carlson, (Economic Research Report No. ERR-49, November 2007): 10.
4. Adrian Nicole LeBlanc," The Price of Parsimony," *New York Times Magazine*, June 6, 2004, 21.
5. Erik Eckholm, "Study Says Education Gap Could Further Limit Poor," *New York Times*, February 20, 2008, A1.
6. Jason DeParle, *American Dream: Three Women, Ten Kids, and a Nation's Drive to End Welfare* (New York, Penguin Books, Ltd., 2004), 231, 239, 243, and 245.
7. Legal Momentum, "Reading Between the Lines: Women's Poverty in the United States, 2006," September 2007.
8. George Gilder, *Wealth and Poverty* (New York: Basic Books, 1981), 72.
9. John Woolman, "A Plea for the Poor," essay, 1764.
10. Erik Eckholm, "States Take Child Support, Leaving Mothers to Scrimp," *New York Times*, December 1, 2007, A-11.
11. Conn Carroll, comments on The Foundry, blog for The Heritage Foundation, "Marriage Breakdown Causes Poverty," http://blog.heritage.org, April 17, 2008.
12. Stephanie Coontz and Nancy Folbre, "Discussion Paper: A (Marriage Proposal) to End Poverty," Council of Contemporary Families, 2003.
13. "Key characteristics of America's Volunteers," *Chronicle of Philanthropy*, May 15, 2008.
14. See note 6, 60 and 133.
15. Heather Mac Donald, "Hispanic Family Values? Runaway illegitimacy is Creating a New US Underclass," *City Journal*, Autumn 2006.
16. David Wessel, "Racial Discrimination Is Still at Work," *Wall Street Journal*, September 4, 2003, A2.
17. Solomon Moore, "Reporting While Black," *New York Times*, September 30, 2007.
18. "Young Black Males Headed for Extinction?" Candidate Watch, The Fact Checker, *Washington Post* blog, October 10, 2007.

19. Erik Eckholm, "Reports Find Persistent Racial Gaps in Drug Arrests," *New York Times*, May 6, 2006, A21.
20. Orlando Patterson, "Jena, O.J. and the Jailing of Black America," op-ed, *New York Times*, September 30, 2007.
21. Michael Fletcher, "Middle Class Dream Eludes African American Families," *Washington Post*, November 13, 2007, A1.
22. Associated Press, "Income Gap Between Black, White Families Grow," November 13, 2007.
23. David Hilfiker, *Urban Injustice: How Ghettos Happen* (New York: Seven Stories Press, 2002), 20.
24. Remarks of Senator Barack Obama, "A More Perfect Union," Constitution Center, Philadelphia, Pennsylvania, March 18, 2008.
25. Pew Research Center for the People & the Press, "Trends in Political Values and Core Attitudes: 1987–2007," March 22, 2007.
26. Remarks of Senator Barack Obama: Apostolic Church of God, Chicago, Illinois, June 15, 2008, http://www.barackobama.com/2008/06/15/remarks_of_senator_barack_obam_78.php.
27. Sudhir Alladi Venkatesh, *Off the Books: The Underground Economy of the Urban Poor* (Boston: Harvard University Press, 2006).
28. Alford A. Young Jr., *The Minds of Marginalized Black Men: Making Sense of Mobility, Opportunity, and Future Life Chances* (Princeton, Princeton University Press, 2004), 54.
29. Katie S. Martin, Beatrice L. Rogers, John T. Cook, and Hugh M. Joseph, "Social Capital Is Associated with Decreased Risk of Hunger," *Social Science & Medicine* 58, no. 12 (December 10, 2003).

CHAPTER 10. **The Charity Myth**

1. Kevin Bonsor, "How Fire Engines Work," http://science.howstuffworks.com/fire-engine.htm (accessed August 3, 2008).
2. Solvej Schou, "Celebs Serve Holiday Meals to the Homeless," Associated Press, November 21, 2007.
3. Editorial, "A Fortress Against Hunger," *Boston Globe*, August 20, 2007.
4. Adam B. Ellick, "The Chicken and Rice Man," *New York Times*, November 25, 2007.
5. Detailed analysis of commodity prices conducted by the Wisconsin Community Action Program Association (WISCAP) at FoodLinks America, TEFAP Alliance Blog, September 29, 2007, http://tefapalliance.org/blog/archives/92 (accessed August 4, 2008).
6. Janet Poppendieck, *Sweet Charity: Emergency Food and the End of Entitlement* (New York: Penguin Books, Ltd., 1998), 209-229.
7. Value of grocery bag estimated by the South Texas Food Bank and based on the US Department of Agriculture Food and Nutrition Service, "Food Stamp Program: average monthly participation by state (households), (data as of November 30, 2007), http://www.fns.usda.gov/pd/16fsfyhh.htm
8. Barbara Ehrenreich, *Nickel and Dimed; On (Not) Getting By in America* (New York: Henry Holt and Company, 2001), 102, 103, and 185.
9. Pew Research Center for the People & the Press, "Trends in Political Values and Core Attitudes: 1987-2007," March 22, 2007.
10. US Department of Agriculture, Food and Nutrition Service, *Food Stamp Program Participation and Costs*, (data as of November 30, 2007), http://www.fns.usda.gov/pd/fssummar.htm (accessed August 3, 2008).
11. America's Second Harvest, fundraising e-mail signed by president and CEO Vicki Escarra, November 8, 2007.
12. Holly Hall and Peter Panepento, "Half of Charity Employees Report Seeing Ethical Lapses," *Chronicle of Philanthropy*, April 17, 2008. Stephanie Strom, "Report Sketches Crime Costing Billions: Theft from Charities," *New York Times*, March 29, 2008, A10.

13. Robert Egger, with Howard Yoon, *Begging for Change: The Dollars and Sense of Making Non-profits Responsive, Efficient, and Rewarding for All* (New York: HarperCollins, 2005).
14. Nora Barton and Peter Panepento, "Executive Pay Raises 4.6%," *Chronicle of Philanthropy*, September 20, 2007, 15. Metropolitan Museum of Art, IRS Form 990, available at http://www.guidestar.org. Salaries listed in Brennen Jensen, Leah Kerkman, and Cassie J. Moore, "Pay Raises for Charity Leaders Keep Pace With Inflation," *Chronicle of Philanthropy*, September 29, 2005. Government funding found on IRS Form 990s, available at http://www.guidestar.org.
15. See note 6, 6.
16. Mark Winne, "Holiday Handouts Don't Solve Hunger Problem in US," (op-ed) *Washington Post*, November 18, 2007, B1.
17. James Graham, *The Enemies of the Poor* (New York: Vintage Books, 1970), 174.
18. Deborah Solomon, "Questions for W. Todd Bassett," *New York Times Magazine*, February 1, 2004.
19. Ben Feller, "Bush Praises America's Giving Spirit," Associated Press, November 19, 2007.
20. Ray D. Madoff, "Dog Eat Your Taxes," (op-ed) *New York Times*, July 9, 2008.
21. Council on Foundation statistics quoted in Heather Joslyn, "Image vs. Reality," *Chronicle of Philanthropy*, October 18, 2007, D-3.
22. Gar Alperovitz, Steve Dubb, and Ted Howard, "New Approaches Needed to Curb Poverty," *Chronicle of Philanthropy*, November 15, 2007.
23. Kenneth D. Ackerman, *Boss Tweed: The Rise and Fall of the Corrupt Pol Who Conceived the Soul of Modern New York* (New York: Carroll & Graf, 2005).
24. Virginia Gardiner, "Free Dinners Add to Cheer for Christmas," *Chicago Tribune*, December 25, 1930.
25. *Chicago Tribune*, November 15, 1930.
26. "FreshDirect, Customer Update," e-mail to customers, December 30, 2007.
27. Tyson Food Web site, http://hungerrelief.tyson.com/ (accessed August 4, 2008).
28. Eric Schlosser, "Tyson's Moral Anchor," *Nation*, July 12, 2004.
29. Sasha Lilley, "Meat Packer's Union on the Chopping Block," Corp Watch, ZNet, April 20, 2005.
30. Phyllis Jacobs Griekspoor, "Tyson Workers File Suit for Pay," *Wichita Eagle*, May 2006.

CHAPTER 11. **How Media Ignores Hunger (Except During Holidays and Hurricanes)**

1. Barbara Ehrenreich, *Nickel and Dimed: On (Not) Getting By in America* (New York: Henry Holt and Company, 2001), 117.
2. Larry J. Brown and H.R. Pizer, *Living Hungry in America* (New York: Macmillan Publishing Company, 1987), ix.
3. Neil de Mause and Steve Rendall, *The Poor Will Always Be With Us—Just Not on the TV News*, Fairness and Accuracy in Reporting, September 7, 2007.
4. Celia W. Dugger, "World Bank Neglected African Agriculture," *New York Times*, October 15, 2007.
5. US Census Bureau, *Income, Poverty, and Health Insurance Coverage in the United States: 2006* (August 2007).
6. Newspaper Guild-CWA, "2006 Reporter Top Salaries," October 2006.
7. Bob Papper, "Seize the Pay," Radio-Television News Directors Association/Ball State University 2007 Salary Survey, June 2007.
8. "What New Yorkers Make: A Survey Up and Down the Pay Ladder of 33 of the Town's Professions," *New York*, November 11, 2000.
9. "Who Makes How Much: An Impertinent Look at Other People's Paychecks," *New York*, September 26, 2005.
10. Loretta Schwartz-Nobel, *Growing Up Empty: The Hunger Epidemic in America* (New York: HarperCollins, 2002), 7.

11. Carol Vogel, "Telltale Art," November 4, 2007; "A Matisse 'Odalisque' Sells for $33.6 Million, A Record for the Artist," November 7, 2007; "A Disappointing Night For Painting Sales at Sotheby's," November 8, 2007; "Dealer's Trove Draws Loyal Collectors and Strong Bids at Christie's," November 13, 2007; "At an Enthusiastic Christie's Sale, 'One Million Dollars Is the New 10 Grand'," November 14, 2007; "Fall Art Auctions Limp to Finish on Mixed Night at Phillips," November 16, 2007; "One Market Remains Sound: Money Is Still There for Best Art," November, 17, 2007, all *New York Times*, Metro Section.

12. *New York Times*/CBS Poll, December 5-9, 2007, Iowa and New Hampshire, N = 1,133; Registered Voters= 1,028, Republican Primary Voters= 266, Democratic Primary Voters= 417, see http://graphics8.nytimes.com/packages/pdf/politics/20071113_POLL.pdf.

13. CNN Opinion Research Poll, interviews with 1,024 adult Americans conducted by telephone by the Opinion Research Corporation November 2-4, 2007. See question 5 at http://i.a.cnn.net/cnn/2007/images/11/07/rel11d.pdf.

14. Brent Cunningham, "Across the Great Class Divide," *Columbia Journalism Review*, May/June 2004. Mary Ellen Schoonmaker, "Keeping Poverty on the Page," *Columbia Journalism Review*, Jan./Feb. 2008.

15. CNN.com, transcripts, Special Event, CNN/Los Angeles Times Host the Republican Presidential Debate, aired March 2, 2000.

16. Jonathan Mahler, "The Bloomberg Vista," *New York Times Magazine*, September 10, 2006.

17. Editorial, "Gotham's Latest Non-Crisis," *New York Post*, December 30, 2006.

18. Alexis Rehrmann, "Defeating Hunger and Homelessness, Step by Step," *New York Times*, December 2, 2007.

19. "Tackling hunger, one turkey at a time," *Park Slope Courier*, November 23, 2007, front page.

20. Kathleen Lucadamo and Greg. B Smith, "Won't Squawk Over Turkey," *Daily News*, November 23, 2007.

21. "Facing Hunger: Feeding America," *CBS Early Show*, April-May 2008, http://www.cbsnews.com/stories/2008/04/28/earlyshow/main4049032.shtml (accessed August 4, 2008).

22. Telegram to Secretary Freeman from CBS President Frank Stanton, 1968, Raymond Wheeler Papers (#4366), Southern Historical Collection, Manuscripts Department, Wilson Library, University of North Carolina at Chapel Hill.

23. Nick Kotz, *Let Them Eat Promises: The Politics of Hunger in America* (Garden City, New York: Anchor Books, 1968), 109 and 110.

24. Letter from Congressman to Dr. Raymond Wheeler, (May 27, 1968), Raymond Wheeler Papers (#4366), Southern Historical Collection, Manuscripts Department, Wilson Library, University of North Carolina at Chapel Hill.

25. E. J. Dionne, Jr., "In Other, Non-Dog News . . ." op-ed, *Washington Post*, August 31, 2007.

Section II — THE SOLUTION

CHAPTER 12. Here It Is: The Plan to End Domestic Hunger

1. Franklin D. Roosevelt, commencement address, Oglethorpe University, Atlanta, Georgia (May 23, 1932) from Samuel I. Rosenman, ed., *The Public Papers and Addresses of Franklin D. Roosevelt* (New York: Random House, 1938–1950).

2. US Department of Agriculture, Economic Research Service, *Household Food Security in the United States 2006*," by Mark Nord, Margaret Andrews, and Steven Carlson (Economic Research Report No. ERR-49, November 2007).

3. Aviva Aron-Dine, "Extending the President's Tax Cuts and AMT Relief Would Cost $3.5 Trillion Through 2017," Center on Budget and Policy Priorities, January 31, 2007.

4. Amy Belasco, "The Cost of Iraq, Afghanistan, and Other Global War on Terror Operations Since 9/11," Congressional Research Service Report to Congress, updated November 9, 2007.
5. Remarks of Senator Barack Obama in Zanesville, Ohio, July 1, 2008 (as prepared for delivery), http://my.barackobama.com/page/community/post/amandascott/gG5xY3 (accessed August 4, 2008).
6. Editorial, "New and Not Improved," *New York Times*, July 4, 2008.
7. Lauran Neergaard, "Medical Clinics Expanding Care to Needy," Associated Press, December 26, 2007.
8. Stephen Castle, "Dutch Move to Limit Big Payouts for Chief Executives," *International Herald Tribune*, May 13, 2008.
9. Thomas Z. Freedman and Jim McLaughlin, "New Attitudes About Poverty and Hunger: The Rise of the 'Do Right Voter' and Other Lessons from Recent Research," polling report for the Alliance to End Hunger, October 30, 2007, 7.
10. Peter D. Hart and Associates, "Memorandum to the Food Research Action Center and the Center on Budget and Policy Priorities, re: Public Support for Food Stamps," June 13, 2007.
11. See note 9, 1, 5, and 7.
12. Pew Research Center for the People & the Press, "Trends in Political Values and Core Attitudes: 1987-2007," March 22, 2007.

CHAPTER 13. Bolstering Community Food Production and Marketing

1. Thomas Jefferson, letter to John Jay, August 23, 1785 found on the Web site of The Avalon Project, Yale Law School, http://www.yale.edu/lawweb/avalon/jefflett/let32.htm (accessed August 4, 2008).
2. Jon Hurdle, "Where Industry Once Hummed, Urban Gardens Find Success," *New York Times*, May 20, 2008.
3. Kim Severson, "Some Good News on Food Prices," *New York Times*, April 2, 2008.
4. Dan Barber, "Change We Can Stomach," op-ed, *New York Times*, May 11, 2008.
5. See note 3.
6. Mary Hedrickson and William Heffernan, "Concentration of Agricultural Markets," Department of Rural Sociology, University of Missouri, January 2005, http://www.foodcircles.missouri.edu/CRJanuary05.pdf (accessed August 4, 2008).
7. Joel Greeno, "Farmers, Consumers Are Getting Milked," *Family Farm Defenders*, Fall 2007.
8. US Department of Agriculture, Economic Research Service, *Structure and Finances of US Farms: 2005 Family Farm Report*, by Robert A. Hoppe and David E. Banker, (Economic Information Bulletin No. EIB-12, 51 pp, May 2006).
9. "Organic food: Buy or bypass?" by Mayo Clinic staff, MayoClinic.Com, December 20, 2006, http://www.mayoclinic.com/health/organic-food/NU00255 (accessed May 23, 2008).
10. Sarah Murray, "The Deep Fried Truth," *New York Times*, December 14, 2007.
11. Raj Patel, *Stuffed and Starved*, (Brooklyn: Melville House Publishing, 2008), 286.
12. Michael Pollan, "Why Bother," *New York Times Magazine*, April 20, 2008.
13. Mark Winne, *Closing the Food Gap*, (Boston: Beacon Press, 2008), 55.
14. Marlene Kennedy, "Garden Solutions Taking Root," *Albany Times Union*, February 8, 2008.
15. US Census Bureau, "American Community Survey, 2006."
16. US Department of Agriculture, Economic Research Service, *Food and Nutrition Assistance Programs and Obesity: 1976-2002*, by Michele Ver Ploeg, Lisa Mancino, and Biing-Hwan Lin, (Economic Research Report No. ERR-48) September 2007.
17. New York City Department of Planning and New York City Economic Development Corporation, "Going to Market: New York City's Neighborhood Grocery Store and Supermarket Shortage," May 5, 2008.
18. Food Trust (Philadelphia, Pennsylvania), Supermarket Campaign, http://www.thefoodtrust.org/php/programs/super.market.campaign.php#1 (accessed August 4, 2008).

CHAPTER 14. **A New War on Poverty**

1. Michael K. Honey, "The Legacy of Dr. Martin Luther King Jr.: Defending the Right to Organize," *Commercial Appeal* (Memphis), February 3, 2008.
2. Harry J. Holzer, Diane Whitmore Schanzenbach, Greg J. Duncan, and Jens Ludwig, *The Cost of Poverty: Subsequent Effects of Children Growing Up Poor,* Center for American Progress, January 24, 2007.
3. Citizens for Tax Justice, "New Data Show Growing Wealth Inequality," May 12, 2006.
4. Remarks of Senator Barack Obama, "Changing the Odds for Urban America," Washington, DC, July 18, 2007.
5. Heather Boushey, "Staying Employed After Welfare," Briefing Paper #128, Economic Policy Institute, June 2002.

CHAPTER 15. **How All of Us (Including *YOU*) Can End Hunger in America**

1. Sufi parable as told by Nazmiye Oral, playwright, "The Veiled Monologues," http://www.stannswarehouse.org/extras.html (accessed August 4, 2008).
2. Pew Research Center for the People & the Press, "Trends in Political Values and Core Attitudes: 1987–2007," March 22, 2007.
3. "The Yellow Fever Visitation—Terrible Scenes in New Orleans and Memphis," Frank Leslie's Illustrated Newspaper, September 28, 1878, found in the Philip S. Hench Walter Reed Yellow Fever Collection, University of Virginia, http://yellowfever.lib.virginia.edu/reed/ (accessed August 3, 2008).
4. B.S. Kakkilaya, The Malaria Site (updated April 14, 2006), http://www.malariasite.com/malaria/history_wars.htm (accessed August 3, 2008).
5. US Department of Health and Human Services, Centers for Disease Control and Prevention, "Eradication of Malaria in the United States (1947-1951)," April 23, 2004, found at http://www.cdc.gov/malaria/history/eradication_us.htm; Content source: Division of Parasitic Diseases, National Center for Zoonotic, Vector-Borne, and Enteric Diseases, http://www.cdc.gov/malaria/history/index.htm.
6. Editorial, "Profiles in Pusillanimity," *New York Times*, December 5, 2005.
7. Remarks of Senator Barack Obama, "Changing the Odds for Urban America," Washington, DC, July 18, 2007.
8. John McCain 2008, "John McCain Statement on Poverty," press release, April 4, 2008, http://www.johnmccain.com/Informing/News/PressReleases/Read.aspx?Guid=ddd2c9b9-d16e-460f-8f50-2d7411cbf15c (accessed August 4, 2008).

APPENDIX B. **Revised Rules for Radical Centrists: Tips for Activists on How to Organize and Craft Messages for Successful Advocacy Campaigns**

1. Pew Research Center for the People & the Press, "Trends in Political Values and Core Attitudes: 1987-2007," March 22, 2007.
2. Thomas Z. Freedman and Jim McLaughlin, "New Attitudes About Poverty and Hunger: The Rise of the 'Do Right Voter' and Other Lessons from Recent Research," polling report for the Alliance to End Hunger, October 30, 2007, 14.
3. Matthew Nisbet, "Communicating About Poverty and Low-Wage Work: A New Agenda," The Mobility Agenda, A Special Initiative of Inclusion, October 2007.
4. David D. Kirkpatrick, "The Evangelical Crackup," *New York Times Magazine*, October 28, 2007, 45.
5. Nick Kotz, *Let Them Eat Promises: The Politics of Hunger in America* (Garden City, New York: Anchor Books, 1968), 161.
6. Jose Antonio Vargas, "A Diversity of Opinion, if Not Opinionators," *Washington Post*, August 6, 2007.

INDEX

activism, food, 259, 263–66, 306
activist behavior, 310–13
activist response time, 306–7
AFDC. *See* Aid to Families with Dependent Children
affirmative action, 187
AFFORd. *See* American Family Food, Opportunity/Responsibility
African Americans
  college rate *vs.* prison rate of, 185
  economic improvement by, 186
  food aid use by, 37
  income among, 187
  in middle class, 186–87
  obesity and, 125
  responsibility of, 187–88
  as welfare recipients, 184
agribusiness, 213, 256
Aid to Families with Dependent Children (AFDC), 162
Alliance to End Hunger, 296
ally development, 307–9
American dream, 155–56, 282
American Enterprise Institution for Public Policy Research (AEI), 111–12
American Family Food, Opportunity/Responsibility (AFFORd)
  EITC and, 239
  eligibility for, 239
  suggestions of, 238–39
  WIC food program and, 239
Americanism
  choice and, 110
  hallmarks of, 13
  myth of rich and, 13–14
America's Second Harvest Food Bank Network. *See also* Feeding America
  food distribution by, 201
  goals of, 200
  statistics of, 16

  study by, 35–36
  survey of, 90
AmeriCorps national service program, 280–81
anthropologists, on race, 69
antifraud techniques. *See also* fraud
  computer matching as, 96
  finger printing as, 95
antihunger conference, of Rumsfeld, 74
antihunger efforts/programs. *See also* hunger
  celebrity endorsement of, 194–95
  creation of, 287–90
  federal, 15–16, 19–20, 25–26, 238–40
  food security and, 269–71
  funding for, 200
  idealism of, 194
  legislation of, 71
  race and, 68–70
  reform of, 285–87
  of USDA, 25–26
antipoverty programs, 20. *See also* poverty
  creation of, 287–90
  food aid and, 252
  grassroots, 283, 288
  reduction of, 192
apprenticeships, 280
armies of compassion. *See* faith-based armies of compassion
aspiration empowerment agenda, 276–77

Barber, Dan, 260
beef production/packaging, 261
Besharov, Douglas, 114, 116–17
billionaires, 128
  number of, 127, 130–31
  as self-made, 144–45
  in US, 15
birth defects, 47
birth weight, low, 47
Blankfein, Lloyd, 152
Bloomberg, Michael, 122

on campaign contributions, 148
on food quality, 273
Bost, Eric, 82
breakfast, school performance and, 97–98
Brown, Larry J., 45–46
    on food insecurity, 48
    on malnutrition, 77
bucket brigade, 192
bulk food, 110
Burger King, 122
Bush, George W.
    on compassionate conservatism, 210
    economy under, 81–82
    on faith-based armies of compassion, 38
    on food banks, 210
    Food Stamp Program budget cuts of, 82
    on hunger, 41
    knee-jerk reaction to, 249
    as liberal, 303
    tax cuts by, 242

CABs. *See* Customer Action Boards
calories, in fast food, 122
campaign contributions, 147–51
    Bloomberg on, 148
    corporate, 152
    of defense contractors, 148
    voting record and, 221
Canadian food insecurity, 115–16
capitalism
    dysfunction of, 141–42
    economic growth and, 155–56
CCHIP. *See* Community Childhood Hunger
    Identification Program
celebrity endorsement, 194–95
Census food stamp data, 34
Census poverty line statistics, 132
Center for American Progress, 275
Center for Responsive Politics, 151
    on Goldman Sachs, 152
Center on Budget/Policy Priorities, 299
Center on Hunger/Poverty, 297
CFED. *See* Corporation for Enterprise Develop-
    ment
charity, 202
    American view of, 191
    claims of, 202–3
    corporate donations to, 213–15
    as donor benefit, 195
    food costs and, 16
    food distribution by, 201
    government effectiveness *vs.*, 201–2
    hunger and, 199–200
    restrictions on, 210–11
    as shield, 214
    superiority myth of, 202–4
    welfare *vs.*, 191, 202
    workforce of, 192

Charity Aid, Recovery/Empowerment Act, 247–
    48
charity system, of Great Depression, 60–64
CHC. *See* Congressional Hunger Center
Check Out Hunger, 193–94
cheeseburger calories, 122
Child/Adult Care Food Program, 75
child care
    cost of, 14
    funding for, 172, 181–82
Child Nutrition Act of 1972, 74
children
    cognitive development of, 47–48
    food insecurity and, 15–16, 30, 123–24
    hungry, 57, 59
    poverty rate of, 157
    school performance of, 96–98
    test scores and, 48
choice, Americanism and, 110
cholera, 284
Churchill, Winston, on democracy, 33
Citizens' Board of Inquiry Into Hunger/Malnu-
    trition in United States, 25, 72
City Harvest, 121
city migration, 56
city stratification, 139
civil rights laws, 291
class bias, 110
    of food activism, 264–66
    hunger and, 231
    in media coverage, 226–27
Clinton, William Jefferson
    administration of, 78
    on welfare reform, 161, 170
CNSTAT. *See* Committee on National Statistics
cognitive development, of children, 47–48
Coke calories, 122
Coles, Robert, 67
college education importance, 179
Commission on Hunger, 112
Committee on National Statistics (CNSTAT), 42–
    43
Commodity Supplemental Food Program, 82
communication, 305–7
Community Childhood Hunger Identification
    Program (CCHIP), 27, 78
Community Food Security Coalition, 266–67,
    297
Community Food Security Initiative, 42, 79, 248,
    263, 271
community garden projects, 266–67
community nutrition, 269–71
community organizing, 161
community support, 312
Community Supported Agriculture (CSA), 263,
    273
compassionate conservatism, 210
Compassion Capital Fund, 211

computer matching, as antifraud technique, 96
Congressional Hunger Center (CHC), 297–98
corporate charitable donations, 213–15
    food insecurity and, 252–53
corporate food distributors, 261
corporate political donations, 152
corporate tax breaks, 145–46
corporate welfare, 145
Corporation for Enterprise Development (CFED),
    299–300
cost burden
    of hunger, 46
    wages and, 133–38
cost of living, 141, 177
    average, 139
    Ehrenreich on, 135
    reduction in, 278–79
crop subsidies, 148–50
    protests against, 151
CSA. *See* Community Supported Agriculture
Customer Action Boards (CABs), 289–90

defense contractor campaign contributions, 148
democracy, Churchill on, 33
democrats, on hunger, 20
DeParle, Jason
    on food stamp benefits, 93–94
    on hunger, 34–35
    on welfare reform, 164–65
Department of Health, Education, Welfare
    (HEW), 26–27
diabetes, obesity and, 124–25
dietary guidelines, 119
disease, government solutions to, 284
domestic hunger. *See* hunger
donations, 152, 213–15, 252–53
Dunbar, Leslie W., 71

earned income tax credits (EITC), 305
    AFFORd and, 239
    costs of, 164–65
    expansion of, 279
    welfare costs *vs.*, 164
eating intervals, 123–24
EBTs. *See* Electronic Benefit Cards
economic growth, 155–56, 217
    African Americans and, 186
economic power, 153–54
economic research, 155
economic stimulation
    by Food Stamp Program, 85–86
    by immigrants, 137
economy
    of Bush, 81–82
    expansion of, 217
    food insecurity and, 45
    strength of, 46

editorial opinions, on hunger, 227
education
    costs of, 280–81
    higher, 179
    importance of, 179
    nutrition and, 245
Ehrenreich, Barbara, 35
    on cost of living, 135
    on food distribution, 199
    on minimum wage, 135–36
EITC. *See* earned income tax credits
Electronic Benefit Cards (EBTs), 85
emergency feeding programs, 16, 38, 197–99,
    206–7. *See also* feeding efforts
Emergency Food Action Center, 251
The Emergency Food Assistance Program
    (TEFAP), 196
employment. *See also* underemployment; unem-
    ployment
    food insecurity and, 50
    food security and, 50
    hourly, 136
    for immigrants, 137
    sexism and, 181
    welfare *vs.*, 168
entertainment spending, 177
entitlement, welfare and, 11, 165
Environmental Working Group (EWG), on farm
    subsidies, 150
estate tax elimination, 147
executive salaries, 142, 252–53
executive windfalls, 252–53

faith-based armies of compassion, 38, 210–11,
    247–50. *See also* religious charity restric-
    tions
    nonprofit organizations and, 248
    Obama on, 249
familial independence form, 158
family farming, 260–62
famine
    in Great Depression, 60–64
    Irish, 55–56
    in Mali, 14
Farm Bill, 177, 242
farming, 260–62
farm subsidies, 148–50
    protests against, 151
farm welfare, 148–50
fast food availability, 121–23
fast food calories, 122
fast food marketing, 123
fatalism, 165–66
FDR. *See* Roosevelt, Franklin Delano
fear
    of agribusiness, 256
    food insecurity and, 108, 110
    food stamp benefits and, 100

federal antihunger safety net programs, 15–16,
    25–26
modernization of, 238–40
success of, 19–20
Federal Emergency Management Agency
    (FEMA), 196
federal minimum wage. *See* minimum wage
federal nutrition assistance programs, 90. *See
    also* nutrition assistance programs
military spending *vs.*, 244
of Reagan administration, 20
spending on, 244
federal safety net programs, 256
antihunger, 15–16, 19–20, 25–26, 238–40
growth of, 75
truth of, 83–85
federal spending, on nutrition programs, 84–85,
    244
Feeding America, 74, 196, 296
feeding efforts, 213. *See also* emergency feeding
    programs
faults of, 215
poverty and, 59–60
support for, 215
feel-good fixation, 227–29
FEMA. *See* Federal Emergency Management
    Agency
female-headed households, 176, 181
government policies regarding, 182
fetal development, 47
Field Foundation, 67–68, 72, 75–76
Mississippi study of, 71
finger imaging. *See* finger printing
finger printing
for food stamp benefits, 94–96
food stamp fraud and, 95
food. *See also* nutritious food access
adequate supply of, 115, 199
as central organizing tool, 271
international, 265
as medication, 124
organic, 264–65
quality of, 273
as social centerpiece, 109
food activism, 259, 263
class bias of, 264–66
media coverage of, 306
food aid, 37, 39–40, 76. *See also* food banks; food
    pantries; school lunch; school meals; soup
    kitchens
African Americans and, 37
antipoverty initiatives and, 252
dependency on, 16, 255
FDR on, 63
government and, 62–63
grassroots, 192–93, 250–51, 257
Hispanics and, 37
to nonwhites, 26

poverty and, 37, 98
social workers on, 62
Thurmond on, 70
volunteer workforce of, 193
food banks. *See also* food distribution; food
    pantries; soup kitchens
Bush on, 210
dependency on, 16, 255
founding of, 196
funding of, 201
shortages at, 17–18
food choices, as determined by food stamp bene-
    fits, 100–102, 119
food consumption survey (1965), 26
food costs, 16, 197–98, 259–60, 270
of nutritious items, 17
food deserts, 119–21
food distribution, 202, 238, 265. *See also* food aid;
    food banks; food pantries; soup kitchens
by America's Second Harvest, 201
charitable *vs.* governmental safety net, 200
by charities, 201
corporate, 261
Ehrenreich on, 199
food stamp benefits *vs.*, 73
organization of, 196–97
pros/cons of, 197
by religious organizations, 197
food drives, 229
food insecurity, 15–16, 28, 30, 80–81, 240–45. *See
    also* food security; very low food security
Brown on, 48
in Canada, 115–16
children and, 15–16, 30, 123–24
corporate role in, 252–53
economy and, 45
employment and, 50
fear and, 108, 110
for female-headed households, 176
health and, 49
homelessness and, 33–34
hospitalization rates and, 45
hunger and, 28–29
illegal housing and, 34
for male-headed households, 176
medication costs and, 50
methodology of, 33–35, 80–81, 113–14
middle class concerns about, 45
in Mississippi, 32
obesity and, 123–24
poverty line relative to, 247
poverty rate and, 33
social impacts of, 48–49
state and, 33, 246–47
suicide rates related to, 49
of two working parent households, 175–76
in US, 15–16, 29, 45
USDA report on, 28

weight loss and, 117–18
with/without hunger, 28–29
food limitation, starvation and, 70–71
food packaging, 261
food pantries, 35. *See also* food aid; food banks;
    food distribution; soup kitchens
    alternate methodology for, 250
    boom of, 76–78
    hunger increase and, 206–7
    increased attendance of, 112
    organization of, 250
    problems of, 197–99
    rationing by, 198
    supplies for, 199
    time spent at, 113
    transportation to, 113
food purchasing power, 242
food rationing, 14–15, 198
Food Recovery/Gleaning Initiative, 79–80
Food Research/Action Center (FRAC), 27, 74,
    246, 298
    on obesity/hunger debate, 118
food security, 89–90. *See also* food insecurity
    affordability of, 241–45
    antihunger programs and, 269–71
    children's test score and, 48
    employment and, 50
    Glickman on, 271
    national summit on, 80
    public policy advocacy for, 271–73
    threats to, 21–22
    very low, 42–43
food shopping, time required for, 102, 109
food spending, 104
    nutrition and, 105–6
Food Stamp Act (1977), 74–75
food stamp benefits, 34, 64, 75, 89, 91, 238, 267,
    311. *See also* Food Stamp Program
    advocacy strategy for, 99
    application for, 90–92
    demographic use of, 86–87
    denial of, 95
    DeParle on, 93–94
    eligibility requirements for, 71, 81–82
    fear and, 100
    federal spending on, 84–85
    finger printing for, 94–96
    food choices with, 100–102
    food distribution *vs.*, 73
    fraud and, 95
    JFK and, 66
    management of, 93
    as medicine, 86
    in Mississippi, 70
    myths surrounding, 87
    Obama and, 291
    participation in, 89, 200
    poverty and, 87

recertification for, 93
seniors and, 86
size of, 88–100
soup kitchens *vs.*, 107
    as supplementary, 100–101
    tax dollars and, 11
    in unemployment, 56
Food Stamp Challenge
    difficulties noticed during, 99
    experiences during, 104–5
    food limitations of, 105–6
    grocery list example for, 101–2
    meal plan example for, 102–3
    operation of, 100–102
    outcome of, 107–10
Food Stamp Program, 85–86, 94. *See also* food
    stamp benefits
    administration of, 91
    budget cuts for, 82
    economic stimulation by, 85–86
    effectiveness of, 88–94
    FDR and, 64
    Frank on, 91
    improvements to, 78
    nutritious food access and, 120
    obesity and, 268
    participation in, 74, 93
    public opinion of, 254
    simplification of, 238–41
    time limits of, 204
    USDA and, 66
    use of, 84
food systems, 262
Ford, Henry, on salary minimums, 46
for-profit work, 206. *See also* nonprofit work
FRAC. *See* Food Research/Action Center
Frank, Deborah, 47
    on Food Stamp Program, 91
fraud. *See also* antifraud techniques
    food stamp benefits and, 95
free trade distortion, 151
Friends of World Food Program, 301

geographical stereotyping
    of hunger, 32
    of poverty, 134
GI Bill, 64–65, 282
Gingrich, Newt, 78
Gioia, Eric, 99
Glickman, Dan
    on food security, 271
    on hunger, 41
    initiatives of, 79–80
God's will, hunger as, 208–9
Goldman Sachs, 151–53
government funds
    charity claims about, 202–3
    charity effectiveness *vs.*, 201–2

entitlement to, 11, 165
for food aid, 62
as hunger solution, 11, 284–85
for recession intervention, 61
government views, on food aid, 62–63
grassroots movement, 310
for antipoverty, 283, 288
for food aid, 192–93, 250–51, 257
Great Depression
breadlines of, 60
charity system collapse and, 60–64
famine during, 60–64
grocery store
consolidation, 262
independent, 261–62
supermarket *vs.*, 120
time needed in, 102, 109
gross domestic product, 275
taxes as percentage of, 243

Hands Across America, 193
Harrington, Michael, 31
health quality, 49
Heritage Foundation
Distinguished Fellows of, 112
funding for, 111–12
on hunger, 29–30, 114
HEW. *See* Department of Health, Education,
   Welfare
higher education, 179
Hispanic food charity use, 37
homelessness, 17
food insecurity and, 33–34
in New York, NY, 34
rise in, 170
Hoover, Herbert J.
on hunger, 61
leadership of, 61–62
Hoover Institution, 62
hospitalization rates, food insecurity and, 45
housing costs, 134
for middle class, 139
for poor *vs.* rich, 135
housing, illegal, 34
housing wage, 134
human behavior, racism and, 185
hunger, 25, 28, 30–31, 34–35, 42–43, 49, 72, 112,
   227. *See also* antihunger efforts/programs
Africa *vs.* America, 13
as alleged, 113
American view of, 18
American *vs.* Third World, 113–15
blame for, 116
Bush on, 41
CCHIP surveys on, 27
charity roles in, 199–200
children and, 57, 59
class bias and, 231

as cliché, 193
commission on, 112
communication about, 305–7
corporate role in, 252–53
cost burden of, 46
democrats *vs.* republicans, 20
DeParle on, 34–35
as domestic problem, 18, 223
economic causes of, 54
effects of, 50
food insecurity and, 28–29
food pantries and, 206–7
FRAC on, 118
geographical stereotyping of, 32
Glickman on, 41
goal for, 237
as God's will, 208–9
government as solution to, 11, 284–85
as handicap, 48
Heritage Foundation on, 29–30, 114
on holidays, 223
Hoover on, 61
idealism and, 194
improvements/increases in, 59, 167, 204
Industrial Revolution and, 53–56
JFK on, 65–67
McCain on, 291–92
McGovern on, 19, 74, 234
media coverage of, 17–18, 218, 220, 231–34
Meese on, 18
in Mississippi, 26
myths about, 36
as nationwide problem, 33, 36
Nixon on, 13, 19, 73–74
as noble, 209
Obama on, 292
obesity and, 116–19
of parents *vs.* children, 30
pattern of, 55
physical growth and, 46–50
as political problem, 18–22
poverty and, 32, 40–41, 50–51
in pre-industrial age, 54
as presidential debate issue, 66
public opinion on, 254–55
racism and, 231
Reagan on, 18, 76–78
in recession, 58–59
rediscovery of, 65–68
religion and, 197, 208–10, 247–50
resources on, 295–302
school performance and, 96–98
Schwartz-Nobel on, 17
soup kitchens and, 206–7
starvation *vs.*, 256
statistics on, 30–31
study of, 224, 254
USDA on, 25–26

volunteer opinions of, 204–5
voting on, 286
Hunger Free Communities Act, 286–87
Hunter, Robert, 57
Hurricane Katrina media coverage, 17–18

IDA. *See* Individual Development Account
idealism, 165–66, 253–55
of antihunger programs, 194
identity politics, 310–11
illegal housing, food insecurity and, 34
illegal immigrants, 137–38
immigrants
economic input by, 137
employment for, 137
illegal, 137–38
resentment towards, 184
risks for, 137–38
income, 14
of African Americans, 187
examples of, 131
of hedge fund managers, 142
increase in, 129
low, 100–102, 116, 119, 189–90, 288–89
median, 128
wealth *vs.*, 277
income gap, 155. *See also* inequality
Individual Development Account (IDA), 277–78
industrial age
in US, 56–60
work conditions of, 56–57
Industrial Revolution, 53–56
inequality, 115, 155, 277
media coverage of, 232
in New York, NY, 130–31, 138–39
in US, 127–31
of wealth, 17, 21–22, 127, 129–30, 277
international food system, 265
interracial dating, 187
Irish famine history, 55–56

JFK. *See* Kennedy, John F
job availability, 137
job training and, 279–80
reduced, 170
transitional jobs and, 280
for welfare recipients, 169
job earnings, 166
job placement, 168
job stimulation, 145–46
job training, 195, 279–80
Johanns, Mike, 94–95
junk food availability, 121–23

Kennedy, John F (JFK)
food stamp program of, 66
hunger view of, 65–67

ketchup, as vegetable, 77
Kiva Microfunds, 302
Kotz, Nick, 27
on racism, 311
welfare description of, 70
Kroc, Joan, 209

language, 312
values and, 305
legislation
for antihunger efforts, 71
for welfare reform, 162
liberalism, 159–61
low birth weight, 47
low-income families, 116
challenges for, 288–89
food choice of, 100–102, 119
networking of, 189–90
luxury items, 161

malaria, 284
male-headed households, 176
Mali, West Africa, 13
culture of, 14
famine in, 14
per capita income in, 14
malnutrition
Brown on, 77
mothers and, 47
on Navajo reservation, 232
Perkins on, 58–60
symptoms of, 58
in US, 25–27, 72–73
in US *vs.* Third World, 26–27
Mays, Benjamin E., 71
Mazon: A Jewish Response to Hunger, 298
McCain, John
on hunger/poverty, 291–92
promises of, 292
McGovern, George, on hunger, 19, 74, 234
media, 222
activism coverage by, 306
class biases in, 226–27
failure of, 228–29
feel-good fixation of, 227–29
food activism, 306
format of, 228
hunger coverage of, 17–18, 218, 220, 231–34
Hurricane Katrina coverage by, 17–18
inequality coverage by, 232
mainstream *vs.* right-wing, 227
pack mentality of, 219
paradox presented by, 221
poverty coverage by, 220, 223, 231–34
presidential campaign coverage by, 225–26
salaries of, 222
statistical distortion by, 31–32

story choices of, 220, 229–31
median household income, 128
Medicaid, 172, 224
medical schools, nutrition in, 125–26
medication costs, food insecurity and, 50
Meese, Edwin
   as Distinguished Fellow of Heritage Foundation, 112
   on hunger, 18
mental illness, poverty and, 49
message repetition, 311–12
Mexican immigrant workers, 137–38. *See also* immigrants
Mickey Leland Memorial Domestic Hunger Relief Act, 78
middle class
   African Americans in, 186–87
   as endangered, 138–39
   food insecurity concerns of, 45
   housing costs for, 139
migrant farm workers, 137
military spending, 244
minimum wage, 133, 283
   Ehrenreich on, 135–36
   surviving on, 134–35
mission conditions, 57, 209
Mississippi
   Field Foundation study of, 71
   food insecurity rates in, 32
   food stamp benefits in, 70
   hunger rates in, 26
   Wheeler on, 68
Mobility Agenda, 300
mothers, malnutrition of, 47
Municipal Lodging House, 57
Muñoz, Jorge, 197

national antihunger programs. *See* federal antihunger safety net programs
National Hunger Awareness Day, 194
National Rifle Association (NRA), 309
National School Lunch Program. *See* school lunch
National Summit on Community Food Security, 80
New America Foundation, 300
New Hope Initiative, 279
New York City Coalition Against Hunger, 38, 289, 295–96
   hunger study of, 224
   media coverage of, 306
   poster of, 308
   supermarket mapping by, 121
New York, NY
   Great Depression breadlines of, 60
   homelessness in, 34
   income examples in, 131
   inequality in, 130–31, 138–39

welfare failure in, 169–70
Nixon, Richard, on hunger, 13, 19, 73–74
nonprofit work, 205–6
   corruption of, 205
   faith-based work and, 248
   for-profit work *vs.*, 206
   government funding for, 272
   private foundation support of, 212–13
nonwhites
   behavior of, 183
   food aid for, 26
   racial profiling of, 185–86
   racism of, 187–88
Nord, Mark, 44
NRA. *See* National Rifle Association
nutrition
   central problem of, 117
   clinical, 125
   for communities, 269–71
   courses on, 125–26
   education and, 245
   food spending and, 105–6
   in medical schools, 125–26
   taste and, 123
nutrition assistance programs. *See also* federal nutrition assistance programs
   federal spending on, 84–85, 244
   Reagan and, 20
   of USDA, 98
Nutrition-Cognition National Advisory Committee, 46–48
nutrition labels, 121–22
nutritious food access, 118–19. *See also* food
   cost and, 119
   Food Stamp Program and, 120
   increase in, 267

Obama, Barack
   on anger, 187–88
   faith-based plan of, 249
   food stamps and, 291
   on hunger, 292
   promises of, 292
   on racism, 187
obesity
   in African Americans, 125
   as compelling anti-hunger argument, 117
   diabetes and, 124–25
   factors in, 123–26
   food insecurity and, 123–24
   Food Stamp Program effect on, 268
   FRAC on, 118
   hunger and, 116–19
   as lethal, 124–26
   in US, 117
Olbermann, Keith, 43–44
opportunity approach, of health, 251
organic food, 264–65

Oxfam International, 302

Perkins, Frances, 58–60
personal responsibility, poverty and, 175
physical growth, hunger and, 46–50
policy goals, 312
politics, 154
    in antihunger efforts, 285–87
    hunger and, 18–22
    of identity, 310–11
    power imbalance and, 153
Pollan, Michael, 259–60
    on community gardens, 266–67
postwar era school lunch, 64–65
poverty, 18, 61, 84, 132, 167, 175, 309. *See also*
    antipoverty programs; War on Poverty
    causes of, 278–79
    communication about, 305–7
    concentration of, 120
    conservative view of, 159
    cost of, 275
    feeding efforts and, 59–60
    food aid and, 37, 98
    food stamp benefits and, 87
    geographical stereotypes of, 134
    Harrington on, 31
    hunger and, 40–41, 50–51
    liberal view of, 159
    McCain on, 291–92
    media coverage of, 220, 223, 231–34
    mental illness and, 49
    myths about, 18
    pattern of, 55
    personal responsibility and, 175
    as presidential debate issue, 153
    public opinion of, 254–55
    race and, 183
    resources on, 295–302
    seniors and, 133
    sexism and, 181–82
    in US, 115, 132–33, 157, 170, 290
    wealth and, 139–43
    welfare *vs.*, 163, 171, 183
    women *vs.* men, 181–82
poverty line, 15
    Census statistics on, 132
    food aid eligibility and, 98
    food insecurity relative to, 247
    hunger and, 32
    methodology behind, 132
poverty rate, 290
    of children, 157
    extreme, 158
    food insecurity rate and, 33
    national, 170
power, 153–54
    differentials in, 154
    politics and, 153

PPI. *See* Progressive Policy Institute
presidential campaigns, media coverage of, 225–
    26
presidential debate issue, 225
    hunger as, 66
    poverty as, 153
private foundations, 212–13
Progressive Policy Institute (PPI), 300–301
protein intake recommendations, 105–6
public policy advocacy, 207
    for food security, 271–73
purchasing power, 242

race
    anthropologists on, 69
    antihunger efforts and, 68–70
    poverty and, 183
    welfare and, 182–85
racial profiling, of nonwhites, 185–86
racism
    human behavior and, 185
    hunger and, 231
    Kotz on, 311
    of nonwhites, 187–88
    Obama on, 187
Reaganomics, failure of, 76–77
Reagan, Ronald
    funding cuts of, 76–77
    on hunger, 18, 76–78
    nutrition assistance programs and, 20
    WIC food program and, 27
recession
    government intervention in, 61
    hunger during, 58–59
reciprocal responsibility, 178
religion, hunger and, 197, 208–10, 247–50
religious charity restrictions, 210–11. *See also*
    faith-based armies of compassion
republicans, on hunger, 20
resource limit, welfare and, 176
revenue loss, tax cuts and, 147
right-wing think tanks, 111
    ignorance of, 304
    propaganda of, 117
Roosevelt, Franklin Delano (FDR)
    on food aid, 63
    food stamp program of, 64
Rumsfeld, Donald, antihunger conference of, 74

safety concerns, 156
safety net programs. *See* federal safety net pro-
    grams
salary minimums, 46
salary, of media, 222
school lunch, 75. *See also* school meals
    federal spending on, 84–85
    postwar era and, 64–65

revised benefits of, 246
social status and, 97
stigma of, 245
school meals, 59, 96–98. *See also* school lunch
benefits of, 97, 246
stigma of, 97, 245
school performance
breakfast and, 97–98
of hungry children, 96–98
Schwartz-Nobel, Loretta, on hunger, 17
Second Harvest. *See* Feeding America
self-made myth, 143–45
seniors
food stamp benefits and, 86
poverty and, 133
sexism
employment double standard and, 181
poverty and, 181–82
Share Our Strength, 298–99
shock value, 307
slavery, legacy of, 187
small farmer. *See* family farming
social capital, 190
social damage. *See also* social capital
of food insecurity, 48–49
of school lunch, 97
of welfare, 177, 179
social networks, 189
social services
budget cuts for, 76–77
cutting, 160
social status, school lunch and, 97
soup kitchens, 35, 76. *See also* food banks; food
distribution; food pantries
food rationing by, 198
food stamp benefits *vs.*, 107
hunger increase and, 206–7
Spargo, John, 57–58
Special Supplemental Nutrition Program for
Women, Infants/Children (WIC food program). *See* WIC food program
SSI. *See* Supplemental Security System
starvation, 60, 64–65, 256
hunger *vs.*, 256
limited food and, 70–71
stratification
of cities, 139
of US, 208
subsidies, of USDA, 148–51
success
as government-aided, 144
as self-made, 143–45
of welfare, 166, 168
suffering, as noble, 209
suicide rates, food insecurity linked to, 49
Summer Food Service Program, of USDA, 203
Summit on Food Recovery/Gleaning, 79–80
supermarkets

availability of, 120
grocery stores *vs.*, 120
mapping of, 121
range of, 120
Supplemental Security System (SSI), 89
system knowledge, 312

TANF. *See* Temporary Assistance for Needy Families
taste, nutrition and, 123
taxation, of wealth, 242
tax breaks, 145–46
tax cuts, 240
by Bush, 242
estate tax, 147
revenue loss and, 147
tax dollars
food stamp benefits, 11
gross domestic product and, 243
lost revenue and, 147
TEFAP. *See* The Emergency Food Assistance
Program
Temporary Assistance for Needy Families
(TANF), 87
AFDC and, 162
changes to, 172
job earnings and, 166
Third World hunger, 26–27, 113–15
Thrifty Food Plan, 101
Thurmond, Strom, on food aid, 70
time records
doctoring of, 136
Wal-Mart and, 136–37
Tyson Foods, 214
food drive of, 229
work conditions of, 214–15

underemployment, 133
unemployment, 133. *See also* employment
food stamp benefits for, 56
United for Fair Economy, 301
United States (US), 13, 15, 19, 43
billionaires in, 15, 127–28, 130–31, 144–45
expenses in, 14
food insecurity in, 15–16, 29, 45
history of, 294
ideology of, 253–55
industrial age in, 56–60
inequality in, 127–31
malnutrition in, 25–27, 72–73
moderates in, 304
as nation of Bill Gates, 13–15
obesity in, 117
poverty in, 115, 132–33, 157, 170, 290
poverty *vs.* welfare, 163
richest *vs.* poorest in, 129
segregation in, 208

stratification of, 208
Third World hunger *vs.*, 113–15
values of, 304–5
wealth inequality in, 17, 21–22, 127, 129–30, 277
United States Department of Agriculture (USDA), 151
  farm subsidies of, 148–51
  on food insecurity, 28
  food insecurity methodology of, 33–35, 80–81, 113–14
  food stamp program of, 66
  on hunger, 25–26
  national antihunger programs and, 25–26
  nutrition assistance programs of, 98
  Summer Food Service Program of, 203
  Thrifty Food Plan of, 101
United Way fiscal scandal, 205–6
upward mobility, 280
USDA. *See* United States Department of Agriculture

values, 304–5
very low food security, 42–43
volunteer work force, 293
  benefits of, 195
  in charity, 192
  demographics of, 183
  of food aid, 193
  hunger opinion of, 204–5
  job skills of, 195
vote-by-mail laws, 154
voter-identification laws, 154
voting, 153
  on hunger, 286
voting record, campaign contributions and, 221

wages
  cost burden and, 133–38
  decline of, 85
  housing and, 134
Wal-Mart time record doctoring, 136–37
War on Poverty, 66
water, running, 40
wealth. *See also* inequality
  disparities in, 129–30
  income *vs.*, 277
  inequality of, 17, 21–22, 127, 129–30, 277
  poverty and, 139–43
  taxation of, 242
weight loss, food insecurity and, 117–18
welfare, 145–46, 158, 162, 167
  charity *vs.*, 191, 202
  conservative view of, 159
  corporate, 145
  dependency on, 178–80, 255
  double standards of, 178–81

EITC *vs.*, 164
employment *vs.*, 168
  as entitlement, 11, 165
  failure of, 169–70
  farm, 148–50
  Kotz on, 70
  as liberalism, 159–61
  payment shifting of, 163–64
  poverty *vs.*, 163, 171, 183
  public opinion of, 160–61
  racial stereotypes and, 182–85
  regulations of, 178–81
  resource limit of, 176
  social damage of, 177, 179
  supporters of, 168
  work requirement of, 179
welfare recipients
  African Americans as, 184
  job placement for, 168
  penalization of, 179–80
welfare reform, 17, 79, 281–82
  changes of, 162–66
  Clinton on, 161, 170
  debate on, 157
  DeParle on, 164–65
  familial independence from, 158
  legislation for, 162
  success of, 166, 168
  vague nature of, 171
welfare-to-work programs, 180
West Side Campaign Against Hunger (WSCAH), 250
Wheeler, Raymond, 67–68
  fan mail of, 69
  on Mississippi, 68
Whitten, Jamie
  complaints of, 70
  hunger in Mississippi and, 26
  hunger investigation of, 233
WHY. *See* World Hunger Year
WIC food program, 20, 75, 238, 309
  AFFORd and, 239
  expansion of, 47
  federal spending on, 84–85
  Reagan administration and, 27
Winne, Mark, 266–67
work conditions
  of industrial age, 56–57
  safety concerns in, 156
  of Tyson Foods, 214–15
work requirement, 179
World Hunger Year (WHY), 74, 299
WSCAH. *See* West Side Campaign Against Hunger

Yankee stadium, 146
yellow fever, 284